Fighting the Mysore Tigers

Fighting the Mysore Tigers
Two Personal Accounts by Officers of H.M. 12th
(East Suffolk) Regiment of Foot in India
During the Anglo-Mysore War

Diary of Colonel Richard Bayly
12th Regiment 1796-1830

Memoirs of George Elers

Historical Record of the Twelfth or
East Suffolk Regiment of Foot from 1793
Richard Cannon

Fighting the Mysore Tigers
Two Personal Accounts by Officers of H.M. 12th (East Suffolk) Regiment of Foot in India During the Anglo-Mysore War
Diary of Colonel Richard Bayly 12th Regiment 1796-1830
Memoirs of George Elers
and
Historical Record of the Twelfth or East Suffolk Regiment of Foot from 1793
by Richard Cannon

First published under the titles
Diary of Colonel Bayly 12th Regiment 1796-1830
Memoirs of George Elers
and
Historical Record of the Twelfth or East Suffolk Regiment of Foot

FIRST EDITION

Leonaur is an imprint
of Oakpast Ltd

Copyright in this form © 2013 Oakpast Ltd

ISBN: 978-1-78282-225-7 (hardcover)
ISBN: 978-1-78282-226-4 (softcover)

http://www.leonaur.com

Publisher's Notes

The views expressed in this book are not necessarily those of the publisher.

Contents

Diary of Colonel Richard Bayly 12th Regiment 1796–1830 7

Memoirs of George Elers 237

Historical Record of the Twelfth or East Suffolk Regiment of Foot from 1793 333

Diary of Colonel Richard Bayly
12th Regiment 1796-1830

Contents

Note	11
Gazetted as Ensign in H.M. 12th Regiment of Foot	13
Joins 12th Regiment at Newport	17
12th Regiment Embarks at Portsmouth for India	28
Cape Town	32
Madras	42
Expedition to Penang	49
Return to Madras	53
March to Tanjore	55
Duel and Death of Colonel Ashton	58
Before Seringapatam	65
Taking of Seringapatam	76
Narrow Escape From Shipwreck	97
Lieutenant Bayly On Leave In England	110
12th Regiment Embarks For Quilon	122
Further Fighting About Quilon	135
Captain Bayly Wounded	146
12th Regiment Returns To Quilon	160
12th Regiment Ordered To Seringapatam	165

Adventures of Captain Bayly   171
Embarks for Active Service In Mauritius   176

Note

Colonel Bayly was the eldest son of John Bayly, Esq., who, with his ancestors, had long: resided at Hambrook, Co. Gloucester.

The colonel's sister, Eliza, married Barré, son of the Rt. Hon. John Beresford, P.C. second son of the Earl of Tyrone, and brother of the Marques of Waterford.

The colonel's son, Edgar J. Bayly, was a captain in the 12th Regiment, under his command in Ireland. He is mentioned in the MS.

This diary was purchased by the officers 1st Battalion Suffolk (12th) Regiment in 1894.

CHAPTER 1

Gazetted as Ensign in H.M. 12th Regiment of Foot

At sixty years of age tranquillity and reflection are generally the only source of amusement from which we derive any transient gratification, in allusion to those who have reached that period free from any very great reproach of conscience; some glide along the path of life uninterrupted by the least remarkable event, others are predestined to move in a sphere clouded by danger, hardship, want and attendant misery. I have participated in one and the other, and my existence prolonged beyond the common lot to those who have continually wandered on the extended theatre of the world; all I knew in my juvenile years are passed away like shadows; the bravest, the kindest, the loveliest, the best are all involved in the gulf of one common grave, the inevitable destiny of mortality.

But let us cease the tedious theme of moralizing, a species of writing fatiguing to the generality of readers, and passed over with apathy and indifference, pronounced as devoid of interest and irrelevant to the subject. I write *pour passer le temps*, caring neither for applause nor censure; the truth shall be published, and nothing but the strictest veracity shall flow from my pen. Historians may make their heroes gods, but I record the acts of men; and although the great captain of the age, the immaculate Wellington, may appear like his fellow mortals in the course of this narration, I declare solemnly that no unamicable or vindictive feeling actuated me in transmitting his actions to the scrutinizing examination of posterity.

I am the son of a country squire who possessed a landed property of about fifteen hundred pounds *per annum*, near the beautiful hamlet of Trenchhay in Gloucestershire, about six miles from the flourishing city of Bristol; he prided himself particularly on his ancient genealogy; so many hundred years had the property descended from son to son, that it would be folly to recapitulate the absolute nonsense that he was accustomed to advance on this dubious point of pre-eminence; suffice it merely to say that I was the eldest son, received an excellent education, was generally denominated the young squire, and considered myself the undoubted heir to an entailed property of £1,500 a year; horses, servants, carriages, hounds and money were at my command until I attained the age of eighteen, when, observing every spirited young fellow clothing himself in red, blustering and talking of battles and their daring exploits, I at once appealed to my father for the purpose of being enrolled among these defenders of their country.

I suggested every plausible argument to induce him to listen favourably to my entreaties, and at length succeeded in the object of my wishes; he purchased me an ensigncy in the Twelfth Regiment of Infantry, at the recommendation of an old schoolfellow of mine, who had, in the short space of four years, been promoted by purchase to the rank of captain in that corps. It was in the memorable year 1796 that I saw myself gazetted to an ensigncy in this gallant and favourite old regiment, then commanded by the young, handsome, gay, and celebrated Lieut.-Colonel Henry Hervey Aston. What delightful emotions filled my young heart on the receipt of a letter from my friend Woodhall, who was then with the corps at Newport, in the Isle of Wight, giving me a description of his success and his various adventures and hair-breadth escapes during the campaign in Holland, under the Duke of York! He promised to give me a meeting at Southampton, at the Coach and Horses Hotel.

How anxiously did I anticipate the moment of entering on the grand arena of chivalry! I fenced and played single-stick under the tuition of Monsieur Chabas, a fencing master, with such spirit and newly excited animation, that at length the poor little Frenchman was driven into the extreme corner of the room, and the brim of his new hat fairly and scientifically cut through; he, however, admonished my inside and outside thigh very frequently, ere I accomplished this feat of arms. The buoyancy of youth and excitement of the exercise banished from my body and mind all sensation of pain; the pastime over, the punishment was forgotten; at bedtime, however, the black and blue marks on the inside and outside of my right thigh brought to remembrance visible evidence that I had suffered considerably in the *gentle* conflict.

The time now approached for my departure from the scenes of my youth; local attachments impress the mind with strong feelings, and I could not view the village church, the babbling brook, the woods, the park, and the old family mansion with the golden Mercury erected over the porched door, surmounted by a superb hatchment (for the recent death of my great uncle), for the last time without sentiments of deep interest, in fact a species of lump in my throat impeding respiration; a convulsive overcoming sensation thrilled through my whole system; speech was denied, but the deep-drawn sigh and flood of tears too plainly demonstrated that I was mortal, like my fellow-creatures. How I could here sentimentalise! but again I openly declare against all such prosing; brevity, conciseness and simplicity are my motto; to these three constituent parts will I strictly adhere in spite of the scoffs of the world and their paltry "*il ne possède pas un grand talent.*"

Robert, my servant, was at the door with the horses; rushing out of the house, after an affecting parting with my father, mother and sisters, I quickly mounted my snorting steed, and with a cursory glance at the old family mansion, that I was destined never again to inhabit, set off full speed for the mercantile city of Bristol, for the purpose of engaging a seat in the Southampton coach. Pursuing my course for about a mile, I accidentally looked round and saw fat Robert, puffing and blowing like a walrus with the exertion of riding so fast. I therefore relaxed my pace and allowed him to approach me, when he observed, "Why, Master Richard, you be in a mighty hurry to get shot, I thinks; blow me, but it makes me sweat to think on't!"

"Why Robert, you don't think all who enter the army are shot, do you?"

"Perhaps not quite all, but a friend of mine just come from Holland tells I that those Frenchers do fight 'nation hard; he lost one leg, and is crippled in the arm."

"But you see, Robert, I may escape and return a general; this will be much better than remaining a squire all my life."

"For my part. Master Richard, I thinks you had better have taken the old squire's advice, to stay at home and marry that sweet little girl of Winterbourne's; why, Lord, how you blushes, sir!"

"Come, come, Robert, this is carrying the joke too far; you will make me melancholy if you talk in this manner; I may also lose a leg, and then she will like me the better for the dangers I have been through."

"I'll be danged, sir, if she do; no, no; the girls likes a man with all his legs on, I'se sure of that."

"That may be; however, you will see me return covered with glory, or never meet me again."

"The doctors tells I that I have only a few months to live, and when we parts, we parts for ever; no, Master Richard, I shall never see ye again." And the poor fellow began to sob and cry with great violence; the fact was, he had been afflicted with dropsy for some time, and in three months after my departure the earth covered his remains.

We shortly arrived at the Bush Inn, where my place having been taken in the Southampton coach, I bade a hasty *adieu* to poor Robert, and having ensconced myself snugly in the vehicle, we rolled away at a merry rate towards the place of our destination; the most pleasing reflections accompanied me during the whole progress of my journey; I both moralised and sentimentalised, but did not trouble my neighbours with either the one or the other, nor will I you, my kind reader.

CHAPTER 2

Joins 12th Regiment at Newport

On the evening of the same day the coach's load of mortality was safely deposited in the comfortable inn, called the Coach and Horses, at Southampton; I immediately enquired if a gentleman from the Isle of Wight had lately arrived, but heard from the waiter that no such person was there. I then ordered dinner, and just as it was placing on the table, in stalked my friend Woodhall. After a warm greeting on both sides, I surveyed him more minutely and found him covered from head to foot with mud and dirt; he smiled and related that in passing over from Cowes to Southampton the wind had been so adverse, that he had resolved to land, and that having lost his way in the New Forest, he had struggled through bushes, mud and mire, for the purpose of being punctual to our appointment, thus accounting both for his delay and miserable plight; he then adonised, and we did honour to the frugal entertainment of our host of the inn.

I was lighted to my bedroom by one of the prettiest girls I ever saw in my life, and to my great annoyance, modest as she was pretty; no entreaties would induce her to grant me even one innocent kiss. Well, I went to sleep and dreamt of pretty Katy the livelong night.

I awoke early in the morning fresh from my slumbers, filled with joy, hope and expectation. In the breakfast parlour was my friend Woodhall and Major Sandby of the Twelfth. Eggs, ham, toast, muffins, etc., were speedily demolished, and we determined to dine together on a fine turbot, which had just arrived per coach from London, and was intended for the mess, but on inspection we found it would not be eatable the following day, therefore *carpe diem* was our motto, and we washed down the delicious turbot and lobster sauce with a *quantum sufficit* of excellent champagne, and retired in rather muzzy condition to our respective rooms.

The next morning Sandby set off to London; he soon after quitted the regiment, and never joined us again. Woodhall and I embarked on the Cowes packet boat, and sailing down the exceedingly beautiful Southampton Water, reached Cowes about four o'clock in the afternoon of the same day. We slept here, and as we were quietly discussing our breakfast the following morning, were suddenly aroused from our agreeable repast by a loud crash of the window and the instantaneous appearance in the room of Lieut. the honourable John Meade, of His Majesty's Twelfth Regiment; he had accompanied a brother officer from Newport to Cowes in a hired gig, and the charioteer being rather *maladroit*, the gig wheel encountered the more substantial one of a waggon, when the honourable lieutenant was dashed out of his gig through the inn window, and his companion gently deposited on a heap of manure, the sweepings of the street; strange to say, no fracture or wound to the personal inconvenience of the travellers resulted from the inexperience of the young Jehu. They ordered breakfast, and we then proceeded to join the headquarters of the regiment at Newport.

The damage sustained by the proprietor of the inn on account of the window amounted to a considerable sum, which was honourably discharged by the involuntary offending parties. Everyone is acquainted with the beauties of the Isle of Wight; a description would therefore be superfluous, but I must add that in all my voyages and travels, either in Europe, Asia, Africa or America, never has the scenery of any one spot afforded me such exquisite delight as the fertile fields and varied landscapes of this incomparable little island. The enthusiasm of youth rarely extends to the natural beauties of a country; objects of a still more interesting nature generally occupy their minds; but here a man must be an absolute statue not to admire such a succession of diversified objects!

Having joined the regiment at Newport, the first individual I met, limping along supported by two light infantrymen, was a Captain Bellairs, who had been run over by his company in a sham skirmish that morning; in advancing at the head of his light company in double quick time, he accidentally tripped and fell, when several men passed over him, and he was materially injured by their muskets ere the impetus of the rear men of the company could be stopped. I now took lodgings under the same roof with my friend Woodhall, and the evening of my arrival he assembled a few of his particular friends of the corps, and we all sacrificed pretty largely at the shrine of Bacchus, imbibing large potations of old Jamaica rum, mixed with hot water, sugar and lemons; unaccustomed to such potent beverage, I was soon laid prostrate under the table, and all sensation failed me until eight o'clock the following morning.

I awoke thirsty, feverish, and afflicted with a violent headache; I contrived, however, to dress myself, and descend to the breakfast room, when to my horror and disgust Woodhall offered me a tumbler into which he had just poured a small quantity of rum. Never shall I forget the nausea this occasioned; an instantaneous faintness, and violent vomiting immediately ensued, and I am convinced that this simple experiment on my nervous system freed me during life from all propensity to that most destructive of all habits, the love of spirituous liquors; they were never after even named to me without creating a sensation of disgust.

But I had not yet passed through the fiery ordeal prepared for me by my considerate friend, who, having introduced me to my commanding officer, Lieut.-Colonel Henry Hervey Aston, perhaps the most elegant, gentlemanly, and handsomest man in England, I was then initiated into all the *arcana* of the various military drills necessary to form a young officer. Individuals unacquainted with the army imagine that there is nothing absolutely to do, but saunter about a town and ogle all the fine girls: but they are egregiously mistaken, for the study of all the essentials necessary to accomplish an officer in his profession requires the progress of many weary years even before he attains a superficial knowledge of the least important part of the innumerable branches of study requisite for his obtaining eminence in his profession.

Thousands are certainly indifferent to this important truth, and lead a life of indolence and ignorance which has become the characteristic of the British Army, in the opinion of those who observe them in garrison towns; but there is no greater latitude of improvement for the mind in any station whatever than in that of the army; for a man may, if he pleases, and has the capacity, become the most accomplished, learned and scientific member of society. The habit of pleasure, however, generally overcomes the most studious propensities, and thus is seen so many idle, illiterate young men, who, just emancipated from the terrors of the birch, plunge into all kinds of vice and debauchery ruinous to their health, minds and morals.

Having attended drills for several days, one morning after breakfast Woodhall told me, with a very grave aspect, that there was now only one trial I had to endure, which was punishment with a cat-o'-nine-tails; to this I positively objected, as officers were never subjected to this species of castigation. He replied that this was by no means the consideration, but as I was in a few days to become a member of a court martial, it was indispensable for me to suffer the pain of a few lashes, in order that I might then be enabled to reflect feelingly on the necessity of apportioning the punishment to the nature of the crime. I asked him if he had ever submitted to the infliction, and having assured me he had, I then agreed that if he would strip and allow me to apply a dozen lashes to his bare back, he should then perform the same operation on me. To my surprise, he immediately assented to the proposition, and as this was now a direct appeal to my manhood, I was actually ashamed to retract; accordingly the drum-major was called, and a cat-o'-nine-tails was shortly after sent to our lodgings.

Woodhall stripped and directed me to tie his hands to the bedpost, as also his feet to the lower parts of them; having performed this preliminary operation, he then said, "Now, strike me fair over the blade bones of the shoulders, and between each lash count five deliberately." My young heart sickened at the idea of thus barbarously inflicting wanton pain on a fellow creature, and that being the most affectionate of friends; so I commenced as tenderly as possible, and having completed the round dozen, his back bore the marks only of a few red weals; I must confess, this mercy was conferred in hopes that he would also spare me. "Come Master Dick, now strip," said he, and off went my coat, waistcoat and shirt, exposing the fair and tender skin of a lad in his eighteenth year; he then tied my hands and legs in a similar manner to that when he suffered. "Are you ready, my boy?" cried he.

On returning an affirmative, *whiz* went the cat, and slap it came on my poor shoulders, with all the force that a strong man of five-and-twenty could give it. I never shall forget the dreadful sensation of that cruel lash; my heart seemed to leap into my throat, the blood to circulate with irrepressible velocity through every vein of my body, and big drops of perspiration started from my forehead, trickling down my face; but before I could recover from the pain and surprise occasioned by this first essay of my friend's vigorous arm, another and then another lash succeeded rapidly.

I could contain myself no longer, but struggled in vain to get loose, exclaiming, "You damned, unfeeling, cruel, inhuman monster, let me loose, or by the great God of Heaven, I'll shoot you the moment I am free!" This only excited a laugh, and he continued his flagellation to the very last lash, in spite of all my vociferations; the dozen completed, he made me promise to be cool if he released me. I would have agreed to the most humiliating stipulation, for I was exhausted with pain and passion.

No sooner were the bonds detached from my wrists and insteps, than I flew at Woodhall with all the fury of an enraged lion; but he was a stronger, more active man, and a more scientific pugilist than I was; the contest was therefore short, and I soon found myself pinned on the bed with the whole weight of his body lying over me. A flood of tears then relieved my exhausted frame, and I continued some time on the bed after he had released me, sobbing like a schoolboy, and almost in an inanimate state. I was, however, soon brought to a sense of feeling, for Woodhall quickly brought salt and water and anointed my back with it, which, though on the first application caused a smarting, tingling sensation, soon produced the most happy effect; this remedy, with a sound sleep of several hours, renewed my usual good humour and elasticity of spirit.

My first reflection on awaking was a comparison of my slight suffering with that of the poor fellows doomed to receive eight hundred or a thousand lashes! I declare most solemnly that I never attended a regimental punishment afterwards without being affected even to tears, nor did I ever vote at a court martial for more than three hundred lashes for the worst delinquent, though often severely reprimanded by the President of the Court Martial for want of consideration on the enormity of the crime, and the inadequate punishment awarded! The remembrance of my own feelings of pain was sufficient, and no menaces ever compelled me to alter my opinion, and I have, thank God, lived to see this diabolical outrage to the mental and personal feelings of my fellow-countrymen partially abolished. Flogging was an indelible disgrace to civilised society, to the Government of England, and the name of Englishman. Every man of sentiment and humanity must coincide in this short observation.

A few days after my salutary trial of flagellation, a little event occurred, which introduced me to the favourable notice of the commanding officer. He was standing at the door of the Sun Inn, Newport, and raising the point of his sheathed sword in an elevated position to point out some object to the person with whom he was conversing; a large mastiff dog passing by at the identical moment, and mistaking the colonel's mode of indication as an act of hostility to himself, suddenly sprang forward with most ferocious intent, to seize on his supposed adversary. I was standing near the door of the inn on the pavement, and with a blow from a stout ground rattan cane (Penang stick), effectually planted on the dog's head, rolled him over and over into the street, where he lay prostrate for a few seconds, and then slunk off. Pleasure and approbation flashed from the colonel's magnificent dark eyes, and he exclaimed, "Well done, my young hero. I see we shall make something of you; you are quite an acquisition to the corps!"

From this instant I never met him without being favoured by a gracious smile and most cordial greeting. In pugilism and all athletic exercises he was a first-rate performer, and scarcely any circumstance could recommend an individual more to his favourable opinion than a little action of this nature. The name and character of Henry Hervey Aston was at that time intimately known to the king, princes, and nobility of England, with whom he associated on the most friendly and familiar terms, and with whom he possessed more influence than any individual of the nation. It was a subject of surprise and regret to his acquaintances, that a man of fifteen thousand a year preferred embarking for India as lt.-col. of an infantry regiment, rather than moving in the elevated sphere of the most exalted society of the land. It was, however, whispered that embarrassment in his circumstances, produced by certain youthful extravagance, induced him to the selection of this act of prudence. I vouch not for the truth of this latter rumour, but certainly no man was ever more calculated for the command of a regiment than the gay, gallant, sensible, but inconsiderate Henry Hervey Aston.

After due initiation into my military duties as an officer, I devoted many hours to the listless amusement of fishing in a small lake at the foot of Carisbrook Castle, but my success was by no means adequate to the ardour with which I embraced the pursuit. Tired one day with the monotony of the occupation I retired earlier than usual, and sauntered towards the town of Newport; and overtaking two well-dressed females, I entered into conversation with them on the beauty of the scenery in the vicinity of the little village of Carisbrook, and various other light subjects agreeable to the female mind.

Receiving an encouraging consent, and being of an amorous disposition (as the generality of young men are at the age of eighteen) I accompanied them into the town, where they knocked at the door of a respectable-looking house, which being opened by a female, I also entered, and humbly requested a kiss of the rosy lips of my amiable companion, which, being conferred, I thought a little gentle violence would not have been received ingraciously; but, alas, for my poor bones, a little scream brought two great brothers into the passage, and without ceremony, one levelled a most ferocious blow at my tender person, which was warded off, and his fist came in contact with the wall, causing a complete excoriation of his knuckles, and planting a well-directed floorer just under my adversary's ear, he fell prostrate at my feet.

The other brother, seeing the discomfiture of his relation, attacked me fiercely, and we struggled manfully for a few seconds; but my prostrate foe having recovered his equilibrium, soon turned the scale of victory, and I fell almost senseless on the floor, where they kicked me without mercy, shouting: "We have long wished for an opportunity of settling some of you damned Redcoats, and now, my lad, you shall have plenty of it!"

In vain I begged for fair play, and one antagonist at a time; but this was not granted, and they continued to kick and pommel me in the most unmerciful manner, until exhausted nature relieved me from all sensation, when my inanimate body was heartlessly thrown into the street, where two soldiers discovering it, I was conveyed by them to my lodgings. A son of Aesculapius soon appeared, and after a copious extract of the vital stream I began to revive; but the process of revivification was by far more painful than the punishment I had experienced. The disagreeable sensation of circulation of blood through my benumbed limbs was excruciating beyond description.

Most people have occasionally experienced the irritating torment of the return of animation to a sleepy leg or thigh, and this description of pain now pervaded my whole body. I had rather remain a corpse than be again subjected to a similar process. The injury of my corporeal system was comprised in a dislocated wrist, two black eyes, the loss of a tooth, with black marks and swellings from head to foot; and for three weeks I was incessantly confined to my bedchamber.

"The devil help you," say the unfeeling! "Who pities you?" says the young beauty! "You deserve it all," says the rigid moralist! I perfectly coincide most cordially in all your opinions, my impartial censors, and am now as ashamed and indignant at my thoughtless conduct as any of you possibly can be. Observe, I do not spare myself, nor will those be spared in the course of my memoirs who have acted in any manner derogatory to the character of a civilised member of society—*La perfection d'une histoire est d'être désagréable à tous: les siècles et à toutes les nations; car c'est une preuve que c'hauteur ne flatte ni les uns ni les autres, et qu'il a dit à chacun ses vérités.*

My friend Woodhall affectionately attended me during my illness; nor am I quite sure that he did not give one of my persecutors a Roland for his Oliver, in a fair field of pugilistic science. I recollect his coming home one day with a few scratches and bruises, but he never mentioned the result of any *rencontre* of this nature. The success might have gratified my feelings of resentment, but would also have encouraged others less conducive to my future welfare, such as arrogance, presumption, and a disposition to pugnacity—a species of amusement to which I was already but too much inclined.

Having completely recovered, I obtained a week's leave of absence, and proceeded round the little romantic island. And in the latter end of May, let all those anxious to gratify their senses with the unvaried beautiful, make an excursion, alias a tour, through this lovely country. The landscapes and apparent rural felicity of the inhabitants would impress the most prejudiced smoke-loving citizen with a desire of participation in the happy tranquillity and pleasing prospects of the luxuriant woods and fields of the fascinating Isle of Wight. I was accompanied by a young officer, Henry Cavendish, in my tour; and one morning, after a long walk, finding ourselves fatigued and hungry, we approached a humble cottage and enquired of an old woman if she could accommodate us with breakfast. She assented to the proposal, and prepared it accordingly.

The butter, though good, was abominably dirty, and on Cavendish asking if she had none a little cleaner, she broke out into a most outrageous passion, and instantly cleared everything from the table, refusing to supply us with a meal in her house, saying: "You be pretty dainty gentlemen, indeed; you comes here hungry and begging, and then pretends my butter is not clean enough for you. Get out of my house immediately, for not a bit or drop shall you touch here. 'Tis true I've never been above three miles from home in my life, and now I am sixty-five. I have heard speak much of you town folks, but have never met with any of you before, and the Lord protect me from seeing any of you again. Fine airs you give yourselves, forsooth; get along with you, I say!"

No apology, no persuasion would induce the old lady to moderate her anger, and we were reluctantly compelled to seek accommodation elsewhere; and at a small hamlet about three or four miles off, we were provided with a very comfortable, clean breakfast. I recollect well we devoured twenty-four new-laid eggs between us, and, oh! simplicity and honesty, we paid only one shilling each for the refreshing and wholesome meal. I could not forbear slipping another shilling into the hand of a little rosy-cheeked boy who accompanied us a few hundred yards, to show us the regular high road. He told us a great fair was to be held at their village the ensuing week, where backsword playing, donkey races, grinning through a horse-collar, and running in a sack for a shift was to take place.

Pleased with this information we returned to Newport, as our leave was expired. I soon communicated the important intelligence of the anticipated fine fun to Woodhall, and we resolved to become actors in the interesting scene. We both understood the art of singlestick to perfection, but had some doubts of our knowledge of backsword. We engaged one of the men of the regiment accustomed to this exercise to give us a few lessons, and in a very short time found ourselves perfectly *au fait* at the game, and ready to encounter the prowess of any country bumpkin. Accordingly, we joyfully proceeded to the village early on the morn indicated for the fair, about seven miles from Newport, on two strong ponies. We were both dressed as common clowns, in conformity to the costume of the adjacent country.

We arrived just in time to be spectators of the commencement of the backsword playing, and must confess I was both amused and surprised at the dexterity and adroitness displayed by many of the combatants, and began to have some doubts of our anticipated success in this athletic exercise. There were two stalwart, fine-looking fellows, from six feet three inches to six feet four inches high, who broke the heads of their adversaries as fast as they approached, and at length cleared the field. They were brothers, and were very nearly adjudged the prizes, when Woodhall and I presented ourselves as competitors for the honour of a broken head. He was a fine-looking, well made fellow, and no despicable adversary, but I was a tall, slim, active lad, and my bumpkin Hercules looked over me with sovereign contempt. To it we went with a noisy clatter of sticks, striking rapidly against each other; and in five minutes Woodhall drew blood from the head of his opponent, and was, with a shout, proclaimed victor, to the delight of all those who had suffered defeat.

But my task was not so easily accomplished. I received two or three staggering blows across the pate which made me reel again. The superior stature of the clown was a great advantage to him, and my youthful arm began to feel evident symptoms of fatigue. However, an encouraging exclamation from Woodhall incited me to exert all my skill and remaining strength, and elevating myself on my toes, I gave a ponderous stroke over the stick of my opponent, my own stick broke, and the end entered his head just above the right ear, from the wound of which the blood spouted with considerable velocity, and I was consequently pronounced the successful candidate. We had, however, to encounter two or three less expert swordsmen, and happily succeeded in our enterprise. I objected to join in the other games, but Woodhall, than whom no man in the universe could throw his countenance into more frightful contortions, though, naturally, a very handsome man, engaged in the comic scene of grinning through the horse collar, and actually carried off the prize. We did not, however, act ungenerously, for the two smock-frocks and two guineas, as awarded to the two best swordsmen, were magnanimously presented to the herculean brothers, and the fine ribboned hat left for the acceptance of the next best grinner.

We often saw the brothers afterwards at Newport, and enjoyed many a hearty laugh in recapitulating the scenes of frolic and fun which passed off so happily in our village adventure. A short time after this affair, the colonel's orderly called at our lodgings and said, "The colonel wants to see you immediately, sir." I was quite alarmed at this sudden intimation, and imagined that I had omitted some part of my duties, and was on the eve of benefitting by a severe whig or lecture; but on my entering his room, there I saw him dressed in a short jane jacket, exercising himself with dumb bells, alias two ponderous lead weights, which he was whirling about with all the ease and dexterity of a professed athlete.

On my approach he laid them on a chair, and said: "Ah, ah! young gentleman; you are just the person I wish to see. It rains fast; and you must now give me a breathing at single-stick. I hear you are a capital performer, and don't spare me on account of my being your commanding officer." A similar jacket to that he had on was produced, and having properly rigged myself, we set to without further ceremony. Never shall I forget the brilliant activity and elegant attitudes of this extraordinary man—his large, dark eye fixed on me with the steadiness of an eagle. Not a motion could I make without his detecting my design. His strength also was almost superhuman, and, in point of fact, I was no match for such a combination of grace, activity, strength, and science.

After about an hour's exercise we parted very good friends, and he obligingly observed that I did credit to my master, Monsieur Chabar.

He frequently, after this, sent for me, and we renewed our pastime until a few days previous to the embarkation of the regiment for the East Indies. About this time a report was circulated that the regiment was destined for the West Indies, and in consequence several captains sent in their resignations, which the colonel would not accept, as he was determined his officers should accompany their corps to all climates and service to which the government should destine them. Some of them did, however, contrive to quit, but to their great regret, when it was made public that the regiment was to hold itself in readiness to embark for the East forthwith.

Previous to arrival of the route I was invited by a brother officer who had been a midshipman in the navy to visit his old ship, then lying at the Mother Bank, off Portsmouth. I accepted the invitation, and we accordingly proceeded to Ryde in a post-chaise, where we took boat, and shortly reached the vessel, a 74-gun ship. I was certainly amazed at the stupendous size of this floating battery, and mounted up the side to the deck with the most pleasurable emotion. My companion was soon down in the midshipmen's berth, and before an hour had passed was filthily intoxicated, and sprawling on the deck, to the great amusement of his friends, the mids, who played him various scurvy tricks whilst lying in this degraded state.

The motion of the vessel, with the nauseous, disgusting scene before me, produced a most sickening effect, and I requested permission to retire on account of indisposition, which was good-humouredly granted me, and I returned to Ryde, and thence to Newport, with all expedition, completely surfeited with aquatic excursions and marine hospitality. Moyna, the officer alluded to, did not return for a week after, and then upbraided me for quitting him. This produced altercation, and at length the gentleman was obliged to beg my pardon for some unguarded expression. He was a vulgar Irishman—(no disparagement to the sons of old Erin). Individuals of all nations are occasionally ill-bred; on the contrary, a well-educated Irishman is kind, generous, openhearted, brave, polite—in fact, a physical and moral model for a friend. I have seen them in the time of danger, hardship, and adversity in almost every situation of life, and ever found them faithful to the general and acknowledged animated and mercurial character of their nation.

CHAPTER 3

12th Regiment Embarks at Portsmouth for India

Although the transient passion of love has never yet deeply affected me, I was doomed, before my final departure from my native country, to experience a feeling of sweet agitation, from the effects of the predominant propensity in the bosom of all human beings. At several balls, held at the Sun Inn, all the *belles* of Newport and the adjacent country were assembled about once a fortnight, and I had frequently danced with a young girl of surpassing beauty, an inhabitant of Ryde. You may talk of gentle blood and the superiority of aristocratic loveliness, but never did a more perfect face and form grace the four walls of an assembly room than adorned this timid rival of the rose. Her head, eyes, nose, mouth, bust, and stature displayed the most perfect model of symmetry; her motions, actions, voice, and elegance of dancing were of the most fascinating description.

With all these powerful attractions, could a young fellow of eighteen resist such inimitable natural perfections? I was humbled, and confessed my admiration; nor will I deny that a sweet smile of approbation encouraged my warm addresses. Even now, my old, stagnant blood circulates with renewed animation at the very remembrance of her surpassing beauty and perfection. Her teeth were white as ivory; her dark brown hair hung with brilliant luxuriance over shoulders and a bosom fair as alabaster; in her complexion the lily rivalled the rose. She might have been deficient in that rich crimson which renders beauty still more irresistible, but when she became interested in conversation, the deficiency was no longer apparent; and to crown all she was equally distinguished for the beauties of her mind, having received the best education afforded at one of the first female seminaries at the Isle of Wight.

But I am prosing, and having declared brevity and incident my first object, must adhere to my motto. Still, our flirtation went on at every ball—and how little did I anticipate the ludicrous termination of this love adventure! At length she informed me she was recalled home to Ryde to attend an infirm grandmother, and added she should feel much satisfaction in a renewal of our acquaintance there. Having separated with mutual favourable sentiments of each other, I returned to my military avocations with depressed spirits, and thought night and day of my charmer; but our various preparations for embarkation prevented my obtaining leave for the purpose of visiting Ryde, and I had not a moment to call my own until we were fairly on board ship, and anchored at the Mother Bank. But I will not anticipate events.

About the commencement of June, 1796, we marched from Newport for West Cowes, accompanied by at least five hundred women, the wives of the soldiers, only sixty of whom were permitted by regulation to embark with their husbands. The lighters were all ready for our reception, and we got on board as expeditiously as possible, to be conveyed to the Indiamen then lying off Portsmouth. The cries and lamentations of the poor women who were destined to separation from their husbands were distressing beyond description; tearing their hair, beating their bosoms, and rolling in the mud and sand on the beach. Who could survey such a scene of misery and desolation without the profoundest feelings of commiseration?

But it must be acknowledged—to the disgrace of our sex—that the husbands of these forlorn creatures were by no means affected with such symptoms of deep distress. They even laughed and joked with imperturbable nonchalance and indifference; *mais telle est la nature humaine*. Variety and novelty predominate over our very strongest feelings of human affection. Away then we sailed, with the shore resounding with "Arrah, Pat! arrah, Dennis! arrah, Terence!" etc., and your unfortunate wives and children will never again see the light of your sweet countenances.

A few minutes sufficed to carry us far from these distressing exclamations, and in two or three hours the whole regiment of eleven hundred men (principally consisting of youths from eighteen to twenty-six years) were on board four Indiamen of 800 tons each, named, the *Melville Castle*, the *Airly Castle*, the *Hawksbury*, and the *Rockingham*, the latter vessel being selected by the colonel as the headquarters ship, containing the Grenadier and Light Infantry companies, with the staff and band of the regiment. Being all settled snugly on our new element, the officers made frequent trips to Portsmouth for the purpose of amusement and of purchases of little articles essential for their comfort on the approaching voyage.

As to myself, I thought of nothing but the delight of once more meeting her to whom my whole soul was devoted, passing my time in gloomy melancholy, and anxiously awaiting my turn for leave, to go on shore. At length the joyful day arrived, and Major Allen, who commanded the detachment of troops on board the *Melville Castle*, to which I belonged, permitted my absence for a few hours to visit Ryde, where I landed, and immediately enquired for the dwelling of my Dulcinea. I was directed to a miserable little thatched cottage in the upper part of the town as her residence. I could scarcely credit the evidence of my senses. A brown, paltry, low, decayed door, and one diamond-paned casement-window filled with nuts, apples, marbles, and gilt gingerbread toys graced the appearance of the humble abode. The door was open, and there, to my horror and distress, stood behind a wretched counter, selling marbles to some children, that lovely and amiable being to whose charms my heart had paid such devoted homage.

The shock was electrical; never did love evaporate with such a sudden flash. I cast one long and lingering look behind, and left her to the contemplation of her gilt gingerbread husbands, and her amiable occupation of selling marbles to little boys. I was too honourable for a project of seduction, and too proud to unite my destiny to that of a woman's employed in such a humiliating sphere of life. My ideas on this subject may be original, but they are at least sincere. I never saw her again. Some years after she was the wife of a healthy, robust, country farmer. Her father had bestowed on this, his only child, the blessing of a good education, but dying in involved circumstances after a real and reputed affluence of many years preceding, his unfortunate daughter was bequeathed to the care of her infirm old grandmother, and the transcendent charms of the girl had induced the old lady to send her to the Newport balls for the purpose, as she foolishly imagined, of bettering her condition in life.

The poor girl was most fortunate in escaping the quicksand of seduction, where so many gallant, gay Lotharios *voltigeaient de fleur en fleur*. I returned to my ship with an agitated mind, brooded over my misfortune, and forgot the very necessaries requisite for so tedious a voyage, having supplied myself with a stock of eighteen shirts only, whereas at least six dozen were almost indispensable. But the characteristic of youth is inconsideration, and nothing but stern experience can remedy the evil.

CHAPTER 4

Cape Town

The magnificent sight of a fleet of men-of-war and Indiamen lying off Portsmouth, must impress every mind with ideas of the power and wealth of the English nation; about a hundred of various denominations were at this time proudly breasting the wild waves, with their flags and streamers waving in the wind. How my young heart gloried in the contemplation of the fame and riches of my country! There was the *Queen Charlotte* of 98 guns (three-decker), with several seventy-fours, and innumerable frigates and minor-sized men-of-war, rolling from side to side within a few hundred yards of our Indiamen, all prepared, at a moment's signal, to spread their wide canvas and put to sea.

I was suddenly interrupted in my reflections by high words between two officers who were pacing the deck. I heard Lt. Price say to Lt. Willock, "I only wish I had you on shore, my boy, you should soon answer for what you have just said"

This was scarcely uttered than a boat appeared alongside, when Willock, pointing to it significantly, replied, "You may now have your wish." Accordingly they proceeded with pistols and their seconds to the nearest land off St. Helen's, to which anchorage we had shifted the day before, and having landed, they fired a brace of balls each without effect, when the affair was amicably adjusted, and they returned to the vessel in the best of spirits and the most cordial humour imaginable, though they had a tolerable long lecture from our major for the military offence of quitting the ship without leave: they were put in arrest for several days, but were released previous to sailing.

On board our vessel we had a Captain O'Brien, a fine, handsome man, a prodigious favourite with the ladies. He is now Marques of Thomond, but at that time had not the most remote idea of ever succeeding to the title, as there were several male branches of the family living, all possessing nearer claims to the Marquisate than himself; however, in a few years afterwards they all quitted this world of woe, leaving him undisputed right to the honour of succession. In November, 1793, he accompanied the flank companies of the 12th Regiment in their embarkation from Cork to the West Indies, as fine a body of men as ever quitted the shores of old Erin. Having served at the captures of the Isles of Martinique, Guadeloupe, and St. Lucia, they were finally left at St. Domingo, from whence he rejoined the regiment with one sergeant and one private, the remainder of the two companies, both men and officers, having perished in action, or by the fatal insalubrious effects of the climate. He was a worthy, good man, with a little pompous twitch of the right leg in walking, just sufficient to denote his expectation of *un haut rang*; his manners amiable and conciliating, with the usual generous propensity of his countrymen.

On the 27th June we started from St. Helen's, Isle of Wight. The day previous to our departure, the fourth mate of the *Melville Castle* undertook for a considerable wager to swim from the vessel to shore—about five miles distant—and return again. He was a tall, athletic young fellow of six feet two inches in height, and an admirable swimmer; but few men can support themselves in water sufficiently long to overcome the space of ten miles. He sprang from a small boat alongside into the sea with the most perfect confidence and self-possession, commencing his arduous career under the most favourable auspices and ardent wishes for his success of the majority of the disinterested, being about two hours in attaining the point of land near Walmer Castle.

He just landed, and again plunged into the water, appearing yet strong and vigorous; every eye and glass were directed towards this interesting individual, who now approached rapidly. When within a mile of the ship he suddenly turned on his back and appeared exceedingly distressed, throwing up his hands as if beckoning for assistance from the ship; four sailors manned the boat lying alongside, rowing expeditiously towards the sufferer, who was brought on board in a complete state of exhaustion. Poor Collins lost his wager, but recovered long ere we had cleared the British Channel.

There is no scene so monotonous as a sea voyage, a succession of the rising and the setting of the sun, with no other object to attract the attention than the blue expanse of sea and sky; for a few days only is the novelty entertaining. The fresh, invigorating breezes, or motion of the ship certainly infuse into the human constitution an extraordinary and almost unappeasable appetite; hearty breakfasts at 8 o'clock in the morning, *tiffin* at 12, dinner at 3, tea at 6, and supper at 8; everyone punctual to the hour and all equally voraciously inclined. Chess, backgammon, cards, fluting, fiddling, and dancing, the principal amusements in the intervals between our meals.

On Saturday nights the armourer was called into the cuddy to sing the old sea song of "Saturday Night." He had a most powerful, harmonious voice, contributing in no slight degree to our joviality. Four or five young ladies on a speculation voyage to the East, added to our sources of amusement, frequently dancing on the deck.

It was now for the first time I was taught the distinction between ranks; the captains and rich civilians were invariably favoured with the fair hands of the ladies, to the entire exclusion of the sighing subalterns. I was quite *enragé*, and daily seated myself in the stern windows of the vessel, shaving for whiskers, for as Captain O'Brien had an enormous pair of red ones, and was particularly favoured by the partiality of the fair, I thought by coaxing the down on my cheeks I might ultimately become a candidate for their preference. But alas! Nature would not be forced into precocity, and I remained a smooth-faced boy to the end of the voyage. In ten days we reached the Island of Madeira, in which latitude all the huge men-of-war quitted us, leaving the little *Fox* frigate as our future convoy. Captain Malcolm (later Admiral Sir Pulteney) commanded her. We shortly afterwards passed within sight of the Peak of the Island of Tenerife, a mountain three miles high, one of the most elevated in the whole globe, with the exception of the Andes, in South America, and Himalayas in the East Indies.

On this day a man fell overboard, and in lowering a boat for his preservation, five others were precipitated into the sea, from the accident of the stern rope hook slipping from the ring of the boat; another boat was lowered instantly, but four of the latter were drowned; the first was saved from a watery grave. We now sailed by the Cape de Verde Isles; a few boats pushed off from St. Jago and supplied us with a small quantity of fruit and vegetables, sufficient for a day's consumption. As we approached the Line, we were favoured by the Trade Winds, moving forward at the rate of five, six, seven, eight, and sometimes nine miles an hour, without rolling or pitching, or any material alteration in the sails for four of five weeks successively; but at length, within a very short distance from the Line, we were suddenly becalmed, and for three weeks not a breath of air agitated the surface of the ocean.

The blubber-fish accumulated to so considerable an extent that the water appeared in an absolute state of stagnation; the fleet also, by the force of bodily attraction, were drawn so closely together, that long spars were produced to fend the ships from each other. The *Henry Addington*, an enormous 1,200 ton Indiaman, with part of the 80th Regiment on board, was one morning discovered with her bowsprit hanging over the stern of the *Fox* frigate. The swell of the sea was prodigious, and one heavy fall of the cutwater and lower part of the bowsprit of the Indiaman would have had a most fatal effect on the stem of our little convoy. Every sail was hoisted by the frigate, boats lowered from several ships, and all tugged manfully with ropes attached to her head, and at length with pushing with spars and pulling of boats the frigate was extricated from jeopardy. If Sir Pulteney's eye ever scanned this description, he would recollect his perilous situation. We were put on short allowance of water, than which, to a seaman, nothing is a greater hardship. Our apprehensions were fortunately soon tranquillised.

One day about 12 o'clock, a cat's-paw was observed to ruffle the smooth surface of the sea, at some distance, which gradually increased into a gentle breeze. What pleasurable congratulations passed throughout the fleet on this happy occasion! We glided gently on to the Line, in crossing which the usual ceremony of shaving with a saw and hurling buckets of water from the masts and yards on all below took place, tricks so often described that it would be superfluous to introduce a recapitulation of what everyone knows. On the 19th September we came in sight of the superb Table Mountain, ten thousand feet high, with its graceful table-cloth, *alias* white cloud, hovering over it; then appeared the Sugar Loaf Rock, and at length the verdant Lion's Rump came in view, with its chequered little fields and plantations, dotted with milk-white cottages. What an agreeable sight to the eye after three months' unvaried view of sea and sky!

As we entered Table Bay, parts of the Dutch fleet were lying there, recently captured by Admiral Elphinstone. The *Fox* frigate fired the usual salute, which was returned from the shore, when the whole fleet were shortly anchored in this dangerous bay, but now smiling with its smooth, glassy surface, as if inviting the mariner to destruction! A certain proportion of the officers were allowed to land, and I obtained a snug, cheap lodging at a Mr. Muller's. Small parties of soldiers were sent on shore daily for the benefit of their health, but the body of the regiment continued on board during our stay at the Cape of Good

Hope.

I now found for the first and last time in my life that the Latin language was useful. My host was a Divine, and spoke Dutch only, but finding I was a Latin scholar, we contrived to communicate our ideas through this medium with great facility, and I was therefore very comfortably situated, going every three or four days on board ship to take my turn of duty, and then again returning to my comfortable lodging, which was doubly attractive on account of the society of Maria Muller (the sister of the *padre*), to whom I paid the most marked attention, for she was really a very pretty, lively young lass, rather too full in the contour of her person, but this was an additional beauty in my poor estimation. We sang, played, and danced together from morn to night, in their dear little stone-floored parlour, and I regretted the direful obligation of proceeding on to India. Youth is so easily biased by present happiness that they rarely reflect on the future scenes of life that may fall to their portion.

We had cricket matches with the officers of the garrison, which then consisted of many regiments, both cavalry and infantry, and in these our Lt.-Col. Aston shone prominent, his skill, graceful attitudes, and activity were all displayed to advantage, the party to which he was attached almost invariably carrying off the prize: all acknowledged his superiority at every athletic game.

In these days the infernal practice of duelling was resorted to on the most trivial occasions; no less than eleven were fought in the governor's gardens. The first week after our arrival one of our officers was shot through the breast (Ensign Jordan) by Lieut. Willock. The latter was the hero of the little skirmish at St. Helen's, from which he escaped more fortunately, as after this quarrel he was compelled to quit the corps. Some said he was hardly dealt with; he was, however, generally esteemed a good-natured, harmless, brave man, and many regretted the result of the decision.

An order having been issued that no more duels should be fought in the governor's gardens, which practice was dangerous to the public, the place of rendezvous was consequently changed, as the townspeople and officers could now walk there without fear of a stray shot. It is astonishing what frequent quarrels occur on board ship; the confinement, the too familiar intimacy, the gambling, all contributed to this direful propensity.

On the 9th of October a most furious storm came on, driving many ships ashore, and others dragging their anchors, and all congregating together in one confused mass. I was happily on shore, from whence I viewed the scene of devastation with feelings of the sincerest regret, inwardly congratulating myself at my fortunate escape, though lamenting the danger to which my brother officers were exposed. The gale continued the whole day; the weather was so hazy that nothing could be seen, the only indication of the perilous situation of the vessels was the incessant discharge of cannon, announcing the extreme danger of ships near the snore. These signals of distress continued at intervals the whole morning, and when the weather cleared up, which occurred about four in the afternoon, the whole coast was strewed with wrecks and dead bodies!

The Indiamen being what is termed excellent sea-boats, weathered the storm, but they were all foul of each other, and had the violence of the wind continued many hours longer, must have all foundered. The day following I put off in a shore-boat for the *Melville Castle;* the sea was exceedingly agitated, in fact, running mountains high; the rise of the ships would draw their cables out of the water with a sudden jerk, for a length of fifty or sixty yards; our little boat passing the head of the *Braave* Dutch frigate, at a distance considered by the boatman as perfectly safe; she gave a sudden and dreadful heave, the boat was canted up in the air many feet; the red coat, plumed hat, new regulation sword and dandy person of the gay officer were all plunged into the briny element: the luxury of blue *surtouts*, as undress, was at this time unknown in the army.

Fortunately I could swim tolerably, but the sudden shock so confounded my intellect that I floundered about for a few seconds almost unconscious of my danger; the active principle of self-preservation soon excited me to exertion, and I eagerly grasped the huge cable with hands and feet, my back hanging towards the sea, and thus warped myself up the stem of the frigate, encouraged by the excited shouts of some English sailors on the forecastle. The undulations of the cable impeded my rapid progress, and had not the timely assistance of honest Jack aided my exertions, my destiny must soon have been decided. Being at length dragged on deck, every attention was bestowed upon me that the benevolence and humanity of a British naval lieutenant could suggest; dry linen, comfortable cordial, with honest congratulation on my escape, came naturally and liberally from my new-found acquaintance. He supplied me with one of the frigate's boats, when my clothes were dry, and I soon had the satisfaction of shaking hands with my comrades on board the *Melville Castle*, with my originally red coat metamorphosed into a deep purple.

The poor shore boatman and his boat were picked up a long distance astern of the *Braave* by another shore-boat, and I afterwards paid the poor fellow a double fare the first time we met on shore. Our Indiaman had, during the terrible gale, come in collision with another vessel; a crash of the quarter galley and the loss of a few ropes and spars was the only damage sustained. Not one of the numerous shipping anchored in the bay had escaped without injury, yet the following day nature smiled as serenely as if such terrible commotion had never taken place: thus the passions of men,—but prosing is prohibited. Well then, after these disasters we formed a picnic party for the Table Land.

Our party consisted of thirteen. We proceeded with the bottle and bag round the western extremity of the mountain, and scrambling over numerous high hills and rocks, at the back of Cape Town, at length reached the desired platform of the Table Mountain. The sky was cloudless, and one of the most magnificent views presented itself that nature ever formed: the long range of blue mountains in the distance; Robin Island, with the bay studded with vessels of all descriptions, at our feet; and the beautiful Cape Town, appearing like Lilliputian range of buildings. From this immense height of ten thousand feet the inhabitants were scarcely perceptible, and the largest ships looked like children's toys.

We left the town at 6 o'clock in the morning, reaching our place of destination at two; eight hours' incessant labour of climbing and scrambling. After a complete survey of the Table Land, *alias*, flat surface of the mountain, we sat down to a comfortable, and, from hunger, delicious repast; the corks flew from the bottles, and the provisions were tumbled from the baskets; pleasure and hilarity predominated over the gay scene, but alas! for the evanescence of human life, not one of the jovial party was in existence four years after this happy meeting except myself. "Away with melancholy!" and we banished her from our minds, and drowned our senses in copious libations.

About 4 o'clock a drizzly thick vapour began to cover the top of the mountain, when we hastily packed up the remnants of our feast and were conducted to the fissure in the rock, leading directly down to Cape Town. My friend Woodhall, who was the prince of good fellows, the life and soul of every gay party, being a little in the wind, or in plainer terms rather overcome with the effects of his too liberal potations, betted highly he would run from top to bottom of the mountain without stopping, and setting off at a gentle pace, proceeded on his perilous enterprise without further ceremony. We called on the mad fellow to stop, but nought availed; away he went, bounding over precipices of twelve or fifteen feet descent; we sometimes lost and then again discovered his rapidly descending form, as he wildly pursued his headlong career. We were all disposed to escape the skirts of the increasing tablecloth (white cloud), and pushed on vigorously, but *malgré* all our efforts, Woodhall had reached the bottom at least half-an-hour before us; there he lay, puffing and blowing like a walrus, with bruised body, skins, knees, arms, and feet, bleeding profusely. He was scarcely sensible, but had perfectly accomplished his undertaking!

Resting a short time after our fatigues, we took the thoughtless fellow between two of us, and thus supported, entered the town just as daylight began to fade; he was left at his lodgings, where he remained several days, a complete invalid. The rest of the party betook themselves to their ships and various places of abode: thus terminated our happy picnic. Not so for several officers, some years afterwards, who, engaging in a similar expedition without a guide, and the clouds suddenly involving the top of the mountain in obscurity, they mistook the regular fissure of descent, fell many hundred feet down a precipice and were dashed to atoms!

Our second lt.-col., the honourable C. Grey, met with a most melancholy fate during our delay at the Cape. He was one day walking in his bedchamber, and suddenly struck his hip against the corner of a chest of drawers; the pain occasioned by the contact was very trifling, and he neglected all precaution of friction or embrocation; about a week afterwards he complained to the surgeon of a very disagreeable sensation in the part affected. On examination an incipient abscess was discovered; in six weeks after he was a corpse. *Sic transit gloria mundi!*

During our stay at Cape Town, an affair of honour occurred between two officers, a Capt. K——, of the 33rd Regiment, and a young lieutenant of another regiment, which did much honour to the humane feelings of a lieutenant of the 12th, named Buckeridge, who was present at the altercation, and engaged by K—— as his second. This captain was a most notorious marksman, striking a shilling or snuffing a candle with his ball at twelve paces distant almost invariably; he had also shot several officers in various hostile *rencontres*. Poor Buckeridge, who was aware of the inevitable fate attending the amiable young man who was to encounter this cool and fierce marksman, by whom he had reluctantly been forced into the duel, determined to diminish the charge of powder in his pistol, so that the anticipated wound might not prove fatal.

This was accordingly done, the ground being measured and every necessary preparation enforced, the adverse parties fired. K——'s ball, as expected, took effect in the side of the young man, and he fell to the ground. K—— immediately turned round to his second and ferociously exclaimed, "G—d d—n you, if you had only put powder enough in the pistol I should have shot him!" Buckeridge turned on his heel, only replying, "I am sorry I was ever engaged as second to a fellow of such a vindictive murderous disposition," and instantly retired from the ground. The young man was borne home and shortly recovered from the injury.

A meeting of the officers of the regiment took place, and we unanimously decided that Buckeridge should not meet K——, who had sent him a challenge for his parting observation, and the officers of his own regiment fought shy of him for many months afterwards, and he ultimately quitted the corps. In the army we call it "fighting shy" when a body of individuals are on cool terms with an officer who has in any manner committed himself unworthily, just sufficient to escape the ordeal of a court martial.

A trifling mistake occurred a few days before the fleet sailed for India, that nearly deprived me of the felicity of viewing those arid shores. I was one morning seized with the most dreadful spasms in the stomach, and on entering the inn, met Buckeridge, telling him the nature of my malady. "I'll cure you in a trice," said he, and taking down a phial from the chimney-piece, emptied it into a wine-glass, which nearly filled it. I took it off without hesitation, and was instantaneously released from pain. I had not swallowed it more than ten minutes when, feeling a drowsiness and benumbing sensation in my feet and legs, I begged him to let me repose on his bed a little time, until these disagreeable feelings subsided.

He accordingly introduced me to his bedchamber, and I immediately flung myself on the bed, and prepared for a good sound sleep; but it would have been the sleep of death, for in about five minutes Buckeridge rushed into the room, exclaiming "For God's sake don't go to sleep; I have given you nearly two ounces of laudanum! The doctor will be here instantly." These expressions made no impression on me; I was already in a lethargic state, wishing him at Old Nick for disturbing me.

Our surgeon soon administered a strong emetic, which had a magical effect, and relieved me from all stupor; they then allowed me to indulge in a comfortable nap, which continued to late in the evening, when I awoke voraciously hungry, but reeling with an intolerable dizziness of the eyes and brain; a good dinner soon restored me to my wonted animation, and I was now ready to hear the detail of my accident. It appeared that Buckeridge had observed our purser, named Booty (a poor, puny, sickly, cadaverous little man, afflicted with constant spasms and indigestion), apply frequently to the contents of the phial, which was invariably an appendage of the chimney-piece, and fully aware that it acted infallibly on the nerves and spasms of the purser, he of course imagined it would produce a similar effect on me, as I was afflicted with the self-same malady. But unfortunately he had never taken notice of the small quantity taken, and seeing me writhing in the most excruciating torment, thought a good dose would effectually relieve me; poor fellow, he was dubbed with the appellation of "Doctor" to his dying day, an epithet, however, that excited his ire exceedingly.

The period now approached for our departure, and my love affair with the bonny Maria was soon to be finally terminated. She would not marry unless I promised to make the Cape my permanent residence. This stipulation was impossible, and a most distressing scene of separation ensued, fainting, hysteric fits, floods of tears affected the love-sick girl, and I must confess myself to have been almost equally agitated. We indulged in the fascination of one long last embrace, I then hurried to the beach, and once more embarked on the *Melville Castle* for another long sea voyage. Before we sailed, the *padre*, her brother, came on board offering a settlement of eighty thousand *rix dollars* if I would reside at the Cape and marry his sister. Major Allen now interfered, pointing out the imprudence and impossibility of my accepting the "proposal without disgrace and dishonour; I then took a melancholy leave of the disconsolate *padre*, and we separated for ever.

CHAPTER 5

Madras

On the 10th November, 1796, the whole fleet was under weigh, with a favourable breeze, majestically sailing out of Table Bay. I saw the fast-receding shores of the iron-bound coast of this part of Africa with feelings of the deepest regret, and lamented not accepting the liberal proposition of the poor *padre*, but my animal spirits soon surmounted this transient depression; the sly jokes of my comrades in arms, and the space of a few days' time soon revived me, but could not efface the remembrance of my superb Dutch *vrow*. A Captain Ending had married one of the young ladies on board the *Melville Castle* during our residence at the Cape; he accidentally met her in a boarding house, was charmed with her appearance and manners, and in a few days after the Gordian knot was tied.

Capt. O'Brien was to his great annoyance removed to another ship, for the accommodation of Mr. Ending, whose sister was on board our ship. This change was a circumstance of an exceedingly disagreeable nature to all under his command. He was haughty, imperious, and excessively jealous; he almost resented the most casual glance at his pretty wife; scarcely any subaltern was permitted to speak to her, and all excluded from the little parties occasionally given in the roundhouse.

No event of material consequence took place for several weeks. We stretched out towards the islands of St. Paul and Amsterdam, and so far to the south that we hourly expected an interruption of icebergs. Meeting with a very heavy gale of wind, the course of the fleet was altered, and we steered directly for Acheen Head, were soon favoured with the Trade Winds, and again crossed the equatorial line. All was now hurry and bustle, exercising the great guns, as we expected to encounter the French frigates at this time cruising in the

Bay of Bengal. Our fleet consisted of the *Fox* frigate and eleven large Indiamen, many of them mounting thirty-six 18-pounders, with three British regiments on board—the 12th, 86th and 94th, or Scotch Brigade. The mode of encounter was to close with the French and board immediately.

After clearing for action several times, we at length anchored in Madras Roads without further impediment, on the 19th of January, 1797, disembarked at Fort St. George the ensuing morning, and the officers were hospitably entertained at dinner by the gallant 74th Regiment, then doing garrison duty there. This night I indulged so freely in their good Madeira wine, that I became disgracefully intoxicated, abused our kind hosts, and was carried to bed insensible.

On awakening next morning in the quarters of Lieutenant Vesey Hill (who afterwards led the forlorn hope at Seringapatam and was killed) I found both my eyes closed, with large irritating lumps all over my body, and in a high state of fever. I then had several apologies to make to the individuals I had so wantonly and ungenerously abused the preceding night at the 74th Mess, and the good fellows were all amply satisfied. They marched to the station of Wallajahbad a few days after, leaving us in quiet possession of the strong fortress of Fort St. George, called Madras. From January to August we were drilled without intermission, and soon became expert in military evolutions, perhaps superior to any King's regiment then serving in India.

I recollect the gallant Col. Baird attending one of our drills and expressing his most unqualified approbation of our movements and high discipline. For six months the regiment was on the Eastern glacis every morning at daylight; I never saw the rising sun so frequently, and probably never shall during my existence. At 2 o'clock the subalterns were paraded in a long verandah of the King's Barracks, giving the word of command of "Ready; present; fire!" in a loud, firm, and distinct voice, to ten files of men placed at ten equi-distant intervals; then at 6 o'clock in the evening we were again manoeuvred on the glacis.

The guard-houses at Fort St. George, under the bomb-proof ramparts, were so infested by clouds of mosquitoes that I have often sat in a chair or paced in front of them the whole night, lamenting my infatuation of entering the army, or thinking on the happiness I might have enjoyed had I but accepted the proposition of my friend the *padre* at the Cape, where love, content and independence would have brightened my future life.

One night, after a constant vigil of this description, and answering the guard and visiting rounds with all due precision, about 6 o'clock in the morning I threw my coat, belt, sash and stock off, in the hopes of getting a comfortable nap. Before opening the gates a dead sleep overcame my senses, and on opening my eyes there was my excellent but severe colonel on horseback with the animal's head hanging over me. I started up in the utmost dismay; no excuse was offered for my apparent neglect of duty, and he rode out of the guard-room observing, "I'll soon teach you, young gentleman, to be more on the alert!"

The sergeant of the guard assured me he had regularly called me three times, and that the guard had been under arms since daylight, and General Sydenham had passed the gate with the colonel for the purpose of inspecting the regiment, and had marked the omission and neglect of no officer being at the head of the guard.

The colonel rode full tilt into the guard-room, crying out, "What the devil! is there no officer to this guard?" which exclamation in a loud tone awoke me, though I could not absolutely distinguish the expression. The guard was soon relieved, and retiring to my quarters, our old adjutant, Joe Moore, made his appearance, asking for my sword and telling me by the colonel's orders I was to consider myself in close arrest until a court martial could assemble. I remained all that day in an inexpressible agony of excitement; no one came near me, a species of desolation and despair pervaded my whole system, the very sight of food was disagreeable; so throwing myself on my rattan couch, I endeavoured to banish my misfortune in the arms of Morpheus, but in vain.

About 10 o'clock at night my staunch friend Woodhall paid me a sly visit, encouraging me to keep up my spirits and that all would be soon happily settled. Feeling great relief from this assurance, sleep soon usurped its undivided empire. At 8 o'clock the following morning I awoke refreshed, and had just begun breakfast when the adjutant entered with a smiling countenance, and acquainted me that on due consideration of my youth and inexperience, the colonel had resolved to release me from arrest provided an ample apology was made to General Sydenham in writing, explanatory of the whole affair. I immediately and cheerfully sat down, describing the manner in which the night was passed and the deep sleep that ensued, with which the general was pleased to express himself perfectly satisfied.

I was next day introduced to Colonel Wellesley on the parade (now the great Duke of Wellington), and presume, by way of encouragement, Colonel Aston described me as a very promising young officer, though smiling archly at the same moment. The officers of our regiment dined several times at the mess of the 25th Light Dragoons, then commanded by Lieutenant-Colonel Cotton, a pretty-faced, active little man of five-and-twenty, but now the war-worn Lord Combermere.

I had an *affaire du coeur* with the beautiful Harriet Lally (natural daughter of the famous French General Lally, of Pondicherry), which unfortunately embarrassed my finances considerably. The amusement of gambling also occupied my mind more than was judicious, and I was at length compelled to apply for assistance to our paymaster, Major Allen, who refused to supply my necessities unless I gave a solemn promise to abstain from this ruinous propensity during my future residence at Madras: the promise was made and faithfully kept, though I lost the affection of my mercenary Dulcinea, in consequence. Some young scapegrace will here exclaim, "A fig for the old fellow and his *amours*, who cares for them?" But how few years will intervene ere this very individual will be suffering under the inevitable infirmities of old age.

We are all, in youth, very presumptuous and thoughtless. We, however, have the same passions. I recollect your original asseverations on the vaunted score of brevity! I submit Mr. Censor, and must now relate some few anecdotes of the frolics or any other epithet that may be deemed more appropriate of the youthful errors of our martinet lieutenant-colonel; I have them from those who heard him relate them; therefore no blame can attach to me if any little inaccuracies may occur in the course of narration. Some years previous to his mania for military fame he had envied the notorious *éclat* of the famous fighting Fitzgerald, who had been successful in some forty or fifty duels, and who was avoided and feared as a complete pest to society.

In order to attain celebrity Aston resolved to encounter this dreadful person, and with this determination proceeded one evening with some friends to where he understood this Irish Achilles would attend. Sauntering along the walks, the man was shortly pointed out. Aston passed him, pushing rudely against his shoulder; the other, imagining the insult was accidental, passed very quietly on without further notice, but on again returning Aston ran violently against him, and fairly drove him off the walk. This was a too plain indication of hostility to escape the resentment of one less inclined to pugnacity than Fitzgerald, who attacked Aston immediately, and a regular boxing match ensued.

The colonel at this period was the best gentleman pugilist in England, and poor Fitzgerald suffered such a severe beating that he at length lay almost insensible on the ground, when Aston, calling to a waiter to bring a lamp, lifted Fitzgerald up and then threw him again on the ground, crying exultingly, "He'll do! he'll do!" and walked off triumphantly.

Six weeks was poor Fitzgerald confined to his bed, so severe had been his punishment The moment he was able to stand a message was conveyed in due form to Aston for gentlemanly satisfaction, and arrangements made for the *rencontre* accordingly. Twelve paces were measured, and two as brave men as ever existed placed opposite each other. The signal was given, and the unerring ball of Fitzgerald passed through the back part of Aston's neck, who instantly fell. Fitzgerald very coolly approached, lifted him in a similar manner, in which he had been so cavalierly treated, and then let him fall on the earth again, repeating his adversary's facetious joke of "Oh! he'll do! he'll do!"

Aston's life was long despaired of, and he retained an erect stiffness of his neck during life, produced by the severe effect of the wound. A long moral lesson might here be introduced, not very favourable to the principles of either party. My object is to narrate facts, and let those criticise, whose venomous dispositions, or superlative sense of the failings of their fellow mortals, may consider themselves justified in throwing the first stone, as Christ said to those who accused the adulterous woman. I only apply the old adage of "*Humanum est errare.*"

On another occasion our colonel acted perhaps still more absurdly, at Honiton, in Devonshire. During an election he was leaning out of one of the upper windows of the inn there, when observing a finely-powdered head thrust out from one of the lower windows, the old tempter induced him to spit on the conspicuous *caxon* below, which flourished so superlatively ridiculous that he could not abstain from the irresistible impulse of fun, for the gentleman clapped his hand to the part affected, and instantly withdrew his offended pate, and five minutes had scarcely elapsed when in burst the M.P. (for so it was rumoured) into the apartment occupied by Aston, vehemently exclaiming, "By God, I'll give five guineas to the man who will tell me the person that spat on my head"

"Put the money in my hand and I'll tell you immediately; the fellow wants to sneak away, so be expeditious," replied Aston. The purse was produced, and the five guineas deposited in Aston's hand; when he said, with the greatest *sang-froid*, "I am the man who did the deed."

"The devil you are," replied the other; "and pray who may you be?"

"I am generally called Henry Hervey Aston!"

The choleric gentleman was astounded, for this name was at that time familiar to every sporting character in England. However, he retired without further altercation, and a meeting of the parties ensued, a brace of balls projected, and the cauliflower-headed hero was shot *au travers les deux fesses, telle est la fortune de guerre*. As an old French general observed on the eve of a battle, on being asked who he thought the Almighty would favour; "Bah!" said he, "*le bon Dieu est toujours pour les gros bataillons.*" Thus in the chances of a duel the most expert marksman generally succeeds, even though decidedly the aggressor, and meriting all the punishment.

One morning, after a two hours' drill on the well-trod glacis of Fort St. George, the sun rose with its usual splendour; the heat was insufferable at eight o'clock. The movements of the men, from fatigue, appearing to the colonel to proceed from neglect and indifference to duty, he kept us on the ground until nine o'clock, when we returned to the fort *tout en eau*. As I entered my quarters I fell suddenly on my face, deprived of all sensation. My servants placed me on a couch; the surgeon was called, pronouncing my malady as a *coup de soleil*. My nose, on which I had fallen, bled profusely, and this circumstance, in his opinion, saved my life. The excessive heat and unusual long drill produced this affliction. The medical men represented the pernicious consequence of the troops being harassed by long drills, exposed to the intense heat of the sun, when an order was issued restricting the exercise to a specified time and hour.

Every day previous to this salutary prohibition, three, four, and frequently five men would suddenly drop down in the ranks, as if shot through the heart by a musket ball, and numbers died under the fatal influence of this severe affliction of *coup de soleil*.

At the commencement of August, 1797, a strong rumour prevailed that an expedition to the Luconian Islands was in contemplation, and Manilla was mentioned as the chief object of the expedition. We congratulated ourselves most heartily on this probability of suspension from our interminable drills. The name of Manilla was familiar to my ear, for during my infancy our family occupied a house at Clifton, near Bristol, in front of which was (and I believe is, to this day) a monument commemorating the names of all the gallant officers who had fallen victims to its capture, under the command of the famous and learned Sir William Draper.

How often during childhood did I amuse myself in endeavouring to decipher the names and inscriptions of this most elegant monument, which is situated at the eastern extremity of Clifton Green, before a well-built freestone house, where Sir William himself had once resided. I will not disguise the feelings of certain palpitations of the heart, when reflecting on the imminent danger attending the capture of an island so strongly fortified by nature and art, but the excitation caused by the representations of the incalculable riches it contained soon tranquillised these unmilitary sensations. The prize-money of a subaltern alone was vaguely calculated at a thousand pounds; and where is the young mind impenetrable to the charms of possessing a rich harvest of gold-dust, the bane and happiness of civilised society? At length the expedition was publicly announced and the day of embarkation officially designated.

CHAPTER 6

Expedition to Penang

The 12th of August arrived, the surf on the Madras coast was particularly and unusually high; the most distant wave commenced about three hundred yards from land, the second about two hundred, and the third breaking with a thundering noise on the sands. The *masula* boats were all ready, and in spite of the forcible representations of the boatmen of the impracticability of reaching the ships, some companies were embarked, and plunged through the shore surf, but on encountering the second, the boats were upset, and several soldiers drowned, when the attempt was given up, and the troops returned to quarters. For three days the sea continued in this agitated state; nor could the men embark until the 17th inst., and then, even, the surf was frightfully high.

There are, however, some few days in the course of a year when the sea beats so gently on the coast that the smallest ship's boats might land with safety, but this is of very rare occurrence, and all European boats invariably anchor outside the farthest surf, individuals and mercantile commodities being then transferred to the *masula* boat for the purpose of disembarkation; heavy ordnance, with other ponderous lading, is deposited in the native boat at the ship's side. Six companies of the 12th, with several other corps, both European and Native, were soon on board the various Indiamen and other transports prepared for the reception of the troops.

I accompanied two hundred men of the 12th on the *Ceres*, an 1,800-ton Chinaman, and a whole battalion of Rajahpoot *sepoys*, consisting of eight hundred, were crowded into the same vessel. No powers of language can describe the scenes of confusion, discontent, and almost mutiny that ensued for several days after each caste, sect, or religion of *sepoys* had embarked their own water and provisions, which, according to their prejudices, would have been contaminated if touched by an European or separate sect.

Every morning there was a regular bazaar on the deck, each sect scrupulously and sedulously avoiding contact with the persons or provisions of their fastidious neighbours; but in a short space of time everything was carried on with the most perfect amenity of temper. On the 23rd, the first division of the expedition proceeded on their voyage, and arrived at Penang, or the Prince of Wales' Island, on the 23rd of September, joining a large fleet containing fifteen thousand men, fitted out from the three Presidencies of Bengal, Madras, and Bombay. The anchorage off this beautiful little island, situated ten miles from the Malay continent, is particularly convenient. The vessels might lay near enough to throw a biscuit on shore, as the sailors significantly express it, so that large portions of the troops were daily landed to bathe in a certain transparent lake of fresh water, and take exercise.

About five miles up the country there is a magnificent waterfall of several hundred feet in height, and the road leading to it through the most romantic and superb avenue of all descriptions of trees. The solitude, the various noises of insects, and the chirping of birds, would inspire the most volatile disposition with a certain involuntary desire of seclusion from the rest of his species. I was not singular in this feeling, as many other officers who had visited the enchanting scene described themselves affected by similar sensations.

We lived principally on buffalo beef, a coarse kind of meat, but wholesome and nutritious. Every morning large herds of buffaloes were seen swimming from the Queda or Malay coast, over the channel that separated it from Penang, for the supply of the army, one small canoe piloting over forty or fifty dun-coloured heads. The scene was novel and interesting, exciting much merriment in their clumsy endeavours to extricate themselves from the toils of their too active conductors, who soon towed them to the slaughter-house.

It was at this island I first tasted those delicious and luscious fruits called *mangostiens* and *rambostieils*. There is a considerable resemblance in their flavour, but their appearance is totally different; the former is about the size of a middling-sized apple, with a rough, crisp rind or shell, which cracks and breaks on the slightest pressure, exposing a fine, light blue, jellied mass, in which is contained a kernel about the size of a horse-chestnut, and might be mistaken for one; the latter is rather larger than a walnut, perfectly round, with rough, knotted, crisp shell, which, when broken, a delicious circular lump of jelly immediately detaches itself, even superior in exquisite flavour to the *mangostien*; but there is no kernel within this fruit. There is also another species of this indigenous fruit growing most luxuriantly, called the *lichi*, whose quality of flavour is far less esteemed. They were, however, relished by the troops, being common and very cheap, whereas the others were extremely expensive.

The island is overrun with a mongrel race of Chinese, who carry on all the poor trade existing there. A filthy place, designated by the name of Bamboo Square, a receptacle for all the abandoned females of the town, was burnt down one night, occasioned by the folly and depravity of some of our wild young heroes, who went on shore for what they called a spree. I agreed with a small party one afternoon, to land on the Malay coast, and accordingly, after an hour's row, we landed on this savage coast, which was covered with a high jungle, with intervals of desert land. A Malay sprang out of the bramble armed to the teeth—sword, javelin, bow and arrows, with a huge buffalo-hide shield. Large rows of shells adorned his person. He stalked majestically towards us, enquiring with a most arrogant air, what business we had there? When told by a *lascar* who accompanied us, that we merely came to see the country, and would shortly return to the ship, he put on a more conciliating demeanour, but appeared particularly attracted by the brilliancy of my gold epaulet, which he demanded without ceremony.

Unwilling to comply with his wish, I was walking towards the boat, when he precipitately advanced, and almost tore the glittering bauble from my shoulder. This was rather too open an avowal of his ignorance of the difference between *meum* and *tuum*. A struggle ensued, and with the assistance of my companions I was extricated from his fierce gripe. He was greatly enraged and poised his javelin in a menacing attitude, when out flew our swords from their scabbards, and pistols were presented. The savage, nothing daunted, advanced on us with ferocious looks. We could in a moment have deprived him of existence, but decided of retiring peaceably to the boat, if he followed alone, and we soon pushed off.

The savage then coolly thrust his spear in the sand, and adjusting an arrow to his bow, shot it into the midst of us, at not thirty yards' distance. It entered the stern of the boat, just by the *lascar*, who was steering. One of our party then fired a pistol. We were, however, too far off to do execution, though the fellow seemed perfectly aware of the nature of firearms, by placing his broad shield before him. He then gave us a parting arrow, and a shout of abuse, and we speedily returned to our vessel.

One of these fierce barbarians "ran amuck" whilst we were off the island, that is, he wildly entered one of the streets and *creesed* every person he met (the *creese* is a short dagger made in the blade to resemble a flame). He had killed several, when he was fortunately bayoneted by a *sepoy*, who met him in his mad career. These occurrences frequently disturb the town at Penang; these fellows either from intoxication, or the ferocious propensity of their nature, are seized with this mania of killing indiscriminately, without respect to friend or foe, which is termed "running amuck."

There is no race of beings on the face of the earth possessed of such vindictive inhuman dispositions as the Malay's. In their attacks on country ships they will neither give or receive quarter, fighting to the very last man; nor will they spare a single individual if they succeed in the capture of a vessel, and many manned with *lascars* annually fall victims to these numerous and ferocious pirates, who infest the sea in every part of the Straits of Malacca, Banda, and about the Malacca Islands.

CHAPTER 7

Return to Madras

A few days after our arrival at Penang, an express sloop anchored, bringing intelligence of an expected rupture with Tippoo Saib, and dispatches directing the immediate return of the troops to Madras and the other Presidencies. We sailed without delay, but encountering constant gales of adverse winds, and finding it unavailing to contend against the north-west monsoon, a meeting of the captains of the fleet took place, deciding our return to Penang. Having suffered three weeks under torrents of rain and successive storms, we again reached this beautiful little island on the 20th October, where we remained in smooth water, and masticating buffalo beef until the 15th November, when we once more encountered the dangers of the ocean stretching across the Bay of Bengal, under the auspices of a favourable breeze, and every stitch of canvas spread, a second despatch sloop having been expedited from Madras to acquaint us with the imminent danger menacing the Company's possessions from the *sultan*, Tippoo Saib, with directions for our instant departure from Penang, and to adopt every judicious means of reaching the Presidency with the least possible delay.

The Chinamen were allowed to proceed on to Canton; the division of the 12th, on board the *Ceres*, had therefore been transhipped to another vessel, the *Princess Mary*, a country ship of 500 tons, manned with *lascars*, or Indian sailors, an active race in fine weather, but exceeding timid, I may say pusillanimous, in a storm or heavy gale of wind. During our last anchorage at Penang we lost a captain, Whinstone, a man addicted to the excessive use of spirits, and although exhausted and dying with a tremendous abscess in his liver, on his death two bottles of liquor were found secreted under his pillow. The most irreclaimable propensities of human beings are certainly gambling and drinking; in the whole course of my existence I have never witnessed one instance of radical cure for these evils.

We were under convoy of a frigate, commanded by the Honourable Captain Murray, and the *Princess Mary*, a sluggish sailer, was frequently signalled to make more sail, but as she was very crank, alias not having sufficient ballast on board, the captain was apprehensive she would upset, if strained under too heavy a pressure of canvas. The frigate fired several shots ahead and astern of her, and at length the arbitrary honourable captain approaching nearer, fixed another shot between the main and mizen masts, cutting some of the ropes close over the heads of the troops. He then hailed us in a furious passion, threatening to fire into us if the captain did not hoist more sail.

This was too much for our little impetuous Major Bellairs, who commanded on board, who, seizing the speaking trumpet, thundered forth: "The person by whose direction the last shot was fired is a damned rascal; and tell your captain that I, Major Bellairs of the 12th, say so!" The frigate sheered off, and no notice was ever taken of this hasty expression. In the course of the passage a sudden squall of wind laid the *Princess Mary* on her broadside, and for several minutes we were apprehensive of foundering. The *lascars* hid themselves, and the exertions of the soldiers alone extricated us from our imminent peril.

CHAPTER 8

March to Tanjore

On the 15th December, 1797, we once more cast anchor in the Madras roads, and landed the same day. During our absence, a French squadron had appeared off the fort, and succeeded in driving an Indiaman on shore, close under the walls, and after exchanging a few shots with the fort, and receiving a shell or two on board, they sailed off to the southward. This squadron consisted of the seven ingrates whose attack we were prepared for in traversing the Bay of Bengal the preceding year on our passage to India. Some few weeks after their appearance off Madras, they encountered three of our seventy-fours in a calm, which, from their unwieldy size, were very roughly treated, being left almost wrecks without the possibility of retaliating. Captain Lucas, commanding the three English men-of-war, was brought to a court martial. The occurrence, *in toto*, broke his heart, and we had the melancholy duty of depositing the remains of this gallant but unfortunate officer in the Vipiray burying ground, near the fort of Madras.

The four companies left behind on our departure had also embarked and sailed, but a signal was hoisted for their immediate return, and they disembarked the following day. The Governor of Madras had fortunately received information of the hostile intention of Tippoo Saib just in time to prevent the final departure of the fleet, which was only barely in sight as the signal was made. The regiment shortly received a route for Tanjore; on the 26th January, 1798, encamped on the island close to Madras, and two days afterwards proceeded on the march to the place of destination. At this period there was a most dangerous and secret mutiny existing among the company's troops, and I fear some individuals of the 12th were not wholly exempt from suspicion of participation in the disgraceful proceeding.

We had accomplished two marches, when four companies, under

the immediate command of Colonel Aston, were ordered to return to the Mount for the purpose of attending the execution of several European artillerymen, who had been sentenced by a court martial to be blown from the mouth of a cannon. They marched back ten miles, and, after witnessing this shocking spectacle, returned to camp. If our men were really implicated the scene had a very salutary effect, as we reached Tanjore on the 1st of March, a distance of 300 miles, without the slightest indication of any mutinous disposition.

Two companies were detached to garrison the old fort of Vellum, eleven miles off, under Major Picton, who was second in command. Three times a week the eight companies at Tanjore met this detachment, on a fine open plain, equi-distant from the two stations, and were there drilled and manoeuvred for several hours. This arduous duty could not last long; five miles' march to the drill ground, two hours' incessant evolution, and five miles home again, under the fierce rays of a tropical sun, was enough to damp the ardour and exhaust the physical strength of the most robust European.

Many men were struck dead by *coup de soleil,* and four hundred lying in hospital afflicted with dysentery, and other severe complaints. The representations of the surgeon on the imprudence of thus harassing the corps was unattended to; our hardy colonel continued the exercise, but he was always on horseback, and felt not the scorching sun; if he did, it was not accompanied by that excess of fatigue and overwhelming exhaustion that affected those who were compelled to march. Many a time have I relieved a poor fainting soldier from the weight of his musket, and carried it myself, wringing the perspiration in streams from my sodden clothes.

On returning to the garrison, either from climate or excess of fatigue, two officers and upwards of one hundred men died, when government interfered, issuing a peremptory order for the prevention of any future meeting between the two separated portions of the corps, the famous cavalry general, Floyd, at the same time receiving orders to inspect both divisions at their actual stations. On the 4th of May he arrived, and after minute inspection issued the following order:—

Tanjore, May 4th, 1798.

Major-General Floyd desires to express to Colonel Aston, his officers, and men, the satisfaction he received on inspecting this day the eight companies of His Majesty's 12th Regiment at this station. In the masterly hands of their commanding officer, there is every reason to expect that His Majesty's 12th Regiment of Infantry will, whenever they are called upon, be ready and disposed to renew in the East the glories of Minden and Gibraltar!

It is a singular coincidence of time and events, that on this very day the following year, at the storming of Seringapatam, the regiment distinguished itself in the most memorable manner, but, alas! poor Aston was not doomed to reap the benefits of his zeal and ardour in the service.

Chapter 9

Duel and Death of Colonel Ashton

Strong rumours of approaching collision with the army of Tippoo Saib daily prevailed, and our youthful heroes sighed for the hour of action. The route soon came, and the 22nd of July saw us on our march towards the fort of Arnee. In passing Trichinopoly, where General Floyd was stationed with the 19th Dragoons, his favourite corps, in the command of which he had so often signalised himself in former battles and skirmishes with the Mysoreans, we were (*id est*, the officers of the 12th) hospitably invited to dine with the general.

On the introduction of Mrs. Floyd, a beautiful young woman of eccentric disposition, to Colonel Aston, she immediately exclaimed: "Good Lord! Hervey, I always understood you were a very handsome man; but you are as black as a Moorman, and the ugliest fellow I ever saw." Aston, who was a very bashful man, blushed scarlet red, and was *pétri de confusion*.

Soon after Colonel Aston was relating one of his most facetious and amusing anecdotes, when the lady burst forth with, "Well, Hervey, that is the greatest lie I ever heard in my life."

"Pardon me," replied he, "I can tell much greater."

"Do, then; I request of you as a favour."

All was excitement to hear the colonel's reply, when he calmly said: "It is, that Mrs. Floyd is the whitest lady I ever met in my life."

The old general shook his sides with laughter, exclaiming: "You deserve it, madam; you deserve it. Ho! ho! ho!"

She cast a petrifying look at her *caro sposo*, rose from her chair in an agony of tears, and left the table, rudely pushing aside the extended hand of the gallant colonel, who offered his services to conduct her to the door. Some time previously, she had amused the general with one of those extravagant tricks which only a woman on the eve of lunacy would have thought of. He was in front of his regiment observing the manoeuvres, when she rode up to him with, her youngest child in her arms, fifteen months old, and begged the old general to take it for a moment, as she felt unwell. He accordingly took the child, when she rode off laughing, leaving the general at the head of his regiment with the infant in his arms. She afterwards visited the presidency of Madras on her way to England.

The regiment entered the fort of Arnee on the 31st December, and here we were destined to lose our brave, liberal, and gallant colonel. He had proceeded to Madras on some private affairs of importance, and during his absence Major Picton, the next senior officer, had convened a meeting of the officers, relative to the mess; and the decision being contrary to the wishes of the colonel, he directed a most offensive order to be issued, commenting on the irregularity and unsoldierlike conduct of Major Picton in assembling the corps without his permission, and canvassing a point contrary to his express wishes.

A letter was then written by Picton, which was returned from Madras by the colonel in a blank cover. Irritated by this contemptuous mode of treatment, and deeming it a palpable insult, the major resolved on seeking gentlemanly satisfaction for the affront. About the same period, Lieut. Hartly wrote a private note to Colonel Aston, complaining of the paymaster, Major Allen, relative to some pecuniary transaction.

In reply, Aston wrote that Allen was a most "illiberal fellow." This was a private communication and ought not in honour to have been divulged; but Hartly read the obnoxious clause to some of his brother officers. Lieut. Nixon reported the nature of the paragraph to Major Allen, remarking, that as his friend, he could not tamely submit to the publicity of such an accusation without imparting the circumstance to the major, who remarked: "As a sense of friendship has ostensibly induced you to communicate this affair, I expect you to carry a message to the colonel from me, on his immediate arrival."

Lieut. Nixon represented that he depended on his pay, and could not, without probable ruin, act in the capacity of second in a duel with his immediate commanding officer, and offered numerous other excuses to extricate himself from the dilemma, when Major Allen, turning from him in disgust, replied: "Mr. Nixon, you represented yourself as my friend, but I can look upon you in no other light than as an invidious enemy, prone to mischief, and malignantly endeavouring to foment a quarrel between your superior officers." He indignantly turned on his heel, leaving the officious personage to no very pleasing reflections.

As illiberality was by no means a characteristic of Major Allen's general disposition, he felt doubly aggrieved at this wanton imputation, and resolved mildly to ask an explanation and some trifling concession. He little imagined he should be compelled to obliterate the stigma by shedding the blood of his most intimate friend. Human beings are certainly impelled by destiny; our profoundest precautions and most amiable intentions are too frequently frustrated, and our greatest omissions as often turn to our advantage. I am of opinion the colonel would never have adopted the expression, had he reflected for a moment, or been impressed with the idea that the contents of a private note could be exposed to public animadversion.

He often condemned his youthful follies in as severe a tone as the most rigid ascetic could have wished; and his general mode of conciliating conduct towards the officers of his regiment evinced a full determination of attracting their regard and esteem. His too ardent zeal for the welfare of the service certainly led him into some little venial errors; the very best of us are but imperfect creatures, and constantly liable to dereliction from the established code of civilised society.

In November, Colonel Aston rejoined the regiment at Arnee, and the following morning a message was delivered to him from Major Picton, requiring an apology for the insult of returning his note in a blank cover. The colonel replied he was not in the habit of making apologies; consequently arrangements were made for the meeting in two hours afterwards.

The distance of eight paces regularly measured, the signal given, when Picton fired his pistol, without effect. "Fire again, major; fire again!" exclaimed Aston.

"Not unless you fire at me," rejoined Picton.

"I have no personal animosity against you, Major Picton, and have only been actuated in my conduct towards you by a sense of good to the service, and therefore cannot fire at you," replied the colonel, and immediately fired the contents of his pistol in the air. No apology was made, and the respective parties returned to their quarters. Picton would not have been justified in firing a second time, according to the established custom of etiquette in the reigning system of duelling, and retired very ill-satisfied with the result of the *rencontre*.

The ensuing day Asst.-Surgeon Erskine waited on Colonel Aston for the purpose of receiving some explanation relative to the hasty expression of "illiberal fellow," contained in the letter to Lieut. Hartly, which he had unguardedly read to the officers of the mess, and in justice and honour ought to have been made responsible for his intemperance; in fact, had he been possessed of an atom of spirit, or generous feeling, he would have come forward, even at the risk of a venial violation of veracity, and borne the whole onus of the affair. On Mr. Erskine's application for explanation, Colonel Aston merely observed: "I certainly did not intend the contents of the note written to Lieut. Hartly for public inspection, and it is rather hard to be made responsible for the indiscretion of another man. However, as circumstances have occurred, what is your further pleasure?"

Mr. Erskine replied, he was requested by Major Allen to demand an apology, or immediate satisfaction for the implied libel on his character. Colonel Aston's high spirit instantly took fire, and he warmly replied: "Tell Major Allen, sir, that I make an apology to no man, and never did. As to fighting, I'll fight the whole regiment if they require it!"

Mr. Erskine said, "There is no alternative. colonel!" and the meeting was proposed to take place at one o'clock the same day. Major Allen, who was one of the mildest of God's creatures, could not refrain from tears on Erskine's representation of the inevitable necessity of a duel with his quondam, friend and commanding officer. He was well aware of the determined spirit of Colonel Aston, and that he would be probably shot if he did not wound him severely; and brave as he was mild, he prepared for the unhappy event, which was ultimately, in its consequences, to terminate his existence. He proceeded to the ground of action; the usual preliminaries were adopted, when Major Allen said in a voice almost suffocated with emotion: "Will you. Colonel Aston, make the slightest apology?"

"I came here to fight, and not apologise!" was the reply.

"Will you only say you did not intend to cast a reflection on my general character as an officer and a gentleman?"

"I shall answer no questions now, so fire away!"

The only answer to this last remark was: "Then your death be on your own head!"

The pistols were then raised—the signal given. A moment's hesitation ensued ere Allen fired. He expected the first shot from his adversary, but being disappointed, drew his trigger, and the fatal ball entered the right side of the colonel, passing through the backbone, and lodging just under the skin of the left side. This was not, of course, discovered until the body was dissected. The colonel stood immovable for a few seconds, with his arm still elevated in the position of firing. He hastily said: "Major Allen, I could now shoot you, but the last act of my life shall not be murder.!"

He then turned round to his second (Major Craigie, who did not know he was wounded) and faintly observed, "Support me; I am going to fall!" Craigie could scarcely believe the evidence of his senses, until supporting the colonel in his arms, he discovered a small spot of blood just under the waistcoat pocket, and then only was convinced something serious had occurred. The colonel had fainted, and in this state was conveyed to his house. The despair of poor Allen was inexpressible. Casting the fatal pistol on the ground, he uttered the most piercing cries of distress, saying he had killed his best friend, and ran off the ground like a maniac; nor was it ascertained what had become of him for many days after. Even Erskine, his second, was ignorant of the place of his seclusion. On recovering from his insensibility, Colonel Aston was surrounded by his friends, all anxious for the preservation of this extraordinary man. On observing the surgeon among them, he calmly addressed him, saying: "You know, doctor, I am not one of those who fear the prospect of death; therefore, tell me candidly and honestly if my wound be mortal?"

The surgeon replied he had not yet sufficiently ascertained the exact nature of the wound to give a decided opinion, but did not hesitate to say that from its situation, there certainly existed extreme danger. "I thank you for your candour," said the colonel; "and now give me something, if possible, to relieve me from the excessive pain I suffer." An opiate was administered, and the following day he was free from any considerable pain. The wound was so deeply situated that probing was judged dangerous; but from his cheerful demeanour, and constant occupation of dictating his will, the most favourable anticipations were entertained of his ultimate recovery.

It was during this period that Woodhall, my old friend and schoolfellow, entered my quarters, saying he had just seen the colonel, who was much better, then presented me with a handsome white feather as a present from him, acquainting me that the colonel had issued an order appointing me to the grenadier company. Who can describe the pleasure of a young officer on being appointed to a flank company? It far exceeds the poor power of language. I experienced all these nameless, indescribable sensations, and heartily prayed for the speedy recovery of this excellent officer, who, had he lived, would have led us on to glory and honour.

But fate ordained it otherwise, for on the seventh day from the infliction of the fatal wound, he expressed a desire to be assisted out of bed. He had scarcely touched the floor with his foot, than, giving a sudden spring up, he fell dead on his bed. I obtained all these minute details from our Asst.-Surgeon Erskine, with whom I was on the most intimate terms, as he was personally and actively employed, both professionally and otherwise, in this interesting affair. There can exist little doubt on the authenticity of this narration, which I have here recorded from memory, after a lapse of time of nearly forty years. The impression of the scene is just as vivid on my imagination at this moment, as if it had only occurred yesterday.

Three days after the decease of the colonel, his remains were conveyed with all due respect and military pomp, from his house about half-a-mile distant, into the fort, and interred in the little cemetery in the eastern quarter. A handsome monument erected to his memory exists to this day, having been repaired a few years since by the benevolent and voluntary interposition of Major Munro, of the company's service, who liberally and generously paid the attending expenses out of his own private funds. Thus destiny disposed of the proud, chivalrous, and gallant Lt-Colonel Henry Hervey Aston. On what insignificant occurrences depends the life of us poor mortals! The gravest events are frequently produced by the merest trifles.

Now for the sequel of this melancholy transaction. The unfortunate Major Allen, who was of a conscientious, religious turn of mind, had hurried precipitately to his quarters, fastened all the doors and windows, everyone supposing from the deserted appearance of the rooms that he had escaped to Madras. However, when the heavy roll of the double drum announced the funeral procession of his lamented friend, he joined the *cortège* in the usual military mourning costume in solemn silence.

Never was alteration in man produced in so short a space of time; from the portly, full-faced, handsome being of six feet high, he was actually reduced to a skeleton, with countenance as pale as a corpse, cadaverous, hollow eyes, unusual stoop in his shoulders, and so weak that he was scarcely enabled to follow to the grave. When the awful sounding coffin was first struck by the descending earth, he fell fainting into the arms of the bystanders, and was in that state conveyed to his quarters. His *dubash*, or head servant, reported that the major had never touched an atom of food since the fatal event. He only asked for water, continually repeating the expression of "Oh, God! Oh, God! I have destroyed my dearest and best friend!"

Major Allen was now put in close arrest, and afterwards brought to a court martial at Pellore, by which tribunal he was acquitted, but without the word "honourably" preceding. The feelings of the court must have been prejudiced on this occasion, as there was, according to the principles of military etiquette, nothing dishonourable in the whole course of the transaction. The duel was fair, and nothing but its origin could be a source of reprehension; and of this, even the world has now ample latitude to form an opinion. Major Allen was never seen to smile again. He would pace his tent for hours, brooding over his unhappy, melancholy destiny, being the first officer who fell a victim to fever, at the commencement of the siege of Seringapatam.

CHAPTER 10

Before Seringapatam

The 12th regiment marched from Arnee on the 31st of December, 1798, and after a delay of some days at different encampments, joined the grand army at Pellore, on the 1st of February, 1799, where Colonel Wellesley, being the senior officer present, issued an order for the most intelligent officers to attend at his marquee daily, for the purpose of being initiated into the principles of extensive field movements. These gentlemen were, of course, selected by the commandants of corps. I was not yet sufficiently experienced for this employment, but had sense of discernment to discover that the most brilliant talents are by no means an infallible recommendation to confidential places. The most distant ramifications of the aristocracy are invariably the objects of promotion to all staff and lucrative situations.

Even in this selection, the family of officers was considered in preference to the adaptation of qualifications. I attended the field days of instruction, and could not but smile at the various blunders committed by these choice, intelligent officers; nor was the honourable colonel himself so great an adept in military evolutions as the world gave him credit for some years after. General Harris joining the army soon after, we were immediately put in motion for the Mysore country.

Previous to our march, a ludicrous, but nearly fatal scene occurred, close to the encampment. Our men were in the habit of teasing the monkeys that swarmed in immense numbers in thousands of banyan trees. An enormous fellow of the baboon species one morning bounded towards a lake or large tank in the vicinity of the camp, pursued by several soldiers, when suddenly taking the water, he thus hoped to evade his pursuers; but one man, bolder, and more imprudent than his comrades, stripped and swam after the huge animal, whom he soon overtook. The chattering and grinning of the enraged beast as he was caught by the tail afforded infinite amusement to the spectators; but this feeling was soon changed into apprehension for the safety of the soldier, whose arm was seized and bit through.

He disappeared under the water for a few seconds, and then was seen swimming towards the shore, assisting himself with one hand only, the baboon escaping to the opposite side of the lake. A more severe laceration of the arm could be scarcely imagined. The teeth of the animal had entered both sides of the upper part of the arm to the bone, the flesh being drawn several inches asunder. He was sent to the hospital tent, several weeks elapsing ere he was sufficiently recovered to resume the duties of his profession.

Before I enter on a very cursory account of the campaign against Tippoo Saib, it may not be deemed irrelevant to the subject to give a description of the provision of a subaltern for six months' consumption, which may convey a pretty correct idea of the magnitude of the followers of an army of thirty thousand men. I had two bullocks laden with biscuits, two with wine and brandy, two with my trunks, and four for the marquee, in addition to which a *dubash*, *maty* boy, and six *coolies* to transport my couch, chairs, and various other little appendages. Thus, I was accompanied by ten bullocks and eight servants, the majority of whom were followed by every individual of their family—grandfathers, grandmothers, uncles, aunts, nephews, nieces, with whole generations of children. This may appear an exaggerated statement, but no less extraordinary than true.

Every officer in the army was thus encumbered, and generally to a more extensive degree. Marching, thus attended, through the Company's territory about one hundred miles, on the 5th of March we entered the Mysorean dominions by the Ryacottah Pass. Scarcely had we ascended the heights when large bodies of cavalry were observed in the distance, retiring leisurely towards the interior. A rocky hill fort about a quarter of a mile high appearing to offer some impediment to the advance of the army, Captain Woodhall proceeded towards dusk to surprise it. After two or three hours' climbing, the Light Infantry of the 12th under his command took possession of the fort on the summit, without opposition.

This fortification, called Neldroog, was then occupied by a company of *sepoys*, and the Light Infantry returned to camp. We were now joined by Lt.-Col. Shaw, an old, gallant officer who was transferred from the 74th Regiment, to replace our late lamented colonel. He immediately issued the following order:—

Camp near Killamungahim.
8th March, 1799.

As the 12th Regiment, from having the honour to be the oldest King's regiment in the army, is more liable to be called on for immediate service than any other corps, the commanding officer expects the officers, non-commissioned officers, and men will be ready by night or day to turn out at the shortest notice, and to get under arms without noise or confusion. On all sudden alarms, the Light Infantry is instantly to accoutre, without waiting for orders, and be in readiness to march whenever its services may be required.

He was a good, honest, hard-drinking Irishman, and had conducted himself most gallantly in former Indian warfare, and selected by the commander-in-chief to take charge of the fortunes of the 12th Regiment. It was determined, before advancing further, to surprise a large cavalry cantonment, fifteen miles out. A large force, consisting of the 12th, with numerous flank companies of other corps, marched all night for this purpose. During this expedition I observed several young soldiers moving with the column, fast asleep, with muskets on their shoulders, and marching as regularly as their more robust and vigilant companions, who frequently amused themselves by a variety of tricks at the expense of the somnambulists. The probability of this circumstance may be questioned, but old soldiers will bear me out in the assertion.

About an hour before daylight we came in view of the fires and lights in the enemy's lines. Fixing bayonets, we hurried on to the expected encounter, and at least ten thousand horse, as represented by our spies; we, however, found the place completely deserted. The enemy having been apprised of our advance had decamped, leaving their fires burning as a deception. General Baird, to whose command the detachment was entrusted, instantly countermarched, and returned to the army. We were, however, assailed several times by the looties, or predatory horsemen of the enemy, before we joined the main army. They kept at a respectable distance after a few straggling shots from our flankers. Nothing material now occurred, except the surprise of one of our pickets of *sepoys*, eighty of whom were literally cut to pieces in a night attack of the enemy's cavalry.

The officer was left among the heap of dead, a figure too horrible to describe. He had been wantonly and barbarously mutilated, with about thirty sabre wounds in different parts of his body, yet he recovered and returned to his native country, to linger on his future wretched existence. At a place called Amboor, previous to our mounting the Ghauts, the army had been joined by a considerable body of the *nizam's* forces—a disorderly set of savage, undisciplined barbarians, clothed in stuffed cotton, and steel chained armour, prancing and skirmishing about the country in every direction, yet wielding their long lances with uncommon dexterity, and managing their horses with grace and ease almost to perfection.

They were certainly an addition to our numerical strength, but in a military point of view of dubious advantage to the invading regular army, whose movements they frequently confused, by dashing through the infantry columns full gallop, being often mistaken for the enemy's irregular horse, and fired at accordingly.

The advance and movements of the army was entirely confided to the management of Colonel Barry Close, who was Adjutant-General to the Forces, a man of extensive capacity, who had displayed eminent talent in both civil and military situations during his long residence in India. He was an ornament to his profession, and had fortune favoured him might have proved a first-rate general; and by his amiable, conciliating disposition, was beloved and esteemed by all who enjoyed the advantage of his society. As we continued our march, the towns and villages were in flames in every direction. Not one atom of forage or food could be procured; every tank or reservoir of water was impregnated with the poisonous milk-hedge, many horses and bullocks falling victims to the deleterious infusion.

About twelve o'clock on the 27th of March we came in sight of the mud-walled fort of Mallavilly, and as the quartermaster-general's department were fixing on the place of encampment, on an extensive plain of sand just in front, the distant booming of heavy ordnance was plainly distinguished. The *lascars* had commenced pitching the tents, when they were interrupted in their occupation by cannon balls bounding amongst them, and immediately fled to shelter. The enemy were posted on an eminence about two miles distant, supported by a long range of numerous heavy artillery.

Our pickets, commanded by Captain Macpherson, of the 12th, pushed on towards their right flank with two twelve-pound gallopers, and the action became brisk in that quarter. Having ensconced themselves in a wood, they were ensured from the attacks of the hordes of cavalry hovering about them, who were saluted with repeated discharges of grape shot from the twelve-pounders.

The right wing of our army now formed on the intended ground of encampment in contiguous close columns, and in this form cautiously advanced towards the eminence in front. The balls and rockets were showered on us, but with ill-directed aim, and doing little execution. As we approached nearer the enemy's position, they were observed to withdraw their guns, and finally disappeared. In this advance, our captain of the grenadiers, I suppose, observing the paleness of my countenance, turned round and offered me a refreshing draught from the contents of his canteen, composed of brandy and water, which I gratefully accepted. The military man may sneer contemptuously at this indication of pusillanimity, but never during all my service did I see soldiers enter on a scene of action with that calm, florid appearance denoting a sense of security and health. Individuals may hector and swagger, but mortal never existed exempt from the feelings of human nature. I affirm there is a palpable evident alteration in every man's appearance at the commencement of a battle. As it rages, this disappears, and the excitement of exertion soon produces the usual effect of renewed animation, with a spirit of recklessness indifferent to all danger.

As our columns approached the summit of the hill, we deployed into line, soon reached the top, and from thence on the plain below, interspersed with several dense woods, saw the formidable army of Tippoo Saib drawn up in battle array. A large body of cavalry was in the act of charging our light infantry, who were skirmishing in front, but now running with headlong speed to rejoin the British line. This wedge-like column of horse, at the nearest angle, was led on by two enormous elephants, having huge chains hanging on their *probosci*, which they whirled about on both sides, a blow from which would have destroyed ten or twelve men at once.

At first we mistook these men for the *nizam's* troops, but as they rapidly approached towards an interval between the right of our corps and a battalion of *sepoys*, we were soon convinced of their intention of passing through and attacking the rear of the 12th. Fortunately, at this momentous crisis, a detachment of the Native cavalry of our army suddenly rode up and filled the interval, when the enemy made direct to the front of the old 12th Regiment. General Harris rode up to the rear, crying, "Fire, 12th! fire!" To their eternal credit, coolness, and unexampled discipline be it recorded, that not a shot was fired, nor even a movement made that indicated indecision.

The men knew it was not the voice of their colonel, who, however, now gave the word, "Steady, 12th, I command. Wait until they are within ten yards; then singe the beggars' whiskers!" This order was implicitly obeyed. At the word "Fire!" a volley was effectually poured into the wedge of cavalry, followed by a rapid and well-directed file firing. As the smoke cleared away a whole rampart of men and horses lay extended on the ground in front of the regiment. The elephants, maddened by pain, were making off, swinging their chains about in the midst of the cavalry. The *howdahs* from which the leading chiefs had directed the charge were dashed to atoms, and some of them falling headlong from the backs of the enraged animals.

Just at this instant two 9-pounders replaced the cavalry on the interval, and fired showers of grapeshot on the discomfited Moormen, who were retiring to the main body crowded in the topes or woods below, who, perceiving the entire defeat of these two thousand chosen men, poured forth their tens of thousands, scouring rapidly over the deep sands. Colonel Wellesley, on the left of the line, had come in contact with the enemy's infantry, and destroyed whole *cushoons*, or battalions of them. The defeat was complete, and Tippoo drew off with all possible haste. Unfortunately a division of the enemy's cavalry had passed round the right of our line into the rear, and destroyed the whole of our sick men.

The rear of the wedge were actually incapable of continuing the charge, so embarrassed were they by the heaps of slain lying in their front, and the elephants, now more sorely goaded from the grapeshot of our guns, excited by numerous wounds, and deprived of the conductors, turned all their fury on the *ilysoreans*, the ponderous chains, which they swayed about with prodigious rapidity, overturning all who opposed them in their retrograde movement.

Three or four horsemen cut through the 12th Regiment, but were instantly shot. To give an idea of the temper, sharpness, and weight of the swords of all these men (who had all drugged themselves with "*bang*," a species of opium, for the encounter), I have only to mention that the barrel of one of the men's muskets was completely cut in two by one stroke. The musket was many years preserved, and shown as a curiosity. It is now only necessary to add that the victory was most decided, the report of a gun booming at periods in the distance being the only indication of the proximity of an enemy. On returning to our original ground of encampment, the left wing of the army had just arrived, and heartily congratulated us on our success. The following orders were issued by the commander-in-chief, General Harris:—

Camp Malleville.
March 27th, 1799.

G.O. Parole, Malleville.

The commander-in-chief congratulates the army on the happy result of this day's action, during which he has had various opportunities of witnessing their gallantry, coolness, and ready attention to orders.

(Extract) Brigade Orders.

Major-General Baird, with the most heartfelt satisfaction, congratulates the brigade on the victory attained this day over the enemy. It is sufficient for him to say that the valour of the troops fully answered his expectations.

The loss of the enemy on this occasion was estimated at 5,000, our own less than so many hundreds. I have curtailed the account of this battle, as my object is principally to detail the fortunes of the 12th Regiment.

On the 24th of March I was ordered for out-picket, about a mile from the line of encampment, where the enemy's cavalry were hovering about in dense masses, ready to pounce on the exposed parts of our alignment. Observing the loads of two bullocks on the ground, near my position, consisting of entrenching tools, the animals having kicked them from off their backs and escaped to the jungle, I thought it advisable, as the whole day was before me, to employ my fifty men in throwing up a species of field fortification, to strengthen my position, especially as the Moorish cavalry became very daring, and menaced a charge, being kept at a distance only by repeated shots from my party. We set to work merrily, and before evening a respectable triangular breastwork, with a deep ditch, secured my pickets from surprise.

Never were exertions rewarded with more complete success, for about half-past twelve at night, the very earth trembled under the trampling of approaching cavalry, who came boldly on to our breastwork, with yells and shouts. I gave them a peppering file fire, which strewed the front of my position with nearly one hundred of their black carcases, when discharging their pistols and carbines, they suddenly wheeled off to the right, and made an attack on one of our *sepoy* pickets, consisting of eighty men, who were literally cut to atoms. The officer commanding them was left on the ground, with twenty-five sabre cuts on his body. Singular to remark, I had not a man of my picket even slightly wounded, whereas, had not the breastwork existed, I must have been inevitably butchered, with the whole of my detachment.

On the 3rd of April the army encamped within four miles of Seringapatam, behind a range of hills. On reaching this ground. General Harris, escorted by the 12th Regiment, reconnoitred the enemy's position from the apex of the hills. There was only a few cavalry in sight; but suddenly a most terrific earthquake commenced; the plains in front were observed undulating like the waves of the sea, which magnificent motion continued for upwards of a minute. Looking back, we saw our own army undisturbed by the extraordinary appearance. The view was really superb; an assemblage of 30,000 fighting men, 300,000 followers, 400 elephants, 1,000 camels, with 150,000 bullocks. Who could behold such a mass of living matter without the most awful and profoundest reflections! In a few short years all would vanish from the face of the earth, like the "baseless fabric of a vision!"

Many remarkable accounts have been related of the surprising sagacity and docility of the elephant, to which, hitherto, I had read and listened with a species of incredulity, but on this march such manifest proofs of their fine nature was evinced, that I became a convert to all its wondrous instinct. One instance only that occurred under my own personal observation is sufficient to display the comprehensive force of their physical and instinctive energies. A 42-pounder, the largest gun in our battering train, was plunged deeply into a slough, with the mud level to the hind axletree of the carriage.

Fifty bullocks were in vain straining with united strength to extricate the ponderous machine from its immersed dilemma, when an elephant was brought up to their assistance. He seized the muzzle of the gun with his *proboscis*, but finding the weight exceeding the power of his strength, he emitted a trumpeting, sonorous sound, on which another elephant in the rear sprang forward to his assistance. The united exertions of both these noble animals lifted the gun and carriage bodily out of the tough clay; the bullocks at the same instant were exerted to their full strength, and thus the unwieldy machine was again put in motion.

This may sarcastically be denominated a traveller's tale—an epithet too commonly applied by the ignorant and sedentary individuals of a country town to every extraordinary event beyond the sphere of their limited comprehension. A thorough knowledge of the Latin and Greek languages is not alone adequate to the investigation of all the mysteries of nature; but, forsooth, because the elephants of Pyrrhus, in his war with the Romans, did not perform these astonishing feats, all modern travellers' accounts are considered as exaggerated. I was relating this very anecdote some years after to an old divine in Brecon, a Mr. Williams, when he apostrophised me with a solemn air, saying:

"Young man, in promulgating such extraordinary events, I would advise you to reflect, and abstain from all narrations of so dubious a tenour, and beyond the bounds of probability, or the name of Traveller will attach to you during life."

His age and profession secured him from my resentment; but I *did* reflect, that a learned ignoramus might exist under the sanctified and solemn garb of a Welsh parson. Having reconnoitred the enemy's position, and taken a distant view of the strong fortified town of Seringapatam in the distance. General Harris, with his escort, retraced their steps to the ground of encampment. Clouds of rocketmen and irregular cavalry soon appeared, annoying us in every possible shape, and it was some hours ere the tents were regularly pitched; and even then the rockets were continually whizzing amongst them, setting them on fire, as also killing and maiming many of the camp followers.

About six o'clock this evening, the 12th Regiment, with the flank companies of the 74th and 94th Regiments (which latter corps was then denominated the Scotch Brigade) assembled under Major-General Baird, for the purpose of beating up the enemy's cavalry camp, and scouring a wood three miles in front. We proceeded at a slow and cautious pace in various directions, without discovering the cavalry, and at length entered the tope, or wood, about two o'clock in the morning. Here we discovered the remnants of fires, with a variety of cooking materials, denoting, evidently, that the place had but recently been abandoned. There was a long ditch with a breastwork of earth on the skirts of the wood nearest to the fortress, from which it was a mile and a half distant.

The night was dark, and after wandering in the mazes of the different pathways, General Baird came to the determination of returning to camp; being bewildered, and observing the lights in Seringapatam, they were taken for those of our encampment. We therefore moved towards them, but had not proceeded far when Major Lambton, who had a pocket compass, assured the general that we were advancing in an opposite direction. A light was procured, and the compass placed on the ground, when he was convinced of the accuracy of the representation, and we speedily quitted our dangerous situation in an opposite course.

Passing a space of about two miles, we were suddenly halted, ordered to fix bayonets, and to advance *au pas du charge*, and were at once in the midst of a large body of the enemy's cavalry. Two shots only were fired from their *védettes*, when the fatal bayonet was actively at work amidst the slumbering horsemen. Here first my maiden sword was stained with the blood of a fellow-being. A man had been passed over by the troops in front, when, as I placed my foot on the spot near him, he rose on his knees, and made a desperate plunge at my body with a short *creese* or dagger. It glanced through my coat, waistcoat, and shirt, grazing the skin just below my breast, making me stagger backwards.

In an instant I made a random blow with my sword, which fortunately came in contact with his shoulder, and struck him to the earth. The dagger fell from his hand, which I seized, and preserved as a memorial of my narrow escape for many years after. I was then hurried forward by the rest of the troops, and nothing but dying groans interrupted the silence of the night, for at least a quarter of an hour. Few escaped to tell the tale of the fatal surprise.

Our men now loaded, expecting a larger body of cavalry to revenge their fallen comrades. Two companies were pushed out on the flanks, and we again moved on for an hour, when suddenly a rushing noise of approaching troops made the column halt. We wheeled into line, and fired a volley in the direction. At the same moment a voice was heard shouting, "Cease firing; cease firing; we are friends!" The flankers had lost their way, and coming on the main body in an, opposite direction to that from whence they had been thrown out, were naturally supposed to be the enemy. Many poor fellows were killed and wounded by this unhappy mistake. The wounded were mounted on our captured horses, and we once more reached camp at dawn of day, just as the general was beating for the march of the army. I was so overpowered by sleep and fatigue that for half an hour, during the martial preparations for marching, I buried my senses in sweet oblivion on the damp ground.

On the 4th of April the army merely shifted their situation a few hundred yards, but on the 5th moved to the permanent encampment for the siege, about four miles, the enemy's rockets hissing through the columns during the whole march. Several of the unfortunate camp followers being entrapped by the unprincipled looties, were sent into camp with noses and ears cut off. We retaliated by hanging those barbarians, whenever they were taken prisoners.

General Order.

Parole Cornwallis.
5th April, 1799.

The commander-in-chief takes the opportunity of noticing the high sense he has of the general exertion of the troops throughout the long and tedious march, with the largest encampment ever known to move with an army in India; and in congratulating them on a sight of Seringapatam, he has every confidence that a continuance of the same exertions will very shortly put an end to their labours, and place the British colours on its walls.

(Signed)

Barry Close,
Adjutant General.

CHAPTER 11

Taking of Seringapatam

The ground of encampment was on the upper part of an inclined plane, at the foot of which, on the opposite bank of the River Cauvery, stood the proud fortress of Seringapatam, at three miles' distance, from whence they already began to throw shot from guns of a huge calibre into camp, and so pestered were we with the rocket boys that there was no moving without danger from these destructive missiles. Pickets were therefore thrown out to drive them off, which soon established tranquillity and tolerable safety in the lines.

At sunset this evening (5th April) the 12th Regiment was suddenly ordered under arms. It appears that General Harris, after due consultation and deliberation with the adjutant-general, who was the *primum mobile* of every military movement, had decided on opening the trenches if possible this night, before the enemy could collect sufficient force to offer serious opposition, for having expected the attack on the other side of the fortress, the whole of Tippoo's army was assembled on the opposite banks of the Cauvery, having been deceived by a demonstration on our part, it occupying that position two days previously.

In accordance with this determination, two separate bodies of troops were ordered to assemble at 6 o'clock this evening, one destined to take possession of the dry sandy bed of a *nullah* or rivulet in front, the other to occupy a wood at some distance on the right of the river (which the detachment under General Baird had traversed a night or two preceding, but had been silently evacuated by the enemy on the approach of the English); both these positions were now completely occupied by strong and select columns of Tippoo's Tyger Sepoys. This circumstance was not, however, ascertained until after the attack. To accomplish these arduous enterprises, His Majesty's 12th Regiment with a battalion of natives paraded under the command of Colonel Shaw, and advanced from the British lines towards the *nullah*.

The other division, under the honourable Colonel Wellesley, consisting of His Majesty's 33rd Regiment and a battalion of *sepoys*, quitted camp half-an-hour afterwards, proceeding in the direction of the wood on the right, each detachment consisting of 1,500 men. It was intended to carry the two posts simultaneously, for the mutual protection and security of the attacking forces, as one position was almost untenable without the occupation of the other, and both were situated about midway between the encampment and the fortress, that is, at one and a-half miles' distance from each. Colonel Shaw's column had marched on slowly and cautiously for three-quarters of an hour, when the whole atmosphere became suddenly illuminated with a brilliant blaze of light from innumerable fire-balls thrown forward by the enemy, who, perceiving the exact situation of Shaw's force, then projected thousands of rockets and saluted us with repeated volleys of musketry, pouring death into our ranks. The sight was brilliant but awful in its effects.

The Tyger Sepoys were plainly observed in heavy masses in our front, and on both flanks pouring in a destructive fire; still, this gallant little body moved slowly on, unintimidated by the numerous foe, although each moment more encumbered by the wounded. The rockets and musketry from upwards of 20,000 of the enemy were incessant. No hail could be thicker. Every illumination of blue lights was accompanied by a shower of rockets, some of which entered the head of the column, passing through to its rear, causing death, wounds, and dreadful lacerations from the long bamboos of twenty or thirty feet, which are invariably attached to them. The instant a rocket passes through a man's body it resumes its original impetus of force, and will thus destroy ten or twenty until the combustible matter with which it is charged becomes expended. The shrieks of our men from these unusual weapons was terrific; thighs, legs, and arms left fleshless with bones protruding in a shattered state from every part of the body, were the sad effects of these diabolical engines of destruction.

Not a shot was returned from our column, nor had the men even loaded their pieces; a caution from our cool old colonel that "All must be done by the bayonet" needed no repetition to ensure obedience. Scarcely had this order been conveyed through the ranks, when an increased and tremendous peal of musketry for several minutes was distinctly heard from the wood on our right, a certain indication that

Wellesley's column was also seriously opposed. This soon ceased, but immediately afterwards the rear of our right flank was turned, from whence the enemy poured in deadly volleys of musketry. Thus situated, it became a paramount object to shelter our soldiers from this fresh accession of fire; they were therefore directed to lie down, as it would have been a wanton and useless sacrifice of the men's lives to stand and confront such a sweeping and formidable desolation.

The enemy supposing from our recumbent posture, which was plainly exposed by the light of the fire-balls, that the majority were annihilated, a heavy column of Tyger Sepoys ventured a desperate attack at the point of the bayonet, and actually drove our *sepoys* in confusion on the Europeans, killing their commandant, Major Colin Campbell, and wounding many officers. As soon as we were liberated from the flying *sepoys*, who scampered pell-mell over our prostrate line, the command, "Up 12th and charge!" was a signal obeyed with alacrity, and we plunged headlong into the ranks of the swarming foe, springing on them like lions.

The effect was magical; for the moment they discovered the white faces of our men, a general cry of "*Fringee bong chute! Fringee bong chute!*" ensued. They were seized with a general panic and scoured over the plain much more rapidly than they had advanced, and they were scattered in all directions. The murderous rockets and musketry still showering from the other quarters, we were soon compelled to resume our prostrate manoeuvre, and thus remained for several hours patiently awaiting the dawn of day.

About one o'clock in the morning the solemn trampling of a body of troops was again distinguished on our right flank, which being attributed to a renewed effort of the Tyger Sepoys to recover their lost honour our gallant fellows again sprang up, prepared for another charge, when a few stragglers from the honourable Colonel Wellesley's detachment rushed in and warned us of the approach of the remains of that force, which had been repulsed from the wood with great slaughter, and were now advancing to join Colonel Shaw. A few minutes after this report Major Shea (second in command to Wellesley), 33rd Regiment, joined us, with several companies of that corps. He stated that Colonel Wellesley was missing, and the force under his command had been completely broken, repulsed, and dispersed; he had traversed the wood in quest of him, but without success; they had stormed an entrenchment lined with the enemy's pikemen with lances at least twenty feet long, and for once the bayonet had proved ineffectual.

The whole detachment was broken and then charged by the pikemen, by whom they had been dispersed in all parts of the *tope*; that the colonel had been seen by some of the men making off in great agitation in the rear towards the encampment, followed by an officer and a few soldiers; having then collected the scattered remains of the force, and the enemy's fire becoming exceedingly destructive, he had abandoned the wood, for the purpose of preserving the lives of his remaining men, and had joined our detachment in hopes of obtaining information and instructions how to proceed.

This distressing intelligence threw a gloom over our gallant little band, which was not diminished on hearing our inflexible old Colonel Shaw reply, that he did not require his services, and recommending him to follow his colonel to camp. How far this laconic admonition was judicious, in the existing posture of affairs is subject of doubt; the hint, however, was immediately complied with, Major Shea and his remaining force retiring towards camp. Indignation here certainly overcame a sense of prudence and self-preservation, as Shaw soon found the Tyger Sepoys pouring volleys on us from all quarters; the stoutest heart in the force predicting a fatal result from such an unequal conflict.

Large quantities of ammunition were forwarded incessantly from camp during the night, to replenish the imagined expenditure of Shaw's column; the oldest soldiers having never heard such a continued peal of musketry, from which circumstance it was naturally apprehended that all our cartridges had been expended; but this tremendous noise had originated in the exertions of the numerous enemy surrounding us, not a man of our force having even loaded for the space of twelve hours. And this tremendous fire continued without interruption, blue lights and rockets illuminating the atmosphere the whole time, beautiful though terrific.

We now only awaited the dawn of day to exhibit one of the most glorious and impressive scenes that ever added lustre to the British annals of military fame. The whole army in the encampment was drawn up, and just as light appeared the 12th Regiment, with the battalion of *sepoys*, were plainly discovered advancing in line towards the bed of the river, opposed by clouds of the enemy, and a heavy cannonade from the fortress of Seringapatam. The resistance was certainly of the most imposing and formidable description, and the result anxiously attended by our gallant comrades in camp, whose glasses and eyes were fixed on the dubious scene in commiserating suspense: every heart thrilled with hopes and best wishes for our success.

At length the 12th, supported by the *sepoys*, dashed into the bed of the river, and all was involved for some minutes in a mass of confusion; the attacking force was absolutely hid from view; crowds of the enemy in front, flanks and rear obscured their apparent existence; our exertions and courage were certainly put to the test. There was not a single idle bayonet: oaths, shouts, and carnage presented a terrible scene of human ferocity; never did men more heroically perform their duty. The conflict was excessively murderous and obstinate, as the Tyger Sepoys were brave, numerous, and well disciplined. For some time the combat appeared dubious, as a considerable body of French troops persevered in most gallant style to lead on Tippoo's *sepoys*; this did not continue of long duration, for Colonel Shaw, attracted by the obstinate resistance of the French, directed our grenadiers to charge them, when they turned and fled with precipitation.

This example was followed immediately by the surrounding enemy, and we pursued them some distance beyond the *nullah*, but the shots from the fort played on us so rapidly that we were soon compelled to return and shelter ourselves under its banks. The admiration of our army was vividly excited, and General Harris was heard to exclaim, "Well done old 12th; why, they are going to take Seringapatam!" We had scarcely taken possession of the bed of the river and sheltered ourselves under the embankment from the thundering cannon of the fortress, when the enemy in the wood (from which Wellesley had been repulsed) opened several field-pieces on us, completely enfilading the position; a mound of earth was quickly thrown up on the right of the regiment to protect us from this destructive fire.

Several of the enemy's battalions also advanced and poured in volleys of musketry; this additional annoyance induced us once more to form line, load, and fire, on which they again retired to the wood, but no human effort would have prevented us being expelled from this exposed situation, had not a brigade from camp marched to take possession of the *tope*, from which we were so cruelly enfiladed. The enemy, on the approach of the British, quietly abandoned the wood, which was accordingly taken possession of without loss on our side, though in retiring they halted, faced about and delivered repeated volleys.

From Shaw's post we saluted them with a sharp fire of field-pieces on their flank, by which or from the guns of the brigade they lost one of the bravest chiefs of their army (Seyd Giaffer). This evening (6th April) we were relieved in the trenches by the gallant 74th Regiment, who lost several men in their approach, and we were heartily rejoiced to regain the encampment after 24 hours' hard fighting, fatigue, and fasting.

In this brilliant affair eleven officers and 180 men were killed and wounded. One of the officers received so extraordinary a wound that I cannot refrain from relating the particulars. As he was entering the *nullah*, a shot from Seringapatam struck him in front of the right hip, lodging between the bone of the thigh. The *dooley* men, or bearers of the machine on which he was carried to camp, complained of the great weight bearing on the right side. On examination of the wound the surgeons could not suppress a hopeless cast of countenance; on which the wounded officer (Lieutenant Falla) requested that he might have a bottle of port wine to keep up his spirits, and die like "one brave soldier" (he was a Guernsey man not very well versed in the idiom of the English language); he was supplied with the strengthening cordial, and soon after died.

The body was opened, and to the astonishment of all in camp a wrought iron shot of 26 pounds' weight was extracted from between the bones of the thigh, which had been completely covered by a swelling of the part affected, so that it was not discovered any ball was beneath the wound until the extraction took place. This almost incredible fact was generally known, and the shot weighed and exposed to the public scrutiny of the majority of the officers of the army.

The perilous adventure of the honourable Colonel Wellesley must be now narrated, although I may incur the malice and hatred of the great duke in consequence. On his column being repulsed and dispersed in the wood, he unceremoniously betook himself to flight, accompanied by one officer and very few of his men. He soon reached camp, and throwing himself on a table inside the commander-in-chief's dining marquee, burst into a violent passion of tears, exclaiming, "Oh, I'm ruined for ever! I'm ruined for ever! My God, I'm ruined for ever! What shall I do? where shall I go?"

His actions were those of a madman, rolling backwards and forwards on the long table without intermission, uttering the most fearful and bitter invectives on the melancholy failure of his ill-fated attempt on the wood; I did not hear these expressions, but had a faithful description of them the ensuing morning from a staff officer who was present at the scene.

At length his physical powers exhausted by excess of agitation produced a profound slumber of many hours. He had previously represented to the commander-in-chief that the whole detachment had been cut to pieces, and that he alone with the few men who accompanied him in his flight had escaped the bloody catastrophe, concluding his statement with the ominous expression that he was ruined for ever; to which General Harris replied with some asperity, "So you are, unless you return and find the troops confided to your command," and then left Wellesley to the indulgence of his reflections, which produced the table scene. His failure was lamented by many officers who really pitied his unhappy situation, but this generous feeling was soon dispelled on the arrival of Major Shea with the most considerable portion of the column. He had been joined by numerous stragglers on his march, so that on enumerating the whole it was discovered afterwards that twelve only were taken prisoners, with very few killed and wounded.

Affairs now assumed a new and unfavourable aspect; the major reported also that in consequence of the desertion of his colonel, and being ignorant of the exact nature of the attack, he had collected the remains of his force, had retired from the wood and joined Colonel Shaw, by whom he had been directed to join his colonel in camp; he was not even apprised that the occupation of the wood was the ultimate object of the enterprise, so that he was perfectly justified in seeking further instructions from a superior officer. The actual statement of this failure was canvassed at headquarters, and so palpably glaring did Wellesley's misconduct appear to General Harris, that a gentle hint was communicated that his presence would be dispensed with until further orders, tantamount to the more open declaration of, "Sir, you may consider yourself in arrest."

This intimation produced a similar paroxysm of despair to that already exhibited on the table of the commander-in-chief's tent, and everyone was persuaded that a court martial would ensue, as the judgment of this honourable tribunal was essentially requisite to clear his character from the odious stigma of cowardice, which was the prevailing opinion attached to his conduct by the whole army. But here, as in every other situation of English society, the influence of aristocratic ascendancy manifested itself most powerfully. Fortune favoured the honourable colonel in this exigency, as she did subsequently in every dilemma of his future eventful career. He was the brother of the Governor-General of India, the Marques of Wellesley, and it required stronger nerves than those pervading the system of poor General Harris to carry on his duties with impartiality and justice. He considered it, for his own interest, judicious and prudent to pause ere he decided on exposing the frailties of a branch of the aristocracy to the ordinary tribunal invariably resorted to on similar occasions.

Any other officer of the British force would have joyfully courted an investigation, in order to clear his character from the suspicions of the malicious, and thus resume his accustomed intercourse of equality with his comrades as an honourable man, or fearlessly braved the direful consequences of conviction. This spirited mode of conduct did not suit the feelings of the honourable colonel. What! are great men to be adjudged by the opinion of ordinary tribunals, where the paltry considerations of truth, justice, and honour prevail? No; a tame submission to such degrading judgment would taint the character of a scion of the aristocracy with eternal infamy; and thus the conduct of Colonel Wellesley was left to the indiscriminate ordeal of public opinion. I know many old officers who declared they would never speak to him again, unless in an official capacity, and they tenaciously persevered in this determination from the most honourable principles, to the great detriment of their future prospects in life. The most efficient regiment in the army was not employed at the battles of Assaye and Argaum, in consequence of the commanding officer adhering strictly to this resolution.

I now come to the morning of the 6th of April, when the brigade was paraded for a renewed attack on the wood flanking Shaw's post. General Harris, fully sensible of the fearful struggle maintained by the 12th Regiment and battalion of *sepoys*, with an enemy ten times as numerous, hastened to relieve the gallant fellows from their perilous predicament, directing General Baird to head the brigade and drive the Tyger Sepoys from the *tope*. This brave and generous officer requested that Colonel Wellesley "might once more try his fortune." This was most certainly Baird's exact expression; however, others may be pleased to clothe it in more elegant or sentimental language. My intention is to relate facts, with the most distant idea of vindicating or traducing characters.

On this appeal General Harris did, or pretended to, ponder some seconds, when he acquiesced, and despatched an *aide-de-camp* to Wellesley. He soon appeared, and was thus addressed by General Harris: "Colonel Wellesley, at the suggestion of Major-General Baird, I am once more induced to allow you to try your fortune at the head of brigade. Take the command, and drive the enemy from the Sultampittah *tope*." The humbled and mortified colonel assumed the command unhesitatingly, and once more advanced with a band of brave men towards the wood, the enemy offering only a feeble resistance to its occupation. As the English approached, they retired, and Wellesley, without loss, took possession of this important post, which hitherto had so cruelly enfiladed Shaw's post, and almost rendered it untenable.

Frederick the Great, and many other renowned heroes have had their impulses of panic, and why should the great captain have been totally exempt from feelings incidental to the common lot of mortals? *Pro tempore*, his reputation was tarnished in the estimation of the old officers with whom he was serving, many of whom avoided his society, but years of future glory have established his fame. The impression of contempt for his failing has ceased to exist; time and death have nearly obliterated the remembrance of this inglorious epoch of his military career. I was on the spot and in the affair, and have faithfully narrated the event without prejudice or any vindictive feeling, well aware that no comment of mine can possibly affect or injure the great duke, whose name must be handed down to posterity, in spite of every malicious representation to detract from his well-earned fame. I only regret that his future conduct to the brave officers serving with him in Spain, who were sometimes accused of venial errors, and dismissed the army by the haughty fiat alone of this extraordinary man, was not of a more conciliatory and considerate nature.

For example, Colonel Peacock, of the 71st Regiment, and various others, will evince the degree of forbearance manifested by the more fortunate duke towards unsuccessful individuals under his command. I could name many who have suffered apparent injustice from the inflexible and inconsiderate, precipitation of this candidate for universal applause, but gratitude and magnanimity are not component ingredients in the qualifications attributed to the hero of the age. Had any other officer in the army before Seringapatam been guilty of similar dereliction from the duties of his profession, no earthly power could have prevented his dismissal from the service; but Wellesley was allied to the aristocracy of England, who can do no wrong, and so escaped the punishment that would have blasted the reputation, and ruined the prospects of any individual moving in a humbler sphere.

After a month's continual fighting and hardships, a breach was reported practicable on the 3rd of May, and the following day was appointed for the storm. Towards evening the troops selected on this interesting occasion moved slowly down to the trenches, under the command of Baird. For nights and days had the troops suffered from excess of fatigue, up to their knees in water, and exposed to the fierce rays of the sun, fired at and rocketed from every direction, and subjected to continual alarms. We were, therefore, all rejoiced at the speedy prospect of a glorious termination to our incessant sufferings, advancing with all that animation and buoyant spirit so characteristic of British soldiers on the eve of a brilliant attack.

At one o'clock p.m., on the 4th inst., Baird, taking out his watch, exclaimed: "The time has expired!" and leaped on the parapet of the trenches, exclaiming in a loud voice: "Now, my brave boys, follow me!" The enemy were at this moment quietly intent on their culinary preparations for dinner, and we experienced little loss, until we were floundering on the rocky bed of the river, when the men began to fall fast. All who were wounded were inevitably drowned in a second afterwards. One step the water scarcely covered the foot; the next we were plunged headlong into an abyss of fathoms deep. Thus scrambling over, the column at length reached the ascent of the breach, where numerous flankers who had preceded us were lying stretched on their backs, killed and wounded, some of the gallant officers waving their swords and cheering our men on.

We dashed forward, and the top of the breach was soon crowned by our intrepid lads, and the British flag hoisted. But this was for a moment only. A sudden, sweeping fire from the inner wall came like a lightning blast, and exterminated the living mass. Others crowded from behind, and again the flag was planted.

At this time General Baird was discovered on the ramparts. On observing a deep, dry, rocky ditch of sixty feet deep, and an inner wall covered with the troops of the enemy, he exclaimed: "Good God! I did not expect this!" His presence of mind did not desert him; he gave his directions in those cool, decided terms that a great man in the hour of danger and emergency knows so intuitively how to assume, and we were soon charging to the right and left of the breach along the ramparts of the outer wall. In the left attack, Tippoo was himself defending the traverses with the best and bravest of his troops.

This impediment caused a sudden halt, but my gallant friend Woodhall impetuously rushed down a rugged, confined pathway into the ditch, and ascended the second or inner wall, by an equally difficult road, mounted to the summit, followed by his company, the Light Infantry of the 12th. Ere he attained a footing, he had clasped a tuft of grass with his left hand, and was on the point of surmounting the difficulty, when a fierce Mussulman, with a curved, glittering scimitar, made a stroke at his head, which completely cut the bearskin from his helmet, without further injury. Woodhall retaliated, separating the calf of the fellow's leg from the bone. He fell, and the gallant Light Bob was on the rampart in a moment, surrounded by a host of the enemy, whom, with the assistance of his company, he soon drove before him, thus relieving General Baird and his column on the outer wall from the destructive fire from the interior rampart, thereby saving hundreds of lives.

How far this deviation from orders can be justified may be subject for discussion, but a brave man does not often reflect on consequences, when assured that an energetic movement on his part will probably ensure a certain victory and the preservation of a multitude of his fellow-soldiers. Tippoo finding his troops fired on from the inner ramparts, hastened to the Sallyport. Here Woodhall and his men were already in the interior of the town, prepared for the *rencontre*, and a sharp firing ensued. The gateway was filled to the very top of the arch with dead and dying. The column under Baird had pursued the flying enemy to the Sallyport, and whilst Woodhall was bayoneting and firing in the front, they were also attacked in the rear. The body of Tippoo was afterwards found amongst this promiscuous heap of slain.

Neither Woodhall nor his men obtained a single article of plunder on the occasion, but a private of the 74th Regiment secured a very valuable armlet, which was sold to Doctor Mein of that corps for a few hundred *rupees*. It was ultimately discovered to be worth seventy or eighty thousand pounds. The doctor purchased the man's discharge, and settled him in Scotland on £100 pension *per annum*. The fortress now became one wild scene of plunder and confusion, but poor Woodhall and his men were appointed to extinguish the flames of some burning houses in the vicinity of the grand magazine of gunpowder, which, had it ignited, would have blown the whole garrison, friends and foes, into the air.

He performed this arduous duty effectually, and although first in the town, his company were the only part of the regiment who did not reap any pecuniary reward for such daring heroism. The rest of the troops had filled their muskets, caps, and pockets with *zechins*, *pagodas*, *rupees*, and ingots of gold. One of our grenadiers, by name Platt, deposited in my hands, to the amount of fifteen hundred pounds' worth of the precious metals, which in six months afterwards he had dissipated in drinking, horse-racing, cock-fighting, and gambling.

Tranquillity was scarcely restored in the fort, when the honourable Colonel Wellesley was sent in to take the command, to the great dismay and indignation of General Baird, who had felicitated himself on the certain command of this acquisition of his gallantry; but he was superseded, and at once delivered over to Wellesley the important fortress of Seringapatam to his future guidance, who next day hung up eighteen poor *sepoys*, found in the act of plunder, contrary to his orders. General Baird remonstrated on the injustice of his supersession, receiving only sharp and irritating replies to his respectful representations from headquarters. It was inferred that General Harris had been furnished with secret instructions from the governor-general, the Marques of Wellesley, to place his brother in command on the immediate fall of the place. General Baird retired in disgust from the army.

He was, however, afterwards employed in, and commanded the famous Egyptian Expedition, crossed the desert, and joined the British Army at Cairo, with the forces he had so judiciously and successfully conducted. Here, again, the all-powerful influence of the aristocracy is demonstrated, and every Englishman must feel the offensive, but just taunt of our gallant neighbours on the other side of the Channel, that we are "an over-taxed set of slaves." I cheerfully abandon politics for facts. The 12th Regiment, after two or three months at Seringapatam, and in its environs, were ordered to prepare themselves for the subjection of a hill fort called Gooty.

But previous to the march, I must relate the effects and appearance of a tremendous storm of wind, rain, thunder, and lightning that ensued on the afternoon of the burial of Tippoo Saib. I had returned to camp excessively indisposed. About five o'clock a darkness of unusual obscurity came on, and volumes of huge clouds were hanging within a few yards of the earth, in a motionless state. Suddenly, a rushing wind, with irresistible force, raised pyramids of sand to an amazing height, and swept most of the tents and marquees in frightful eddies far from their site. Ten *lascars*, with my own exertions, clinging to the bamboos of the marquee scarcely preserved its fall. The thunder cracked in appalling peals close to our ears, and the vivid lightning tore up the ground in long ridges all around. Such a scene of desolation can hardly be imagined; *lascars* struck dead, as also an officer and his wife in a marquee a few yards from mine.

Bullocks, elephants, and camels broke loose, and scampering in every direction over the plain; every hospital tent blown away, leaving the wounded exposed unsheltered to the elemental strife. In one of these alone eighteen men who had suffered amputation had all the bandages saturated, and were found dead on the spot the ensuing morning. The funeral party escorting Tippoo's body to the mausoleum of his ancestors, situated in the Lai Bagh Garden, where the remains of his warlike father, Hyder Ali, had been deposited, were overtaken at the commencement of this furious whirlwind, and the soldiers ever after were impressed with a firm persuasion that his Satanic majesty attended in person at the funeral procession.

The flashes of lightning were not as usual from far distant clouds, but proceeded from heavy vapours within a very few yards of the earth. No park of artillery could have vomited forth such incessant peals as the loud thunder that exploded close to our ears. Astonishment, dismay, and prayers for its cessation was our solitary alternative.

A fearful description of the Day of Judgment might have been depicted from the appalling storm of this awful night. I have experienced hurricanes, typhoons, and gales of wind at sea, but never in the whole course of my existence had I seen anything comparable to this desolating visitation. Heaven and earth appeared absolutely to have come in collision, and no bounds set to the destruction. The roaring of the winds strove in competition with the stunning explosions of the thunder, as if the universe was once more returning to chaos.

In one of these wild sweeps of the hurricane, the poles of my tent were riven to atoms, and the canvas wafted for ever from my sight. I escaped without injury, as also my exhausted *lascars*, and casting myself in an agony of despair on the sands, I fully expected instant annihilation. My hour was not, however, come. Towards morning the storm subsided; the clouds became more elevated, the thunder and lightning ceased, and nature once more resumed a serene aspect. But never shall I forget that dreadful night to the latest day of my existence. All language is inadequate to describe its horrors.

Rather than be exposed to such another scene, I would prefer the front of a hundred battles. It will be now necessary to record the melancholy fate of the twelve captives of the 33rd Regiment who were taken prisoners in the attack on the *tope*. They were destroyed by order of the *sultan*; and when dug up after the fall of the fortress, a small hole was discovered in the crown of each man's head, and in one of the orifices a large nail was discovered, which had evidently been the instrument of destruction to the whole.

It was reported that this nail had been deliberately hammered into the skull of these unfortunate beings in presence of the cruel *sultan*. Two days after the capture of Seringapatam, the river filled, swelled by the rain that had fallen in the distant mountains. Had this occurrence taken place previous to the storm of the town, our army would have been compelled to abandon the siege, and retire towards Madras, as at the time only two days' provisions of rice remained for the sustenance of the troops; the battering train must have been destroyed, the carriage bullocks having almost all died from scarcity of fodder. Nearly fifty thousand of these animals were lying in a state of decomposition in the precincts of the encampment.

Such an innumerable assemblage of putrid carcases produced the most inveterate fever; the mortality amongst the camp followers was quite devastating, many of whom perished by famine. The troops were affected, and many fell victims to the putrescent, unwholesome state of the atmosphere. Amongst others poor Major Allen terminated his miserable existence from the effects of these noxious vapours. A few days prior to the fall of the place, famine had extended its ravages to so fearful an extent, that mothers publicly offered their female children for sale for a few *fanams*, or a small portion of rice. The calamitous consequences of a retreat under such deplorable circumstances were happily obviated by our brilliant success, which produced the usual order of thanks to the troops.

G.O.

Camp near Yarriagoranelly, June 3rd, 1799.

The colours or standards taken by the following corps from the enemy during the late service to be sent on without delay to the adjutant-general, in order to their being lodged at Seringapatam until they can be forwarded to the presidency.

By His Majesty's 12th Regiment, 8 colours.
By His Majesty's 74th Regiment, 3 colours.

B. Close, Adjutant-General.

By the above memorandum, it will be recorded in pages of history how gloriously these corps conducted themselves in this memorable attack, which terminated in the destruction of the most formidable power that ever opposed British prowess in the conquest of our Asiatic possessions.

Some time after, whilst the honourable Colonel Wellesley was in command of Seringapatam, two religious sects, or castes of natives, had assembled on the Carrighaut Hill, about three miles distant, where they were from time immemorial accustomed to meet, on a certain day, for the purpose of celebrating their religious rites. These castes were of opposite persuasions, called the Right and Left-hand castes. During the different ceremonies on the occasion, disputes frequently occurred, which produced manual struggles, and even bloodshed, ten or a dozen on each side falling victims to the power of fanaticism.

On one of these orgies. Colonel Wellesley resolved to suppress the strife in a most summary and novel manner. Having been apprised that the adverse parties had actually come in contact, and that many thousands had engaged in the conflict, he directed several field-pieces to be placed in the Lai Bagh Garden, close at the base of the Carrighaut Hill, and immediately opened showers of grape shot on the miserable enthusiasts. The carnage amongst them was dreadful, and the astonished multitude dispersed on all sides in the most fearful agitation, leaving the hill covered with dead and dying. How far he might have been justified in this wanton display of tyrannical experiment by government I could never ascertain. He frequently related the anecdote, with manifest self-applause, exulting in the happy knack he possessed of terminating religious differences.

On the 12th of June, 1799, Colonel Shaw, with his own regiment, the 12th, accompanied by a battalion of *sepoys*, and a battering train with a proportion of artillerymen, proceeded towards the strong fortress of Ghooty, which still held out for the Mysore chieftains, many of whom had assembled there on the dispersion or disbanding of the army. After about one hundred miles' march in that direction, and whilst encamped at a place named Sera, information was conveyed to Colonel Shaw that General Harris, then on a tour of survey, was surrounded by a large body of Mysorean cavalry, in a small mud fort, about forty miles off.

The light infantry of the 12th Regiment, with every disposable officer mounted, to the number of thirty, instantly marched off to the rescue. So rapid was our progress, that at sunset the same day we came in sight of the place, and prepared for an assault. The *banditti* had, however, obtained information of our approach, and silently retired, thus relieving the besieged general from his dangerous position, who soon met us with cordial expressions of approbation for our prompt succour, and we regained our camp on the following day without leaving a man in the rear.

A march of eighty miles in two successive days, in a tropical climate, had never before been achieved by Europeans, and, I believe, scarcely ever since this remarkable occurrence. Proceeding on our march, over sandy plains, through dense jungles, and various *nullahs* and rapid rivers, we encamped in a wood about fourteen miles from Ghooty, when a courier brought despatches announcing that Colonel Gowdie had succeeded, with a small force, in compelling the *kellidar* of the fort to capitulate, and consequently our aid was not required.

Our route was now changed to Bangalore, where halting a few days, we then proceeded on to the cantonment of Wallajahbad. At one of the halting places, during this march, being completely surrounded by an impenetrable jungle on all sides of the arena of our encampment, a soldier of the 12th Regiment, named Hudson Taylor, discovered some animal in a thicket, from whence he was in the act of cutting a switch. It appeared to him so mild and inoffensive that he hissed at it, as we generally do to intimidate a cat, when the ferocious beast suddenly sprang on him, fixing its claws in his breast.

The man, who was of strong, muscular proportions, nothing daunted, clasped the brute around with his arms, hugging him tightly to his body, threw him on his back, struggled with him on the ground, and then perforated his neck with repeated stabs from the knife he held in his hand at the moment of the attack. They rolled over each other several times, but still the man preserved his superiority, and was uppermost in the conflict. Had they been uninterrupted, he would have eventually destroyed his adversary, but another soldier, who was loitering in the vicinity, being attracted by the noise of the scuffle, rushed to his assistance, and despatched the cheetah, or young tiger with his bayonet.

Taylor was then conveyed to camp, with the whole of the skin torn from his breast, exposing the bare surface of the bone, and his arms bitten through in several places. The surgeon gave faint hopes of his recovery, as few escape from the effects of the lacerating claws of a tiger, generally dying of tetanus, or a locked jaw. In two months afterwards his wounds were perfectly healed, and he lived many years, always distinguished by the significant epithet of Tiger Taylor. He died in the Isle of France, in 1815, of a liver complaint, and was interred at the military post of Flaig. Fortunately for him, the tiger was very young, as one blow from the paw of a full-grown royal tiger would annihilate the strongest man that ever existed.

In crossing the wide sandy bed of a river near Wallajahbad, the regiment very narrowly escaped perdition. We were in the centre, and had at least a hundred yards' distance to wade through a heavy sand, with partial streams of water, ere we attained the opposite bank, when the cries and confusion of the camp followers attracted our attention; but a more serious and appalling danger speedily indicated the actual cause of the tumult. A huge, white, foaming surge was distinctly observed approaching with incredible velocity from the source of the river, not a thousand yards off. *Sauve qui peut,* was the sudden impulsion of every heart; breathless and panting, we reached the bank of safety, the rear of the column being breast high, as their comrades in front assisted them on shore. Fortunately, the most numerous body of the *lascars* and *coolies* were far in the rear, and had not yet entered the bed of the river, or the major part must have been swept away; as it was many perished in the swollen torrent.

This river is accounted as one of the most dangerous in India. Without any perceptible cause, and on the finest day imaginable, inundations of the most extraordinary impetuosity and force rush down the mountains, some forty or fifty miles distant, overwhelming thousands of the natives annually in a prodigious column of water, that descends on the unwary traveller with such rapidity as to render escape absolutely impossible. Wallajahbad is surrounded by an immense extent of paddy, or rice-fields, where the finest snipe shooting, perhaps, in the universe, may amuse a sportsman indifferent to the fatigue and danger of wading for hours up to his knees in slushy, black mud, covered some inches with water, and exposed to the fervid heat of the sun.

Many fall victims in pursuit of this favourite pleasure; how can it be otherwise? They are generally attended by black servants carrying water, with several bottles of brandy and Madeira wine, with which they repeatedly quench their insatiable thirst, induced by the intolerable heat and fatigue to which they are exposed for many successive hours; one individual alone has frequently been known to consume the contents of three bottles of brandy in the course of a morning's excursion, independent of repeated tumblers of *sangaree* (a tumbler of Madeira, sugar and nutmeg, diluted with a wineglass of water). I defy the most robust European constitution to resist the effects of such excessive excitement, yet the fatality occurring in consequence is invariably attributed to an insalubrious climate.

Nothing can be so inconsistent and unjust, for I am perfectly persuaded that diseases are neither more numerous nor inveterate than in Europe, provided we pursue that regular course of living generally adopted by our countrymen in England, from which they consider themselves licensed to depart in a warmer clime, and thus become victims to their own imprudence rather than to the noxious vapours or climate of India.

Having received £400 as my share of prize-money for the capture of Seringapatam, as a lieutenant, so large a sum became exceedingly troublesome; I therefore came to the resolution of attending the Mount Races, held about thirty miles distant from Wallajahbad and ten from Madras. Big with the fascination of this wise determination, I obtained a month's leave and proceeded to the seat of pleasure held at the Mount, filled with all those indefinable emotions that predominate over the mind of youth in the anticipation of novelty.

I arrived, betted largely on the pacers, and was by no means unsuccessful; excited by this incipient smile of dame Fortune, I ventured a few *pagodas* at the *faro*-table, and was again fortunate; but the attractive piles of gold and banknotes heaped together indiscriminately in the circle on the hazard-table soon induced me to attempt a higher chance, and I boldly entered on the ruinous game for several hours with variable success; at length, a protracted run of ill-fortune deprived me of every penny of my prize-money, and I had contracted a debt of 100 *pagodas*, borrowed from a brother officer, who kindly cautioned me to be more wary and desist; I accordingly adopted his advice for the day and returned to my abode with sensations easier imagined than described—the reward of six months' danger and fatigue had disappeared in the space of a few hours, I had neither gold nor silver remaining to retrieve my loss.

Throwing myself on my couch in an agony of despair, I passed a sleepless night of incessant agitation, and remorse. The following day I once more visited the gay gamblers, and for some time regarded the scene with a species of gloomy apathy, the consequent effect of my misfortune. Crawford, my kind creditor and adviser, observing the distressed state of my mind, approached, and offered me the loan of a 50-*pagoda* note, on condition if I lost it, that the venture should be my last. I joyfully accepted the boon and hurried to the fascinating game.

Throwing my note into the magic circle, I exclaimed: "Who sets the jolly caster?" The note was immediately covered by another of equal value, and I rattled the dice with the air of a maniac. Seven is the main! eleven is the nick! I won. "Who sets the jolly caster again?" A 100-*pagoda* note was instantly jerked into the circle. Six is the main! huzza, twelve is the nick! And thus once more I succeeded; my fortune prevailed, doubling every time to the eighth throw, when I had

6,400 *pagodas*, all my own in the circle. Vain of my repeated success, I braved my companions once more to cover this enormous sum.

Everyone was intimidated, I therefore swept the amount towards me; throwing a 50-*pagoda* note into the ring, which was again covered. *In toto* I threw in 11 times successively, and might have retired with upwards of £2,500 in my pocket, but continuing to play, capricious Fortune no longer favoured me, and towards evening, I found myself a winner of about 1,200 *pagodas* only (nearly £480). Retiring to my room, I there made a most solemn vow never to touch a die again, to which I have invariably adhered through the progress of life, ever bearing in mind the acute sensations experienced on the result of my first untoward experiment. I repaid Crawford, with boundless thanks, and hastened my departure from the scene of temptation.

A few days after my arrival at Wallajahbad, I was inadvertently involved in a most unpleasant affair. At the mess a discussion arose relative to the height of one of the officers, and a bet was offered that he did not measure six feet. I procured a foot-rule, and was marking a standard against the wall when Crawford snatched the instrument rather rudely from my hand. I as hastily recovered it, perhaps with rather more violence than the nature of the circumstance required; he immediately turned on his heel and retired from the mess-room. And thus from this foolish affair originated a duel! I had just laid down for the night when Lieutenant Eustace entered my quarters, demanding an apology or satisfaction for the insult I had offered Crawford. He had certainly been the first aggressor, an apology was therefore unhesitatingly refused, and an appointment agreed on at six o'clock the following morning, in the cemetery, for our *rencontre*, Woodhall attended as my friend, and at eight paces' distance I was placed opposite my quondam friend and counsellor to be shot at, for the most frivolous offence that ever occurred.

I was exasperated at his want of feeling, but fired without aim, of course wide of the mark; he continued at the present, covered me deliberately, and I must have fallen had not his pistol flashed in the pan. "Captain Crawford," I exclaimed, "that cannot be considered as a shot, therefore fire again." He objected to the proposal, and on being assured that he intended no personal affront to me in attempting to seize the rule I immediately made the *amende honorable*, by apologising in due form for my intemperate conduct. Duelling may, in some instances, be a necessary evil, but is too often wantonly resorted to, on the most frivolous occasions, and ought to be discountenanced by every honourable character.

The following fact will evince the abundance of snipes at Wallajahbad. General Macdowel and Lieut. Hartly, of the 12th, engaged, for a wager, to destroy one hundred brace of these innocent birds in twenty-four hours. The task was accomplished by six in the evening, within two pairs, when Hartly, hearing a rustling noise in the overgrown grassy bank of one of the paddy-fields, fired at random, killing six birds. It was dusk at the time, and the wager would have been lost but for this happy accident.

I defy the descriptive powers of the most brilliant genius to dilate on the beauty of the scenery of India. One vast plain of sand, with rocks rising abruptly to the height of many hundred feet; little circumscribed *topes* or woods, impenetrable jungles, and extensive paddy-fields, are the general features of this uninteresting country; certainly on the Malabar coast are interminable forests of the most magnificent timber trees, inhabited by elephants, tigers, and every species of animal and noxious reptile that pester the face of the earth; but there is a total absence of verdant grass-fields.

Even the scanty portions of grass requisite for the subsistence of horses are toiled for daily by poor women, who in twenty-four hours' grubbing under the shady sides of hedges and banks can only collect, each, from 12 to 20 pounds of this scattered vegetation, so that it may easily be conjectured what numbers of these wretched creatures are absolutely indispensable for a regiment of cavalry.

In no situation of the universe can a king's military officer be so uncomfortably and unprofitably employed. After an arduous service of from 20 to 40 years, he returns to his native country with a broken constitution, unprotected and unnoticed, on the half-pay of a lieut.-colonel (of £200 *per annum*); he cannot associate with his equals in worldly knowledge, and is too proud to court the society of those with equal incomes but inferior education; he therefore becomes an isolated being, and too frequently terminates a wretched existence in a manner repulsive to the feelings of a conscientious and honest man; he may sell his commission for £4,500, but this alternative, if adopted, would be a means of circumscribing his comforts to a still more confined degree, and, unless he has a rising family to provide for, should never be resorted to; he must therefore console himself with philosophy, fortitude, and patience, in lieu of the *otium cum dignitate* so ably advocated by the poet Horace.

The company's officer is differently situated and more liberally provided for; in 20 or 25 years he may return at volition to his native home on full-pay (of £800 *per annum*), independent of the little pickings accumulated on staff-appointments during his service in India (from which king's officers are excluded), which may, without exaggeration, be estimated as fully equivalent to the annual amount of his pension; thus, with an income of £1,600 a year, he is enabled to *rouler carosse* and enter into all the enjoyments of civilized society, during the decline of life, and leave a handsome competence to his family at his decease, when his wife succeeds to a humane and liberal provision, derived from a fund established by married officers in the Indian army, of £400 *per annum* during her existence.

The *honour* and *glory* of king's officers must hide their diminished heads on comparison with the more fortunate destiny of the enviable situation of those employed in the service of an English company of merchants: the recompense is indubitably merited, but how lamentable that the sharers in all their dangers and privations should be so inconsistently exposed to humiliation and degradation at a period of life when the comforts of old age are so imperatively requisite to render existence supportable!

CHAPTER 12

Narrow Escape From Shipwreck

A severe affection of the liver complaint, for which I was repeatedly blistered, bled, and surfeited with poisonous calomel, compelled me to seek relief from change of climate, and I proceeded with an intimate friend named Seton, who laboured under a similar disease, to St. Thome, a sea-coast village three miles from Madras. Here I was honestly told by the faculty that unless I proceeded to England immediately I should shortly fall a victim to the malady. A fleet of Chinamen being at this time in the roads of Madras, our passage was taken on board the *Ceres*, the same vessel I had embarked on four years ago for the expedition against Manilla. Seton and myself were the only passengers on board (except two officers of the Company's cavalry— Lieutenants Hamilton and Bryant); we agreed with the captain as the price of our passage home for £300 each, and sailed from Fort St. George the beginning of October, 1799.

After touching at the beautiful island of Penang or Prince of Wales' Island, we proceeded on to Malacca, off which settlement the fleet anchored for several days, to repair some damages experienced from a violent thunderstorm, during which a ball of fire had fallen on our anchor, killing two *lascars* and ten pigs; volumes of smoke ascended from the vessel for several minutes, and a general conflagration was apprehended, but we fortunately escaped this direful calamity. Several other ships had lost masts, yards, etc., without sustaining any mortality. One morning, as I was landing, the surf on the flat shore was excessively violent; I observed a boat upset close to ours, in the midst of the breakers. The screams of a female attracted my attention, and I leapt into the sea to attempt her preservation.

We now continued our voyage, but in the midst of the China seas were overtaken by a tremendous typhoon or hurricane, in which the

Talbot, of 1,200 tons foundered during the night just ahead of the *Ceres*. Our ship was drawn down with such force in the vortex occasioned by her sinking, that she plunged almost midships deep into the raging ocean; a heavy sea then took us in the stern, washing in the dead-lights, breaking down bulkheads, and dashing everyone out of their cots and berths on the deck in the wildest confusion. Arms and legs were broken., and all of us below floating for some time from side to side as the vessel heaved and laboured. By the exertions of the crew we were soon relieved from our distressing situations, and the wounded taken under the surgeon's care.

As the morning dawned a most appalling scene presented itself the whole fleet scattered and dismasted, except the *Carron*, a teak ship built at Bombay, which, from being perfectly new and on her first voyage, had weathered the storm. The *Scarborough* shoal was seen about four miles distant, a high rock, abruptly rising out of the sea some hundred feet high, with breakers dashing over it, foaming and roaring most terrifically. The wind had completely subsided, leaving an enormous swell mountains high, driving us towards the fatal rock, where a Chinaman called the *Scarborough* had been wrecked some years before and every soul perished (parts of the wreck having been afterwards discovered by sloops sent in search of her), from whence the shoal derived its name.

During the day we were gradually drifting towards the awful breakers; every heart quailed at the fearful prospect of inevitable destruction; boats were hoisted out to tow the head of the ship in a different direction. But what are human efforts opposed to the rage of the mighty ocean? The vessel still inclined bodily towards the attractive object, and every hope of preservation was abandoned. Towards evening I descended to the great cabin in the fond hope of indulging in a few hours' oblivious slumber previous to eternal annihilation, but the heavy-treading footsteps of the captain in the round-house above must have fearfully timed with the pulsations of his heart, if I might judge by the accelerated motion of my own, which justly accorded with every falling tread he took.

All prospect of sleep was utterly banished; the ship rolled yardarm under, and I scrambled into my swinging cot as a relief to the sickening motion, and involved in the profoundest reflection, passed the weary, tedious hours of the night; the loud flapping sails and creaking bulkheads alone interrupting the monotony of the dreadful interval.

Am I, then, to perish, so young and far from friends and relations, abandoned by Providence and every human resource; my body to be shattered to atoms against this terrible rock, and then to become food for the fishes of the sea? So perhaps exclaimed those before me in the ill-fated *Scarborough*, who were equally young and tenacious of life; but alas! they were deserted by Providence and never heard of more. What right, then, have I to expect an interposition of Divine favour? My creation and destruction are equally incomprehensible. I submit with resignation for the very reason my predecessors have ever yielded: that of dire necessity. For after all our philosophy, Nature asserts her rights, and us mortals are ultimately doomed to one common lot, experience demonstrating that Providence is equally indifferent to our fate in the hour of danger, as at the inevitable moment of death, or why was the *Scarborough*, and the thousands and tens of thousands of other vessels with their despairing crews, engulfed in the raging bosom of the remorseless ocean?

These might be erroneous reflections, but they were those of the pressing moment, and under such impressions at the dawn of day I ascended to the deck. What a forlorn, superb spectacle presented itself; about five hundred yards off towered the majestic barren rock with sea-fowl screaming in every direction; the swelling billows gliding beautifully almost to its very summit, and there bursting out into showers of foam and mist at periods, shrouding its terrible precipices from our view; the ship plunging and rolling from side to side at the mercy of the waves, or rather swell, for it was a perfect calm; the tremendous motion having been produced by the irresistible effects of the preceding typhoon; everyone gazed with horror on the dreadful but magnificent scene.

I entered the cuddy, or dining cabin, where the captain was leaning in a disconsolate attitude, with his elbow on the table supporting his head with one hand, sitting on a chair and holding on with the other by a lashing that secured the legs of the table to the deck. He smiled, mournfully exclaiming, "I fear our time is come; no earthly power can save us!"

At this identical moment the first mate entered, abruptly crying out, "A breeze aloft, sir; a breeze, the head sails are filling!"

The captain leaped from his despairing position and was on the quarter deck in a second; hope pervaded every bosom; the top-gallant sails were bellying with the gentle gale, and the ship slowly answered her helm; in ten minutes the sluggish movement was evident and we were gradually receding from the abyss of destruction. In a short time the lower sails were affected, and we were rapidly wafting o'er the blue ocean, and then bounding and dancing over the rippling, foamy heads of the merry little waves. Towards evening a large black body appeared right ahead, which was at first taken for another shoal, but on nearing the object it was discovered to be a huge Chinese *junk* or ship, of at least 1,000 tons burden, totally dismasted and in a most helpless condition.

Our captain generously offered to tow her into the Canton River, provided they agreed to defray the expenses of the wear and tear of the different ropes or hawsers necessary for the operation. To this they decidedly objected, the expense being estimated at four hundred dollars or £100; she was consequently left to the management of her crew, but supplied with a few spars from the *Ceres*, or she never could have accomplished her voyage, and even these the mercenary wretches objected to pay for. In a few days we entered the picturesque mouth of the River Tigris, leading to Canton, studded with small islands clothed with wood to the margin of the sea; the scenery was inimitably beautiful as we glided close to their bases. Passing an innumerable assemblage of these little mountainous islands we safely anchored off the Portuguese settlement of Macao.

The usual chops or permits having been granted, we then proceeded through the Bocca Tigris, our keel cutting through the soft mud and discolouring the water with a dingy tint as the vessel slowly advanced. Previous to passing through the channel between the two high rocks denominated the Bocca Tigris, where the current runs with increased rapidity from its compressed situation of a few yards only, we scaled our guns. The effect of the explosions on the Chinese on board was ludicrous in the extreme; they fell flat on their faces, crying "Oy oh! oy oh! I dead! I dead! What for make such bobbery!"

On explaining to them the necessity of scouring the guns they were at length tranquillised, and soon recovered from this unmanly pusillanimity. The sailors were infinitely diverted at their uncouth antics and gesticulations. The following day we reached Wampoa—the customary anchorage of the China fleet of Indiamen, about fifteen miles below the populous city of Canton, where the ships were completely dismantled or unrigged. My friend Seton and self were obliged to hire a small factory at the exorbitant rent of £100 during the season; this was a most unexpected increase of expense, as the captain had not notified nor stipulated in our passage agreement for this additional charge; it was represented as customary, and we were therefore necessitated to submit without further remonstrance: a hint to young travellers to be more scrupulous and exact in terms of negotiation, in which military men are so generally careless that they become dupes to the very lowest crafty mechanic.

For several miles below Wampoa, and the whole course of the river from thence to Canton, the stream is absolutely covered with *junks* and boat-houses, for under no other description can these latter be denominated, being wide, flat-bottomed boats on which are erected various dwelling apartments, similar to the stages of a house, one above another, occupied by hundreds of thousands of the aquatic genus of Chinese; ten or twelve tiers to these nondescript habitations line both sides of the river for a space of at least twenty miles. The sonorous gongs, which are innumerable, with the display of every variety of flag and streamer of all the gaudy colours of the peacock or rainbow, give a most interesting effect to the animated and gorgeous scene. The thundering noise of the gongs is, however, top powerful for the nerves of individuals unaccustomed to the succession of such constant disagreeable vibrations of the air.

On reaching Canton you are first attracted by a long row of magnificent houses, called factories, which present themselves within fifty paces of the margin of the river. The national colours of English, French, Dutch, Portuguese, Danes, Swedes, Prussians, Russians, and Americans are all flying, of best Chinese silk, in front of the different factories; each colour distinguishing the house appropriated to the mercantile speculations of each nation; a broad, flat gravel area in front of the line of houses is unceasingly perambulated by the acute speculators of mercantile emulation. After landing and taking possession of our factory, which consisted of three rooms with bare walls, we were obliged to hire furniture, which was charged at an enormous high rate by the Chinese, than whom no people in the world are greater adepts in imposition.

Having satisfactorily provided ourselves, an invitation from Mr. Hall, chief English supercargo, and the gentlemen of the factory, was handed to us, to consider their dining-table as our own during our residence at Canton, of which we partially availed ourselves. The weather was cold and stormy; hail and snow prevented us attending the company's hospitable board so often as we were inclined, when we indulged in the luxurious treat of fat pork chops. Such delicious food I never tasted; superior in flavour to any ever produced in any other part of the world. Sir George Stanton and Alexander Baring (now

Lord ———) were at this time members of the community of supercargoes; Urmstone, Parry, and William Baring were also of the number; pleasant, agreeable young fellows, but alas! how politics and interest change the dispositions of us worldly mortals; in thirty years the man of twenty is not recognisable for the same individual, either in person or mind; facts that require no further illustration.

As the Chinese destroy all deformed children, they are a most perfect race of men in bodily proportions; such clean-made, stout-legged fellows I never saw. If the mind but accorded with the outward man, from their great population of three hundred and thirty-three millions, and physical strength, they might conquer the world! The oppressive conduct of the government and insulting style of language, addressed towards all foreigners in mercantile transactions, will ultimately incur the indignation of some of the great European powers, when the country will fall an easy prey to the first invader, from the total inaptitude of the natives to our enlightened mode of warfare.

The country circumadjacent to Canton is flat and marshy, intersected by innumerable rivers and canals, so that from any slight elevation a complete panoramic scene is offered to view; thousands of vessels sailing in every direction, apparently through green fields and deeper-tinged verdant foliage of trees. The markets are quite an abomination; baskets of little dogs (for bow-wow pies), horses slaughtered, the limbs and bodies dissected in the most disgusting, filthy state, monkeys, snakes, and various reptiles, all intended for the nourishment of the populace. They are an ingenious and plodding race, expert at models, and with a large plate of glass placed on our best pictures, will copy them so exquisitely exact that nothing but the more vivid colouring of their brilliant paints could detect the copy from the original painting; they excel also in miniature resemblances to an inimitable degree of perfection.

A captain of one of the Indiamen, whose countenance was proverbially ugly, employed one of these artists. When the miniature was completed he objected to purchase it, on the plea of failure in likeness. Spoilum (the artist's *nom de guerre*) insisted on the evident representation, but the indignant captain retired unconvinced, when the sly fellow drew a gallows, to which he attached the head of the captain, then exposing it in the window of his shop, exciting the risible nerves of all who passed, as the resemblance was so perfect that the captain was known at the slightest cursory glance; the success of this *finesse* was soon communicated to him, and he hastened to pay his five dollars (the price of each likeness), thus terminating the public diversion.

We remained at Canton during the months of November and December 1800, and sailed from Wampoa the beginning of January 1801. As Seton and I had engaged the factory for the season, it was optional to retain occupation three months longer, when all the merchants would have retired to Macao—Government permitting them a residence only five months of the year at Canton. No deduction of rent was admitted on our vacating the premises previous to the expiration of the season. The payment of a hundred pounds for two months was therefore a serious consideration to two unfortunate subalterns, but patience and submission was our only consolation.

In descending the river, floating along at the rate of five miles an hour, our keel touched a sandbank, giving the vessel one fearful heel to the starboard. Every person and thing was tossed suddenly against the downward side; a most ludicrous confusion ensued, but the ship sustained no material damage, and we pursued our voyage through the Bocca Tigris towards the Straits of Sunda. For nine days the fleet, consisting of eleven Indiamen and a Portuguese brig, was completely enveloped in dense fog; any observation of the sun was impossible, not having seen its cheering rays once since our departure.

The nautical gentry were apprehensive of the Pracelle, a dangerous shoal, near which it was supposed we were then sailing. About twelve o'clock at night I was quietly reading a book of Blair's Memoirs when an alarm gun was fired by the Portuguese brig two miles ahead; everyone was now on the alert, but the thick haze completely obscured even the nearest object from view. Soon the loud report of guns from various other vessels convinced us that danger was near in some shape or other, and the ship hove to. The sails scarcely flapped in the wind ere the rustling sound of breakers within a short distance was plainly distinguished. The first mate, Mr. Durnsford, hastened to the head of the vessel, and the captain cried, "Let go the anchor! let go the anchor!" when the loud voice of the veteran mate from ahead shouted, "If you do, we shall instantly swing on the rocks that are not forty fathoms off."

The sails were again filled, and in about a quarter of an hour passed another vessel, by whom we were hailed, and warned that rocks were also discovered not far distant in the direction we were proceeding. We again lay to, impatiently expecting the dawn of day; at intervals the booming of cannon was repeated during the night. At six o'clock in the morning the sun rose most resplendently, chasing the foggy vapour away in rolling volumes of light clouds. Not till then were we conscious of our perilous situation; in steering wide of the Pracelle shoal the fleet had approached too near the Cochin China coast, and was embayed within a reef of high pyramidical rocks on all quarters, except the one by which it entered the bay; a steep, rugged, iron-bound coast was on the right and a range of picturesque rocks on the left and in front, as can well be imagined, some rising several hundred feet high, terminating in small sharp peaks, others gradually descending towards the sea, of a similar but more diminutive form, and thus in alternate elevations, resembling the steeples of churches.

The water within the reef was perfectly smooth and transparent, but the waves outside raging and breaking over various parts of the more depressed situations of the rocks in tremendous glittering sheets of water, on which the sun acted in a peculiar manner, forming innumerable irises or rainbows, of inexpressible beauty of variegation. The hills and prominent heads of the mainland were covered by an innumerable concourse of natives, shouting and waving flags, ready to pounce on their expected prey and bear off the rich plunder from the wreck of our inestimable fleet; the wild shouts and fierce gesticulations of these barbarians were really terrific, on observing the vessels once more regaining the open ocean.

In beating out of the bay we several times approached within a short distance of the shore, where thousands of boats appeared, manned, in perfect readiness to avail themselves of our slightest disaster. A signal gun from the commodore for the fleet to close had the sudden effect of dispersing this mighty multitude of pusillanimous, but ferocious wretches, and we thus happily escaped this imminent danger, continuing our voyage towards the Straits of Sunda with a pleasant breeze and flowing sail. I am not an adept in nautical expressions, which imperfection is very pardonable in a soldier's description of maritime events. Passing between the islands of Banca and Billiton, a canoe was discovered which had been driven far from land; two feeble creatures appeared in its hull, making signs with their paddles. We steered towards them, and observed two emaciated Malays, who, from complete exhaustion, were unable to hold on by the rope thrown to them from the ship.

A boat was then lowered and the poor wretches assisted up the side to the deck. Having several natives among our heterogeneous crew who spoke the language fluently, we obtained the particulars relative to the miserable plight in which they were discovered. A fortnight previously they had been fishing off the coast of Banca, and with seven others in the canoe had been forced to sea by a violent gale of wind far from sight of land. These latter had died of famine; the two had supported existence by devouring the putrid carcases of their companions, and in this horrid state, wallowing amidst the decomposed, mutilated forms of the dead, we found them complete animated skeletons. The canoe was immediately cast off, drifting to sea with its disgusting lading; one of these poor fellows died some days afterwards; his comrade, however, became in a few weeks one of the most active sailors on board, appearing perfectly contented and happy during the voyage.

We now entered the magnificent channel between the extremities of the islands of Sumatra and Java, called the Straits of Sunda, filled with shoals, sunken rocks, and clusters of volcanic isles, clothed with superb timber trees to the water's edge. Every precaution was adopted to ensure our safety, sailing by day under topsails and regularly anchoring every evening at sunset. The nightly view was certainly of the most imposing nature; various volcanoes bursting from the summits of the conic-shaped surrounding islands were in full action, casting glaring streams of red, lurid, light across the intervening expanses of sea.

Tremulous motions of the ship frequently occurred, as from an earthquake; roaring sounds from the craters, low moaning, rumbling concussions, apparently from underneath the sea, with fearful gusts of a hurricane wind that laid the fleet gunwale under, were the usual accompaniments of our nocturnal anchorage; incessant torrents of rain, with thunder, lightning, and balls of fire crowned the awful scenes. Near this latitude the French frigates *L'Astrolabe* and *La Roussole*, commanded by the gallant, scientific, but unfortunate La Perouse, were wrecked; the crews perished, not even a solitary individual escaping to recount the dreadful tale. Some years ago a portion of the wrecks of these vessels was discovered, but never yet has any authentic account been obtained of the actual fate of the doomed crew.

Once extracted from the labyrinth of the Sunda Straits, a watering party was landed on the Sumatra coast to replenish our exhausted stores. After shipping a few casks, the menacing attitude of the natives, who approached in considerable numbers, induced the party to relinquish a further supply, and so pressing was the exigency that many empty casks were left on shore, several of the sailors narrowly escaping with their lives from the ferocious attack of these miscreants. About the middle of March the fleet reached the rocky island of St. Helena.

Deep cultivated valleys, craggy precipices, and lofty barren rocks are the principal features of this renowned isle, where the greatest hero that ever graced or tortured the face of the globe died a state prisoner, to the eternal disgrace of the envious, heartless, and cowed ministers of Great Britain; what a pity we cannot blot this indelible stain on our magnanimity from the annals of history!

One week's continual gaiety soon expired; dancing, music, and flirtation occupied our whole time, my lodging and board amounting to one guinea *per diem*, independent of other extravagances. Here was I once more fated to exhibit the effects of my intemperate disposition. Some days previous to our arrival at St. Helena, Lieut. Bryant, one of our passengers, during dinner was presented with a glass of wine which I had called for some minutes before; he certainly smiled significantly at the time, as if aware that the waiter or attendant had mistaken the person.

Irritated at the imagined insult, I rose from the table, descended to the great cabin, and prepared swords for an immediate adjustment of the affair. Bryant soon appeared; I handed him a sword, but he prudently declined the combat *malgré* all my taunting expressions, as ridiculous as unjustifiable, for he was brave to a fault, and equally cool and determined, which he evinced in after years in India, where he performed prodigies of valour when surrounded by a host of the enemy.

Having thus tamely submitted to all my insulting propositions, we mutually avoided each other's company; however, on my landing at St. Helena, I was soon brought to my senses; a message was delivered by Lieutenant Hamilton, and a meeting arranged for satisfactory explanations. Lots were drawn for the first fire, which fell to me; I took deliberate aim, but a better feeling prevailed, and I elevated the muzzle of the pistol so that the ball passed far over my adversary's head. I fully imagined this sudden motion was undetected, but Bryant's keen eye must have caught the generous intention, as he instantly discharged his pistol, the contents of which flew innocently wide of its mark; I then approached him, exclaiming, "Bryant, I have acted like a foolish, thoughtless boy throughout the whole of this affair, and hope the friendly intimacy that has hitherto existed between us may be once more renewed," when a cordial shake of the hand again reinstated me in my own good opinion.

How strange that men possessed of the most amiable generous feelings should sometimes, by an unaccountable fatality, be involved in such disgraceful dilemmas! Not a mortal existing is certain of his line of conduct for the ensuing 24 hours, some sudden impulse or capricious emanation from the brain hurries him on to the commission of absurd and even criminal actions, repugnant to his very nature when, on mature consideration, he reviews the origin of his sensations, if possibly discoverable. Some author has asserted all mankind to be mad, and I am inclined to accord in the opinion. Saints may moralise, but let them studiously analyse the events of their life, and where is he who can conscientiously proclaim himself exempt from the foibles of his erring brethren?

A schooner was forwarded to the Isle of Ascension to turn turtle, and on the seventh morning after our arrival we departed from St. Helena; 86 turtles had been entrapped before we lay to off Ascension, ten of which were apportioned to the *Ceres*, two of them of the ponderous weight of 850 and 900 pounds! Such enormous dimensions are by no means rare in the turtles found on this solitary island, which, was at one time unoccupied and uninhabited, and appeared like one huge mass of cinders, the coast on all sides covered with the white excrement of innumerable water-fowl, and the sea swarming with fishes of every description.

From a single bucketful of sea-water a hundred lively little turtles might be extracted; the surrounding ocean resembled a moving accumulation of animated matter. This extraordinary appearance has greatly altered since the occupation of this dormant volcano by the English; the frequent passing of fleets and ships has now dispersed and exhausted the concentrated multitude of aquatic generations, which have probably tranquilly moved in the liquid empire since the origin of the world!

About three weeks before our arrival at the Land's End, I was sitting quietly in my cabin, ruminating on the delightful prospect of a speedy arrival in old England, which from the existing favourable gale we were unitedly anticipating, when my reflections were unpleasantly interrupted by a piercing cry of "Oh! God, my eye; oh! God!" I rushed into the adjoining cabin from whence the sound proceeded, and discovered my young friend, Seton, writhing in the agonies of excessive pain, with his left eye scooped out of its socket and the glutinous substance of the eye streaming down his face mingled with a flow of blood. I caught him fainting in my arms, and bore him to the surgeon; the upper part of the nose was cut through and the eye-lid hanging by a particle of skin, which was immediately detached; dressings being applied, I returned to the cabin for some explanation of the mysterious accident.

Lieut. Hamilton had purchased a Chinese bow during his residence at Canton, which Bryant and Seton were assisting him in stringing. Having with the united strength of the three, bent it and adjusted the string, the word "all ready" was given, but the string slipping off, the bow recoiled with prodigious force, springing from the deck, and thus deprived the unfortunate Seton of his left eye. He was some years afterwards killed at the Battle of the Pyrenees, fighting gallantly in his country's cause, or rather for the aggrandisement and supremacy of our aristocracy.

These Chinese bows are bent with the greatest facility by a single individual of that nation by some peculiar knack, but require the combined efforts of three or four Europeans to bring them into proper shooting form. Singular to relate, the wound occasioned by the accident was completely healed in the course of three weeks; but he was ever after compelled to wear a black band to hide the voidless socket of the eye; it did not prevent him, however, from, engaging the affections of an heiress, who bestowed her fair hand and wealth on the gallant soldier, in some measure recompensing him for the freaks of Fortune.

On entering the British Channel we were hailed by several men-of-war, proceeding with troops on board to reinforce the Egyptian Expedition. After eleven months' passage we anchored in the Downs, having nearly circumnavigated the globe, for had we sailed round Cape Horn instead of the Cape of Good Hope, the *Ceres* would have accomplished this arduous and interesting enterprise.

Next morning, 2nd June, 1800, we tided to the North Foreland, in sight of Margate. An unusual gale at this season of the year assailed us from the German ocean; the mountain waves soon drove the ship from three anchors, drifting her by the fleet at a rapid rate towards the Goodwin Sands; they were plunging and pitching forecastle under, and sympathised with our distressing situation without the possibility of affording relief. I see them now, in my mind's eye, waving their hands as a token of final *adieu*. The intense friction of the cables in the hawseholes had fired the forecastle, in addition to our other misfortunes; this inauspicious circumstance employed half the crew in handing buckets of water to extinguish the conflagration.

The lumpers (or men received on board at Deal to work the ship up the river) were actually paralysed, falling on their knees, invoking the Deity, and lamenting in loud vociferations the miserable destitution of wives and families in the event of being wrecked. Down splashed the last anchor, snap went the cable, and all hope forsook us; the raging breakers on the Goodwin Sands became every second more intimately familiar to our senses, when we were suddenly brought to by a jerk that shook the very frame of the vessel, her head deeply under, and a diabolical wave at the same instant swept along the whole deck from stem to stern, committing sad havoc; two men had each a thigh broken, and another had been literally cut in half on the descent of the last anchor, having awkwardly entangled himself in the coils of the cable; his head and breast was instantaneously lying on one side of the deck and his lower extremities on the other, a frightful example of the evanescent tenure of mortal existence.

The actual cause of our preservation originated in the stout temper of the iron of the remaining flue of the sheet-anchor, the other had been torn asunder and separated from the stock by the repeated concussions occasioned by the heavy waves beating in rapid succession against the bows of the vessel.

It is really incomprehensible to landsmen how a small piece of iron, not six inches in diameter, could resist the drifting weight of upwards of 2,000 tons, with the additional propelling onus of the enormous waves; but thus were we situated when the gale only partially moderating, we were hailed by the incomparable boatmen from Deal, with their equally incomparable boats, to say they were laden with cables and anchors for our service. The customary nautical operations were then adopted to secure the acceptable assistance; a weather-beaten, jolly-looking fellow having discharged his burden, proposed to take any of the passengers to Margate for five guineas each.

Happy to escape by any means from our floating prison, Seton and myself availed ourselves of the reasonable offer, and with a single portmanteau each, were soon landed at the gay watering-place; immediately after ensconcing ourselves in a post-chaise, we soon reached the New Hummums in Covent Garden, and for a few days enjoyed all the luxuries incident to those just escaped from the odious privations ever attendant on a long voyage, even in the best provided ships.

CHAPTER 13

Lieutenant Bayly On Leave In England

London, thou source of wealth, luxury, extravagance, and depravity; what a scene of temptation thou offerest to the voluptuary! what a gulf of perdition to the youthful, unsophisticated mind! but I have forsworn all effusions of sentimental prosing. Making my bow at the Horse Guards, I obtained a three months' extension of leave, paid my respects to the colonel of the 12th, General Picton, who distinguished himself at the famous Battle of Warburg, or Minden. Knocking at his door in Bond Street, an old grenadier corporal ushered me into his master's drawing room. In a few minutes a huge form entered, of at least six feet four inches, the floor trembling at every advancing pace from the weight of his enormous proportions; a suit of snuff-coloured habiliments covered his gigantic person, the flaps of his waistcoat reaching almost down to his knees, from the pockets of which he continually extracted large handfuls of loose snuff, besmearing his nose, chin, and whole surface of the front of his person to the waistband of his small clothes; he was bordering on eighty years of age. Extending his cramped, gouty hand towards me, he growled out in a thundering intonation,. "Well, lieutenant; I am glad to see you. I understand the 12th Regiment has again distinguished itself at the siege of Seringapatam?"

I assented to the observation, when he plunged his hand into his reservoir of snuff and suffused his whole person in clouds of the titillating dust; this operation he repeated at least a dozen times during the short interval of a quarter of an hour, which was the most tedious I had ever endured. At length, rising majestically and bowing stiffly, he saluted me with a "Good morning," and best wishes for future success in my profession. I strolled towards my hotel, rejoicing in the happy termination of my ceremonial visit. In St. James' Street, Captain Ruding congratulated me on my escape from the horrors of India, where he had sojourned one year only, whilst our six companies voyaged to Penang.

The gay Aston and Lord Hobart, Governor of Madras, had paid too much attention to the pretty Mrs. Ruding. The husband on his return remonstrated ineffectually; he then obtained leave of absence, and ultimately retired from the service. I was invited to dinner next day at Limmer's Hotel, Conduit Street; our party consisted of four officers of the Guards beside ourselves. Burgundy and champagne, with every edible rarity the season could produce, appeared in sumptuous profusion on the board; Ruding became disgustingly inebriated. The officers, after the splendid repast, accompanied his wife to the opera, and I retired to my comfortable hotel to sleep off the fumes of the luscious grape.

At 8 o'clock the next morning the waiter knocked at my chamber door to say that a servant in livery had brought a note requiring an immediate answer. As I knew no one in London, I was convinced some mistake had occurred; however, to satisfy the importunity of the impatient waiter I opened the door, took a glance at the note, and was but too soon assured by the address that I was the unfortunate *homo* for whom it was intended.

Having twice perused its contents, I perfectly comprehended the modest request of the writer, who being involved in an expensive lawsuit and disappointed in remittances from his father, who was then in the north, would esteem it a *particular* favour if I could send *one hundred pounds!* which should be punctually returned to me in two or three days; signed "Yours most faithfully, Walter Ruding." Now, although I was by no means an adept in the crooked path of the great world, and completely ignorant of the unblushing effrontery of those involved in the mazes of pecuniary distress, this exorbitant requisition for the pleasure of a single good dinner struck me most forcibly as a palpable attempt to impose on my credulity and youthful inexperience; had the amount of the sum been one-tenth, I should have had no hesitation in accommodating my libertine acquaintance, although until our accidental *rencontre* in St. James' Street I had ever been on the most distant terms with him.

The note was therefore answered politely, but sincerely explaining the impossibility of meeting his wishes in his existing exigency.

We met next day in the course of my perambulations, but a frigid nod of recognition was the only salutation deigned. I had no peculiar penchant to renew a transitory intimacy, and thus we parted for ever; however, his wild career merits a cursory narration. He had a handsome allowance as an only child of £1,500 *per annum* from his father, who possessed an entailed estate of several thousand pounds' revenue.

Finding this allowance inadequate to defray the expenses of his thoughtless mode of living, he had imprudently mortgaged both this and his father's property to Jews and money-lenders on *post obit* bonds; consequently, on the decease of his only parent, his mother dying many years before, he became an absolute pauper, escaped from his various creditors on the Continent, and there perished in miserable indigence.

The newspapers of 1834 announced a certain disgraceful swindling transaction committed by his unfortunate wife, and thus terminates a record of the follies and result of direful extravagance which might superinduce fifty pages of moralising in conformity to the existing system of book-making. A distant relation of my friend Seton arriving from Aberdeen, and occupying a house in Baker Street, Portman Square, he was invited there, and thus I was left in my solitary hotel, from whence I proceeded almost daily to the India House, where my baggage had been detained on account of a discovery of prohibited goods, which ridiculously enough, consisted of forty pairs of old white nankeen pantaloons that had been stained or dyed a salmon colour for the voyage.

Under this frivolous pretence I was detained in town upwards of a month, and even then only procured it by addressing a saucy letter to the secretary of the department. My threadbare trousers were actually sold at public auction for £20, and the amount handed to me accordingly; so indifferent was I to the restitution of these articles that I determined if they had been restored to offer them as a present to the first needy adventurer.

On my arrival at Bristol I discovered that our family circumstances were not in that affluent state so flourishing previous to my departure from Hambrook. My father was residing in a handsome house in Portland Square; his establishment consisting of a man servant and two horses only—a sad falling off from his accustomed splendour. No explanation was proffered. I was received affectionately, and considered it an impertinent interference to attempt a categorical investigation of affairs, over which I could as yet have no control; but hunting, coursing, and open table for a set of jolly country squires, I was well aware, could not have improved the patrimonial estate, and the accustomed equanimity of my father's disposition had completely abandoned him, plainly evincing the progress of some evident domestic calamity; he merely told me that he had speculated in an iron mine association in Wales, to which he had advanced £10,000, and another in cotton mills at Keynsham of £4,000, from both of which he anticipated the most fortunate results.

Some few years afterwards the director of the first absconded to America and the second became insolvent, so that he was ultimately defrauded of the whole amount and involved in the intricacies of a lawsuit, which entailed a further expense of several thousand pounds. Gentlemen of landed property should ever abstain from mercantile speculations, as neither habit nor experience adapt them to the occupation, consequently they are liable to the imposition of every designing knave, who may delude them with brilliant theories. Such was his case; and I have only to regret the infatuation which ruined my prospects in life, by rendering my profession a source of emolument, instead of a display of patriotic enthusiasm.

Meeting with an old schoolfellow, by name Willoughby, of the 27th Regiment, who had attained the rank of captain by purchase, and just sold his commissions, we attended the Clifton balls regularly, and I might easily have repaired my broken fortune by an eligible marriage, but the usual sensitive delicacy of uniting my destiny to that of a female for the mere dross of wealth was repugnant to my feelings, and for some months we continued our frivolous and unprofitable amusements.

One evening I quitted the assembly earlier than usual and returned to Portland Square, leaving Willoughby, at the time, perfectly sober, and enjoying the giddy dance. The following morning at six o'clock a post-chaise and four drove furiously up to the door; a thundering knock roused the family from their slumbers. Willoughby leaped from the vehicle, requesting an interview on the most important occasion. I hastily dressed, and descending to the drawing room, found him pacing backwards and forwards in an unconceivable state of agitation. He soon explained the nature of his visit at so early an hour, relating that he had drank deeply after my departure from the assembly, and entering the ballroom in an indecent state of inebriety, had wantonly insulted one of the Dean of Bristol's daughters by rudely attempting to kiss her, for which he had been immediately knocked down by her brother, a lieutenant of the 7th Fusiliers, who he had agreed to meet at eight o'clock this morning, requesting me to attend as his second.

On a deliberate review of this affair, I candidly exposed the probable consequences of his intemperate conduct, and expressly refused to accompany him unless he consented to make the most ample apology to Laird (who was an intimate acquaintance of mine), as also to his sister, if she could be prevailed on to accept it.

Outrageous as he appeared, my arguments overcame his vindictive feelings. I deposited my pistols in the carriage and we proceeded to Windmill Hill, near Clifton, the place appointed for the duel; Lieutenant Laird and his friend were already on the spot. I soon explained my intentions, and the affair was adjusted, but not in so satisfactory a manner as I anticipated. Laird positively refusing any amicable recognition of a friendly feeling towards a man who had so wantonly transgressed the acknowledged laws of civilisation; the parties coolly bowed and thus the affair terminated.

I now endeavoured to gradually disentangle myself from any future intimacy with my old schoolfellow, but could not succeed until poverty aided my design; in the course of six months he had squandered the produce of his commissions, a sum of nearly two thousand pounds, on which he retired to his father's domain, called Wick, about four miles from Bristol, on the Bath Road. I was invited to dine with the old gentleman, who was most hospitably disposed, which a princely income enabled him to gratify.

After dinner his son became so intoxicated that he upset the table, broke the chandeliers, and hurled a decanter at his father's head. For this outrageous conduct he was dismissed the house, which he did not quit without a severe struggle with the domestics, one of whom he nearly killed. Having at length been expelled, he retired to a mean lodging, from which I received various applications; first for a guinea, then half a one, then an old coat, hat, etc., etc. Finally he embarked on board a West Indiaman as a common sailor; in a few months returned, and then enlisted as a soldier in a marching regiment; deserted, and was ignominiously flogged on being secured. He then accompanied his corps to the West Indies.

On his passage he was made permanent cook; another brother (of whom there were five living), a captain, was proceeding by the same conveyance to join his regiment, then stationed in one of the islands. Pacing the deck one morning, he gazed steadfastly at the man officiating at the caboose, or cooking machine, and attracted by a resemblance to his brother he approached nearer, and falteringly inquired if his name was Charles Willoughby. He instantly replied in the affirmative.

No electric shock could have excited such an irrepressible impulse; the captain at one spring leaped from the deck into the sea, sinking without an effort to preserve existence; *telle est la vie, mais le vrai n'est pas tou jours le vraisemblable!* The brother gazed on the passing scene with a stupid, vacant stare of insensibility; the continual excitement of spirituous liquors had eradicated every finer feeling of humanity and affection from his torpid system, continuing his degrading occupation without even a passing expression of regret.

On reaching Jamaica he was the first man of the regiment who fell a victim to the yellow fever: an additional proof that the vices of gambling and habitual inebriety are the two most irreclaimable errors of our life. Free from the persecutions of my tormentor I again entered into that delightful society that constitutes the principal happiness and misery of us mortals—the fascinating pursuit of lovely woman. I adopted the code of Chesterfield, as most men of the world do, and never discovered my folly until too late to remedy the evil.

On a shooting excursion I well remember the salutation of an honest country farmer, who was blessed with a family of several buxom, rosy-cheeked, healthy girls, to whom my devoirs were warmly directed. Observing us gaily romping, he exclaimed "Now I don't mind you red-coats a bit; for you tells I plainly you'll kiss my daughters if you can, and we knows what to do; but dang it, there's no knowing what to do with the black-coated parsons, who comes sneaking in and talking vine things about religion and morality and all that, when we suddenly find ourselves grandfathers before the proper time; romp away my lads and lasses; I'll look ater ye!"

No man is really virtuous until proved so by this fiery ordeal: the wealthy bloated sensualist or the independent philosopher may express astonishment at the crimes of the poor, but had they moved in a similar sphere of life, surrounded by every species of excitement and temptation, who could decide on the absolute preservation of that negative virtue, which is erected principally on the basis of wealth? My short leave having expired, I was now employed on the recruiting service, and in collecting the Army of Reserve for the actual defence of our coasts, then menaced by the all-conquering army of the immortal Napoleon Bonaparte, who were encamped on the heights near Boulogne, and the encampment plainly distinguished from Dover and the adjacent sea-ports. Including volunteers the English could have opposed a numerical force of 400,000 men, but could they have effectually resisted the veteran troops of France?

Fortunately this dubious query was never put to the test; the sons of old England were at this period complete children in the art of war, with respect to military operations, and therefore if the French could have landed 100,000 men, London must have been in their possession 48 hours from the period of debarkation. Old officers were of this opinion; the ignorant multitude argued differently; happily for them the experiment was never tried.

At Wells, in Somersetshire, I had collected about 200 substitutes for the Reserve Army, each of whom were to receive from £40 to £60 for their services. A very small proportion was allowed the men at the time of enlistment, and the officer was responsible for the grand deposit, which, on reaching Chatham, was to be handed over to the commandant of that station. I was therefore possessed of several thousand pounds in bank bills on their account, which I had carefully sewn in the lining of my regimental cap, considering it hazardous to confide it to country bankers. I had written to the War Office representing the dangerous responsibility to which I was subjected, but no notice was taken of the appeal; I was therefore in a constant state of agitation, with my cap either on my head or placed close to my elbow.

The peculiarity of my vigilance had attracted the attention of an old rogue of a sergeant named Holroyd, and one morning, having quitted my room for five minutes on some urgent occasion, he had availed himself of my momentary absence to abstract both bills and lining from my cap. I did not make this discovery until at least an hour afterwards.

Who can describe the sensations of horror I experienced on lifting my cap, when I saw its contents had vanished! My landlady informed me she had seen a fat sergeant enter my apartments an hour since, from whence he had again rushed with extreme precipitation. Well aware of the character of the man, from various little pecuniary transactions passing between us, in paying the soldiers, I despatched several couriers in quest of him without effect. Suspecting desertion, I enquired at the coach office if a person of his description had recently applied for a seat in any of the coaches? The clerk—an intelligent fellow—informed me that a burly looking man, with Yorkshire accent and dressed in a huge drab coat, had paid for an outside passage and set off towards Bath about two hours ago. I had no hesitation now in declaring my suspicions of the delinquent, and mounting a beautiful, young, fleet, blood bay mare, a present from my father, I quitted Wells full gallop in pursuit of the miscreant.

So rapid had been my progress that just as I entered Bath, my mare gave a sudden plunge forward and fell dead at my feet, on which I had most conveniently alighted, my charger having relaxed her pace at the foot of the bridge leading into the city, so that in her expiring plunge I was only slightly propelled towards her head. Hastily disembarrassing myself from the stirrups, I applied instantly at the coach office for information as to the different passengers from Wells, and learnt from the coachman that a man of the description I stated had quitted the top of the coach about a mile before their entering Bath, and was observed to take the direction of the Bristol road, afoot. Commission, reputation even, from the stigma of embezzlement, and honour were all at stake.

Depending on my success in the apprehension of this unprincipled villain I had already travelled thirteen miles *ventre à terre* in thirty-five minutes, and now resolved to scour the country in and about the Bristol road. Whilst the hack was preparing I was seated in a window of the White Hart Inn, nearly opposite the pump-room; a stagecoach came rattling up the street. Looking from the open window I recognised the base fellow on whom my future destiny depended, sitting on the hind seat of the Bristol coach on its way to London. As it was passing directly under the window at not six feet distance below, I sprang on my prey without hesitation, shouting, "Stop coach! stop coach! a thief! a thief!" He trembled in every joint, and became pale as death. The dastard fell on his knees, acknowledged that the money was about his person, and offered to restore it if I would promise not to hang him. He was taken into a private room, and after a minute search the bank notes were discovered in his neck-cloth, still wrapped up in the old lining of my cap; a military escort soon attended, and he was marched off prisoner to Wells.

My poor mare was discovered bathed in blood, flowing from her mouth, completely dead; she was only three years and a half old; the extraordinary exertion had ruptured a blood vessel, or, according a vulgar expression, broken her heart; by which sad event I lost at least ninety guineas, a sum I had been frequently offered for her. Had the result of my exertions been unsuccessful I must have inevitably fallen a victim to false appearances; even my appeal to the War Office would have been construed into a premeditated plan of operation with the sergeant to defraud the public; nor would the event of his desertion palliate the odium attached to my character; an ignominious dismission from the army and eternal stigma on my reputation would have been the inevitable consequences of a failure on the apprehension of this man.

On my return to Wells I rejoiced to find the honourable Captain Maude had assumed the command of the detachment. I immediately handed him over the money, and thus was relieved from a state of most oppressive agitation that ever mortal endured. The sergeant was brought to a court martial, broken and flogged; a sentence from Civil Law might have been more severe in its ultimate results, but slower in operation, and less efficacious in a military point of view.

※※※※※※

After recruiting in several towns with considerable success, I once more visited Bath. Forty years ago our views were not so mercenary as they are in the rising generation. I was therefore extremely anxious to meet this lovely creature, and promenaded the streets for several days without being rewarded for my perseverance. The house being pointed out where she resided and lodgings conspicuously announced in the same premises, I engaged apartments on the same floor with the beauty; but what was my surprise and rapture in meeting her on the stairs to recognise Miss Marston, the lady I had so opportunely saved from a watery grave three years ago at Malacca. On her arrival in England she had been received by her aunt with every demonstration of affection, who, living on a handsome jointure, was enabled to support her in that style of splendour she had been accustomed to from her infancy at Calcutta.

But alas! the goods of this world are of a perishable nature; the aunt had been improvident, disbursing the full extent of her annual income, so that at her death six months previous to our meeting the whole wealth of my lovely friend consisted of less than a thousand pounds, derived from the sale of her aunt's effects, after discharging the demands of various creditors. I remained several weeks in my present abode in constant intercourse with this attractive female, and in spite of all my friends could say, love, all-powerful love, overcame every prudential consideration, and in eleven months I became the proud father of twins, and in seven years the distressed but still happy husband of this amiable woman, with a family of nine children.

I held many serious consultations with my father on my existing difficulties, without avail; he was ardent in the cause of the evils arising from primogeniture, and I once more determined to brave the sea and horrors of war, for the maintenance of those I had so cruelly involved in the intricacies of my unhappy destiny. I applied to rejoin my regiment, was ordered to the Isle of Wight, and in October, 1806 once more embarked with an aching heart for the shores of India.

To crown my misfortune my wife was doomed to confinement with her fourth child one week only previous to sailing. I was therefore reluctantly compelled to abandon her with my children at Newport, and two months after my arrival at Madras she rejoined me with my family, the expenses of her passage amounting to £500! True, I had been promoted to the rank of captain in 1805, and was therefore enabled to support my wife in some degree of respectability had I been fixed in a permanent station; this was not the case, as the regiment was at Cannanore, on the opposite side of the peninsula, at nearly five hundred miles' distance; not a syllable of complaint or regret did this amiable woman ever utter amidst all our distressing difficulties.

In this long march I lost one boy at Uscottah and two other children at Seringapatam. Proceeding on through the Wynaad country, I at length reached my destination, rejoining my old corps at Cannanore in June, 1807. A handsome breakfast had been prepared, and the band met my small detachment of 18 men three miles from the station, and if music and a friendly reception from my brother officers could have conferred happiness, I had every reason to be contented. The regiment at this period was in a most deplorable state; they had been recently ordered for Seringapatam, where 500 men had been afflicted with the yellow fever, so that in their march from that unhealthy fortress to Cannanore, upwards of 400 soldiers had been conveyed in *doolies*, a species of rude *palanquin*, appropriated to the use of the sick in India, and at the time of my arrival several hundreds were still suffering in hospital from the effects of climate.

I now passed several months free from care and privation; we had a constant succession of friendly parties, given by the married officers of the cantonment, and my wife experienced all those little amiable attentions that a young and beautiful woman invariably receives from the liberal, polite, and generous military; parties to Mahe, Tellicherry, and Billipatam varied the delightful scene. The hospitable mansion of Mr. Baber, a civilian at Tellicherry, was ever open to our reception, and we passed many weeks with him and his amiable wife, in a round of friendly intercourse. He then occupied a bungalow on a high rock overlooking the sea, from whence could be seen several of the Laccadive Islands, one of the most enchanting spots ever formed by Nature.

Soon after a rumour prevailed that hostilities had commenced between the Rajah of Travancore and the company. Two of our battalions of *sepoys* having been surrounded by a host of the enemy at a place called Quilon, near Cape Comorin, stationed there as a friendly subsidiary force to the *rajah* of that country. It was represented that nothing could save them from destruction but a prompt succour of a regiment of Europeans, and as we were nearer the scene of action than any other King's corps our anticipations were shortly realised.

I must here introduce a few lines on the fate of my friend Woodhall, who fell an early victim to the climate, which is certainly not congenial to all European constitutions. In 1800 he purchased the majority of the regiment, and then married a Miss Cochrane. In a year after he died, leaving one child, who soon afterwards followed him to the grave. His wife then determined on her return to England. Just before her embarkation she had the bodies of her husband and offspring disinterred from the Madras Cemetery, and carefully packed in a box, for the purpose of depositing them in a vault belonging to Woodhall's family at Ratcliff Church, Bristol, his native town.

On her passage home, a young lieutenant of dragoons (Sir G. Tuite) paid his addresses, and she once more ventured on the experiment of matrimony ere the remains of her former husband were committed to its final abode; so much for the affection and caprice of women. Speculative opinions on constancy after death are absurd and unnatural; few females can withstand the persevering attentions of an elegant and accomplished young man, although previously devotedly and romantically attached to an object that no longer exists. The dictates of Nature must ever predominate over our better resolutions, for we preach to the winds when actuated by the irrepressible force of human passions. The relict of the hero and the clown are alike subjugated by the indiscriminate shafts of almighty love. Why then, should my friend's wife rise superior to the common lot of humanity?

Whilst at Cannanore a young officer named Jenkins joined us from Bombay under peculiar circumstances. He had accompanied the 56th Regiment to India under a feigned name. Sir Thomas Picton had procured an ensigncy for a young man, who declined accepting it, when Jenkins was offered the situation provided he changed his name to Phipps. This stipulation was accordingly agreed to, and for several years the surreptitious plan succeeded admirably. He had gradually mounted to the head of the subalterns of the 56th.

But this state of things was not doomed to last, for one day a large party having been invited to the mess, an old schoolfellow of Jenkins' was among the guests, and was excessively astonished on an introduction to Lieutenant Phipps. "Well," said he, "I certainly will never again depend on the evidences of my senses, for you resemble an old friend of mine so perfectly that I could have sworn to his identity on being introduced to you."

Jenkins assured him that he was mistaken, and the dinner passed over with continual observations on the miraculous resemblance. Jenkins was so shocked, and his mind so agitated at the disgraceful necessity of the subterfuge, that he applied to his colonel the following morning to resign his commission, which was accordingly granted, and he joined us as plain Mr. Jenkins, strongly recommended to Colonel Picton for the first vacant ensigncy that might occur.

CHAPTER 14

12th Regiment Embarks For Quilon

On the 24th December, 1808, the 12th Regiment at length received orders for embarkation, with positive instructions to the commandant of the station to have them conveyed in the most economical manner to Quilon, in the Travancore country. By the 26th the preparations were so far advanced as to enable the commandant of the garrison (Colonel Ouppage) to commence the embarkation, and in the course of the same day the whole battalion was on board twelve *patamars* (open boats from 40 to 100 tons' burden), and the flank companies on an old country-built brig. With the exception of four boats the others were all leaky, consequently not seaworthy. The orders were to proceed forthwith to Cochin, and ultimately to Quilon, in the dominions of the Rajah of Travancore, a distance of upwards of 300 miles. The vessels were excessively crowded, as a proportion of followers, consisting of cooks, *Lascars*, and officers' servants, accompanied the troops.

Thus situated, a signal was made from the fort of Cannanore for the little fleet to sail, which was immediately obeyed. Rice, salt fish, and arrack were the only provisions provided for the voyage. In two or three boats there was a quarter-cask of arrack; the others were unprovided with this essential article, which, when properly diluted in water, contributes materially to the health of the soldiers. The unequal distribution of this liquor caused much inconvenience and distress during the voyage, for when the fleet stood out some distance from the shore, the agitation of the sea became so great as to prevent all communication, so that those boats unprovided with this essential stimulant were necessitated to remain without it for several days.

The situation of the troops was distressing in the extreme, from this confinement to one position, without the possibility of reclining the body in a recumbent posture or taking any refreshing slumber, being absolutely wedged together, without awning or covering to defend them from the scorching rays of the sun (which are reflected from the sea with redoubled fierceness), or the baneful and heavy dews of night, which, with the deadly land winds blowing off the shore, were sufficient to injure the most robust constitutions in a very few hours; the natives, when exposed to the influence of this wind during night, are frequently deprived of the use of their limbs during life, which are withered and distorted in a most awful and unaccountable manner.

The short and rapid motion of the vessels produced the most violent sensations of nausea; the disgusting effluvia proceeding from those affected soon compelled those of stronger stomachs to yield to the prevailing malady, and thus sitting opposite each other in a cramped, confined position the scene that ensued beggars all description; even whilst labouring under the effects of these complicated miseries these gallant sufferers refrained from the expression of the least complaint, except a little regret for the loss of the accustomed dram of *arrack* which might have cheered their spirits amidst the evils they endured.

Although the most positive instructions had been issued for the boats to preserve hailing distance and keep as closely together as possible, consistent with safety, it was soon discovered to be impracticable; for during the first night they were assailed by sudden squalls, so that at dawn of day the following morning only four of the fleet were visible, which reached Cochin the same evening, but had scarcely approached the offing of the harbour when an express boat rowed out with despatches from Lieutenant-Colonel Macauley, British Resident in Travancore, requiring the immediate continuance of our voyage to Quilon, as he had just received information that the two *sepoy* battalions stationed there were completely surrounded by at least 40,000 Travancorians.

The four *patamars* instantly put to sea again and reached Quilon on the 29th inst. The coast appeared completely deserted, for although the canoes of the fishermen were plainly discerned lying on the beach, no one approached to communicate with the *patamars*, and we remained several hours in a state of the most anxious suspense. At length several British officers were observed exerting themselves to launch a boat; these incipient symptoms of a friendly disposition were joyfully acknowledged by our unfortunate sufferers with a general cheer. The officers soon came alongside, representing that the whole country was in arms, and every individual prohibited from affording assistance or furnishing provisions to the British, and further that the moment an European soldier landed would be a signal for driving the whole invading force into the sea.

In defiance of this imposing menace the four companies were disembarked the same day, but with the greatest difficulty, as the small canoes employed for the purpose were only calculated to contain three or four soldiers at a time, and managed rather awkwardly by the *lascars* who accompanied us, for the inhabitants had all deserted the coast. The troops fortunately were unmolested and landed without accident; opposition was naturally expected and prepared for, as this proceeding was in direct violation of the treaty subsisting between the *rajah* and the Company's Government, which specified that the landing or marching Europeans on the Travancore dominions would be considered an open declaration of war.

Having happily effected the disembarkation of the four companies, one of which I commanded, we immediately joined the *sepoy* force, commanded by Colonel Chalmers, though most precariously situated, yet no positive act of hostility had occurred previous to our arrival. The peninsula of Quilon is exceedingly populous, and the moment the first detachment of Europeans touched the shore a general howl prevailed among the inhabitants, who abandoned their habitations in every direction. Horses, elephants, *palanquins*, with numerous retinues of the principal natives, were observed moving off with the greatest expedition. These ominous indications induced Colonel Chalmers to detach a force to occupy an eminence that commanded the *dewan's* palace (*duan* or *dewaun, alias* prime minister of the *rajah*) and the grand bazaar, to ascertain any hostile movements of his forces (large bodies of whom were stationed in the vicinity), and anticipate any sudden attack from that quarter. Captain Clapham, with four companies of *sepoys* and one 6-pound field-piece, marched to perform this important service.

Our officers had been hospitably invited to share the dinner of the mess of one of the *sepoy* battalions, where we were comfortably imbibing our Madeira wine after a scanty meal, which pleasant occupation was interrupted by the report of artillery and successive volleys of musketry, which made us start from our seats and join our men. The Europeans, not anticipating an attack, had, as customary in India, procured liquor and indulged to such an excess that of seventy men of my company I could only collect four capable of shouldering a musket; the others were scattered about on the sandy plain in a beastly state of intoxication.

The rapid succession of firing, however, soon brought the majority to a proper sense of duty; had the enemy been aware of the actual state of our army, they might have annihilated the whole force almost without opposition. Captain Clapham, having been instructed in the most impressive terms to abstain from an attack on the *rajah's* troops unless they openly opposed his occupation of the post, which alone insured the safety of the left flank of the British lines (which consisted of a high artificial mound of earth, apparently accumulated with the intention of forming a battery), advanced cautiously to accomplish the object in view, but ere he reached the bazaar a strong body of matchlock men and archers suddenly filled the road in front.

In conformity with orders, he acquainted the chief that no hostility was intended; if, however, they impeded his progress, he should immediately fire on them. This intimation had no effect; they pushed on, and were within a few yards of the *sepoys* when a resort to arms became indispensable for the preservation of the troops under his command; a round of grape shot was therefore discharged among them with deadly effect. This chastisement of their temerity did not intimidate them. Still advancing with undaunted resolution, several successive showers of grape were now poured into the adverse column, which with a smart volley of musketry at length cooled their ardour, and the post was occupied without further resistance.

During this affair, in which the enemy lost a hundred men (sixty of whom lay dead on the spot), the troops in camp bivouacked and remained under arms all night, as authentic intelligence had been communicated that upwards of 30,000 of the *rajah's* regular army were close to Quilon, and meditated an attack on the British camp. Our army consisted of 270 men of the 12th Regiment, with 1,500 *sepoys*. On the morning of the 31st Dec. the *dewaun's* palace was taken possession of by another detachment; eight guns, all pointed towards the principal entrance, and each doubly charged with round and grape shot, were captured. It was a most fortunate circumstance that the palace was not attempted the preceding night, for one discharge from these guns would have destroyed the whole detachment, as they must have marched up a short avenue fronting these engines of destruction.

On the occupation of the palace, the detachment advanced towards the banks of the Backwater, where columns of the enemy were crossing to retake the palace. Major Hamilton (commanding our troops) arrived just as the *rajah's* troops were midway over the ford. A smart fire of musketry commenced, and some showers of grape following, the enemy, after sustaining a heavy loss, regained the opposite shore, from which they kept up an incessant cannonade.

Whilst this scene was acting about five miles from the encampment (appearing, from the awful booming of the heavy ordnance, much more serious than it really was), the enemy had passed the Backwater in great force to intercept Major Hamilton's detachment. I was ordered with my company to attack them and join the major; this was effected without loss, for the *rajah's* troops on the approach of the Europeans retired without firing a shot. I pursued them to the banks of the Backwater, where they were crowding into canoes for the purpose of returning to the opposite shore; the surface of the water was beautifully animated by several hundreds of the little craft filled with troops.

As they did not fire, I continued my route towards the major's detachment, but a few volleys of grape shot obliged me to shelter my men more inland amongst the cocoanut trees. Having joined Major Hamilton, I found him retiring, for, being separated from the enemy by an arm of the sea, which flowed through the beach and formed the Backwater, and under a heavy cannonade from the opposite peninsula, without a possibility of offering any effectual resistance, he had decided on returning to camp, though ignorant of the ambuscade intended for the destruction of his party until I apprised him of the menacing posture of affairs. He resumed his original position at the palace, and I rejoined the army without further interruptions.

The situation of our encampment was on a small sandy plain, rather more than a mile in circumference, about four hundred yards from the sea, surrounded by a forest of lofty cocoanut trees; we had four 6-pound field-pieces, three of which were unserviceable, and mounted on sandbanks without carriages. The guns captured the preceding evening at the *dewan's* palace were useless, as the calibre was not calculated for our shot. Towards evening, 31st December, an insulting message was delivered by the *dewan's* herald that unless the Europeans were re-embarked immediately he would that night drive the English force into the sea, and if any were taken prisoners they should be trampled to death by elephants, and whilst the conference with Colonel Chalmers was going on our pickets were driven in, and numerous battalions of the enemy appeared on all sides, indicating a combined attack. Flags flying from the cocoanut trees around, with distant musketry, the spent balls falling rapidly among the English force, plainly denoted the commencement of a general action; had they persisted in this design, success must have attended the enterprise.

We had only twelve hundred bayonets, with one 6-pounder, against 30,000 of the enemy, supported by numerous heavy artillery; the disparity of force was too obvious. At this perilous moment a *sepoy*, despatched by Major Hamilton, arrived, and mentioned that the *dewan's* troops had crossed the different ferries on the Backwater and had entirely surrounded the palace. Under these circumstances, pressed on all sides by a powerful and vindictive foe, it was considered judicious to retire from the encampment and take up a strong position on the left in the remains of an old Dutch fort at the extremity of the peninsula, about four miles distant, which had been dismantled, but still retained the advantage of a commanding situation. Two of the dismounted guns were replaced on the decayed carriages, and at dusk our army proceeded towards the dilapidated fort; the camp was left standing for the purpose of deceiving the enemy; the soldiers' caps, pockets, and pouches were filled with ball cartridges, and in passing the *dewan's* palace the guns taken there were spiked by Hamilton, whose detachment now joined us in the retreat.

Every precaution was adopted to prevent the annoyance of the force in its retrograde movement during the march to the fort, which lay through a heavy sandy road, lined on each side by mud walls, breast high, behind which an impenetrable forest of cocoanut trees secured us from any regular attack from the enemy. Loud shouts were distinctly heard around. However, about nine at night, after many awful halts, the force took up a position on the ruins of the rampart without impediment. Scarcely had we reached our destination when a tremendous storm arose, accompanied by torrents of rain, which continued the whole night, rendering the ammunition unserviceable, and the small arms completely rusty.

The force being unsheltered and exposed to the full inclemency of the weather, so violent was this unseasonable storm (for it was the time of year when the season was proverbially mild on the Malabar coast) that the wrecks of several vessels were cast on shore, and the carcases of many wretched victims to the fury of the unrelenting element strewed the beach around the fort. Our poor soldiers, perched on the rocky fragments of the ramparts and exhausted by the incessant fatigue to which they had been subjected since debarkation, and yet labouring under the cramping effects of their miserably constrained position during three days' voyage, slept soundly amidst this jar of contending elements, officers and men lying indiscriminately together.

As they thus slumbered the rain had completely saturated their caps and clothing; the cartridges were consequently dissolved, tinging their persons with the blackest hue, so that at the dawn of day, when the hats and caps were suddenly required and precipitately placed on the head, the Europeans were scarcely distinguishable from the *sepoys*. During this miserable night I drank the contents of a whole bottle of brandy without the least ill effect—indeed, the preservation of my life may be justly attributed to the revivifying cordial. Soaked to the skin, and shivering on the rampart, exposed to the fury of the gale, nothing could exceed the misery of our deplorable situation. The morning of the 1st January, 1809, was ushered in by the most lamentable scenes than can be imagined.

Let the man of feeling picture to himself a small dilapidated fort, a mile and a-half in extent, of triangular shape, over two sides of which the sea was dashing its raging billows with irrepressible fury, and on the ramparts fifteen hundred British troops, exposed to all the inclemency of a storm of wind and rain, beyond the comprehension of those unaccustomed to a tropical climate; fifteen thousand followers, principally the wives, children, and families of the *sepoys*, occupying the area of the triangle (where they had sheltered themselves all night from the dread of a still more remorseless enemy), running about in the wildest confusion, and uttering the loudest lamentations of despair, which with the roaring of the sea, the wrecks and dead bodies scattered on the shore, and he will have a faint idea of one of the most impressive and terrific scenes that ever history recorded.

At five o'clock the troops were paraded amidst torrents of rain, without a single dry cartridge to defend themselves from any attack In this hopeless predicament it was resolved to regain the ground of encampment at the point of the bayonet, and accordingly we moved off along the road we had traced the preceding evening. The van consisted of the four companies of H.M. 12th, pushed forward towards the *dewan's* palace, which was reoccupied immediately. Just beyond this spot sixty or seventy of the dead bodies, interred on the night of the 30th December in superficial graves, were dragged out by the jackals, who were in the act of devouring the *delicious* repast as we hastily proceeded by the infected atmosphere. These animals interrupt the silence of night with the most hideous and appalling howling, assemble in numerous droves, and disinter bodies from the deepest graves, satiating their voracity on the flesh, although in a state of the extremest putridity.

These animals are more numerous in the vicinity of Quilon than I recollect in any part of India. When within a few hundred yards of the original ground of encampment, ten or twelve poor fishermen rushed towards us, who had just had their noses and ears cut off, with faces streaming with blood; the *dewan's* spies had detected them selling fish to our troops, and this mutilation was the brutal punishment inflicted. From these wretched objects it was ascertained that the *rajah's* army had been deceived the preceding evening by our retrograde movement, suspecting our sudden departure as a *ruse de guerre* to attack them in some unexpected quarter during the night; the enemy had consequently concentrated their whole force on the opposite bank of the Backwater, at least five miles distant.

On this information our little force soon reached camp, but a scene of desolation presented itself, almost as distressing as that so recently abandoned; every marquee and tent was level with the ground; boxes and liquor cases broken open; wearing apparel and empty bottles scattered in all directions. The depredators were but too evident, as many of them were lying about in the most beastly state of intoxication and insensibility; the more prudent, but not less iniquitous, had escaped with the more valuable portion of the articles. However, on mustering these miscreants (our own camp followers) we fortunately recovered the principal part of our clothes, but the wine, brandy and gin were irrecoverably gone. The magazine and all public stores remained uninjured and precisely in the state they were abandoned the preceding evening.

As the English force was destitute of every species of conveyance, especially the Europeans who had so recently landed, all their baggage had been left to the mercy of the enemy, and several officers possessed only the wet clothes on their backs; this evil was, however, soon remedied by the generous contributions of those who had not sustained such severe loss.

Whilst busily employed in regulating our encampment, an ostentatious flag of truce arrived from the enemy, with propositions of the most insulting description, no less than the surrender of the British force, and that vessels should be provided for immediate embarkation, without which we were to suffer complete annihilation, as the forces of the Rajah of Cochin had united with those of Travancore, thus augmenting the confederate army to 60,000 men! Our danger was certainly imminent, and Colonel Chalmers returned a temporizing reply to these menaces, which produced a partial suspension of hostilities. On the 6th January the *dewan* forwarded a dispatch from the governor-general to Sir George Barlow, Governor of Madras, expressive of a decided disapprobation of invading the territories of the Rajah of Travancore.

This letter had been originally forwarded by Colonel Macauley, Resident at Cochin, to Colonel Chalmers, and so arranged that it might be seized by the *dewan's* spies; it was actually intercepted and opened by him, and on conviction that our government was averse to warfare, had suspended his meditated attack until the morning of the 7th. The resident at Cochin, well aware of the perilous situation of the diminutive force of English at Quilon, had ingeniously contrived to mislead the enemy by this insidious experiment. At six o'clock the sandy plain on which we were encamped was surrounded by the confederate forces, and at least thirty guns were plainly distinguished among the cocoanut trees.

Our tents being struck, and the line drawn up judiciously to oppose this hostile indication, at this instant an elephant was seen emerging from the confines of the wood, striding over the plain, most gorgeously caparisoned, a *howdah* on its back, with a distinguished chief called the *Coodry-poochy* (or Master of the Cavalry). An *aide-de-camp* from Colonel Chambers advanced to a conference. This chief demanded in an insolent and haughty style an explanation of the unaccountable conduct of the English in landing Europeans in Travancore contrary to treaty and in violation of the sentiments expressed in the governor-general's letter? pompously enumerating the strength of the *rajah's* army, and full determination of attacking our force, if not withdrawn in the course of the day.

Colonel Chalmers merely replied that he had not the power of entering into any political discussion, and requested a suspension of hostilities until final arrangements could be proposed by the British Resident, intimating that he had positive orders to respect the *rajah's* troops unless he was attacked. In the course of the morning a letter was received from the *dewan* expressing his irrevocable determination of attacking the British the following day.

Timidity and irresolution existed on both sides, but the perilous position of our little force admitted some apology for equivocation, and we were rejoiced to observe the multitude of the enemy retiring from the woods to a more respectful distance. Whilst they were moving off, our remaining fleet of *patamars* was discovered, augmented to the number of fifteen or twenty. The 18th Regiment of Native Infantry had embarked at Cannanore and joined the six companies of our regiment at Cochin; these vessels soon anchored, and the troops disembarked the same evening, with four 9-pounder field-pieces and a howitzer. This seasonable acquisition infused fresh courage into our exhausted troops, who had been seven days and nights under arms! Our army now amounted to upwards of three thousand effective men, seven hundred of whom were Europeans.

Fifty men of the 12th Regiment had been left at Cochin for the protection of the resident, Colonel Macauley, as an attempt had been made to assassinate him. On our first four *patamars* passing Cochin, many covered boats were lying in a creek not a mile distant from the residency, filled with armed men for the purpose of a concerted attack on the colonel's person, and it appears a singular anomaly that he should have been so deficient in authentic intelligence as to be totally ignorant of transactions agitating so close to the very place he had selected himself, as combining security with facility of action.

Had he been aware of this premeditated treachery, he would not have evinced such anxiety for the speedy departure of the four companies of the 12th, who appeared almost designed by Providence for his protection. The resident's most confidential servants were implicated in the plot, as they hourly communicated with the *rajah's sepoys*, secreted in the covered boats; the arrival and departure of the Europeans were perfectly understood, which will account for the determined confidence with which they persisted in quest of the object of their revenge.

The Travancoreans were influenced by sentiments of peculiar inveteracy towards the resident, whom they considered as the author of the existing troubles, and in whose death they anticipated the happiest results, forgetting in their native ignorance that this outrage would effectually preclude the possibility of amicable adjustment. Another remarkable occurrence also escaped the resident's observation. On the evening of the 28th December, as he was indulging in social intercourse with a few select friends after dinner, a native was introduced who possessed several tame hawks, which by a variety of tricks afforded infinite amusement to the jovial party; several pebbles were thrown up and arrested in the air by the rapid flight of the birds; although the attention of the guests was principally directed to the pastime, yet the commanding mien and scrutinizing observation of the man was not totally disregarded; it was remarked on his retiring, that a performance of this description had never previously been exhibited at Cochin, and admiration was expressed at the superior, dignified countenance and stature of the native; no suspicion was, however, entertained of the probability of any extraordinary event arising from so apparently trivial a circumstance. It was afterwards ascertained that this very individual was one of the leading characters of the force destined for the attack on the resident's person.

At 12 o'clock the same night a partial fire of musketry was heard proceeding from the colonel's bodyguard, consisting of a few *sepoys*, several of whom were killed, and the remainder soon overpowered by numbers. This slight resistance, although ineffectual, gave timely notice to the resident, who, roused from his sleep by the noise of the conflict, opened a window, enquiring the cause of the firing, when he was most disagreeably saluted by a volley of musketry, upwards of twenty balls penetrating the Venetian blinds of the very window he had opened; this species of reply to his enquiries could not be misunderstood, and convinced him no time was to be lost in effecting a retreat.

A party of the foe was already at the door, demanding admission and using every exertion to force it open; hastily revolving innumerable plans of no use, his fertile imagination suggested one as infallible, that of descending into the hole of a privy situated at an inconsiderable distance from his bedchamber. Eligible as this resolution might have appeared to the agitated resident, it was certainly a disgusting refuge, a lamentable and awkward predicament for a British Resident! To this high-flavoured sanctuary he was, however, indebted for the preservation of his existence; scarcely had he ensconced himself, when the doors of his mansion were forced open.

Every mode the ingenuity and cunning of the natives could devise was resorted to, in full expectation of ultimately securing the object of their detestation and sacrificing him to their fury. Rooms and closets underwent the minutest examination, nor did they omit an inspection of the place of his actual retirement—one of them even thrust a torch down the hole, but, by a most miraculous intervention of good fortune the resident remained undiscovered; thus disappointed, they dashed the trunks, globe lamps, and other costly furniture of the proprietor to atoms.

They then attacked another house, in which the resident sometimes resided, at this time occupied by an inoffensive German in the employment of the Company; he barricaded the doors and offered a resolute resistance, but his efforts would have been ineffectual, had not the arrival of several boats at the mouth of the river, represented as filled with Europeans, spread such terror amongst the assailants that they precipitately retired; the old German, having overheard their conversation and aware of the cause of sudden retreat, availed himself of the occasion to effect his escape and communicate intelligence of this fortunate event to the agitated resident, who without purification procured a canoe and was received with every demonstration of commiseration which his recent misfortune entitled him to, on board a *patamar*, five of which, with a proportion of the 12th Regiment, had so opportunely arrived, thus releasing him from durance vile, and never was the acceptation of the term more appropriately exemplified!

Several of the *patamars* had been dashed to pieces on a sand-bank near Cochin, in the gale of the 29th December; the troops waded to shore, without the loss of a single man. Two *patamars* were missing, supposed to have foundered in the gale. However, just as the remainder of the regiment was quitting Cochin, one of them appeared and accompanied the fleet to Quilon.

Never were troops more scantily attended or equipped than the army in Quilon, not a single bullock or conveyance for guns or baggage of any description; thus we were exposed to the united efforts of the armed population of Cochin and Travancore, without the possibility of retaliation, in the event of obtaining any partial success, which could not be taken advantage of, for want of carriage. As the remaining companies of the 12th Regiment were landing, the enemy made some movements in front, in order to prevent the operation, but such was the activity and exertion of the boatmen that the whole force was safely on shore by six o'clock in the evening. We now reposed in perfect confidence, striking the tents at three o'clock every morning, the troops resting on their arms until daylight, when line was formed in preparation for any attack the enemy might contemplate, and this plan was pursued with undeviating uniformity until the cessation of hostilities, a period of three months.

The troops were fully occupied until the 12th inst. in landing stores and artillery, which latter, from the small size of the canoes, was impracticable; fortunately the *Piedmontaise* frigate arrived, and with the assistance of her boats the object was accomplished. Captain Foote, having tendered any further service, proceeded with Colonel Macauley, the resident, who was on board, to reconnoitre the enemy's positions on the coast. In passing near Anjenga, the frigate was attacked by nearly two hundred canoes filled with armed men; as the wind had ceased almost to a perfect calm, they safely approached the vessel, but when near enough to feel the effects of grapeshot, a whole broadside was poured amongst them, destroying at least forty canoes, dispersing the remainder, and covering the sea with dead bodies. From motives of humanity a repetition of the iron shower was not resorted to, or nearly the whole squadron might have been exterminated.

Poor devils, they had no more idea of the tremendous battery of a frigate than the savages of America, for they had actually contemplated the capture of the vessel! During the resident's short visit to Quilon, he had officially notified to Colonel Picton the melancholy fate of the *patamar* supposed to have foundered in the gale, on board of which were 33 men and the second sergt.-major of the 12th Regiment (Sergt. Tillesley); they had escaped the fury of the storm, and anchored in the roads of Aleppi, which was unfortunately taken for those of Quilon. Canoes pushing off from shore, they landed without hesitation or suspicion, rejoiced to be relieved from their miserable and dangerous confinement.

On reaching the bazaar, they were informed that the British Army was only five miles distant; having deposited the arms in a large room, pointed out as the temporary barracks for the Europeans, they afterwards strolled about the town, and the inhabitants supplying them with *arrack* free of expense, they all soon became intoxicated, and extended in the streets in a complete inanimate state, and were thus secured by the Travancoreans, who first cruelly broke their wrists, and then, tightly tying their arms behind them and neck and knees together, plunged them headlong into a deep, unwholesome dungeon.

In this shocking condition they remained four days and nights, and, on the fifth morning taken separately, in a deplorable state of exhaustion, to the Backwater, about three miles distant (surrounded by the exulting populace), where it was many fathoms deep; heavy stones were then attached to the neck of each helpless wretch, who was instantly hurled into the water amidst the barbarous shouts and music of the remorseless natives! The second sergt-major was the last victim to this unprecedented tragedy; he repeatedly called for a sword, that he might die like a soldier, but all in vain; he was precipitated, in spite of cries and struggles, into the watery grave already shared by his miserable comrades. These particulars were communicated by a cook boy, who had accompanied the detachment and had been an eyewitness of the whole inhuman transaction. Aleppi is 30 miles from Quilon.

CHAPTER 15

Further Fighting About Quilon

At two o'clock in the morning of the 15th January, 1809, a cloud of hissing rockets was thrown into camp, followed by a discharge of artillery from the front and both flanks. I leaped from my rattan couch, as several cannon balls passed through the marquee, one striking the couch from which I had the instant before risen, and dashing it to pieces. The whole power of the enemy's guns was directed towards the Europeans, whose situation they had minutely ascertained, and before the 12th Regiment could wheel into line several men fell dead; the intervals between the companies were literally ploughed by cannon balls. The sandy particles of the ground driven into the faces of the soldiers, so confused them that much difficulty was experienced in forming line.

So completely had the range of our regiment been taken that it became indispensably necessary to advance at least a hundred paces, before we were clear of this terrific cannonade. The night was exceedingly dark, and the enemy still continued to fire on the exact spot from which we had advanced, until the light of morning exposed the fresh position of the British army. It appeared that the *dewan* had advanced his guns during the night, with profound silence, to within a quarter of a mile of our encampment, an operation easily effected under cover of the dense forest of cocoanut trees that surrounded the British force, not one of which had yet been felled, from motives of respect to the enemy's religious prejudices, who are peculiarly attached to their preservation, considering the destruction of a single tree as a crime of the most unpardonable nature. The onset was so sudden, and proceeding from so many directions, that no decisive plan of operation could possibly be adopted until the enemy's position was reconnoitred.

At six o'clock (after three hours' cannonade from at least 40 pieces of ordnance showering round and grape shot on the encampment, piercing almost every tent, and some literally torn to pieces by the innumerable balls passing through them) daylight now enabled the British commander to make arrangements of defence. Five companies of the 12th, with a battalion of *sepoys* advanced to the front attack, a similar proportion to the left flank, and a battalion of *sepoys* to the right. At this moment our pickets came rushing in, followed closely by the enemy. Colonel Picton, who directed the front line, charged them at the point of the bayonet, but on entering the wood, two guns opened on him, killing 20 grenadiers; the guns were however captured, the gunners bravely defending them until bayoneted on the spot. Unceasing volleys of musketry were interchanged in this quarter, whilst Colonel Chalmers, commanding the left attack, was advancing into action.

I was in this division, and we halted to give the enemy a round of grape in reply to several 18-pounders which annoyed us exceedingly. As nine artillerymen were dragging the field-piece into position, a ball struck the first man at the rope near the hip, and carried off the lower extremities from the bodies of the eight men in his rear. We had not more than 30 artillerymen in our whole army, this was therefore! a most serious loss, and deprived the left flank attack of all aid from the gun during the battle. I was ordered to advance with my company towards a low sandhill, from whence several guns were vomiting their iron showers, committing sad havoc among our men; my brave fellows pushed on, and in five minutes the battery was in our possession, with loss of two killed and my lieutenant slightly wounded, a round shot passing between his thighs, slightly grazing both of them.

I maintained my position until joined by the rest of the division, in spite of many thousand archers, whose arrows were bristling about us like the short straws of a stubble-field. The battle now raged on all sides. The right attack was but feebly opposed, the battalion of *sepoys* in that quarter, having lined the banks of a ditch, kept the enemy at bay; they had, however, introduced themselves into our encampment along the seashore, and wild shouts of success soon announced that all our baggage was captured, and the British force completely surrounded.

For several hours the roar of cannon and peals of musketry were incessant, the enemy bravely contesting every inch of ground, nothing appearing to intimidate them but the charge of the Europeans. The five companies of the 12th of the left attack gallantly pursued a large body through the woods, when a battery of four guns opened on their rear from the opposite side of a low marshy ground several hundred yards to the left; a causeway of four feet wide was the only mode of approach to the battery, which Colonel Chalmers determined to storm; our five companies retraced their steps under a heavy fire from this formidable obstacle, and on arriving at the near side of the causeway, observed at least 10,000 of the *rajah's sepoys* drawn up on the opposite bank in support of the guns.

Although by no means of a desponding disposition, I could not view this disparity of our force without certain disagreeable sensations; even the veteran Chalmers hesitated. The *sepoys* again joining who we had left in the rear for the protection of the captured guns, the command "Charge, 12th!" was given. I was the leading officer and rushed forward at the head of my company (the causeway admitting a formation of four deep only), followed by the rest of the division; the battery of four guns was immediately in front, the enemy's *sepoys* a few yards to the left.

One volley from such numbers was sufficient to have annihilated us; as we advanced at full speed they appeared panic-struck, gave one loud shout of "The Europeans, the Europeans!" and disappeared amidst the trees without firing a single shot; the battery was also deserted, as I mounted the eminence on which it was erected, where some dozens of mangled corpses were extended around. We pursued the fugitives, but a few straggling shots were the only indication of the proximity of an enemy in this quarter. The fire was still brisk where Colonel Picton was engaged, we therefore recrossed the causeway to his support, but observing the forlorn situation of our encampment crowded by the enemy, who were plundering and unprepared for an attack, we charged in amongst them, and such a scene of slaughter ensued as no pen can describe.

They fought desperately, man to man, foot to foot; all was one wild confusion. They were at least ten times our numerical strength, but at length victory crowned our efforts, and they abandoned the encampment and the principal part of the baggage, but in this conflict our troops had suffered too severely to return to the assistance of Colonel Picton, who was yet fighting in front. His gallant division did not fortunately require our aid, or the battle might have terminated to the disadvantage of the British. He had successfully resisted every attack and taken ten guns after seven hours' hard fighting, and just as our division had driven the enemy from the camp, he had stormed several houses occupied by the *rajah's* troops, every one of whom perished; one house, in particular, offered such a resolute resistance that it was fired after an ineffectual offer of quarter, and not a soul escaped.

Our soldiers were animated with a degree of fury beyond any I have ever known; as they charged they encouraged each other by the expression of "Remember Aleppi, my boys" and one of them plunged his bayonet with such force through the body of a Travancorean that it remained firmly fixed in the back-bone, from which in his hurry he could not withdraw it, he therefore unfixed it, leaving the carcase in that state. The *sepoys* emulated the Europeans in this day's glorious action by various remarkable instances of bravery. In almost every charge with the bayonet they were close by our side, cheering on with the usual exclamation of "*Ding! ding!*" or "Charge! charge!" A languid fire of musketry was now kept up by the enemy, who by five o'clock in the afternoon had disappeared, leaving 1,500 dead and upwards of 2,000 wounded on the field of battle.

The battalion of *sepoys* that defended the right flank of our line had conducted themselves gloriously, having captured four small field-pieces and repulsed the enemy with considerable slaughter; this was an unparalleled instance of gallantry in a native corps unsupported by Europeans, except a few artillerymen, who served the gun attached to the battalion. The loss of the British was under 200, with only four officers wounded, two of whom belonged to the 12th Regiment. It is necessary to observe that the English force in this conflict had encountered the impetuous efforts of an unconquered people, who a few years before had successfully repulsed the invading army of Tippoo Saib. The Nairs or Travancoreans may be justly considered the bravest race in the peninsula of India, and had their knowledge of military tactics equalled their natural animal courage, the East India Company could never have conquered this inaccessible country.

The *dewan*, previous to this action, had issued especial directions for the destruction of every European, and all prisoners were to be bound neck and knees together and cast into the sea. Many thousand natives had ropes tied round their waists for the purpose; some of these were lying wounded, and explained the intended use of the cords. In the course of the evening I took a survey of the field of battle; the dreadful realities of war and all its concomitant miseries were never more fearfully displayed; the enchantment of the word glory may, at a distance, delude us poor mortals, but we cannot be dazzled or deceived on the fatal plain where the wretched victims of ambition are writhing and groaning life away.

But brevity is my motto, and I will merely describe a few of the shocking wounds I observed: one man both thighs shot away yet still alive; another both eyes shot out; others with legs, arms, and thighs wounded and the splintered bones protruding through the flesh in various directions; as to heads and bodies dashed to pieces, this was a happy fate to that of the mutilated wretches who were all crying in a feeble voice for water.

One poor fellow in particular attracted my notice; his face was completely carried away, and nothing visible but a small hole, once forming the back part of his mouth; he was leaning against a tree pointing to the orifice, intimating a desire for water, which I myself poured into it from a small leathern bottle having a tin pipe attached to it; he was taken to the hospital tent, but died in a few hours. *Bellum! horridum helium!* the Latin poet expressively denominates it, and doubly horrid when opposed to barbarians, who recognise neither the laws of honour nor humanity.

As I was surveying these spectacles of wretched mortality, my beautiful little spaniel came frisking and fawning at my feet, then jumped up, placing its paws against my knees, then ran off a few yards and again returned, repeating this several times. I followed him to the site where my marquee had stood prior to the battle, but dragged many yards from thence by the enemy; the dog began scratching the sand and then ran to a chatty or large earthern cooking vessel lying upside down; I kicked the chatty over, and under it recognised the black head of my *dabash* or principal servant buried up to the chin in the sand; with this dirty black pot he had covered his head and thus escaped detection.

I extricated him from this living grave, on which he pointed out several places where he had also buried all my trunks, and the carcase of a fat calf that had been killed and skinned in my tent, the evening before; to the latter object my sagacious little dog had directed all his attention. I presume the natural instinct arising from a good appetite produced this excitement, rather than any remarkable instance of sagacity. Having disinterred my baggage, re-erected my marquee and cooked a piece of veal, several of my acquaintances assisted me in doing justice to the fatted calf, which was soon divided amongst them, and stewed down to curries, our invariable food in camp.

In the course of this night a heavy fall of rain took place, which destroyed many of the wounded who were left on the field. So improvident had the government been, that the force was not supplied with a single *dooly*, consequently the wounded were all borne to the hospital tent on the shoulders of their comrades. The soldiers were by no means insensible to this shameful neglect, observing "that they were always ready to perform their duty for the honour of His Majesty, and wished only to be treated as Christians and not as dogs!"—alluding to the helpless condition of those who lay weltering in blood without prospect of removal or surgical aid.

Had the force been properly supplied with common conveyance we could have pursued the advantages of our victory the following day; but there we remained, without a single beast of burden and exposed to the continual assaults of the enemy, who were perfectly apprised of our helpless condition, and resorted to every means of annoyance by day and night; sometimes our army was three or four times under arms during the 24 hours, these false attacks being repeated by successive parties of the *rajah's* troops, in order to harass us as much as possible, to tame the indomitable spirit of the Europeans. The following order was issued by Colonel Chalmers on this brilliant occasion:—

Quilon, Jan. 16th, 1809.

D. M. O.—It is with the greatest satisfaction that Lieut.-Colonel Chalmers congratulates the troops that he has the honour to command on the glorious success obtained yesterday against the attack of an enemy whose force did not amount to less than 30,000 men. He begs leave to offer his most particular thanks to Lieut.-Colonel Picton, who commanded in front with a wing of His Majesty's 12th Regiment, and to the officers, and non-commissioned officers, whose gallantry and high discipline have on all occasions appeared conspicuous. He begs leave to offer his thanks to Major Muirhead and to the European and Native officers, non-commissioned officers and privates of the 2nd battalion 18th Regiment, as also to Captain Newhall and the officers both European and Native, and to the non-commissioned officers and *sepoys* of the 1st battalion 4th Regiment, for the gallantry with which they repulsed the attack made on them.

Lieut.-Colonel Chalmers begs leave to offer his thanks to Major Hamilton, who commanded on the left with a wing of His Majesty's 12th Regiment, and to the officers, non-commissioned officers and privates, whose gallant conduct needs no further comment than that they belonged to His Majesty's 12th Regiment. Captain Mackintosh and Lieutenant Lindsay of the artillery are also thanked, and Captain Pepper of the 13th Native Infantry.

We learnt from some of the prisoners that the four first companies of Europeans landed were to have been massacred the night of their arrival, but the plot was frustrated by the spirited conduct of Captain Clapham at the *dewan's* palace. The English now divested themselves of all false delicacy for the religious prejudices of the natives, and the axe was applied without ceremony to every cocoanut-tree that impeded our operations. Three large batteries were erected, and the 26 fine guns taken placed in them; thus these venerated trees became one of our principal sources of defence, independent of which they afforded a most nutritious vegetable to the troops.

At the summit of each tree a species of cabbage grows, of a porous, succulent nature, and when just detached (which operation requires the force of an axe) its flavour resembles that of the finest filbert, and when boiled that of a cauliflower, the size varying according to the bulk of the tree; it is generally from three to four feet long and two in circumference. As no other vegetable was procurable at Quilon, this substitute was a most acceptable and unexpected luxury.

On the 18th a heavy cannonade was heard in the direction of Aleppi, and a few hours after the *Piedmontaise* frigate was again anchored off Quilon with the resident on board. As all communication had been rejected at Aleppi, Captain Foote had cannonaded the town, as an intimation that the barbarous murder of the 33 men of the 12th was not forgotten. On the arrival of the resident, he immediately addressed to Colonel Chalmers the following letter:—

Circular.

Sir,—I had the honour of receiving your short note of the 15th, acquainting me with the brilliant and glorious conflict of that day with the united forces of the *dewan*; this important intelligence was without a moment's delay forwarded to government. Whilst at sea I received your letter of the 16th, communicating the details of that victory, an achievement that reflects signal honour on the discipline and animated valour of the troops under your personal command, and sheds fresh lustre on the British arms. I beg leave to offer you and the officers and men of the force serving in Travancore my cordial congratulations upon an event so highly honourable and beneficial to themselves and to the public interest.

The details were also transmitted without delay to the honourable the Governor in Council, who will, no doubt, be disposed in his discharge of the obligations of public duty on this occasion to regard you and the troops under your command on the 15th instant as well entitled to the public gratitude and applause.

  (Signed)   C. Macauley, Resident.

Captain Foote announced to Colonel Picton that he had, with the assistance of Lieutenant Gilmore, commanding a small cruiser, completely destroyed the whole of the enemy's vessels in the Port of Aleppi, upset the guns in their batteries, and set fire to part of the town, the troops drawn up on the beach receiving several broadsides of grape from the frigate, which dispersed them in the greatest confusion, with a loss of some hundreds killed and wounded.

Another tragical event was communicated by the resident. Colonel Chalmers, at the commencement of hostilities, had forwarded his wife and her two children (by a former marriage) from Quilon to Cochin, under the escort of Surgeon Hume, by the Backwater. On the passage they were taken prisoners by a detachment of the *dewan's* army, but after thirty hours' confinement Mrs. Chalmers and her family were permitted to proceed, suffering most indecent verbal abuse, and reached Cochin in safety. Mr. Hume was detained three days, and then told he might depart. Conceiving himself at liberty he walked off, but ere he had proceeded many yards, several shots were fired at him, one of which took effect and brought him to the ground.

In this state he begged for a drink of water, and a green cocoanut was presented him filled with its milk, but as he was pouring it into his mouth, and held his head back for the purpose, one of the savages struck him across the throat with the edge of his sword, and nearly smote the head from the body. This act was merciful, had they not mutilated the carcase in a manner too horrible to relate, and then scattered the remnants as food for vultures and jackals.

On the 22nd January, we received information that the detachment of fifty men of the 12th, under Lieutenant Thompson, left at Cochin for the defence of the town, had been attacked by the troops of the *rajah* of that country. The fortifications of the place having long been blown up and dismantled, the enemy entered the streets from every quarter, driving some hundreds of the Company's *sepoys* before them at daylight on the 19th January, and established themselves in full possession of the town, except the quarter where the detachment of the 12th was posted. Here our flying *sepoys* rallied under the command of Major Hewitt, and, led on again by the Europeans, a dreadful conflict of many hours occurred in the streets. No sooner was the enemy driven out of one street than they assembled in another; nothing, however, could resist the charge of the English bayonet.

At length Lieutenant Thompson of the 12th fell pierced with wounds; one ball entered his face just below the left eye, penetrating the cheek bone, passing through the roof of the mouth, and lodging in the back of his neck, four of the fingers of his left hand were shot off, and a ball through each thigh. Fifteen of the men of his detachment also fell. Captain Read of the 17th Native Infantry was shot through the head. The *sepoys* now began to waver, and many threw away their arms and military clothing, appearing in the simple dress of the common native (a scanty cloth tied round the loins, peculiar to the peaceable inhabitants of India), in order to impress the enemy with an idea that they were common *coolies*, under which disguise they hoped to escape the anticipated massacre.

The undaunted firmness of Major Hewitt, and the conspicuous prowess of the remaining Europeans soon changed the aspect of affairs, infusing renewed confidence through the ranks. Order was once more restored, and those who had shamefully deserted their post again eagerly joined their companies, officers being too seriously occupied to notice individual misconduct. The 2nd Battalion 17th Native Infantry engaged had but recently been levied, which in some measure palliates this deficiency of intrepidity, which in an old corps might have been considered an indelible disgrace. The first essay of the best trained troops in an action, where the numerical strength is so obviously in favour of the enemy, generally depresses the spirits and causes temporary irresolution.

The gallant 12th, heading every charge, at length cleared the streets of Cochin, impetuously pursuing the advantage to the open country; but here, several batteries opening on them, they were compelled to take refuge behind the ruins of the walls of the town, which had been dismantled and blown up some years before by the English, when the place was taken from the Dutch. Two guns brought close to the walls fell into the Europeans' possession, which they dragged into the streets in spite of a heavy cannonade. The Rajah of Cochin, having coalesced with the Dewan of Travancore, had advanced with 4,000 men, supported by ten guns, to take Cochin, and the enterprise was certainly carried into execution with unusual gallantry by the *palliate* (or *dewan* of the Cochin *rajah*), who led on the attack.

The plan was to have annihilated every soul in the town. The inhabitants gratefully acknowledged the services of the 12th, whose exertions and courage saved them from the contemplated massacre; 300 Company's *sepoys* against 4,000 of the enemy, armed and disciplined like themselves, would have easily been overpowered, but the stimulating energy of this handful of Europeans (of whose presence the *palliate* was ignorant, understanding they had all embarked for Quilon) changed the fortune of the day, and preserved the place from a melancholy scene of indiscriminate slaughter.

Barricades were now thrown up at the entrance of each street to prevent the effects of enfilade, as the enemy continued a furious cannonade; and in this situation they remained several days, until the arrival of the *Piedmontaise* frigate and a Bombay cruiser relieved them from their difficulties. The cruiser, on entering the port, ran aground on a sandbank; the enemy, taking advantage of the circumstance, poured volleys of grape and musketry into her, so that after fruitless efforts to extricate the vessel they were at length reluctantly compelled to abandon her. A bar at the entrance of the river prevented the frigate's co-operation. Whether the loss of the cruiser affected the spirits of Lieut. Gilmore, her commander, or some other latent cause excited him to insanity, was never ascertained. His recent misfortune might have been the cause, as he immediately became gloomy and despondent, and in three days after the event terminated his existence, by applying a pistol to his head and blowing out his brains. It was confidently reported that he committed this rash act in consequence of some misunderstanding and altercation with Capt. Foote who had severely reproved him for unjustly abusing a *sepoy* who was on duty.

On the loss of the cruiser, the boats of the frigate were actively employed in landing part of the crew with two 18-pounders; which having been mounted on an eminence, the enemy's cannonade was returned with some effect. Just at this time two 6-pounders fortunately arrived from Calicut, accompanied by a detachment of artillery, which enabled the British to act offensively. The *palliate* (who had been instigated by the *dewan* to join in the war against the Company) now made overtures of a pacific nature, a proposition, under the existing state of affairs, too satisfactory to be neglected.

A negotiation was therefore commenced, and speedily terminated on the most advantageous basis for the interests of the Company. The Cochin troops were immediately disbanded and separated from those of Travancore. On their march afterwards through the Cochin country, they were guilty of the most horrible excesses, massacring a thousand native Christians and several Portuguese priests, who had sought sanctuary with their proselytes in a church; they were surrounded by these disbanded miscreants, and burnt without mercy.

The inoffensive inhabitants were also doomed to suffer every indignity of wanton cruelty from these bands of lawless *banditti*, and the innumerable dead bodies floating down the river by Cochin evinced but too clearly the agitating desolation carrying on in the interior of the country; I willingly abstain from enumerating all the horrors that ensued in consequence of the political arrangements of the resident, and once more return to a detail of the operations at Quilon.

CHAPTER 16

Captain Bayly Wounded

The termination of the confederacy of the two *rajahs* relieved the British force at Quilon from the effects of the operation of at least 10,000 men, who were now withdrawn by the Rajah of Cochin, from the *dewan's* army. The enemy, notwithstanding, attacked our pickets daily, driving in the working parties, and giving us nightly alerts without intermission, so that an entrenchment round the camp was considered indispensable, where the troops could repose free from danger, and even in this snug berth a stray shot from the woods would sometimes find a victim. This nightly bivouac was attended with intolerable suffering; the men cold, shivering and wet to the skin from the intense dew which fell like thick light rain, dispelled only by the morning sun.

The sudden transition from cold to heat affected the troops with inveterate dysentery, so that the hospital soon became crowded with patients. We had by constant labour cleared a considerable extent of ground, by felling the cocoa trees around, which at length gave our batteries a full command of a large sandy plain some distance beyond the wood, where immense bodies of the enemy's infantry were encamped just beyond the range of our guns.

In addition to our privations we were now menaced by a still more serious calamity—that of famine. All the little bullocks running wild about the woods were soon consumed, as also the scanty provision of stores landed with the army; every article of provision was excessively dear, and at length nothing but "*paddy*," or rice in the husk, was issued for the nourishment of the troops. On the 28th January, 1809, a supply of various descriptions arrived on board some *patamars*, expedited by the indefatigable exertions of Mr. Baber, collector of Tellicherry, who may be justly esteemed the saviour of this little deserted army, thus preserving them from the most terrible of all disasters.

John Bull never fights so well as when the inward man is properly fortified; scanty meals, in which musket balls were not unfrequently forcibly inserted, did not promote the health or spirits of our harassed troops, but, thanks to the exertions of Mr. Baber, we were again properly primed for action. On the 31st January, 1809, the *dewan* once more advanced to an attack. Our troops lying snugly in the trenches were assailed at break of day by the usual salutation of rockets, grape and musketry, which for some time passed harmlessly over our heads.

On the nearer approach of the enemy on the open sandy plain in front, our batteries began to play on them with fearful execution. Their glittering bayonets, gorgeous colours, striding elephants, and compact columns were beautifully displayed as the brilliant sun fell with full lustre on the pompous array; a more splendid scene could scarcely be imagined. Our batteries continued to vomit death and destruction into this armed population, still advancing solemnly and slowly in our front. They then dragged their guns to the summit of elevated sandhills and commenced a furious cannonade on the encampment, but these were shortly dismounted by the superior fire of our batteries. A simultaneous attack on our flanks now compelled us to expose the line of defence.

On mounting the entrenchments the enemy gave one loud and lengthened shout, rushing forward with intention to charge; our grape shot, however, made such fearful breaches in their columns and line that they were thrown into the utmost confusion. One long line further to the left, beyond reach of our batteries, was seen advancing rapidly to charge the battalion of *sepoys* stationed there. When within a few yards, they mistook the *sepoys* for Europeans, from being clothed in blue cotton trousers, and immediately retired, with the usual cry of "*Feringee! Feringee!*" A curious circumstance now occurred. Our howitzer was fired; the shell circled round and fell in rear of the gun amongst our own troops.

Fortunately the fuse was extinguished ere it reached the ground or many Europeans must have suffered. The attack on the right was more successful, the battalion of *sepoys* in that quarter was driven in on the 12th Regiment, a wing of which instantly advanced to the support, and in five minutes took four of the *dewans'* guns and drove the enemy into the woods, where, hiding themselves behind the trees, they galled our troops insufferably for several hours. We were then compelled to adopt a similar system of warfare, and skirmished with success, defended by the trees.

About two o'clock the enemy began to retire slowly in all quarters, I must say with great firmness and regularity, forming a respectable rearguard of several thousands of their choicest troops, bearing off their dismounted guns and innumerable wounded men. It was conjectured that the loss of the enemy was as great on this day as on the 15th instant, 1,500 dead having been buried in the plain where they had commenced the action. Never was victory obtained over so numerous a foe with such insignificant loss—five men killed and twenty wounded were our only casualties. We had repulsed the enemy, but could not pursue our advantage; what more could be expected from a handful of troops so miserably equipped?

Many French families, settled at Quilon, when they heard of this second defeat of the *dewan's* army, were pleased to denominate the British troops by the significant epithet of "The Band of Heroes." This from the mouth of an enemy was certainly subject of exultation for those to whom it applied. We now continued the system of field fortification with redoubled ardour, as the enemy still annoyed us day and night by a repetition of volleys of musketry from the woods, which though not very fatal in its effects, harassed the army exceedingly, as we had not an hour's peace.

On the 12th February the following order was promulgated by the Madras Government:—

> Fort St. George, 6th February, 1809.
> The honourable the Governor in Council has recently received a favourable account of the action that took place on the 15th of January between the British troops and the troops of Travancore, in which, after a long contest, the Travancore troops were defeated with heavy loss. From the extent of the combined force which was opposed to the British troops, this signal victory reflects the highest honour on their discipline and valour, and the Governor in Council has great satisfaction in expressing his strongest approbation of their meritorious conduct.
> The Governor in Council accordingly conveys to Lieut.-Colonel Chalmers, who commanded the British detachment at Quilon in this distinguished action, his public thanks, and Lieut.-Colonel Chalmers is requested to convey the thanks of the Governor in Council to Lieut.-Colonel Picton of His Majesty's 12th Regiment, Major Muirhead, Major Hamilton, Capt.

Newhall, Capt. Pepper, Capt. Mackintosh, Lieut. Lindsay, Lieut. Arthur of the Engineers, and the officers of the staff, Capts. Cranstoun and Achmuty, width the other officers and troops of the detachment who bravely signalised themselves on the occasion.

The honourable the Governor in Council also takes this opportunity of expressing his warm approbation of the conduct of a detachment of troops stationed at Cochin, under the command of Major Hewitt, who with great skill and bravery repulsed a numerous and united force of the troops of Travancore and Cochin in an attack which they made on the British detachment on the 29th *ult.* The Governor in Council has particular satisfaction in expressing to Major Hewitt, and to the officers and troops under his command, his public thanks for their highly deserving conduct.

(Signed)   G. Buchan,
Secretary to Government.

The gallant conduct of Lieutenant Thompson, of the 12th, is not alluded to in this order, though he charged nearly 4,000 of the enemy seven distinct times with only 50 Europeans, and at length fell covered with wounds and glory. This omission of justice to the deserts of so brave a man had an immediate effect, for after joining the force at Quilon and listening silently to the reading of the order, his agitation was so great that a fever seized him and he was a corpse the next day. On dissection, one of the balls with which he had been wounded was found lodged in the back of his neck, after passing through the cheekbone and roof of the mouth; thus perished a gallant officer, a martyr to the neglect of form in an official document.

Sir George Barlow was at this time Governor of Madras, a man devoid of every honourable principle, and by his tyrannical conduct ultimately drove the officers of the Madras establishment into the most fearful and dangerous state of opposition to his vindictive proceedings, and had not their sense of honour for the welfare of the nation superseded every other feeling, the Company's possessions in the East must have been lost for ever.

From the contemplation of this ungrateful subject, I return to one of a more brilliant and consoling nature, in reference to the persevering and successful efforts of the gallant little army at Quilon, who still maintained their ground in defiance of the united force of the *dewan*, who had now assembled the armed population of the country to the amount of nearly a *lac* of men (100,000) and concentrated them in the environs of the British encampment, which they kept in constant alarm—in fact there was no relaxation from incessant labour and hardship; what with felling the trees, working the batteries (to keep the enemy at a respectable distance), digging trenches and repelling partial attacks of the *dewan'* s troops, our force, now reduced to little more than 2,000, was fully occupied.

Seven times when on these working parties, on different days, I was attacked by superior numbers and compelled to retire before the numerous hordes that pursued me; on the *eighth* I was completely surrounded, and fell amidst my men, deeply wounded in the small of my back and knocked down by the fall of a tree, several of which were nearly felled as the skirmish commenced; the firing becoming unusually brisk, support was sent from camp, which alone extricated us from our difficulties. I was borne wounded to my tent, and remained an invalid for many months. On the 7th of February, 1809, His Majesty's 19th Regiment of infantry, accompanied by a detachment of artillery with several field-pieces, arrived in *patamars* from Colombo (island of Ceylon). This reinforcement was exceedingly acceptable, for our troops, after a month's exposure to the inclemency of the weather and the incessant efforts of an active and vigilant enemy of at least thirty times their numerical strength, were rejoiced to find relief from part of the arduous duty they were daily, I may add hourly, called upon to perform.

The hon'ble. Lieut-Colonel Stewart, commanding the 19th Regiment, from the apparent tranquillity of the country, could not be persuaded of the proximity of an enemy, so the evening of his arrival he was permitted to advance to the front, with two guns, some shrapnel shot and a detachment of his regiment, to reconnoitre; he had not proceeded above three miles when he was attacked and soon compelled to regain the army, with a loss of several killed and wounded. The following morning despatches were received from the Rajah of Travancore with propositions for peace, provided no other European force was permitted to land. This was rejected instantly, as from the nature of the overture it was evident that the 19th Regiment had been descried as they coasted the shores of the country on the passage from Colombo; the inhabitants, in order to ascertain this point had sent off canoes filled with poultry and fruit, which were offered for sale to the vessels as they passed.

A most seasonable supply of stores and provisions were brought by this detachment from Ceylon, for our force was again deficient in almost every necessary of life, having speedily consumed the contents of the *patamars* expedited by the active Mr. Baber. Although thus reinforced, an attack on the enemy's entrenchments, about four miles off, was not yet considered prudent, nor to make an advance movement until the old dilapidated triangular fort of Trangacherry was fortified for the reception of our sick and wounded, and the protection of the inhabitants dwelling in the vicinity, who had been menaced with destruction by the *dewan* for assisting the English.

Having accomplished this important object, and left four companies of *sepoys* for its defence, the army having received another supply of provisions and a scanty number of bullocks for the conveyance of the baggage, prepared for an attack. Prior to the movement, a message arrived from the *dewan* enquiring why the English did not come and fight him? sarcastically observing that if they came to subdue the country it was an extraordinary mode of effecting it by merely occupying one position in a state of inactivity. We were not alone liable to these taunts from the *dewan*; a suspicion derogatory to the honour and courage of the force possessed the minds of many individuals in India, who were unacquainted with the innumerable disadvantages under which the troops laboured; for how could any progress be made in the interior of a country never before trodden by European foot, without a proper *matériel?* for we had neither food, conveyance for ammunition, or baggage, and had to thread the inextricable mazes of a forest of cocoa trees on all sides, defended by an enemy twenty or thirty times more numerous than our force; the experiment must have been attended by inevitable destruction.

On the 11th February a despatch arrived communicating the gratifying intelligence that an army under the command of the hon'ble. Colonel St. Ledger was on its march from Trichinopoly towards the Arambooly lines, a range of fortifications situated on the opposite extremity of the Travancore country, which was intended to be carried by a *coup de main*; no doubt was entertained of complete success, as the principal force of the *dewan* was all concentrated in the environs of Quilon, at least 200 miles distant from the point of attack. The day following the receipt of this despatch the *dewan's* army was observed in motion, and we were again drawn up in position for another action; but all remained quiet during the day. Information was now obtained that the *dewan* had quitted his entrenchments with the major part of his force on his march towards the Arambooly lines.

At daylight on the 21st February our force moved out in two divisions by separate roads to attack the enemy's works, which were carried almost without opposition. Seven old excavated guns fired on the advancing columns, killing and wounding nine men of His Majesty's 19th Regiment; the *dewan's* troops then abandoned the fortifications, which were immediately occupied by our army. The next morning we advanced, with four days' provisions carried by each man, through interminable woods towards Trevandrum, the capital of the *rajah's* dominions, to form a junction with the force under Colonel St. Ledger. The following official document of the above affair is founded on the report of the resident:—

> Headquarters of the Army, Choultry Plain,
> 9th March, 1809.
>
> G.O. by Government, Fort St. George, 3rd March, 1809.
>
> The Resident of Travancore, in a despatch under date the 21st *ult.*, having communicated an account of the spirit and gallantry with which a part of the British forces encamped at Quilon, under the command of Lieut.-Colonel Chalmers, consisting of two columns under the respective commands of Lieut.-Colonel Picton, of His Majesty's 12th Regiment, and the Hon. Lieut.-Colonel Stewart, of His Majesty's 19th Regiment, assaulted the batteries and works erected by the enemy in front of that position, and after having silenced and carried the batteries, captured seven guns, the honourable the Governor in Council has great pleasure in recording the high sense which he entertains of the skill and judgment evinced by Lieut.-Colonel Chalmers in the arrangements made by him to secure the success of the attack upon the enemy's position, and requests that Lieut.-Colonel Chalmers will convey to Lieut.-Colonel Picton, to the hon. Lieut.-Colonel Stewart, and to the officers and men who served under them, the public thanks of the honourable the Governor in Council, for their meritorious exertions on this occasion.
>
> (Signed) A. Falconer,
> Chief Secretary to Government.

The first day's march towards Trevandrum was about three miles, having only conveyance sufficient for one tent per company for the soldiers' accommodation. On the arrival of the army on the ground of encampment, the villagers hoisted white flags on the trees, indicating their disposition to submission, and many ventured into camp voluntarily offering supplies of every description, provided a guard of protection was accorded them; this trivial stipulation being cheerfully acceded to, we soon found ourselves in the land of plenty. Having for several days traversed swamps jungles, woods, rivers and almost inaccessible mountains, by miserable pathways, where sometimes the whole force was compelled to march in single file, we at length reached an open space near a village called Attingurry. I accompanied the army in a *dooly* or *palanquin*, as my wound still incapacitated me from participation in active military duty.

I one morning sheltered myself near the door of a Nair's house from an approaching thunderstorm, which are more frequent near Cape Comorin than in any part of the peninsula of India; in this temporary refuge I was in the act of drinking some water, when a flash of lightning shivered the tumbler to atoms, leaving the solid bottom of the glass only in my hand; a huge column of teak wood, many feet in circumference, close by my side, supporting the verandah of the house, was at the same instant rent asunder, and split into countless splinters, scattered in all directions; not an individual with me escaped unhurt except myself, several retaining black marks on their bodies for many weeks after.

Disasters of a more melancholy complexion often occur in this turbulent climate, where scarcely a day closes without the distant growl of thunder. The curious formation of the rocks, surrounded by scattered fragments at their bases, evince the irresistible power of the lightning. Many natives annually become victims to the effects of the contending elements, and a still greater number are deprived of sight by this dreadful scourge.

On the 28th February two native troopers came full speed into camp, announcing that the Hon. Colonel St. Ledger had marched through the country and was encamped near Trevandrum, without experiencing opposition except at the entrance of the Arambooly lines, which were feebly defended. Capt. Syms, of His Majesty's 69th Regiment, was the only individual killed, and this appeared accidental, proceeding from one of his men in rear, who in the night attack mistook him for one of the enemy. It may not be considered superfluous to introduce the official letter from Colonel St. Ledger to the government on this occasion; though exceedingly prolix, it does justice to the honourable and gallant feelings of many brave officers.

Extract of a letter from the honourable Lieut.-Colonel St. Ledger to the Chief Secretary of the Government, dated 10th February, 1809.

Sir,—I had the honour to convey to you this morning, by express, a small note in pencil, written for the information of the honourable the Governor in Council, by which you were made acquainted with the satisfactory intelligence of the British flags being flying in every part of the Arambooly lines, as well as the commanding redoubts to the north and south.

It is impossible for me to convey in language sufficiently strong, the obligations I feel under to the personal exertions of Major Welch, commanding the 3rd Regiment of Native Infantry, and the detachment for escalade under his command. The southern redoubt, which presented a complete enfilade of the whole of the main lines as far as the gate, was the object of Major Welch's enterprise, an enterprise which from the natural strength of the approach appeared only practicable to the exertions and determined bravery of British troops led on to glory by Major Welch. It was ascended under cover of the night, and our troops had absolutely escaladed the walls ere their approach was suspected, and the ascent was of such great difficulty as to require six hours of actual scrambling to reach the foot of the walls.

On consideration of the brilliancy of this achievement, I feel a pleasurable duty in detailing, for the information of the honourable the Governor in Council, a list of the names of the officers who accompanied the detachment for escalade; it consisted of two companies and the picket of His Majesty's 69th Regiment, commanded by Capt. Syms, and it did not require that confirmation which Major Welch has conveyed to me in the most handsome manner to convince me that to have accomplished such an object every man must have done his duty. In the list of gallant fellows that accompanies this despatch, I have to lament the fate of poor Capt. Syms, of His Majesty's 69th Regiment, whose wound I fear is mortal, depriving his country of a brave and valuable officer.

When Major Welch had once effected his security in this commanding position, I despatched to his assistance, by the same arduous route, a company of His Majesty's 69th Regiment and three companies of the 1st battalion 13th Native Infantry, under

Capt. Hodgson, to reinforce and give confidence to his party. As soon as this addition was perceived, a detachment from his party stormed the main lines, and by dint of persevering bravery, carried them entirely, and the northern redoubt was abandoned by the panic-struck enemy, who fled in all possible confusion in every direction, leaving me in possession of their strongest lines, and I am now encamped two miles interior of the Arambooly Gate. I had ordered the remainder of the detachment to be under arms at midnight, and marched to the most convenient position, either to secure Major Welch's retreat or furnish him support, and when daylight permitted, Major Welch had the satisfaction to see his friends at hand ready to support him.

It would be injustice in me not to express the active services I received from Lieut.-Colonel Macleod, of His Majesty's 69th Regiments they were such as might have been expected from an officer of his reputation and experience—in bringing forward his regiment in support of the attack with the most willing zeal. I feel it a duty I owe, from the report of Major Welch, of the Pioneers, who accompanied him, to express my entire approbation of their conduct, and that of Lieut. Bertram who commanded them.

In short, I feel highly satisfied with the conduct of the officers and men who composed the detachment under my command. I am in possession of the arsenal, well stored with arms, ammunition and military stores, with a quantity of valuable ordnance on the works. I have not yet been able to ascertain the loss of the enemy, but it must have been considerable.

It will be perceived that Capt. Syms alone fell in the storming of the Arambooly lines, and this accidentally from the fire of his own party; darkness prevented his men from distinguishing objects perfectly. No doubt was entertained from whence the fatal ball proceeded, as the enemy were all in front, and he received his wound from the rear. He was fully conscious of this acknowledged truth prior to his death a few hours afterwards. Two or three companies of the *dewan's* Camatic brigade alone defended the Arambooly lines, that required a force of at least 20,000 men to occupy the works. The moment the British ascended the walls the enemy fled without offering the slightest resistance, and how the Hon. Lieut.-Colonel, in his official letter, could assert that their loss was considerable can alone be explained by those engaged in this affair.

This dubious fact cannot, however, detract from the gallant and meritorious conduct of those who so nobly ventured their lives on the occasion; but had the *dewan's* army been present instead of acting at Quilon at the time, the daring enterprise might indeed have been attended by a serious loss on both sides, and few of the heroic escalading party would probably have survived to recount the fearful tale. The Hon. Colonel St. Ledger marched on to Trevandrum almost without opposition. The loss of three men of his army in the advance were the only casualties that occurred; his principal impedimenta were the natural obstacles of an unexplored country of forest trees and jungles, and intersected by deep *nullahs* or rivers, with spacious swamps.

The two British forces having communicated, by permission of the Rajah of Travancore, who declared that the war had been waged by the *dewan* without his sanction, that he had excited the people to revolt and acted in defiance of the *rajah's* orders, this unfortunate man therefore became a doomed victim to the duplicity of a faithless sovereign. The English Resident first stipulated for the *dewan's* head. As a preliminary to negotiation, a large reward was offered for his apprehension, and parties of *sepoys* despatched to scour the country in pursuit of him. During the encampment of the Quilon force at the village of Attingurry, I obtained leave to visit Anjenga, about five miles distant, proceeding down a beautiful river studded on both sides with luxuriant cocoanut trees. Mere curiosity actuated me on this excursion to take a view of the birthplace of Sterne's Eliza Draper.

A humble cottage thatched with *cajan* leaves, close to the sea-shore, shaded by trees, was pointed out as the dwelling of her parents and where she was born. That she was endowed with rare mental perfections, and a considerable share of personal attractions, must be admitted by all who have perused Sterne's letters, and those of the Abbe Raynal; but in an infatuated moment she neglected her reverend friend's sage admonition of "reverence thyself," for on her return to India she abandoned age and austerity, in the shape of an old husband, seeking congeniality of sentiment and equality of temperament in the protection of a young officer who appeared all her vivid fancy imagined. Thus the seductive charms of sensibility overcame the dictates of a matured and superior mind. I could almost apostrophise—may the errors of such a heart be venial in the eye of Heaven! Her hope of permanent felicity in this sentimental experiment was delusive, for on more intimate acquaintance with the object for whom she had thus sacrificed her reputation she too late discovered that his mind was not of the refined texture her fond imagination had pictured.

This reflection soon rankled in her bosom and embittered every fleeting moment; a few short months subsequently to her dereliction from duty she silently reposed in the land of her ancestors, dying of a broken heart in her thirty-third year. A stone is pointed out near the Court-house at Tellicherry, under which her mortal remains are represented to have been deposited. I recollect a glowing inscription to her memory, on a neat white marble monument, on the right-hand side of the entrance to Bristol Cathedral; she evidently was not interred there, as she quitted England in her thirtieth year to revisit her native country and rejoin her superannuated husband. On her passage out she formed the unfortunate liaison with the young officer mentioned in one of her letters to Laurence Sterne, and never returned to England afterwards.

Having frequently mentioned the Backwater, a cursory description of this singular phenomenon may not be inapplicable. The shore from Calicut to Anjenga, a distance of 200 miles, is at various parts overflown by the sea at certain periods. The Cochin and Travancore countries are for several miles inland exceedingly low and marshy, so that these successive inundations have formed innumerable lakes of all dimensions, connected by narrow deep channels. The water assumes a most beautiful lucid appearance, and on passing over its surface the sand is clearly visible, and the eye is amused by the diverting gambols of various species of the finny tribe, which abound in incredible shoals. Frequently these lakes and channels are within 10 yards of the ocean, and only separated from it by a low bar of sand; in other situations they are 10 or 20 miles inland, and surrounded by majestic forests and frowning rocks, forming *in toto* one of the most picturesque countries on the surface of the globe.

Some of the lakes, especially near Aleppi, are so extensive that the opposite shore is not visible; the water is, however, so shallow that the most violent tempest causes but a superficial rippling on its tranquil bosom. Here the reflection of the sun from the glassy surface is almost insupportable; complete rolls of skin are parched from the face of an European, and the natives in mid-day run their canoes ashore, seeking shelter from the scorching heat under the umbrageous cocoanut-trees, which line the shore in all directions; under the agreeable shade of this Indian blessing they generally repose until the cool of evening again enables them to resume their hardy labours.

Innumerable little islets dot the lakes, which are generally highly cultivated and converted into gardens, giving the scene quite a magic appearance; these beautiful and interesting objects are not, however, the invariable features of the country; sometimes stagnant swamps of interminable extent, covered with high reeds and coarse grass, interrupt the harmony of the scene; a narrow ditch of green, filthy water intersects these swamps, along which the boatmen row for many leagues, through hosts of alligators and mosquitoes, all around a dense fog of loathsome and pestiferous exhalation is both seen and inhaled. The natives always exert every muscle to extricate themselves as speedily as possible from these gloomy and unwholesome regions. Emerging from these the voyager is again enchanted with scenery of the most unrivalled beauty.

The English, although addicted to the improvement of their native soil, are, most unfortunately, absurdly indifferent to that of a foreign land, and so deep-rooted is this unaccountable prejudice, that though the soil is evidently, in most situations in our Eastern possessions, three-fold as prolific as that of Great Britain, and capable of producing every species of tree, fruit, herb, vegetable and leguminous root, and some in a higher state of perfection than in our native country, yet all these obvious and incontrovertible facts are either neglected or despised. The rich gifts of Nature are generally disregarded by the Anglo-Asiatics, their whole soul being devoted to the hasty acquisition of a heap of gold, no matter by what means, which they as speedily dissipate on returning to Europe; I must therefore contend that individuals of all other European nations have a far more rational, consistent and humane mode of managing their foreign possessions than the sons of old England.

In Cochin and Quilon there are several Dutchmen who have embellished their little establishments with the most enchanting beauties; grottoes, shady walks, cool, artificial rivulets conducted through the garden, arbours, groves, with every agreement denoting content and happiness. Now, every town on the Coromandel and Malabar coasts is a tacit reproach to our mercenary agents, who linger out a ten, twenty or thirty years' monotonous, solitary existence in a barren bungalow, oppressing the natives by every fraud and injustice for the purpose of accumulating a portion of paltry gold.

In the Dutch, Danish and French possessions, the ties of society are cemented by every endearing method, and the Governors, instead of acting the tyrant, become the mild friend and anxious father to those entrusted to their fostering care. But "*this is my home, here am I to live and die*," cannot be impressed on the mind of an Englishman; pride, avarice, and a speedy return to his native land are the characteristics of our Anglo-Asiatics. In all foreign settlements the bazaar or market is admirably arranged; there every article is astonishingly cheap, the regulation of the police is just and humane; the numerous native adherents, an honest, sober, industrious, humble race, who seek their old masters in the very gulf of adversity, demonstrate this fact; but I never recollect one individual instance of attachment from an Asiatic to an Englishman.

At Cochin, on the termination of the Travancore War, I was repeatedly charged a double *fanam* only (4d.) each for a visiting set of *palanquin* boys, four in number; after an arduous day's labour, they would in the evening receive this mite with content mixed with humility. Now, at Madras, a boisterous, drunken, ungracious crew assail you, who for the same time and number of bearers demand one *rupee* and a half each (three or four shillings), which, on payment being made, they regard with manifest symptoms of discontent, looking sulkily and saucily, with the usual exclamation of "Master's favour," *id est*, an additional *rupee* for the purpose of purchasing ardent spirits.

During the period a fleet of Indiamen is riding in the Madras Roads, *palanquin* bearers are not procurable under a *pagoda* each (or eight shillings) *per diem*, as the sailors fully employ this insolent, exacting tribe, who pillage them in the most shameful manner; these subtle natives, fully aware of the foibles of our honest, imprudent tars, humour their penchant for females and intoxicating liquors, and thus easily deprive them of their superfluous gold, the recompense of many a stormy day's service.

CHAPTER 17

12th Regiment Returns To Quilon

During our encampment at the village of Attingurry, pending the negotiations between the resident and the Travancore *rajah*, the various aquatic excursions of the officers of the army were the principal recreation in the passage down the river to Anjenga. The enormous size of many of the canoes attracted our attention. I had the curiosity to ascertain the dimensions of one of them, which was 11 feet wide and 60 long, scooped from the trunk of a tree of prodigious magnitude. This may appear an exaggeration, but those who have traversed the vast forests that clothe the Malabar coast will vouch for the probable accuracy of this statement.

On expressing my surprise at the amazing size of this canoe to an old Dutchman, a resident at Anjenga, he assured me that when he visited Rangoon, in the Burmese country, he had measured one 23 feet in width and 90 feet long. I have no object in imposing absurdities on the credulous mind, but appeal to common sense and liberal investigation of natural history for an elucidation of circumstances that may appear fraught with extravagant representation. Presumptuous European! why wilt thou ever attempt to prescribe limits to the works of a divine Being, and openly assert that all that exceeds the standard of thy shallow comprehension must be impossible? Unfortunately, the apprehension of criticism from these self-opinionated individuals, causes the suppression of many an interesting publication. I cannot refrain from relating a curious anecdote of a Scotch surgeon, who was proceeding to India with one of His Majesty's regiments; he was a learned and clever man, according to the general acceptation of the word.

Some person having casually mentioned the astonishing feats performed by the jugglers at Madras, and amongst others that of swallowing a sword two feet long by an inch in breadth, and keeping it in that position for upwards of a minute, the shrewd Scotchman could no longer contain the expression of his incredulity. "By God! sir," addressing the narrator in his broad dialect, "it must be a trick, a regular imposition on the senses; I have studied the formation of the human body with the profoundest attention, and declare that the intestines are incapable of receiving such an instrument, it must therefore be a delusion."

The reply was, "I shall soon convince you of your error."

The man of science, irritated at such apparent pertinacity, exclaimed, "I'll bet £50 it's a deception, and that I detect it,"

The bet was accepted, and on the arrival of the ship at Madras I was fortunately present at the period of decision. The juggler was introduced with his apparatus into the mess-room; the surgeon smiled most confidently, took the sword in his hand, rubbed it, bent it, struck it against the wall to ascertain its temper and sound. All appearing satisfactory, He returned the instrument to the juggler, but with his eye fixed steadily on it, to prevent the possibility of an exchange; the juggler then, without a moment's delay, placed the point of the sword in his mouth and glided it gradually down his throat up to the very hilt. Whilst in this posture, the doctor compressed the lower part of the abdomen, the end of the sword was perfectly perceptible to his hand.

He was confounded, convinced, and lost his wager, to the great mirth and gratification of those officers who were present at the learned disquisition in which he had attempted to prove its impossibility; a salutary lesson to those who judge infallibly from the narrow sphere of an isolated academical education, without the necessary indicative aid of practical worldly knowledge to perfect the foundation of theoretical study, to eradicate these prejudices and errors, the invariable attendants of close study. The army occupied the ground of encampment at Attingurry until the 31st March, when the British Resident, having terrified the timid *rajah* into compliance with, all his exorbitant requisitions, arrived in camp, and announced that final arrangements had been entered into for the partial evacuation of the Travancore country.

The 12th Regiment was then ordered to Quilon, and the 19th Regiment in pursuit of the unfortunate *dewan*. In a few days after our arrival at Quilon, where we again encamped on the old fighting ground, and flattered ourselves with the pleasing anticipation of reaping some solid pecuniary advantage (as a recompense for the toils and dangers so recently endured) in the shape of prize-money, we were suddenly astounded at an official notification from the resident (Colonel Macauley), that the Madras Government had decided that all pretensions to prize-money were inadmissible, as the war was undertaken against the *dewan*, and the English forces had merely aided the Rajah of Travancore in quelling a rebellion, which had originated in the revolt of a turbulent minister, unsanctioned by the approbation of his master. Never was a more lively sense of astonishment and indignation excited than arose from this unprincipled declaration, unfounded in truth and devoid of all justice; a base finesse for the express purpose of defrauding a gallant body of men of their just claims.

We were, however, obliged to relinquish all our booty, amounting to nearly £100,000, the plunder of the *dewan's* palace, etc., etc. Now it is a fact beyond controversion, that the armed population of the Travancore country, from the age of fifteen to forty, had been called upon and actually put into action to repel the English, sanctioned by the authority of the *rajah* himself, and at the termination of the war the Madras Government had seized on all warlike stores throughout the *rajah's* dominions.

Nor did the capital itself (Trevandrum) escape the scrutiny, from whence several hundred pieces of ordnance and 20,000 stand of arms, with other stores, estimated at an incredible value, were actually taken possession of by the Company's agents; every hill fort was plundered and dismantled, which augmented the acquisition to at least 1,500 guns of various calibre, and 100,000 muskets and stores in proportion, which the Madras Government ludicrously represented were only to be preserved in *trust* for the future service of their faithful ally the Rajah of Travancore! This mean and illiberal subterfuge of the Governor of Madras (Sir George Barlow), for the purpose of obtaining possession of incalculable wealth, without burdening his employers with the expense of granting an equivalent to the army, whose blood had been profusely shed in its acquisition, as also to enhance his niggardly merit for economy in the estimation of the East India Company, reflects disgrace on his name both as a man and a politician.

He compelled the constituted prize agents of the force to refund heavy sums of money arising from the sale of large quantities of pepper, with all the furniture of the *dewan's* palace. Now, as this individual had been publicly proclaimed a rebel, his captured property was decidedly an evident claim to the army. Independent of these circumstances, another palpable proof of the fraudulent practices of the Madras Government, to deprive the military of their hitherto uncontested due, was the fact of the *rajah's* being compelled to defray the whole expenses of the war, and an enormous heap of treasure was also rapaciously extorted in addition; thus the richly replenished coffer of this *old* and *faithful* ally, which for so many years had been accumulating in security, was converted to the use of the Company and completely exhausted.

Upwards of a million sterling was thus nefariously plundered (I speak from the prevailing reports on the subject), and yet the mercenary Sir George Barlow, with unblushing effrontery, publicly proclaimed that war had not existed between the Company and the *rajah*, and therefore a division of prize-money was inadmissible. The *dewan*, fully sensible of the implacable hatred of the resident, and that he must eventually fall a victim to his machinations and power, sought refuge with his brother and a few faithful adherents on the mountains, and for some time eluded detection. The unceasing perseverance with which he was pursued had obliged his friends to desert him from sheer want of nourishment; at length a party of *sepoys*, aided by the local knowledge of the *rajah's* troops, overtook him, and having surrounded a small hut in which he had secreted himself, broke open the door and there found him weltering in his blood, with his throat cut and entrails obtruding from another ghastly wound which he had inflicted in his abdomen; his brother was standing close by, whom he had entreated to despatch him, should he have failed in the attempt on his own life.

This faithful, affectionate relative had promised due observance to his dying request; and when the party entered the hut, headed by a British officer, he pointed to the deceased minister, exclaiming emphatically, "If you seek the *dewan*, there he is!" This was a truly affecting scene for the officer, who had been intimately acquainted with him in more prosperous days. The brother was then taken prisoner, and the body of the *dewan* hanged on a tree by the side of the highway, by direction of the resident, but what advantage this unfeeling exposure of the body of his enemy was intended to produce I could never ascertain; if to impress the inhabitants with the fatal consequence of rebellion, the act itself was manifestly absurd, as all the country were fully aware that the *rajah* had not only sanctioned but approved of all the proceedings of this unfortunate minister, until the defeat of his army, when a victim being indispensable, of course the weakest suffered.

Thus fell a man generally acknowledged as the most enlightened in that part of India. His person was uncommonly fine and commanding, with an insinuating address and remarkable share of natural abilities; he had also imbibed a confused notion of European politics from the casual conversation of some intelligent Frenchmen residing at Quilon, and when war with the English appeared inevitable, he despatched ambassadors to the Isle of France for a reinforcement of Europeans, and at the very period His Majesty's 12th Regiment landed at Quilon it was hourly expected, and during our encampment a French privateer had been observed hovering about the coast, but on the appearance of the *Piedmontaise* frigate her probable destination was prevented.

A few weeks after the *dewan's* melancholy fate, two other chiefs attached to his interests were apprehended and hanged on the banks of the Backwater, near Aleppi, directly over the spot where the inhuman massacre of the 33 men of the 12th Regiment had been perpetrated. Popinapilly was head collector of pepper, and principally concerned in this atrocious act; he therefore merited his punishment, and was exhibited in chains for many months. The other delinquent, called the *Coodry-poochy* (or General of Cavalry), against whom no crime could be alleged, but that of bravely leading on his followers in the battles of Quilon, by especial command of his sovereign, at the place of execution remonstrated on the injustice of his fate, demanding boldly for what offence he was doomed to die? "I commanded the *rajah's* horse and have acted in submission to his will." His hands being tied behind him, assistance was offered to enable him to mount the ladder to the gallows, but he indignantly refused all aid; advancing with a firm and majestic air, he seized the steps of the ladder between his teeth and thus ascended. The rope was then fixed round his neck, when, upbraiding the injustice of his enemies, he leaped off and expired in a moment.

Several British officers who were present at the execution asserted that not a single muscle of the body quivered, so effectual was the shock of this resolute leap to eternity. Another *dewan* having been nominated by the resident, the Rajah of Travancore now became a humble dependent on the East India Company and the country resumed its previous state of tranquillity, with the exception of daily explosions in and about the capital (Trevandrum), caused by the destruction of the finest guns in the *rajah's* possession, a brilliant instance of the good faith of the Madras Government, in reserving them for the future exigency of his service.

CHAPTER 18

12th Regiment Ordered To Seringapatam

In the month of May I proceeded to Cochin by the Backwater, passing almost under the chains that suspended the bodies of the *Coodry-poochy* and Popinapilly, for the purpose of conducting my family to Quilon, where the 12th Regiment were to be stationed for some time. Arriving safely at this town, I hired a small boat of about seven tons, and with one of our officers, named Eustace, put to sea with three boatmen, intending to reach Tellicherry the following day; but alas! we were doomed to encounter a misfortune that tried our moral and physical strength almost beyond human endurance. For several hours after our departure the weather was unusually serene, the sea calm as a lake, with light airs just sufficient to waft us on at the rate of a mile an hour; but towards evening heavy black clouds appeared to lower about the land, and the rumbling of distant thunder proclaimed an approaching storm. About seven o'clock in the evening a furious gale came off shore, accompanied by torrents of rain and vivid lightning, which continued all night.

All the sails were lowered and the head of our little bark directed to windward, but the waves broke over the half-deck repeatedly, and all hands were busily employed in baling out the water. Without intermission this deplorable scene continued until the following morning, all our exertions scarcely keeping the vessel afloat. In vain, at daylight, we looked for land, the tempest had driven us far beyond its view. With one day's provision, without compass or nautical skill, there were we exposed to all the horrors of submersion or famine, the sea running mountains high and the boat receding at a rapid rate from all prospect of salvation. For two long, long days were we in this lamentable and perilous situation; on the third a dead calm ensued. Poor Eustace was seized with an epileptic fit, and lay on the deck agitated by the most frightful contortions, with three native boatmen looking on in the wildest despair. We had exhausted all our water and provisions, and nothing but inevitable destruction stared us in the face.

In the middle of the third day another gale came on, from the opposite quarter to the preceding one, but equally furious, when some hope of safety inspired us with renewed exertions. Eustace still continued unconscious of all our dangers, sometimes beating himself most violently against the sides of the vessel and moaning in a frightful manner. Two more horrible days passed over, and land was not yet seen. We regarded each other with cannibal looks; hunger overcame every feeling of humanity. I acknowledge without disguise that I could have sucked the blood or devoured part of the spare carcase of one of the boatmen with the most voracious appetite; they, however, regarded me with similar symptoms of voracity, and I instinctively grasped my sword closer to my side in expectation of attack. Such is self-preservation, though I need not have apprehended their enmity, for we were all so exhausted that at length we lay in the boat in an almost inanimate state.

Eustace at length awoke from his trance demanding water; I feebly told him we had none. "Where am I?" said he; I then imparted to him our horrible situation. He made an effort to throw himself over the gunwale, but fell back quite overcome by the exertion; I had not sufficient strength to assist him, and he appeared once more to relapse into an utter state of insensibility. All I now recollect is, that about twelve o'clock the sixth night a tremendous crash of the boat against some hard substance awoke me to a sense of existence; it appears a huge wave had thrown us on the sand some few miles from Tellicherry, high and dry.

On awakening, as if from a dream, I found myself in a native hut with Eustace lying by my side; a pan of rice with water was offered us, which we greedily devoured, and in a few hours became sufficiently collected to make inquiries, and discovered that two *palanquins* had been sent for us by Mr. Baber, to bear us to Tellicherry when strong enough to proceed there. One of the boatmen had died, the other two were convalescent, though unable to move. In a few hours we recovered our strength, by the humane attentions of Mr. and Mrs. Baber, who forwarded us every species of delicate nourishment, and shortly reached their hospitable mansion, when to my great disappointment

I found my family had already proceeded to Cochin, some days prior to our unfortunate voyage. Nothing could be more vexatious, independent of which I was again compelled to encounter the deceitful elements from whose fury I had so narrowly escaped.

Remaining only three days at Tellicherry, I once more embarked on a *patamar*, and in 36 hours entered the Cochin River, and found my family snugly lodged in one of the best houses of the town, and in about a week proceeded via the Backwater to Quilon. Scarcely had we arrived, when I was doomed to suffer the most excruciating torments from my wound; the lower part of the backbone having been materially injured, several small portions of the fractured bone obtruded, which required a surgical operation to extract. I was confined to my bed many weeks. How I dreaded the daily probing, cutting and dressing; the application of the cool plantain leaf alone gave me any relief from agony the most intense.

To increase my nervous irritability, an order suddenly arrived on the 15th of May, 1809, for the 12th Regiment to march without delay from Quilon to Seringapatam, through the Travancore country. The monsoon had already commenced with incredible fury; torrents of rain, thunder, lightning, and hurricanes of wind succeeded each other without intermission.

No one, who has not visited a tropical climate, can form an idea of the brilliant illumination caused by the lightning at night; it flashes incessantly from every direction, so that sometimes you may see to read, or pick up the smallest article without inconvenience, the light of the sun even not being more powerful or regular. No spectacle can possibly be more beautiful or awful, but accidents of the most distressing nature often occur. I recollect one morning eight *sepoys* being struck dead on returning from a guard relief, the bayonets and barrels of the muskets having attracted the electric fluid, which at once annihilated them. The distance from Quilon to Seringapatam is about 460 miles. The idea of once more revisiting this latter station was by no means consolatory, as two years before the regiment suffered there so severely from the fever (which resembles that of the West Indies, the corpse of either white or black men being invariably tinged with a deep yellow colour) that the body of the regiment (that is, the most numerous part) were borne to Cannanore in *doolies*; to encounter this detestable malady once more was, therefore, repugnant to the feelings of every individual of the corps.

A long march through an unexplored country, in the very height of the monsoon, was also an enterprise of no common occurrence; both officers and men were, however, compelled to abandon their comforts and recently constructed huts on the banks of the Backwater, and once more expose themselves to the inclemency of the elements.

On the 20th May, 1809, the regiment began the march (leaving me at the old fort of Trangacherry, dangerously afflicted with the consequences of my wound and completely bedridden), in defiance of the rain, which poured down in torrents, and wind that snapped the stoutest trees. With extreme difficulty and danger four short marches were effected, when the whole marshy part of the country having become inundated, presented an insurmountable obstacle to the further progress of the regiment, until a partial cessation of rain should enable them to proceed. It had not been without the greatest efforts of courage and perseverance that even this short distance had been accomplished; the provisions, tents and new clothing had been all destroyed, and many of the officers lost every atom of their baggage. So thoroughly saturated was every denomination of stores and wearing apparel, that not a single article remained free from a state of utter decomposition, lying absolutely in smoking piles, with muskets, bayonets and other arms all so rusty that, in the existing humidity of the atmosphere, it was impossible to preserve them from the corroding filth.

For three weeks, the regiment occupied one little hillock, surrounded by floods of water and exposed to incessant torrents of rain, the trees and a few old Nairs' huts being the only shelter in this unprecedented and deplorable situation. The last morning of these disastrous four days' march the regiment passed over a river, the sandy bed of which was visible, the water flowing in several small rivulets not knee deep; an hour after the whole bed was filled to a depth of more than twenty feet, sweeping away in its impetuous torrents every one and every thing crossing at the time of the sudden swell. The baggage, camp equipage, many followers and cattle, with several Europeans attached as guard to the equipage, were all involved in one common ruin; and had the body of the regiment been passing at this identical period, but a small proportion would have escaped a watery grave.

Information having been conveyed to the commandant of Quilon of the perilous state of the 12th Regiment, elephants, bullocks, and camp equipage were speedily forwarded, if possible to mitigate the sufferings of the corps. The boats laden with provisions were almost all swamped in the passage up the Backwater, by which accident ten *sepoys* were drowned. Tents and provisions were at length supplied, but too late to preserve 30 or 40 Europeans, who had already been carried off by dysentery, of which disease 300 more were affected, promiscuously strewing the ground with their dying carcases; it, however, preserved them from actual destruction.

Many officers were also seized with this inveterate malady, to whom the humane indulgence was granted of proceeding to the place of destination; one of them, however, died before the *palanquins* arrived for their conveyance; the others, who were on the confines of the grave, availed themselves of this considerate permission, and thus extricated themselves from the fatal spot, near which a hospital was now formed for the reception of 280 men afflicted with fever and inveterate dysentery, with whom a surgeon was left to superintend.

The remainder of the regiment (after five weeks' unexampled exposure and suffering), taking advantage of a day's partial cessation from rain, made a forced march and succeeded in reaching the Coromandel coast, to which the influence of the Malabar monsoon did not extend. Another halt then ensued, as the soldiers still continued pressed with disease, and a representation of the inefficient and exhausted state of the corps was despatched to Madras, when an order was in a short time received changing its destination to Trichinopoly, one of the most salubrious stations in India. The grand details of war are generally most ostentatiously published, but how very few of what is commonly denominated the petty details of warfare ever meet the public eye.

What miseries, sufferings, dangers and privations of every species attend an army in a protracted warfare, and with what astonishing apathy and indifference are these minor relations viewed by those who have never encountered the various dangers and hardships of war. A glorious victory, a long list of killed and wounded, for a moment attracts attention, and then all is soon banished from the memory, except that a battle of a certain name had once taken place. It certainly is a most incomprehensible infatuation in the British character, that a man should spend four or five thousand pounds to attain rank and be constantly exposed to scenes of danger and hardships, and if he escape, to retire at the age of 50 on a bare sufficiency to preserve him from actual pauperism, *id est*, as a lieut.-colonel he will (for his half-pay) be entitled to £200 *per annum*, after devoting 35 years to the service of his country, and sometimes the principal and generally the major part of that period passed under the enervating sun of the torrid zone.

Now, an officer of similar rank in the Company's service retires on an income of £365 *per annum*, without having expended a fraction in promotion to the different ranks, and that after 23 years entitles them to the retirement on full pay of their actual rank, which, with the pickings they have accumulated in snug staff situations, enables them to pass the remnant of life in ease and even affluence. There can never be any cordial co-operation between the King's and Company's army whilst the present inefficient system exists; how can harmony be established where such discordant principles prevail?

The *sepoy* army is undoubtedly the great machine that maintains our dominions in the East, but the post of honour is invariably accorded to the Europeans, without whose powerful stimulus our possessions would soon be invaded and overrun by the other native princes inimical to our extensive government; the King's officer should therefore be considered as entitled to some remuneration beyond the paltry modicum of his bare half-pay. A retired colonel on the effective list of the Company's army, entitled to the advantages of the officers' reckoning fund, has a magnificent allowance of nearly £1,300 *per annum*; a King's colonel has merely his £200, let his services be ever so extensive.

Let those, then, who are desirous of prospering in the pecuniary and more substantial acquisitions of life enter the Company's army; honour is a gaudy toy, but wealth secures or at least conduces to the permanent happiness of our declining days.

Chapter 19

Adventures of Captain Bayly

After a month's suffering at Quilon (since the departure of the regiment), I hired a covered boat, resolving to rejoin at Seringapatam as speedily as possible. Passing the Backwater rapidly towards Chitwa, on the second day, when in the midst of the extensive lake near Cochin, a gale of wind towards evening compelled the boatmen to seek shelter by running the boat on shore under a thick brushwood that overhung the water; here we prepared for our dinner, which had been delayed in consequence of the boisterous weather. We had scarcely commenced cooking, when the voices of a numerous body of men were distinctly heard at a very short distance from our little harbour; drums and other warlike instruments accompanied their loud vociferations.

Now, as the bands of the licentious Cochin Army had not yet dispersed, we considered it judicious to extinguish our fires, lest they might attract the attention of these lawless depredators. I rubbed up my pistols, in the event of attack, and we vigilantly kept watch the whole night without further interruption, though sometimes the voices appeared within a very few paces of our place of shelter.

Towards morning they had discovered the mast of the boat, when a hideous shouting denoted the coming storm. We had scarcely shoved the boat off the sand, when several hundred armed men approached, threatening to fire on us if we did not immediately return. The poor terrified boatmen were so intimidated that they appeared inclined to comply with the command, when I presented a pistol and compelled them to row on, and they certainly exerted themselves manfully, for in a few minutes we had gained a distance of at least forty yards from shore, when a well-directed volley of musketry from these miscreants killed two of the boatmen and shattered the oars to atoms, splintering the gunwale seats and covering. I then fired my two pistols, which, though at too great a distance to produce much effect, certainly surprised our adversaries, who ceased firing for several minutes, during which I detached the sail wound around the mast and then hastened to the tiller, thus saving the whole party from the inevitable fate of a most inhuman massacre.

I had no assistance whatever in this operation, as the other boatmen and all my servants had crouched down in the hull of the boat paralysed with fear. Several other volleys of bullets came now rapidly amongst us; one ball struck the tiller from my hand and others penetrated the sails and covering in all directions, and I was compelled to lean over the stem of the boat to keep her head, by the rudder, towards the desired point. Whilst in this position, another ball passed through the stern board and penetrated the upper part of my right thigh to the very bone.

I was affected with a dizziness and numbness that for an instant obliged me to let go the rudder, but the reiterated shouts from shore soon awoke me to a sense of our peril, and I once more clung with agonising tenacity to this our only hope of preservation, and though bleeding profusely had still presence of mind to retain my hold until beyond reach of their continued volleys; at length one of the boatmen, finding the danger over, came to my assistance, and I fell insensible to the bottom of the boat, from whence my wife and servants moved me to the shelter of the covering or large cabin, in which, though completely riddled, my family had escaped uninjured.

My two little boys, of three and four years old, were looking as pale as death; they had been in the arms of their mother during the whole of this eventful period, lying on the cabin floor, which accounts for the miraculous escape, for had they been either sitting or standing, they must have fallen victims to this wanton and barbarous attack. We arrived at Cochin a few hours afterwards, when my old friend Colonel Hewitt, who commanded there, sent out parties for the detection of the miscreants, and they were hunted down until the whole had dispersed, though none were taken prisoners.

For three weeks I was confined to my bed; the ball was cut out of my thigh about five inches below the wound, and several small splinters of the bone extracted, which relieved me from pain. We received every possible kindness and attention from the garrison, and many of the wealthy inhabitants of the town (more regularly built and resembling an European style of architecture than any I have seen in India); but the innumerable swarms of mosquitoes, produced by the surrounding stagnant swamps, renders it a most ineligible residence for the English, though the Dutch prefer the situation to any other on the Malabar coast.

I cannot refrain from the relation of one fact that came under my immediate observation. The first night of my arrival the clouds of mosquitoes that infested my bedchamber were so dense that respiration was impossible without inhaling a multitude of these noxious little pests, and as our curtains were not mounted, my pillow appeared like one mass of black living matter; so closely had the mosquitoes assembled together on it, that the point of a pin could not have been inserted amongst them without destroying some of the nest. This may be considered exaggeration, though a faithful representation of the actual state of my bedchamber.

A disease prevails here called the "Cochin leg," a serious species of elephantiasis, deriving its origin from the unwholesome nature of the water, producing malignant fevers generally terminating in an enormous swelling of the legs, and continues thus during the remainder of existence, and although from the knee downwards they are equal in size to the body, still it offers no impediment to activity and motion; the spectacle is disgusting, appearing like huge masses of blubber, and I may venture to affirm that one individual in every six at Cochin is afflicted with this disgusting disease.

I was therefore anxious to quit a place whose noxious atmosphere might render me an object of future derision, and before my wounds were well closed I once more embarked in an accommodation boat for Chetwa, where my friend Mr. Baber having placed relays of *palanquin* bearers, I proceeded on towards Seringapatam *via* Paulghantcherry. Arriving at Coimbatore, I was delayed a few days from excess of fatigue. During this halt my *palanquin* boys asked for a present of a few sheep, and giving them a *pagoda* (8s.), they soon brought thirteen lean sheep, as I imagined to select one for the money, but to my excessive astonishment they had purchased the whole of them for the eight shillings, and told me they could have selected eight of the fattest sheep from a flock for the same money; they had, however, preferred the thirteen, as more adapted to accompany us on a march.

I was entertained at Coimbatore most sumptuously by a *dubash* belonging to Mr. Riddle, who, although his master was absent, had directions to receive every passing European officer and provide them with every accommodation his bungalow could afford. Such an instance of liberal hospitality is rarely heard of in these degenerate days.

Having first halted at a *choultry* near the town, this faithful *dubash* came towards me with many humble *salaams*, inviting me to take possession of his master's bungalow. I objected to this immediately, from motives of delicacy, naturally imagining that a family would be too great an encumbrance for a bachelor's house; but the poor fellow assured me, if I did not accept the invitation his master would be angry and dismiss him from his service, when I reluctantly acceded to his wishes.

We therefore proceeded to this bungalow, having the appearance of a superb palace; the roof was supported by white polished columns of highly finished *chunam*, floors of the same material, on which it was almost dangerous to walk, from its extreme beautiful polish; mirrors of superb splendour ornamented each room; ebony bedsteads, fine net mosquito curtains, with magnificent beds made of floss cotton, chairs of the most elegant satinwood, and in fact every luxurious article of furniture that imagination could suggest adorned this unique mansion.

The beds, although two or three feet thick and immensely long and wide, weighed only eight or ten pounds, so light was the material they were composed of, with sheets like the driven snow; never shall I forget the delightful sensation I experienced when I extended my wounded and exhausted body on this mass of luxury, where I passed a most delicious week of heavenly repose. Though envying the happy lot of an East Indian civilian, I internally prayed for the welfare of my liberal absent host. Champagne, claret, Madeira, an excellent English pale ale were all profusely placed on the hospitable board, accompanied by curries, ragouts, beef, mutton, and a variety of vegetables prepared by a first-rate cook.

In my life I never passed seven days so agreeably; at the termination, and on the eve of departure, I was inclined to be most munificent to the domestics, but could not prevail on them to accept a solitary *rupee*; the *dubash* signified that his patron would be "too much angry" if he accepted presents; he only required a *chit* (note) to prove that he had done his duty. This of course I wrote, expressing in the warmest terms my high sense of the extreme hospitality I and my family had received, with a pressing invitation to the mess of the 12th Regiment, should Mr. Riddle ever pass over our station. Alas! poor fellow, I never saw him; he died some few years afterwards. Pity that men of such liberal, humane principles could not live to eternity!

I now proceeded on to Seringapatam, crossing the rapid and dangerous River Bowanny in basket-boats, and then mounting the stupendous Gazzeletty Pass into the Mysore country. On the summit of this mountain in the road three huge dead elephants were lying, represented to have died of old age. The vultures, kites, jackals, and other birds of prey were regaling themselves with a most abundant repast; on our approach they fled screaming away into the depth of the jungle. It was near this spot an old acquaintance of mine, an assistant surgeon by name Morgan, had a most miraculous escape. He was on a shooting excursion, when a large bear appeared, trudging off with all speed, but being fired at with small shot, he returned and charged his adversary.

A short struggle ensued, and Morgan's head was completely scalped by one of Bruin's paws; at this moment a little spaniel that followed him flew at the bear's heels, who instantly quitted his prey for this fresh enemy, but the animal was too nimble for him and' escaped, when the bear re-entered the jungle and disappeared. Morgan was discovered by some of his party in the most deplorable state, with the scalp covering his face and insensible from loss of blood; he was, however, cured, though a fever shortly after terminated his earthly career. The poor little faithful dog was lying close to his master when he was found, whining in the most piteous manner, and licking the wound.

The latter end of July, 1809, I entered Seringapatam, taking up my quarters *pro tempore* with my old friend Major De Haviland, of the Company's Engineers. After some days I rented a house overlooking the eastern side of the fortification, from whence I had a commanding view of the adjacent country, and where I was destined to view a scene that quite confounded my senses. I here learnt that the regiment was at Trichinopoly, but in daily expectation of moving to Wallajahbad; I therefore considered it prudent to remain a short time at my present station until my corps had reached the latter cantonment, and consequently forwarded a sick certificate of my actual inability to join.

However, on an intimation that the garrison of Seringapatam, then under command of Lieut.-Colonel Bell, of the Company's artillery, had taken possession of the fortress and were openly resisting the Government of Madras, directed by Sir George Barlow, I became exceedingly anxious to extricate myself from this dilemma. Everything being in confusion, I was unable to procure *palanquin* bearers or coolies, and was reluctantly necessitated to remain in this dangerous and equivocal position until more pacific times offered the means of removal.

CHAPTER 20

Embarks for Active Service In Mauritius

Le règne du despotisme fut toujours le règne de la confusion, car le caprice n'a que des mouvements et point de rues. In order to account for the mutinous state of the garrison of Seringapatam, a retrospective view of the state of government affairs from the commencement of the year 1809 is requisite to explain this unprecedented phenomenon of a British army in open rebellion to the existing civil authorities of the country. I abstain from any extensive reasoning on the subject, and let those draw conclusions whose abilities may be considered adequate to decide on the *ars gubernandi* of fickle mortals in temporary power.

About the latter end of 1808, the commander-in-chief of the Madras Army, irritated by an unjust dismissal from a seat in council, determined to revisit his native land. A few weeks previous to the embarkation of the General (Macdowal), he issued the following order:—

Headquarters, Choultry Plain,
28th Jan., 1809.

G. O. by the Commander-in-Chief.
The immediate departure of General Macdowal from Madras will prevent his pursuing the design of bringing Lieut.-Colonel Munro, quartermaster-general, to a trial for disrespect to the commander-in-chief, for disobedience of orders and for contempt of military authority in having resorted to the power of the civil government, in defiance of the judgment of the officer at the head of the army, who had placed him under arrest on charges preferred against him by a number of officers com-

manding native corps, in consequence of which appeal, direct to the honourable the President in Council, Lieut.-General Macdowal has received a positive order from the chief secretary to liberate Lieut.-Colonel Munro from arrest. Such conduct of Lieut. Colonel Munro being destructive of subordination, subversive of military discipline, a violation of the sacred rights of the commander-in-chief, and holding out a most dangerous example to the service, Lieut.-General Macdowal, in support of the dignity of the profession and his own station and character, feels it incumbent on him to express his strongest disapprobation of Lieut.-Colonel Munro's unexampled proceedings, and considers it a solemn duty imposed upon him to reprimand Lieut.-Colonel Munro in general orders, and he is hereby reprimanded accordingly.

(Signed) S. Macdowal,
Assistant Adjutant-General.

It appeared that Lieut.-Colonel Munro had involved himself in delinquencies amenable to the cognizance of a military tribunal, in consequence of which charges of a serious nature were preferred against him by several officers, not only of elevated rank but of unsullied reputation; accusations thus advanced and forwarded to the commander-in-chief, it was deemed expedient to place the arraigned delinquent in arrest, the usual mode of procedure on all similar occasions, a mode established by law and recognised by custom. Under this impression, General Macdowal could not have anticipated any interference from the civil government, an event that did not even suggest itself in the remotest manner to his imagination, as his rights were defined beyond a doubt, and his authority in this respect certainly exclusive; the officer who had disgraced himself by misconduct was therefore placed in arrest, and a few days would have substantiated either his innocence or guilt by that most honourable of all tribunals, a court martial.

Conscious, however, of having acted a flagitious part, he abjectly sheltered himself under the protection of the civil power, by whom, it was rumoured, he had been instigated to set military authority at defiance; thus supported, he was released from that durance to which every officer of untarnished honour is ambitious of aspiring when unjust accusations have been disseminated to the prejudice of his character. From this circumstance it was generally considered that an evident collusion must have existed between Lieut.-Colonel Munro and Sir George Barlow, the Governor of Madras, as no military man had ever before appealed to the civil power on a similar emergency, nor would such an unprecedented application have been attended to by any governor unbiased by prejudice.

From this interference it appeared that the Madras administration had views in contemplation inimical to the interests of the army, especially as General Macdowal had been suddenly deprived of a seat in council, the invariable right of every preceding commander-in-chief. Lieut.-Colonel Munro was accordingly released from arrest, *malgré* every representation of the unheard of injustice of the innovation on military arrangements. Affairs thus situated, with the additional mortification to General Macdowal that 15,000 men had taken the field without his knowledge, but actually within his command, perceiving himself an absolute cipher, and that Sir George Barlow had virtually assumed the command of the army, he instantly sent in his resignation of the shadow of the high situation he held, and previous to embarkation for England issued the order before transcribed. What latent cause originated the antipathy of the Governor of Madras towards the commander-in-chief has never been distinctly explained, but it is evident that this innovation on the rights of the army gave rise to the most dangerous commotion that ever menaced our Asiatic possessions.

The strong appeal of General Macdowal to the feelings of a body of enlightened men soon produced its effect, insinuating a species of venom into their very nature not easily suppressed, and which manifested itself in evident symptoms of anarchy and a respectful memorial from the officers of the army, of which I shall have occasion to refer hereafter. General Macdowal, on the publication of his order, ought certainly to have awaited with manly fortitude the result of his appeal, instead of which he hastily embarked and sailed previous to the promulgation of the following order from Sir George Barlow:—

Adjutant-General's Office,

Fort St. George.
31st Jan, 1809.

G. O. by Government.
It has recently come to the knowledge of the honourable the Governor in Council that Lieut.-General Hay Macdowal did, previously to his embarkation from the presidency, leave to be published to the army a general order, dated 28th inst., in the

highest degree disrespectful to the authority of the government, in which that officer has presumed to found a public censure on an act adopted under the immediate authority of the Governor in Council, and to convey insinuations grossly derogatory to the character of the government and subversive of military discipline, and of the foundation of public authority.

The resignation of General Macdowal, of the command of the army of Fort St. George, not having been yet received, it becomes the duty of the Governor in Council, in consideration of the violent and inflammatory proceedings of that officer, on the present and on other recent occasions, and for the purpose of preventing a possible repetition of further acts of outrage, to anticipate the period of his expected resignation, and to annul the appointment of Lieut.-General Macdowal to the command of the army of the presidency.

Lieut.-General Macdowal is accordingly hereby removed from the station of the Commander-in-Chief of the forces of Fort St. George. The Governor in Council must lament with the deepest regret the necessity of resorting to an extreme measure of this nature, but where a manifest endeavour has been used to bring into degradation the supreme public authority, it is essential that the vindication should not be less signal than the offence, and that a memorable example should be given that proceedings subversive of established order can find no security under the sanction of rank, however high of station or however exalted.

The general order in question having been circulated, under the signature of the deputy adjutant-general of the army, it must have been known to that officer, that in giving currency to a paper of this offensive description he was acting in direct violation of his duty to the government, as no authority can justify the execution of an illegal act, connected as that act obviously in the present case has been with views of the most reprehensible nature. The Governor in Council thinks it proper to mark his highest displeasure at the conduct of Major Boles, by directing that he shall be suspended from the service of the honourable Company. The general order left by the commander-in-chief for publication, under date the 28th inst., is directed to be expunged from every public record, and the adjutant-general of the army will immediately circulate the necessary

orders for that purpose.
    (Signed)   G. Buchan,
                           Chief Secretary to Government.
The honourable the Governor in Council appoints Major General F. Gowdie to the command of the army of this presidency until further orders.

I am of opinion that Sir George Barlow would not have dared the promulgation of the above order had General Macdowal been actually on the spot, or he might have *nolens volens* been placed in a Masula-boat and sent over the surf; for although the army be not a deliberative body, yet in emergencies of this nature a question may arise as to the necessity of interference which might tend to the prevention of a complication of serious disasters, that comprehensive and reflecting minds foresee as the inevitable consequence of unprecedented and dangerous innovations.

The poor general was, however, on his passage to Europe, which. he was fated never to reach. A hurricane off the Isle of France sank three large Indiamen; in one the ill-fated general and his staff went down, happily for the investigation of the conduct of Sir George Barlow, as an account of the transaction was now consigned to his fertile imagination, and representations made with impunity that otherwise might not have been so successful. As Major Boles had a wife and family, and was by the arbitrary suspension from rank and pay now left destitute, the officers of the army entered into a handsome subscription for his relief—a subject of grave offence to Sir George Barlow, who animadverted on their conduct in unmeasured terms.

At the mess-table of the Madras European Regiment, then stationed at Masulipatam, two young lieutenants, refusing to drink the health of Sir George Barlow, were banished to some unhealthy hill-fort and the regiment ordered to embark on English frigates, to act as marines; but the whole corps, supported by a battalion of *sepoys*, flew to arms, and declared they would not serve on board His Majesty's frigates, as they had been especially enlisted for the Company's service, and that embarking them on king's ships was a direct violation of the tenor of their attestations; they were, however, ready to proceed on any Company man-of-war cruiser, declaring they thought it very hard to be punished for the thoughtless expressions or acts of two young inebriated officers.

A communication was soon conveyed of the proceedings at

Masulipatam to the whole coast army, every part of which evinced a disposition to resist the excess of tyranny resorted to by Sir George Barlow, and every Company's regiment on the Madras establishment now came to the determination of resisting any oppressive measures that might emanate from the authority of Sir George, who now issued a paper for the signature of all officers, who professed allegiance and fidelity to his government, and those who refused compliance were directed to be imprisoned in hill-forts and other ineligible stations, until a revolution should be effected in their refractory spirits. The following is the spirit of the *test*, as it was denominated test, or pledge of obedience:

> We, the undersigned officers of the honourable Company's service, do in the most solemn manner declare upon our word of honour as British officers, that we will obey the orders and support the authority of the honourable the Governor in Council of Fort St. George, agreeably to the tenor of our commissions, which we hold from that government.

This document was considered by the army as an additional insult and was almost universally rejected, except by a few irresolute, timid characters who affixed their names, incited most probably by the hope of succeeding to lucrative employments that might become vacant by the secession of their brother officers rather than with a view of any beneficial result in favour of the government from this line of conduct; several hundred officers were consequently sent on to Pondicherry, and still greater numbers to hill-forts in the interior of the country. Whilst these proceedings were in agitation, the Company's troops had seized on various fortresses and commenced operations for the junction of armies, and amongst others the town of Seringapatam was selected as a rendezvous, and two battalions of *sepoys* commenced marching from the strong fort of Chittledroog, to form a junction with the garrison of Seringapatam, the different stations of Company's troops having now all unanimously resolved to resist the wanton punishment resorted to by Sir George Barlow. As I was present at Seringapatam, confined by my wounds and general debility, I could coolly and dispassionately survey the various proceedings in the garrison as they progressively transpired.

On the 28th July, 1809, a rumour was circulated that the fort was destined to an attack from the Mysorean Army, including His Majesty's 69th Foot, and the 25th Dragoons; this information was conveyed to the garrison by an officer friendly to the cause. The place was consequently armed at all points, and perfectly prepared for the contemplated assault; but all remained tranquil until the 4th of August, when the two companies of His Majesty's 80th Regiment, composing part of the garrison, were directed to vacate the fort, to prevent collision between them and the *sepoys*, one of the drunken men having applied the epithet of *mutineer* to a *matross* of the Company's artillery. This precaution was indispensably necessary to prevent an immediate effusion of blood, as the *matross* had knocked down the offender, and several individuals on both sides had prepared to decide the dispute at the point of the bayonet; an officer timely interfered, endeavouring to pacify the parties, and partly succeeded, but could not eradicate the deep-rooted resentment this unfortunate transaction gave rise to.

Colonel Bell, the commandant, deemed it prudent to place an insuperable barrier to future disputes and the probable massacre of His Majesty's troops, and these two companies were accordingly directed to quit the fort, and join the besieging army outside. He also requested a suspension of hostilities until the arrival of Lord Minto, the governor-general, who was hourly expected at Madras, by whom all differences were expected to be adjusted. No reply was returned to this request, and an awful pause of several days ensued, when, on the 10th August, 1809, an encampment was perceived on an eminence about two miles to the eastward of the fort, considerably within range of the guns, consisting of the 25th Dragoons and 59th Foot, just arrived from Bangalore.

At six o'clock the following morning a cannonade was distinctly heard in the same quarter, though at a considerable distance; however, it was soon ascertained that the two battalions of *sepoys* from Chittledroog were approaching, surrounded by a horde of Mysorean cavalry, with whom they were warmly engaged, formed in one large square and repulsing the attacks in every direction with the coolest intrepidity, arriving within two miles of the fort, in spite of every obstacle.

At this momentous crisis, two squadrons of the 25th Dragoons galloped up to the spot, drawing up opposite the gallant battalions; a pause of a few minutes ensued, when the dragoons, forming with the Mysorean cavalry, charged the square, who, on the hostile approach of the British, threw down their arms and hastened towards the fortress pursued by the cavalry. They had dispersed in obedience to previous orders, that if attacked by the King's troops they were to offer no resistance; the officers and *sepoys* were only preserved from indiscriminate massacre by a few shots from the garrison plunging amongst them; they soon gave up the pursuit.

The remains of these battalions were soon admitted into the fort, and explained the extraordinary scene that had just occurred. It appeared that Lieut. Jefferies, of the 25th Dragoons, had advanced before his squadron extending in his hand a white handkerchief; imagining this a signal for a conference, a *sepoy* officer stepped forward, but ere they had approached each other sufficiently near to effect an explanation, Lieut. Jefferies wheeled round his horse and rejoined his men, when a simultaneous charge of the British and Mysorean horse was the immediate result.

It proved that Lieut. Jefferies, on his advance for the professed purpose of offering terms of accommodation, received a slight scratch just below the right ear, from whence or by what weapon could not be ascertained; this circumstance induced him to gallop off and represent himself wounded, and an immediate charge was the consequence. Now, 3,000 Mysorean horse, with a considerable body of matchlock-men, had been skirmishing with the battalions the whole of the morning, and were actually firing at the instant this flag of truce was proffered; it is probable a random shot from this rabble might have occasioned the hurt. The *sepoys* certainly did not fire on the 25th Dragoons, as the lieutenant's was the only casualty that occurred; the wound was so superficial that scarcely a tinge of blood was discovered. On the entrance of the dispersed *sepoys* into the garrison, they exclaimed loudly that they had been betrayed by their officers, and the other troops joining them, all was anarchy and confusion, as they insisted on being led immediately against the King's troops.

The distressed commandant, anxious to preserve the lives of the officers, at length promised that in a few hours they should be satisfied, and the same evening several field-pieces and howitzers were drawn up on the island near the banks of the River Cauvery, placed so that the shot and shell might sweep the rear of the British encampment without doing any execution. This disposition of attack gratified the *sepoys*, who were not, however, aware of the humane intention of Colonel Bell for the preservation of His Majesty's troops.

The commanding officer of the Chittledroog battalion suffered severely in the conflict, having received three sabre wounds and being taken prisoner by the Mysore horse; he was compelled in this miserable plight to march from the place of slaughter to Mysore, a distance of twelve miles, goaded on with the points of their sabres.

Though bleeding profusely and almost exhausted, he contrived to support himself until within a mile of his destination, when his vile treatment being announced to the British Resident, the honourable Arthur Cole, a *palanquin* was forwarded for his accommodation, and he was thus preserved.

Mr. Cole had a few days previous, injudiciously despatched the Mysorean cavalry for the purpose of preventing the march of the *sepoys* from Chittledroog, with positive orders to the native chief to attack them if they persisted in the advance to Seringapatam. This verbal command being disregarded, the two battalions were harassed during this long march of 160 miles, in continued skirmishes, and although the horse charged repeatedly in heavy bodies, they were incapable of making the least impression on the square of infantry, who would certainly have accomplished their object had not the charge of the 25th Dragoons dispersed them, which was submitted to in obedience to the instructions of the officer who commanded them.

The whole baggage was plundered and the wives of the *sepoys* treated most brutally, many of them suffering amputation of nose and ears for the valuable gold rings that they usually wear on them, a circumstance that exasperated the misled *sepoys* more than any other, except the order to throw down their arms in the event of attack from Europeans, which impressed them with the idea that they had been betrayed by the officers who commanded them, asserting with every appearance of probability that if they had been permitted to repel the attack of the 25th Dragoons by a volley of sharp file-firing, they could have reached Seringapatam with one-tenth of the loss they actually experienced, as a few yards only intervened between them and the marshy *paddy* or rice-fields, where the cavalry could not have acted without the horses plunging knee-deep in mud at every step.

Discarding further comments on this ungrateful subject, it is now only necessary to observe that the skirts of the British encampment were fired on that night, without injury, in order to appease the resentment of the *sepoys*, several hundred of whom were dying in the hospital of the wounds received on this disastrous day.

Information was shortly communicated that Lord Minto had arrived at Madras, and that the Company's officers of the other stations had all submitted to his authority, and consequently, as there was now no question of Sir George Barlow, the fortress was immediately given up cheerfully to the besieging force. Several officers were brought to a court martial and restored to their rank, except Lieut.-Col. Bell, who was dismissed the Company's service; the army, however, subscribed, and made a munificent provision for him during life. He was accidentally thrown into a perilous and unfortunate situation, but was beloved and respected, for his honourable and benevolent character, by all who had the advantage of his acquaintance. As Lord Minto declined the responsibility of acting in the Madras Government, from motives of delicacy, the ensuing account of the foregoing affair was promulgated to the army:—

Fort St. George, 18th August, 1809.

G. O. by the honourable the Governor in Council.

The Governor in Council has received intelligence that the troops at Chittledroog, consisting of the 1st battalion of the 8th and 15th Regiments Native Infantry, seized in the latter end of July the public treasure at that station, deserted the post entrusted to their care, and, in obedience to an order they received from a committee who have usurped the public authority at Seringapatam, marched, on the 6th inst., to join the disaffected troops in that garrison, plundering the villages on their route.

The British Resident and the officer commanding in Mysore prohibited in the most positive terms the advance of the troops from Chittledroog, and demanded from the European officers a compliance with the resolution of the Governor in Council of the 26th *ult.*, by either declaring that they would obey the orders of government according to the tenor of their commissions or withdrawing for the present from the exercise of authority.

The officers having refused to comply with his requisition, and having persisted in advancing towards Seringapatam, it became unavoidably necessary to prevent by force their entrance into the garrison. In the contest that ensued, a detachment from the British force, under the command of Lieut.-Col. Gibbs, aided by a body of Mysore horse and 1st battalion 3rd Native Infantry, entirely defeated and dispersed the corps from Chittledroog. During this affair a sally was made from the garrison of Seringapatam on Lieut.-Col. Gibbs' camp, but was instantly driven back by the pickets and 5th Regiment Native Cavalry, under the command of Captain Bean, of His Majesty's 20th Light Dragoons, in charge of that regiment. Nearly the whole of the rebel force was destroyed, while one casualty only was sustained by the British troops. Lieutenant Jefferies, of His Majesty's 25th Light Dragoons, having zealously offered to carry a flag of truce, which Lieut.-Col. Gibbs, anxious to prevent the effusion of blood, was desirous of despatching to the rebel troops, was slightly wounded in the execution of that duty, by a volley fired by the express command of an European officer.

While the Governor in Council participates in the feelings of sorrow that must have been experienced by the British forces in acting against the rebel force, and deeply laments the unfortunate but imperious necessity which existed for that proceeding, he considers it to be due to the conduct of the British forces to express his high admiration and applause of the zeal, firmness and patriotism they displayed on that most distressing occasion; their conduct affords a further proof of the superior influence in their minds of the principles of virtue, loyalty and honour over every other consideration, and eminently entitles them to public approbation. Lieut.-Col. Gibbs, Lieut.-Col. Adams, Major Carden, Captain Bean, and Lieutenant Jefferies availed themselves of the opportunity on this occasion of serving their country.

The Governor in Council is also happy to distinguish the zeal and loyalty displayed by the 5th Regiment Native Cavalry, the 1st Battalion Native Infantry, and the Mysore troops, who all manifested an eager desire to perform their duty. The Mysore horse on one occasion put the column of the Chittledroog troops to flight, and took two guns and both the colours from one of the battalions, a memorable proof of the weakness of men acting in the worst of causes.

That a body of officers should deliberately disobey the orders of their government, seize the public treasure under their protection, abandon the post entrusted to their charge, march to join a party of men in open opposition to authority, plunder the dominions of a British ally, and finally bear arms against their country, must excite grief and astonishment, but the conduct of these officers in urging innocent men under their command, who had the most powerful claims on their humanity and care, in the guilt and danger of rebellion, constitute an aggravation of their offence that cannot be contemplated without feelings of the deepest indignation and sorrow.

The Governor in Council is very far from wishing to aggravate the misconduct of these deluded and unhappy men, but he earnestly hopes the example of their armies and of their fate will still impress on the minds of the officers who have joined in their plans, a sense of the danger of their situation, and the propriety of their endeavouring by their early obedience and future zeal to efface the deep stain that has been cast on the honour of the Madras Army.

In announcing to the native troops the distressing events described in this order, the Governor in Council must express his concern that any part of the native army should be so far deluded by misrepresentation, and so lost to a sense of the obligations of fidelity, honour and religion, as to act against the government which has long supported them. The general order of the 3rd inst., and the conduct that has been observed towards the native troops at the presidency, the Mount Villore, Trichonopoly, Bellary, Gooly and Bangalore, must convince the whole native army of the anxiety of government to promote their welfare, and save them from the dangers into which they were likely to be plunged. The Governor in Council still places the greatest confidence in the fidelity and zeal of the native troops, and is convinced that they will not willingly sully the high reputation which they have so long enjoyed by joining in the execution of plans that must end in their disgrace and ruin.

The Governor in Council trusts that the unhappy fate of the Chittledroog battalions, who allowed themselves to be engaged in opposition to their government, will have the effect of preventing any other part of the native army from suffering themselves, under any circumstances, to be placed in a situation adverse to their duty and allegiance.

The Governor in Council avails himself of this occasion to express in the most public manner his high sense of the zeal, moderation, energy and abilities displayed by the Government of Mysore and by the British Resident and commanding officer during the transactions that have recently occurred in that country. The British Resident and commanding officer in Mysore did not permit the adoption of coercive measures until every means of expostulation and forbearance had been exhausted, and until they were compelled to embrace the alternative of employing force to prevent the most fatal evils to the cause of their country.

The Governor in Council requests that the honourable Mr. Cole and Lieut.-Colonel Davis will be pleased to accept the expression of his highest approbation and thanks for the moderation, firmness and ability which they manifested on this unprecedented and distressing occasion.

    (Signed)   H. Falconer,
                           Chief Secretary to Government.

The foregoing order is excellent, if the misstatements and fabrications contained therein did not disgrace the authority from whence it issued. I speak from ocular proof, having viewed from the ramparts of Seringapatam, which my house overlooked, the whole hostile proceeding that occurred on the eminence where the pretended conflict took place, and I solemnly affirm that the Chittledroog battalions did not fire a volley, but dispersed on the immediate charge of the dragoons, without resistance; if they had fired, more fatal effects must have ensued than the scratch of one individual officer.

It was proved also, at the court martial held at Bangalore on Colonel Bell, at which I was summoned and present, as an evidence that, the test was never *offered* for signature to the officers at Chittledroog, consequently they could not have refused compliance. It was also proved that the Mysore horse had plundered the villages, and not the Chittledroog battalions, as represented in this order; nor did they lose guns or colours during the march, until they were attacked by the dragoons before the fortress, when everything was abandoned in obedience to previous instructions from their officers.

It appears to me that undue interference by Sir George Barlow in the acknowledged rights of the army occasioned all this anarchy and confusion, and certainly at the commencement of the affair both King's and Company's officers were equally indignant on the occasion; but lucrative commands and splendid promises seduced the commanding officers of the King's regiments to adhere to the cause of Sir George, or he must have been dismissed from his government or our Indian possessions would have fallen to military authority and perhaps been for ever lost to the mother country. I still retain documents to prove this position, but my principal object is to narrate the events of a long life, without involving myself in the arcana of politics.

At the conclusion of Colonel Bell's court martial I had quite recovered from the effects of my wounds, and in May, 1810, arrived with my family at Wallajahbad, where I was congratulated by all my friends on my escape from friend and foe, though it was significantly hinted that after so long an absence I had some symptoms of the rebel about me; and with these jocular observations I soon resumed my usual routine of military duties, not however very well pleased with Sir George Barlow, who had certainly occasioned my protracted delay and caused me many disagreeable sensations during my residence at Seringapatam, from whence I was compelled to forward monthly sick certificates to the regiment, to evince my actual inability to quit the garrison.

In May, 1810, the flank companies of the 12th were ordered to march from Wallajahbad to Madras, to compose part of an expedition fitting out for the attack on the island of Bourbon, the French squadron from Mauritius and this isle having captured and destroyed innumerable vessels belonging to the East India Company, and obtained treasure to an incalculable amount; about 2,000 Europeans and a like proportion of *sepoys* were embarked and proceeded on their voyage towards this island. The passage from Madras was favourable, and they reached the small island of Rodriguez on the 20th June, 1810, which had been taken possession of some weeks previously by Colonel Keating, by a force under his command, with which he had attacked and plundered the town of St. Paul's in Bourbon, burning the arsenal and public stores, and conveying away a rich booty.

The French denominated this a wanton act and a barbarous innovation on the acknowledged system of civilised warfare, comparing Keating and his force to a set of *flibustiers* or buccaneers; certainly the island might have been at once carried without unnecessary experiment, which added no lustre to our national glory. The requisite arrangements having been completed, the expedition proceeded under convoy of the *Boadicea* and *Nereide* frigates, commanded by Captains Rowley and Willoughby, two gallant officers, the latter a terror to the inhabitants of the Mauritius and Bourbon, around which he had been cruising for many months, landing frequently with parties of his crew and carrying off many respectable habitants, to the great disgust of the chivalrous Frenchmen.

On approaching the island, they were joined by three other English frigates, the *Sirius*, *Magicienne* and *Iphigenia*, and came in sight of Bourbon on the morning of the 7th July. It was decided to attack the capital (St. Denis). The principal part of the force, under Colonel Keating, was to land at the village of St. Marie, five miles to the eastward of the capital, and the remainder of the force at Grande Chaloupe, six miles to the westward, under the command of Colonel Frazer, who were directed to disembark two hours before the headquarters party. This they effected about 12 o'clock, and ascended the side of a tremendous ravine, again descending on the other side of the steep rock, several ravines offering almost insurmountable obstacles on the road to St. Denis, of an equally barren and frightful description.

The main force, under Keating, attempted to land at St. Marie, but the swell of the sea caused such a high surf on the beach that for some time they were unsuccessful; the gallant Willoughby, in a small schooner, at length drove on shore, which example was imitated by many of the ships' boats, and about 200 men effected a landing, but in a most deplorable condition, almost without arms, with the greatest proportion of the ammunition saturated with seawater; many lives were lost and the schooner and boats dashed to pieces on the beach.

The distressing and perilous situation of those on shore was obvious, for had the enemy, who were strongly posted in the vicinity, attacked them, they must either have been annihilated or taken prisoners of war. The commodore (Rowley), perfectly conscious of the precarious situation of these gallant men, made signal for one of the large transports to run on shore, which was accordingly executed; but this had not the desired effect, a few boats only being enabled to land some few men under shelter of the transport's side, and only 300 *in toto* were safely got on shore, many perishing in the last attempt.

Aware now of the impracticability of further aid to this party, they were left to their fate, and Colonel Keating proceeded with the remainder of the army to Grande Chaloupe, to prosecute the attempt on that side, leaving the *Boadicea* frigate off St. Marie. During the night the surf had considerably subsided, when an additional force was landed from the frigate, and they were instructed to march towards St. Denis, for the purpose of co-operating with the attack on the western quarter under Colonel Frazer, who, having disembarked without opposition, proceeded on as before described over the rocky and mountainous road towards St. Denis, and in the afternoon reached the brow of a lofty precipice overhanging the plain near the town, from which it was about a mile distant; here he halted during the night.

The following morning Colonel Frazer descended by the zigzag road into the plain below, under a heavy cannonade from the town and field-pieces attached to a body of Frenchmen of about 400 drawn up on the plain. These were instantly charged and driven over the river, and he took possession of a redoubt which supported their right flank; this they abandoned at once. During this little affair Colonel Keating had arrived, and a flag of truce being advanced, he was admitted into the town; a short conference ensued, and the island was transferred to the dominion of the English. Lieut. Munro of the 86th was killed in the attack, and Lieut. McCreagh severely wounded in the shoulder. The party from St. Marie had reached the town as the terms of surrender were agreed to. Lieut. Spink, of the 12th, had been shot through the leg, and a few men wounded on the night after the distressing debarkation; had the French known their miserable plight, they must all have been made prisoners.

Mr. Farquhar was now installed as governor, having accompanied the expedition from Calcutta for the purpose. It was now determined to annoy the good people of the Mauritius. The four frigates, *Sirius, Magicienne, Iphigenia* and *Nereide,* which were crowded with troops, attacked and carried the small fortified barren rock at the entrance of Grand Port called the Isle de la Passe. The *Nereide* was stationed near the rock, and the other three frigates cruised off Port Louis. During their absence three French frigates, with two captured Indiamen, their prizes, appeared off Grand Port, standing straight into the harbour, into which they passed, except one, and then receiving a broadside from the *Nereide,* the smallest of them struck her colours, but being supported by the other frigates, cut her cable and followed the other vessels.

The *Windham* Indiaman, being a heavy sailer and not yet quite within the reef, tacked on hearing the firing and put to sea, but was afterwards taken by our squadron. Three French frigates and a captured Indiaman were thus enclosed in Grand Port harbour, without a possibility of escape, the *Nereide* being anchored in the mouth of the entrance of the reef, not 100 yards wide, supported by the strong battery of the Isle de la Passe, which was not 20 fathoms from her. Had the English only waited patiently for the grand expedition, which was hourly expected from India, the French squadron must have surrendered at discretion, as well as that riding in the harbour of Port Louis, without additional bloodshed; but this judicious procrastination did not accord with the energetic, fearless disposition of the gallant Willoughby, who signalled for the other three frigates, which in a few hours entered the narrow channel of the coral reef and brought up close to the *Nereide.*

A consultation of the captains ensued; the senior, Pym, was averse to the project of attack, but after some warm altercation, and an assurance that a pilot was ready to conduct them through the sinuous intricacies of the reef that intervened between them and the French, a space of at least five miles, the fiery arguments of Willoughby at length overcame the better judgment and prudence of his more temperate, judicious, and equally brave commanding officer. Every possible precaution was then adopted that human foresight could suggest to ensure the success of the enterprise. The enemy had in the meantime erected several batteries on the most projecting points of rock and filled their vessels with soldiers, despatched from Port Louis by General Decaen, for the purpose of assisting in the defence of the squadron.

As the English came within range of shot the action commenced, but suddenly the *Iphigenia, Magicienne* and *Sirius* grounded on a coral bank, thus leaving the unfortunate *Nereide* exposed to the destructive fire of the enemy's concentrated force. The three stranded frigates had fired a broadside or two, when the French cut their cables and were driven on shore; but now perceiving the helpless situation of the three gallant vessels, who were too distant to be seriously damaged by their fire, every effort was directed to destroy the *Nereide*, which had anchored close to them; in a few hours she was a complete wreck—mast, yards, and rigging cut to atoms, with the whole crew killed or wounded on the decks. The hills around were crowded with spectators, viewing this novel spectacle, and afterwards did ample justice to the chivalrous bravery of the British sailors.

About 10 o'clock at night, finding the *Nereide* fire silenced, the French ventured to board her, and there found the heroic Willoughby on the deck, lying amongst his gallant officers and crew, all weltering in their blood, the upper part of his cheek bone carried away by a ball and several wounds in his body. The frigate was a complete wreck, pierced through and through by hundreds of cannon balls; in the annals of naval history never was a more frightful scene recorded.

The *Magicienne* and *Sirius*, after many hours' exposure to the fire of the French batteries, and losing many men, were reluctantly abandoned; the former was burnt by the crew, the latter sank in deep water. The *Iphigenia*, after incredible exertion, was warped off the reef, but too late to afford aid to the deplorably situated *Nereide*, and received on board the remainder of the officers and men of the other two frigates, and regained the anchorage near the Isle de la Passe; having provisioned this post, she proceeded to the Isle de Bourbon.

The French, recovered from the panic occasioned by this rash attack (which would certainly have succeeded had not our ships touched the coral reef), resolved to retake the important battery of the Isle de la Passe; but our troops did not surrender it until they had exhausted all their water, with which the rock was totally unprovided, except the casks left by the shipping. After repulsing the enemy several times, they were at length reduced to the necessity of capitulating, to be sent to Bourbon, but they were most dishonourably forwarded to Port Louis and there detained as prisoners of war. The official letter on this unhappy affair, from Captain Pym to the government of Bourbon, dated 24th August, 1810, may be referred to in Note No. 1, and as I have never seen a copy of his despatch in the English language, nor a detailed account of the loss of these frigates, the extract was copied from the *Bourbon Government Gazette*. The bravery of Captain Willoughby was eulogized by the following distich:—

> *Au brave Willoughby, commandant la Nereide frégate de sa Majesté Britannique:*
> *A la grandeur du vrai courage*
> *Tous les peuples rendent hommage:*
> *Reçois le nôtre, Willoughby!*
> *Du grand Nelson tu montras la vaillance,*
> *Le ciel le fit semblable à lui*
> *Et sur les traits voulut aussi*
> *Du même sceau marquer la ressemblance.*

It was well known to all civilized nations that Nelson had lost an eye. Willoughby had also an eye shot out in some previous action, of which the French took advantage in conveying this pretty compliment.

The result of this calamitous affair gave the French a decided superiority in these seas, and sailing immediately for Bourbon with four frigates, blockaded the *Boadicea* (Capt. Rowley) in St. Paul's roadstead with the *Otter* sloop of war. At this eventful period the English frigate *Africaine* (Capt. Corbet) arrived, and in conjunction with Commodore Rowley proceeded to attack the French squadron. The *Africaine*, sailing admirably, at once engaged the French, taking up a rash position between two of their frigates. A calm came on, and after a most desperate defence the *Africaine* was taken in sight of the *Boadicea*, then five miles astern. Capt. Corbet lost his leg, and when informed of the capture of his ship, furiously tore off the bandages of his wound, and thus fell a victim to his too ardent courage and zeal for the service. A breeze springing up, the French, who had been roughly handled, made off, leaving the *Africaine* to be recaptured by Commodore Rowley, by whom she was towed into St. Paul's, completely dismasted and with several feet of water in the hold.

A short time afterwards the *Ceylon* frigate, with General Abercrombie on board, was passing Port Louis on his voyage to Bourbon, when two French frigates gave chase; he was overtaken by *La Venus*, and after a gallant action both vessels were dismasted; the other Frenchman coming up, he was compelled to submit, and struck his colours accordingly. Commodore Rowley, hearing the distant cannonade whilst lying at St. Paul's, put to sea, and was fortunate enough to capture the two dismasted frigates, the other French frigate sheering off at his approach.

Thus three dismasted frigates were now anchored off St. Paul's, but by the unceasing exertions of this prudent and gallant officer were all ready for sea in an incredibly short space of time, and being joined by the *Nisus* (Capt. Beaver), with Admiral Bertie on board, they sailed to cruise off Port Louis. In the last action between the *Ceylon* and the French frigate General Abercrombie had a very narrow escape. As he was sitting and arranging his official papers to be thrown overboard, a ball struck his writing-desk, shivering it into a thousand pieces; he succeeded, however, in destroying all documents of importance.

The squadron continued to cruise some weeks off the mouth of Port Louis harbour, but the French evinced no disposition to move from their secure anchorage, nor did any event of material consequence occur until they joined the grand expedition at the Isle of Rodriguez, except the capture of a French schooner from France, which was gallantly boarded by the crews of some boats, who carried her in the highest style; she made a stout resistance, and did not surrender until the two officers and many of her men were extended on the deck. It was discovered by the papers on board that four French frigates were on their voyage from France, filled with troops for the reinforcement of the Mauritius.

This squadron was a few weeks afterwards encountered by the brave Capt. Schomberg, with four of our frigates; two of them were taken after a hard-fought action near the coast of Madagascar, the other two escaped, after innumerable dangers and difficulties, to the mother country, where the captains were not very honourably received by the great Napoleon; one of them, in an agony of desperation, shot himself in consequence, and the other was ingloriously dismissed from the service, so it was reported by the inhabitants of the Isle of France; but as no race of men are more ingenious in the fabrication of news than the French, I will not vouch for the authenticity of this statement, which, however, is very probable, for had they properly supported the frigates engaged, they might have turned the scale of victory, as they were all larger ships and heavier metal than the English.

On the 20th August, 1810, Colonel Picton received the following letter from the Presidency of Madras:—

> Fort St. George, 19th August, 1810.
> Sir,—I have the honour of acquainting you with the instructions of His Excellency the Commander-in-Chief, directing that you will hold His Majesty's 12th Regiment in readiness to march for Fort St. George on or about the 28th inst. That corps is placed under orders for foreign service, and will, of course, retain no men who are unfit for that purpose, and it may be convenient to place the latter in Poonamallie during the march of the corps from Wallajahbad.
> (Signed) W. Blacker,
> Quartermaster-General.

At the specified period we marched, reaching the Mount on the 30th of the same month. The 21st September proceeded to Madras, and embarked on board the *Russell* (74); frigates, *Clorinde*, *Cornwallis*, *Cornelia*, *Bucephalus*, and *Hesper*. I was placed on the old *Russell* with my company. Having assembled my men on deck, the Admiral (Drury) ordered the ship's crew from below and addressed them thus:

> I expect, as the troops are now serving with you, that both officers and men will carefully avoid all interference with them in any shape whatever, and if any complaints should exist, let them be immediately reported to me; but I positively forbid any altercation between you and the soldiers.

Nor had we, after this judicious caution, the slightest disagreement during the voyage to the island of Rodriguez, which was fixed on for the rendezvous of the fleets from the three Presidencies of Bengal, Madras and Bombay. We experienced fine weather during the passage, with the exception of a slight gale of a few hours' continuance, when every cheek was blanched in the crazy old *Russell*; she was so worn out that only a few weeks preceding, in a short cruise from Bombay, she was literally discovered in the act of foundering bodily by the head, and nothing but the most active exertions in lightening her saved the crew from perdition. In this gale she worked so frightfully that the seams between the planks would open and close alternately as she rolled from side to side.

We were all rejoiced when anchored in the roadstead off Rodriguez, where we arrived on the 20th October, 1810.

The admiral having here been apprised of the disastrous affair of the loss of four of our frigates at the Isle of France, landed the 12th Regiment at Rodriguez and proceeded with the men-of-war for the purpose of re-establishing our supremacy in those seas, and if possible capturing some of the French squadron; but in a few days he fell in with Admiral Bertie, his senior officer, and to his great disappointment and vexation he was ordered back to Madras. The old man was so irritated that he wished some of the captains to carry a message to Bertie, but they were more reasonable and prudent than the admiral, and of course declined so hazardous an enterprise. I must here observe that during the three weeks my company was on board the *Russell* the greatest harmony prevailed between the two services.

Major-General John Abercrombie now arrived at Rodriguez, were we had been several days living on measly pigs and salt meat. The good fellows of the *Russell* had left us a cask of Cape Madeira, part of our united stock, but which was generously relinquished and made over to us, on their observation of the abandoned and deserted state of the island. The general inspected the small detachments of troops on the sands, and made arrangements for the expected divisions from the other Presidencies. The Bombay fleet soon arrived, but day after day passed without receiving the least intelligence of the Bengal fleet, when, on the 26th November, the general came to the determination of proceeding to the attack without their assistance, as the period of the hurricanes was fast approaching and it was considered dangerous to delay a moment longer.

The 12th Regiment had been crowded on board one ship, the *Castlereagh* Indiaman, and we were just sailing off when the Bengal fleet appeared in the offing, led by the *Illustrious* (74), Commodore Broughton. All the arrangements had been previously made by the general, so that we were only detained a few hours, for some little communication of orders, and then were wafted on with a gentle breeze towards the point of destination.

The island of Rodriguez is about 12 miles long and five broad, several hundred feet above the surface of the sea, clothed with wood and inhabited only by three or four French families; it had been in our possession ever since the expedition to Bourbon, and was at the time of our arrival garrisoned by a company of *sepoys*. A reef of coral rock surrounds the whole island, extending on all sides, at least a mile from the mainland, covered by a depth of water two or three feet, through which the blue, red, and purple coral is seen distinctly, and has a very pretty effect; at the outside of the reef the sea is many fathoms deep, so that a ship can approach so near as to rest her side against it.

There are many deep fissures separating the coral bank, through which vessels may approach close to the shore and lie in tolerable security from partial gales of wind. The appearance of the different branches of coral under water resembles the heads of cauliflowers, variegated by a profusion of colours; the oysters and other shell-fish are of a poisonous nature on all these banks. Seventy-eight men of the fleet were severely affected and many died in consequence of eating them during our stay at the island.

Towards sunset of the 28th of November, 1810, we caught a view of the high mountains of the Mauritius, and on the 29th November were sailing direct towards Cap Malheureux by the Isle of Ronde, and about 11 o'clock a fleet of 100 sail anchored in the narrow channel between the small isle of the Mire de Coir and Cap Malheureux. This passage had been surveyed by the officers of the navy, but was previously considered by the French as impracticable. At 12 o'clock we were all ready for debarkation; the flat-bottomed boats were hoisted out, and under the brave and celebrated Captain Beaver the descent was speedily accomplished, and I had been appointed brigade-major to the 1st Brigade. Our men had no sooner assembled than we moved off the ground towards Canonier Point, alias Pointe de Canonier, skirting La Grande Baie.

A tremendous explosion took place at the Battery Canonier as we approached it; we then entered a narrow road towards the interior of the island, which led through a wood skirted by an impenetrable jungle on both sides. Hitherto no opposition whatever was offered to our progress, and we accordingly hastened on to gain an open space if possible, before the enemy could offer any serious impediment to our progress. When about halfway through the jungle a sudden halt took place, and a scattering fire of musketry was scarcely distinguishable proceeding from the front of the column led on by General Warde (afterwards Sir Henry), with the light infantry of the 12th Regiment, who coming suddenly on one of the enemy's posts, a short skirmish ensued, and they were driven from their position at the point of the bayonet.

Several of our men were killed, and Lieut. Ashe of the 12th had his thigh broken; so closely had the encounter been that the sleeve of his coat had been scorched, arm severely wounded, and his face disfigured in a shocking manner by the explosion of the fire-arms. Ashe had vigorously cut down two of his opponents ere he fell.

As we soon moved on, dying with heat and thirst, we passed the headless body of one of the light infantry of the 12th; some of the young soldiers of another corps, being too minute in their inspection of this miserable object, had assembled around it in a crowd and were with some difficulty brought to a sense of duty, as they delayed longer than consistent with the energy required by their profession and actually for a few minutes interrupted the line of march. Having overcome this obstacle, it was dusk before we debouched from the wood and were unable to ascertain the position of the enemy. The column was here halted, and we took up our ground in the midst of an extensive maize-field, where we remained during the night. We had all exhausted the contents of our canteens, and the troops were exceedingly overcome from the heat of the march and the absence of all water during the course of the march.

There was only one little well at the skirt of the field, near a cottage; the soldiers crowded eagerly towards it, swearing, pushing, and fighting for the precious liquid; even the general was thrust rudely aside on begging a drop, so intemperate is the sense of self-preservation. "Water! water! water!" was the continual cry of all this dreadful night; men even in their slumber were mumbling this irrepressible want. The confinement on board ship had the effect of rendering the fatigue and failure of water doubly oppressive, and a gallant captain of one of the Indiamen, who had volunteered his services, died through fatigue and exhaustion, his death being attributed to a *coup de soleil*; the rays of the sun on that day were as fierce as any I ever recollect, even in India.

At the dawn of day on the following morning we moved forward, and as the *manioc*-fields appeared with the broad leaves of the shrub covered with sparkling drops of dew, the men simultaneously burst from the ranks, devouring eagerly the scanty refreshment. At length we reached a large open plain, on the left of which the French had erected powder mills, called "*Moulin au Poudre*," through which flowed a beautiful transparent stream of water. We had scarcely taken up our position in two distinct lines, when the rivulet was swarming on all sides with the exhausted soldiery; a king might envy them their delicious draught. Although they had only marched five miles this morning, they were soon lying fast asleep on the soft turf; but the nap was speedily interrupted, for about 12 o'clock a large party of horse, headed by General Decaen, advanced to reconnoitre our army.

Unfortunately, a picket in front was dispersed on a plundering excursion, and were cut to pieces before they could effect a retreat; the conduct of Lieut. Prendergast, who commanded them, was highly censured, and he very narrowly escaped the ordeal of a court martial. The picket of the 12th stood the brunt of the attack, and being joined by the rifle company of the 59th, under the gallant Capt. Darby, soon dislodged the enemy's marksmen from the old houses and barns in front. General Decaen had a shot through his boot, when, having rode along the front of our line, he retired towards Port Louis and left us unmolested the remainder of the day. We were now amply supplied with provisions from the fleet, and the troops fared sumptuously, comparatively speaking; I do not mean to assume that we fed like the pampered bodyguard in St. James's, but we had sufficient good wholesome food to satisfy the cravings of nature.

On the 1st December the army was once more in motion, the numerical strength consisting of about 10,000 or 11,000 men *in toto*, including several battalions of Bengal *sepoys*, with a small proportion of Madras native troops, neither of whom had ever been employed on foreign service since the projected expedition to Manilla in the year 1797. No resistance was offered until we came to the Rivière de Pamplimonsis, when a sharp firing of guns and musketry commenced. The enemy were strongly posted on the opposite side, supported by guns, to oppose our further progress; they had completely destroyed the bridge, leaving the huge beams alone, which they had not time to remove. We skirmished for some time, when two field-pieces being advanced and pouring a few volleys of grape among them, they retired without further opposition at this point.

We now passed rapidly over several of the remaining beams of the bridge, and our guns were dragged through the bed of the river (then containing little water) by the active exertions of a body of sailors, who had been landed from the fleet for the purpose of helping us on with our artillery. About this time Major O'Keeffe of the 12th Regiment was observed hanging his head on his bosom and supported by the arm of his servant, complaining of sickness and exhaustion; he had been unwell on board, and possessed of a presentiment of his approaching fate; he was heard to observe, "I have been actively employed in the reduction of most of the West India Islands, but never experienced those sensations that now oppress me." He was recommended strongly to remain behind, but he persisted in placing himself with the leading division of the regiment, and thus supported by his servant continued the march. We advanced about a mile further when the column was annoyed by the enemy's *voltigeurs*, and our flankers were detached to oppose them, who soon silenced the daring fellows.

As we approached the River Seche, a battery on the other side showered volleys of grape shot up the road by which our column was slowly approaching. Just at this period the 12th had about 60 men mowed down. I was close to poor Major O'Keeffe, who received a large ball on the upper part of the left temple, carrying off the top of his skull; a column of blood of the size of my arm spouted from the wound and he fell back a dead man; he heaved one deep-drawn sigh alone, as an indication of any bodily suffering, and lay on his back like a person asleep, without that ghastly hypocritical countenance, the usual appearance in a natural death.

At this instant the regiment just in front was panic-struck, turned, and bore down the two front sub-divisions of the 12th Regiment, when General Abercrombie came galloping down vociferating, "Slaves! cowards! what the devil are you doing? advance 12th, advance, and take the place of these fellows"! We accordingly moved to the front, and, as the ground widened, deployed into line, rushing forward to take possession of the enemy's battery in front; the little River Seche intervened, and though the charge was executed with celerity and regularity, under a heavy discharge of musketry and grape, we could not reach the battery in sufficient time to use the bayonet.

They immediately abandoned their guns and fled in all directions, leaving several field-pieces and a howitzer in our possession. The lieut.-colonel of their artillery was left bleeding near the post, wounded in the groin; he appeared in great bodily fear of our soldiers, begging protection from the officers, exclaiming "*Ah! messieurs vos soldats sont si féroces, protégez moi je vous en prie.*" The 12th Regiment were now ordered to ascend the Montague Longue and storm the fortification of the flag-staff. We were about an hour executing this manoeuvre; a few straggling shots was all the opposition offered; the moment we gained possession a naval officer began to work the signals, specifying to the inhabitants of the island that the English were beaten off, and that the colonists might return to their dwellings.

Our navy had long possessed the whole code of signals of the French, and now very judiciously availed themselves of the secret. Whilst we were thus employed, the army had advanced very near the enemy's lines and were saluted by an incessant heavy cannonade from a tremendous battery of 20 or 30 guns, from a hill on the right of their lines. The deputy adjutant-general (Lindsay) was now seen riding full speed towards the Montague Longue, at the foot of which he shouted out that the general intended to storm the lines immediately, ordering the 12th Regiment to descend and join without delay. I was directed by Colonel Picton to hasten to the general to say that the instant we could assemble our detachments, who had pursued the enemy to various precipices and ravines on the mountain, we would immediately rejoin the army.

I hastened down and approaching the general, who was seated on a conspicuous white horse, with the cannon balls ploughing the earth up on all sides of him, I delivered my message, when he desired me to tell Colonel Picton to keep possession of his post, as he should defer the advance on Port Louis until the morrow. I was rejoiced at this short detention, for never were balls thrown from such a distance with such nice precision; I was several times covered with sand and earth during this short conference; the general calmly smiled, desiring me to hasten off with the message.

Away I went, and nearly stumbled over a wounded French soldier lying about midway between the rear of the army and Montague longue; he started up, and I was in the act of cutting him down, having my sword drawn, when he cried out "*Grace, monsieur grâce; je ne suis qu'um pauvre mâitre d'école, j'ai été forcé de prendre les armes par monsieur le Général Decaen, je suis blessé comme vous voyez!*" I saw that he was severely wounded by a musket ball, gave him a drink from my canteen and pursued my route; he, poor fellow, was found dead the following day on the spot where I had left him. Having delivered my message to Colonel Picton, I was again despatched with directions to obtain food and water for the regiment.

Having communicated with the commissariat, I again ascended the mountain for the third time during the day. Completely overcome with fatigue, I now plucked a goose, made a fire, and dressed it for Picton and myself. This was my only plunder at the flag-staff; we ate the delicious morsel with that *goût* that hungry men alone know how to appreciate, and then flung myself on the hard rock to take a few hours' refreshing slumber.

I had scarcely courted the aid of Nature's balmy restorer, when I was shook roughly by the shoulder and ordered to descend the hill once more, and acquaint the general that the enemy were assembled in considerable force at the farthest extremity of the mountain, with an evident intention of regaining its possession. This was too much for my strength and I appealed to the humane consideration of my colonel; he was himself completely overcome by one ascent, and accordingly admitted that a fourth trip was too much for me.

A sergeant and drummer were therefore despatched with a letter to the general about seven o'clock in the afternoon; as to myself, I could not have passed over a less space than 20 miles that day, and accordingly slept very soundly until about three o'clock in the morning, when I was suddenly awoke by repeated peals of musketry from the encampment below us.

The regiment was under arms in five minutes, expecting an attack; the firing continued for about a quarter of an hour in camp, when it suddenly ceased and all was quiet again. We were extremely anxious to ascertain the cause of this disturbance, expecting the return of the sergeant and drummer; they never returned, having been both shot in the false alarm. It appeared afterwards, that a small party of the dispersed French soldiers had in the night mistaken their way and entered the encampment; the sentinels had fired on them, which was returned, and the English troops thus unexpectedly attacked awoke half-conscious of their situation, and mistaking their comrades for the enemy had fired on each other for several minutes, until the general and his staff stopped the murderous proceeding at the imminent hazard of their lives; our couriers fell in the *mêlée*. It was afterwards computed that as many men were killed and wounded in this unfortunate affair as we lost in the attack on the island.

We descended the Montague Longue this morning, and were spectators of the effects of the preceding night's calamitous firing; there were the poor sergeant and drummer lying close to each other shot through the bodies, with the general's answer to the letter in the sergeant's cap. One *sepoy* I met proceeding to the hospital, a ball having passed through the windpipe; he could not speak, but in his endeavours to do so the breath escaped at the orifice of the wound, and crowds of wretched men were borne off the field for the surgeon's scientific ingenuity. This poor *sepoy* was, however, completely cured, and I saw him some weeks afterwards on duty at Grand Port. Had I descended the mountain for the fourth time my career in life would most probably have been terminated. The following order was issued by General Abercrombie on the success of the preceding day's operations:—

Headquarters, Port Louis,
1st December, 1810.

G.O.

Major-General Abercrombie is most perfectly satisfied with the steadiness and gallantry displayed by the flank battalion and grenadier company 59th Foot, in the affair which took p]ace this morning, and he is desirous to express in this public manner the sentiments which he entertains of their exemplary good conduct. The Commander of the Forces is fully persuaded that the flank battalion will sincerely participate with him in the severe loss which His Majesty's Service has sustained in the death of that valuable and excellent officer, Lieut.-Col. Campbell. Major-General Abercrombie is also happy to acknowledge the steadiness shown by His Majesty's 12th Regiment of Foot, and he feels himself particularly grateful to the zealous exertions of the detachment of seamen landed from the squadron under the directions of Captain Montague, and he requests to offer him and the officers and men under his command his sincere acknowledgments for the services which they have rendered the army.

Nothing can be so discreditable to troops as a dangerous and unnecessary expenditure of ammunition. Major-General Abercrombie observed with great regret that some corps showed a degree of unsteadiness in this particular, which disappointed the hopes he had formed of their discipline. All shooting in the line can only be permitted amongst local and irregular troops.

(Signed) W. Nicholson, Adjutant-General.

Now, Colonel Keating commanded the flank battalion, and every allusion to his conduct is sedulously avoided in the foregoing order. In leading this choice corps he descended from his horse as the firing became brisker, and complained that the wound in his leg gave him great pain. All who heard him were much surprised, as previous to the existing moment he had never come in contact with the enemy; but on the surgeon inspecting the wound, it appeared like a small puncture of a small-sword through the calf of the leg, which the public decided to have been perpetrated by his own sword. General Warde rode up and said, "Colonel Keating, if you will not or cannot lead on the flank battalion I will;" and then placing himself at their head moved on with Colonel Campbell.

The latter officer was shot through the head five minutes after, and at the termination of the affair the gallant Colonel Keating retired to hospital, where (on visiting some of our officers who had been severely wounded) I saw him in apparently great pain; this was the same Captain Keating of fighting notoriety when at the Cape of Good Hope in the year 1796.

At ten o'clock on the morning of the 2nd December, 1810, the day after the action. General Decaen despatched a trumpeter to the British lines, proposing terms of capitulation for the surrender of the island, which were so preposterously extravagant that they were at once rejected, and a schedule returned of the terms on which General Abercrombie would admit the capitulation. As no answer was returned during the day, everything was prepared and arranged for storming their lines.

At daybreak on the 3rd, a French officer rode into camp proposing an immediate suspension of hostilities, which was agreed to, and after some trivial alteration in the proposed terms the capitulation was finally adjusted. This happy termination to our fatigues and dangers having been soon bruited through the camp, the flank battalion was ordered to march to take possession of Port Louis, when to the astonishment of the whole army the gallant Colonel Keating was seen gaily prancing on his charger at the head of these brave soldiers; but had we been compelled to storm he would have been found in luxurious occupation of his snug berth and bed in the hospital, where he had lain almost inanimate until the intelligence of capitulation revivified him, and springing actively from his dormant state, declared himself well enough to head his division. It was rumoured that he had acquired immense property in the plunder of the Isle of Bourbon, and was not therefore anxious for his heirs to reap the benefit of his dangers and hardships so speedily after the acquirement.

The Isle of France or Mauritius had been represented as another Gibraltar, clothed with hill-forts and batteries, and we of course expected to lose several thousand men in the attack; but the capture was achieved at the moderate loss of 200 killed and wounded; the courage and talents of the famous General Decaen had also been greatly overrated, as evidently appeared in his feeble dispositions for the defence of the island. His principal reason for so precipitate a surrender was, he asserted, the appearance of our Cape squadron; but unfortunately for his veracity this division of our army was not visible until some hours after the capitulation had been signed. It consisted of the 72nd and 87th Regiments, with 100 artillery, and although too late to participate in the honour of the fall of the place, yet shared in all the advantages of prize property equally with their comrades of the actual invading force.

We had scarcely taken possession of the town, when a smart firing of musketry was heard in the direction of the port. Our poor sailors, who had. been formerly taken prisoners and confined in prison-ships, were so rejoiced on discovering the British flag flying on the ramparts of Port Louis, they rose on their guards and disarmed them. Several French frigates sent armed parties on board, and these poor fellows were accordingly massacred without mercy; the affair was, however, of so intricate a nature that no investigation took place. It was dubious how far the French were justified in firing on these men after the surrender of the place, but would the English similarly situated have tamely submitted to this mutinous conduct on the part of the French?

In a week after the capitulation, the French troops (about 1,200) were embarked on some of our transports for France, the principal part of our army returning to the Presidencies, to be employed in the contemplated expedition against Batavia, leaving the 12th, 72nd, and 87th Regiments to garrison the Isle of France. The 12th were stationed to the windward of the isle, at a place called Grand Port, where we had unhappily lost four frigates a few months before, and the topmasts of the *Sirius* were at the time of our arrival seen plainly above the surface of the water, a melancholy memorial of the temerity of our brave tars.

The morning after the arrival of the regiment at this station our bugles, as usual, having sounded for parade, the inhabitants were observed rapidly deserting the small town and making off to the interior of the country with great expedition; they had mistaken this signal of parade for one of attack, and it was with considerable difficulty they were persuaded of our peaceable disposition through the means of the *commissaire civile*, who at length explained the cause of alarm, and we soon became on the most friendly terms, though they were very indignant at a government order requiring them to deliver up all their arms, which they pretended were absolutely necessary for personal defence against the slaves; and so far had they carried the spirit of resistance that the whole of the adjacent country had assembled one morning at a few miles' distance, fully armed, to contest the justice of the requisition; however, on the approach of the 12th Regiment they abandoned their intention, moving off very quietly to their habitations just as we were preparing to charge them.

After this little discontent the respectable planters became very hospitable, and invited the officers to their romantic habitations, where I hesitate not to assert there were some of the most beautiful young females in the whole universe, though the consummate ignorance in which they were brought up amongst these wild woods and mountains rendered them unfit for civilised society. One of these lovely creatures, one day after dinner, enquired if the English did not always get intoxicated and box with each other after dinner? Another was anxious to know if England was equal in extent to the Isle of France? with various other ridiculous and naive questions, that afforded extreme amusement to our young officers, some of whom, however, became fascinated by their personal charms and committed the grand error of matrimony, an experiment never conducive to the permanent happiness of an Englishman, even though united to the best educated French female, for domestic comfort is literally uncongenial to their nature, *mais pour passer le moment passager il n'y a point de femmes comme les francaises!*

An old French gentleman who had been particularly active in repelling the incursions of the gallant Willoughby, who frequently landed small bodies of sailors from his frigate and surprised the peaceable inhabitants, for the purpose of obtaining fresh meat and vegetables for his crew, paid me the most obsequious attention, inviting me to his habitation, five miles from Grand Port, and introducing me to his charming family. Monsieur Cherval, the name of this insidious old fellow, would, after our jovial repasts, sometimes declaim in warm language on the renown of the great Napoleon, in whose praises I joined as a generous enemy, in acknowledging his transcendent military abilities One evening he addressed me with tears in his eyes, deploring the want of one real friend, and enquiring if I would assist him in his difficulties?

I replied, "Certainly, so far as my means admitted," imagining he alluded to some pecuniary embarrassment; when to my excessive astonishment he disclosed a plan of operation for recapturing the Isle of France, and wished me to inspect a voluminous correspondence with his associates in different quarters of the island, by which he assured me I should be convinced of the practicability of the project, as 10,000 persons were implicated in the design. My indignation at first deprived me of all utterance, which quiescence he mistook for a tacit approval of his iniquitous plan, and approached me to seal the contract by a hearty shake of the hand.

I recoiled from the contagion, exclaiming, "*Vieux coquin, comment oses-tu me proposer une telle bassesse? Je te méprise. Je te hais je te déteste, monstre execrable; toi et tes camarades seraient les premiers de me mépriser si je me prêtais a tes desseins.*" Thus far I had proceeded in French, and then a volley of English abjurations closed the conference. I thanked him for all his hospitality, at the same time intimating that his roof alone protected him from the sharp point of my sword. I afterwards had several warnings from friendly negroes to beware of riding out alone, as Monsieur Cherval had spies in various directions, in ambush, to give me a sly shot, and for months afterwards I always travelled with a brace of loaded pistols in my holsters.

I related my adventure to Colonel Picton, who called him a damned old ignorant fool, and advised me to take no further notice of the ridiculous affair. This same Cherval in one of Willoughby's incursions held out a flag of truce, and on Willoughby's approaching to a conference the traitor and his party fired a volley on them, killing two of his men and penetrating his clothes with several balls, in fact the French themselves despised him for this act of treachery; this anecdote I learnt only after his abominable proposition.

The officers of the regiment frequently visited the famous Isle de la Passe, at the margin of the coral reef, for the purpose of fishing for shells, and obtained innumerable olives, double harps, *tétons de venus*, and a great variety of other beautiful, rare and valuable specimens of conchology. I have perused books in which were representations of invaluable shells having been discovered on the seashore; but these accounts are erroneous, as all shells thrown on the sands are shortly tarnished by the heat of the sun and destroyed by the constant action of the water. In order to preserve the glowing polish and perfect shape which forms the principal value and beauty of shells, they require to be fished up with hooks from several fathoms deep, and then buried under ground for many weeks; when disinterred, the fishy blubber is decomposed and the shells appear in all their original lustre and beauty.

I inspected a variety of collections belonging to French planters in the vicinity of Grand Port, the most beautiful I had ever seen, all accumulated in the foregoing method, and valued at many thousand pounds. Our surgeon, Mr. Erskine, offered 5,000 dollars for a minor collection; however, the owner assured him he expected to obtain double that price on exportation to France. Shells are certainly beautiful, but a display of large quantities fatigues the eye and bewilders the imagination, though admiration and wonder at the infinite variety so incomprehensibly formed by that transcendent Being, the Author of all things, must strike the beholder with deep reflection on the plentitude of his power.

I frequently amused myself in wandering through long avenues of mango trees of many miles in extent, closely planted on each side of the road, which rendered it almost impervious to the rays of the sun striking down at pleasure the exquisitely delicious fruit, which is as wholesome as luscious, never cloying the appetite. I have eaten 50 mangoes during a morning's walk without experiencing the least ill effect. The verdant *manioc* fields spreading widely over the adjacent country, the brilliant little red cardinals hopping cheerily on the twigs, the prattling *moynas* scouring along in countless flocks, the woods, deep ravines, volcanic rocks, and distant murmur of the sea breaking on the coral reef formed a scene that the most romantic imagination could have desired.

The cardinal is about the size of a canary bird, of a gorgeous vermilion colour and abounding in all districts of the Mauritius. The *moyna* resembles our blackbird, destroying all species of insects. A planter, one season, shot all these latter birds that approached his fields; the consequence was, that his crops failed from the uncontrolled depredations of insects, and the *moyna* has ever since been held in high estimation by the inhabitants.

The *commissaire civile*, Monsieur Letort of Grand Port, was one of the most laughter-loving, jolly companions that Nature ever formed; he would sing and play antics at our mess the live-long night, sometimes to the great destruction of our tumblers and wine-glasses, nine of which, in the flourish of the arm, previous to the commencement of "O, Richard! O *mon Roi!*" he swept majestically from the table one evening. I had invited him to dine with me; we had a large party of French, and they all preferred sipping cherry brandy to the more salubrious beverage of claret and Madeira, they were all therefore rolling on the floor in a beastly state of intoxication in an hour after the cloth was removed, and nothing heard but ejaculations of "*Ah! que les anglais sont de braves, gens; vivent les anglais, ce sont de braves gens,"* and old Letort would thunder forth his indecent song of *"Pierre en revenant du moulin renontre fille en chemin,"* etc., etc.

The next morning I never saw a more miserable looking set of wretches, apostrophising our gay lads with *"Ah! mes amis, vous en avez tués j'ai un mal de tête a faire mourir,"* sacréing the cherry brandy without mercy.

In one of my morning excursions among the wild rocks and ravines, having selected several delicious mangoes, I sat down on the fragment of a rock commanding a deep ravine with a limpid brook flowing below; I was luxuriously engaged in extracting the exquisite pulp from the fruit, unconscious of danger, when bang went a rifle from the opposite side, the whizzing ball striking the mango from my mouth, grazing the forefinger of my left hand and covering me with blood. I leapt from my perch, ensconcing myself behind the rock, lest another shot might salute my *pericranium*; scarcely had I sheltered myself, when I observed a slave making off with a musket or some species of firearms in his hand, but could not distinguish his features. I then recollected the menaces of my old acquaintance Cherval, and this retreating fellow certainly imagined he had executed his master's commission most effectually, as my sudden disappearance from the rock must have impressed him with the belief of the fatality of his aim.

I was not above two miles from the barracks, to which I hastened on assurance of safety, which was evident now from the hasty retreat of my intended assassin; the wound, or rather the cicatrice, is still on my forefinger to this hour, as evidence of my veracity on this occasion. In my long rides my pistols always accompanied me: an attack so immediately in the vicinity of the station was however rather unexpected.

I had little necessity for future precaution, being summoned to my staff duties at Port Louis the following day, and confess my gratification to have been thus removed 35 miles from my suspected vindictive foe. In about five months after the capture of the island my family arrived, but the health of my wife was fearfully changed. She had insisted on accompanying me to the place of embarkation from Wallajahbad only ten days after her confinement; on the march we were overtaken by one of those short but sweeping storms of wind and rain that are only known in tropical climes, and just as we arrived at a *choultry*, the storm forced open all the windows and she was compelled to remain in the deluged room upwards of an hour, and was soon after affected by the disease of *hydrops pectoris,* which in a few months after her arrival at Port Louis conducted her to that bourne from whence no traveller returns.

She was interred with military ceremony in a vault near Fort Blanchaving, leaving me three young children (having lost five others in India), rather an awkward appendage to the baggage of a military man. I settled my two boys at the Colonial College, and then, accompanied by my infant girl, I proceeded to the Isle of Bourbon on the staff, and again returned to the Mauritius on promotion to the majority of the regiment, by which I forfeited my staff situation.

I had scarcely landed at Port Louis when an order transferred the 12th Regiment to the Isle of Bourbon, and I was stationed at the seacoast town of St. Paul's in command of a district of 90 miles' extent, with four companies, every post of which was to be inspected once every three months, with strict injunctions to prevent the disembarkation of slaves from the Isle of Madagascar, in which traffic the Bourbonese were extremely active. Near St. Paul's the grave of the devoted Capt. Corbet, who gallantly fell on board his frigate, the *Africaine,* in the action with the two French frigates, was pointed out to me by an inhabitant; a heap of sand near one of the batteries was all the indication of the mortal remains of the brave fellow who sacrificed existence in defence of his country. If this be glory, it is that of oblivion, *mais tel est le destin des militaires.* At this post I passed a monotonous period of two years.

I made a tour of the island, and in passing the *pays brut,* on that part of the coast, of about nine miles extent, covered with huge masses of lava that were emitted from the volcano two years before, I suddenly lost the track of the pathway that led through the mountains of lava, as also the negro slave who accompanied me to take care of my horse. The evening was rapidly closing, my horses' shoes became detached and he fell dead lame, from his continual scramble amongst the cinders; I was therefore compelled to dismount and lead him by the bridle, and whilst in this unpleasant situation on the summit of a lava ridge I fortunately discovered my absent negro, a few hundred yards off, making signals for me to descend towards him. Having with some difficulty accomplished this disagreeable task and joined him, he communicated the joyful intelligence that a pathway leading close to the sea was practicable, by which we could proceed to an oasis where a hospitable French family dwelt at about a league distant from our actual position.

At half-past eight o'clock we arrived at the house, which was surrounded by a few hundred acres of fertile sugar-cane land, encompassed in every direction by ridges of lava. I was received with every demonstration of cordiality by the proprietor, who directed his forgeman to shoe my horse, and his servants to prepare supper. Several blooming girls, his daughters, were introduced, and with the amiable society of *madame* his wife I passed a most delightful evening. One of the sons played the violin, a *quadrille* was formed, and we danced till two o'clock in the morning. In the course of conversation my host related many amusing anecdotes, all local; at length he enquired if I was acquainted with a Madame Desforges? From this enquiry I almost suspected he knew me as commandant of St. Paul's; however, his ensuing relation convinced me to the contrary.

He began with a history of her life, and finally detailed the affair of the battery at St. Paul's, where the commandant was observed to dismount from his horse and in company with Madame Desforges retire for upwards of a quarter of an hour. I could no longer retain my indignation, and exclaimed, "Whoever told you this piece of scandal is a vile, detestable liar; I am the commandant of St. Paul's, and declare to you on the honour of a gentleman that no occurrence of this nature ever took place, and that I am now on my road to St. Suzanne to solicit the honour of her alliance!" Never was poor man so dumbfounded; he apologised a thousand times his indiscretion in mentioning the circumstance, assuring me the report was current throughout the island, and that two days before a passing traveller had related the tale in presence of his family.

I could attach no blame to my host, retired to bed, and at five o'clock was on my old Arab, proceeding slowly towards my place of destination. Being suddenly intercepted by a deep ravine and hearing the loud neighing of a horse, I cast my eyes on the opposite precipice, and there discovered a horseman on one of the most beautiful mountain ponies I ever saw, long mane and tail floating in the wind and wildly neighing with unceasing clamour. The scene was quite picturesque. On passing the ravine and joining the cavalier, I expressed my admiration of his elegant little steed, when he offered him for sale at 120 dollars. I closed with the bargain, mounted my negro on him, gave an order for the money and pursued my journey, after taking breakfast at the owner's habitation, who entertained me most hospitably.

On reaching a wide sandy plain, I was so pleased with my recent purchase that an irresistible fancy seized me to mount him and try his paces, which hitherto only appeared a short shuffling amble, sidling and arching his pretty, full, round, muscular neck the whole time; I therefore dismounted, and delivering my Arab to the negro's care I boldly mounted the little mountaineer, who curvetted and pranced proudly with his new burden.

Wishing to try his speed, I gave him a loose rein and off he shot at full speed, followed closely by my old Arab (who a few years before had won everything at the Madras Races and had been sold to Major-General Sir William Nicholson, for 740 *pagodas*, of whom I purchased him at Port Louis for about half that sum). Pursuing our course *ventre à terre* for about a mile, I was desirous of a little relaxation from this breathless speed, tugging and jerking at my snaffle-bridle to moderate our rapid movement. These operations only served to increase his headlong course, attended by various kicks behind and floundering plunges forward; when, almost exhausted by my vain efforts to restrain his impetuosity, the cord girths of the rough straw-stuffed saddle suddenly cracked asunder, and in an instant I lay extended on my back, with a shock that shook my heart to my breast, flat on the sandy soil over which we had so long been scouring.

The scene did not terminate with this disaster. I had scarcely time to extricate myself from my recumbent posture ere I saw my sleek, shining black steed attacking my old Arab with the fury of a little devil; they were both bolt upright on their hind legs, biting and pawing most gracefully. The negro soon slipped off the Arab, and *malgré* our united efforts the battle royal continued with a ferocity exceeding all belief, for several minutes. My Arab's nature was savage beyond expression; one day, whilst in the stable, I was gently patting his back when by some unaccountable impulse his eyes became fiery red, he seized me by the breast with his teeth and tore off my right nipple, and had I not taken shelter under the manger and laid perfectly quiet, he would certainly have destroyed me.

Another time, whilst my grenadier groom, Richardson, was cleaning him, he bit the man terrifically in several parts of his body, and having got him down, went on his knees to complete his conquest. The poor man, conscious of the ferocity of his antagonist, as his lust chance of escape, seized hold of the horse's lower lip between his teeth, and held on so tightly that the animal became suddenly as docile as a lamb. On another occasion, this same man was leading the Arab for me to mount, on the Champ de Mars, at Port Louis, when, bending down to brash off a white mark on the horse's knee, he was unexpectedly caught up by the waistband of his pantaloons, and the animal bounded off with him, throwing his head up and down as if he had an infant only between his teeth; he bore him at least a hundred yards in this manner, curvetting and galloping the whole time.

The grenadier was upwards of six foot high, and weighed 13 stone. The waistband of his pantaloons giving way after this short frolic, the man was released from, his perilous predicament, and strange to say the horse returned to the original position from whence he set off and allowed me to mount him without further trouble. I merely relate these little anecdotes to evince how formidable an antagonist little blackey had met with. The fight continued for nearly a quarter of an hour, when the youth and activity of the mountaineer appeared to prevail; the Arab turned tail, lashing out most fearfully in his mad progress as he was closely pursued by his vindictive foe, whose head was several times closely shaved by the Arab's strong heels.

They shortly reached a rock overhanging the sea, which washed its bold base 20 feet below; the Arab sprang off, plunging deeply in the waves, followed instantly by his terrible persecutor. When I arrived at the rock they were both swimming towards a sandy beach on the left side of the rocky promontory, the Arab many yards ahead, appearing to swim with much greater facility than the other. On touching the sand, he sprang on, and hastened to the spot where I stood, allowed me to mount him, and we set off full speed to escape from the little persevering tiger, who soon pursued us. I ensconced myself behind a small clump of trees, my charger trembling and snorting from fear and exertion, with his neck near the mane covered with a row of large round excrescences, some as large as my fist, caused by the severe bites he had received in the conflict.

In about a minute my new purchase came rushing at headlong speed towards our shelter, rose on his hind-legs, and pawing the air with his forefeet at length settled them on my knees, seizing the Arab's ears and biting most unmercifully. I now drew my sword, as my life was in absolute jeopardy, and struck several blows with the flat of the blade, but this produced no effect whatever; I then gave point, and thrusting it into the mountaineer's nose he retired a few paces, when the Arab reared and again attacked. Clinging to his mane, I preserved my seat. Both horses were now in nearly the position of the lion and the unicorn, as represented on the King's arms.

At this critical moment the negro came up, and catching the bridle of the loose nag he desisted from further violence, permitting the man to mount him with as much docility as if he had been just led from the stable. To my great satisfaction, his neck was as closely studded with large round lumps as the Arab's; he had also been severely punished by deep lacerations on the flanks and thighs, from the lusty heels of his opponent. I have seen a cavalry field-day of entire horses in India, when frequently 40 or 50 would rear on end and dismount their riders, whose legs and arms were sometimes broken in the fall, with dislocations of hips, etc., but I never witnessed so ferocious an encounter as that which occurred between my two horses.

Some few weeks after my arrival at St. Denis, I was compelled to part with the little mountaineer, as he became so vicious that the most expert rider was unhorsed in endeavouring to train him, as he either reared and fell back or would rush wildly to the nearest precipice and plunge headlong down, to the imminent hazard of the rider's life. So much for the fascination of a beautiful exterior. But all is delusion in this world of insanity; we all aspire to immortality, though clothed in mortal trammels!

A short time after this event I lost my command at St. Paul's, and a salary attached thereto of upwards of £200 *per annum,* by one of the most singular and unprecedented circumstances that ever involved a British officer in the mazes of diplomacy. Having received repeated orders and instructions from the Lieutenant-Governor of Bourbon (Colonel Keating) to seize all newly-imported slaves in the act of disembarking on the coast of my district, I successfully opposed this illicit trade, and at various periods captured between 40 and 50, for which active exertions I was thanked in public orders by the Lieutenant-Governor of the island. Soon after a proclamation appeared in the *Isle of France Gazette,* prohibiting all interference on the part of officers commanding stations with this traffic of the inhabitants, and that any future seizure of slaves should be attended by the expense of their maintenance falling on the captors.

This notification of the governor of the Mauritius, Mr. Townsend Farquhar, was transmitted me by Colonel Keating, with positive instructions to continue my unremitted endeavours for the suppression of the slave trade, for which he was responsible, as it was in direct opposition to the laws of the legitimate Government of England, and that no local colonial governor could be justified in conniving or acting inertly when this illicit traffic was carried on in the immediate precincts of any officer's command, and that though he was subordinate to Mr. Farquhar, he would still act according to his conscience, and the known laws of the British Government, by opposing every possible obstacle to the introduction of fresh importations of slaves into the island of Bourbon.

I instantly detected the difficulty of my situation, as disobedience to the orders of either power must eventually cause my dismission from command; I therefore resolutely came to the determination of supporting that authority sanctioned by the laws of the mother country, naturally concluding that the onus of opposition would rest with the Lieut.-Governor of Bourbon, by whose positive written orders I was fulfilling an imperative duty. About a week after these inconsistent and opposite instructions, a large brig and schooner appeared off the roadstead of St. Paul's, crowded with slaves, and I accordingly made arrangements for their capture, which I effected the same night. I pushed off from shore with four boats filled with forty soldiers of the 12th Regiment; it was perfectly calm, and after two hours' rowing over a distance of some seven or eight miles, we reached the vessels just as the slaves were lowered into boats for the purpose of being landed.

A few shots only from the brig, which fell harmlessly, was the extent of opposition offered, and, on ascending her sides, followed by my soldiers, I found the deck deserted, whilst Captain Read attacked the schooner as successfully. Having left a small party of men to retain possession of each vessel, I pursued the boats that were making off rapidly towards shore, and by our united exertions 80 slaves were seized; the remainder (nearly 200) were safely landed and immediately carried off by the inhabitants to their different estates. Having lodged and fed the miserable lacerated beings, whose legs and arms were ulcerated and bleeding from the pressure of the iron manacles by which they had been so long confined, I wrote off to the lieut.-governor, communicating the success of my enterprise, and for instructions how they were to be disposed of?

For ten days I waited anxiously for some information; at length I was directed to deliver them up to the proprietors, and that the expense of maintaining them during the interval of detention was to fall exclusively on myself. I accordingly assembled the slave merchants, desiring them to select the slaves belonging to them, giving me a receipt for the number consigned to each claimant, whose insolent smiles of successful villainy excited my indignation much more than the loss I had sustained in the maintenance of the unhappy victims of these mercenary planters. The following day I was directed by order from General Sir Alexander Campbell to join the headquarters of my regiment at St. Denis, without any comment or reference to the proceeding, and was accordingly relieved of my command by a junior major of the corps.

Sir Alexander was commander-in-chief of the forces on the two islands, and was of course compelled to act in the affair according to the suggestion of the governor, Mr. Farquhar, and my only consolation from Colonel Keating was that I should certainly be ultimately justified by the authorities at home for the honourable share I had taken in the transaction; but neither remuneration for my losses nor justification for my conduct ever solaced me for my disinterested exertions. Due performance of my duty being the exciting cause that actuated me on the occasion, I must have been insensible not to have felt, as every individual does, when labouring under the oppression of arbitrary power.

Four frigates arrived at the Isle of Bourbon in the name of Louis XVIII., bringing Bouvet de Lozier as governor; the same evening a French regiment landed and immediately relieved the guards of the 12th Regiment at the different posts, and before the expiration of two hours the whole French guards were so completely intoxicated with what they denominated "*le petit vin du pays*" (*alias arrack*) that *they* were rolling about in a mad state in front of their guard-rooms, abusing the English as *foûtres* and Louis XVIII. as a *vieux coquin*. We kept our men confined to barracks, to prevent collision with these inebriated fellows, and after giving a handsome dinner to the French officers, who considering it an indispensable etiquette to drink a glass of wine with every British officer who had invited them to take wine, some of them swallowed 20 or 30 bumpers ere the cloth was removed; the consequence may be naturally imagined, and four of our lads conveyed the Governor Bouvet de Lozier to the Government House in as glorious a state of intoxication as ever disgraced human nature.

The ensuing morning the 12th Regiment marched down to the beach, preparatory to embarkation; the French guards as we passed turned out, and were still so drunk that several of them levelled their pieces at our men, exclaiming "*Sacré, il faut tuer un anglais!*" and if they had, not a Frenchman would have been left to tell the tale, for in defiance of the most rigid discipline our men would certainly have rushed from the ranks and have bayoneted the whole guard. Fortunately their forbearance was not put to the test, and the embarkation took place without accident.

In the year 1817, towards the latter end of August, after 15 months' monotonous duty at Port Louis, Grand Port and Flacq, the three principal military stations on the island, we suddenly received orders to prepare for embarkation on three transports, to return to old England. Just before our march from Flacq, as I was one evening taking a solitary walk in the environs of the cantonment, I observed the summits of the distant mountains tinged with a fiery hue, and then the whole atmosphere in the direction of Port Louis became of a deep, glaring red colour. The whole regiment assembled to view this extraordinary phenomenon, which was attributed to the sudden eruption of a volcano; but the following morning intelligence was brought that an accidental conflagration had completely destroyed the town of Port Louis, and in a day or two after, when the regiment marched into the place, such a scene of melancholy desolation I never witnessed.

A complete ruin of smoking embers, with the tottering walls of 11,000 houses, which had been destroyed in one night, proved the fury of the devouring element. French claret was flowing in rivulets down the streets, from 10,000 pipes that had exploded, intermixed with casks of brandy. Soldiers and inhabitants were lying about promiscuously, actually dead drunk, with various mutilated bodies, arms and legs burnt to the very trunk, and some without heads. I never shall forget the horrid scene to the latest day of my existence.

The whole Champ de Mars was covered with tents, pitched for the purpose of sheltering the houseless, ruined inhabitants, who were roaming about in the wildest state of despair. The powder magazine, where 15,000 bands of gunpowder were deposited, was surrounded by burning houses; wet blankets were continually thrown against the door, and but for the indefatigable exertion of the troops, then in garrison, the whole town must have been blown to atoms with all the shipping in the harbour. At one time the door of the magazine was actually in flames. This dreadful calamity of explosion was, however, spared the poor inhabitants, who were already suffering the extreme of misery. So brilliant was the conflagration, that the illuminated atmosphere was distinctly seen from the Isle of Bourbon, at 90 miles' distance.

The evening previous to this unfortunate occurrence, the governor gave a splendid ball at the Government House, where nearly 300 beautiful young females were assembled from all quarters of the island, the majority of whom lost their superb dresses; this to the affluent may appear subject of little consequence, but to those who labour by the sweat of their brow for the good things of this life, the loss was severely felt, and years of economy were necessary to replace the finery. I have often observed ladies at the governor's balls whose dresses were estimated at 1,500 or 2,000 dollars each, yet the families of whom they formed a portion were by no means in affluent circumstances, and could ill afford to repurchase these splendid decorations.

Whilst the ruins of the town were still smoking and smouldering, the 12th Regiment embarked on three transports and proceeded on the long voyage to old England, touched at the Cape of Good Hope and reached St. Helena about the middle of September, 1817. The greatest man that ever the world produced was here confined as a State prisoner, Napoleon Bonaparte, Emperor of France, whose deeds are transmitted to posterity by such a multitude of excellent authors that the renown of Alexander, Caesar and all the ancient heroes is comparatively of trifling consideration to that of the conqueror of the civilized western world. The envious aristocrats may denominate him as a brigand and his troops robbers, but still they cannot detract from his merit as a great military hero and consummate politician; he paralysed the whole continent of Europe, and made England tremble so that the timidity of her government tarnished her glory for ever, in banishing her magnanimous foe to the solitary rock of St. Helena.

On our arrival the emperor was residing at Longwood, and we forwarded a request for the honour of an interview, and in reply the emperor appointed the following day for the officers of the 12th Regiment to be presented to him. Alas! we never had that honour, for as we were all dressed in our best and just landing, a note from General Montholm was delivered to the commanding officer, signifying that the emperor was so indisposed as to be incapable of receiving us. This did not prevent my taking a walk to Longwood, and from the entrance gate I observed this great man (in the common acceptation of the word) amusing himself at a billiard table, though I could not distinguish his features; this cursory view satisfied my curiosity and I reflected that I should not have been so anxious for such proximity had he been surrounded by his gallant army.

At dawn of day the ensuing morning our little fleet again sailed, anchored a few hours on arriving at Ascension, and after experiencing a severe gale of wind off the Western Isles, reached Portsmouth on the 11th Nov., 1817, and two days afterwards received orders to proceed to Ireland without landing in England. This was rather severe work after a three months' voyage; however, the regiment was transhipped into one large transport, from the three in which the passage from the

Isle of France was accomplished. In this huge hulk we lay nine weeks more at the Mother Bank off Portsmouth, detained by contrary winds and several tremendous gales, and did not arrive at Cork until the latter end of January, 1818.

The most deplorable part of a British soldier's life is certainly his long confinement on board transports; the misery and privations are indescribable. It is pretended that seasickness is of a salubrious nature; some strong constitutions may resist its effects, and others laugh at the deadly Sensations accompanying this malady. There have been many come under my own observation whom I have seen die under the agony of the most excruciating torments, especially two who fell victims to it the second day after our departure from the Mauritius, soldiers of the most robust and powerful frames—in a word, the most healthy-looking men in external appearance of any in the corps.

On landing at Cork we were at once marched off to Athlone, in the midst of winter and after 20 years' service in India and six months' imprisonment on board transports. This was a fearful trial of the constitutions of the poor soldiers, many of whom died on the road and others were deposited in hospitals, from whence they never escaped with life. Wading through miry roads, sleet, snow and rain for more than 100 miles, we reached the old town of Athlone the latter end of February. Here a Bond Street major-general, by name Buller, commanded the garrison. The regiment was thrice a week paraded for his inspection, waiting sometimes for two hours and upwards, with the snow driving in the men's faces, in heavy marching order on parade, when an *aide-de-camp* would dash up on a fine prancing horse, informing the commanding officer that the regiment might be dismissed, as the general was indisposed.

A repetition of this stale trick soon disgusted all the old wounded soldiers, and they applied to a man for their discharges, which, as they had completed their period of service, they were entitled to, so that in six months the corps consisted of a set of raw boys, just fresh from the plough. I never shall forget the first morning this major-general inspected the regiment. After riding down the line, he pompously exclaimed, "Thank God, I am once more among real soldiers; I never saw a steadier corps." This was quite ludicrous from a man whom we all knew never heard a shot fired in his life, except as adjutant of one of the regiments of Guards, when the men were practising at target exercise. He certainly had a martial, blustering air, and was a handsome man, nor is there a doubt if he had ever been seriously opposed to an enemy he would have evinced the characteristic animal courage of an Englishman.

Tired of the worrying parade scenes of this blustering would-be hero, I resolved to retire from the army, as in time of peace there is no prospect of promotion for those who are not intimately connected with the aristocrats.

Having obtained three months' leave of absence, I hastened to my paternal home, expecting at the decease of my father to succeed to our entailed estate of £1,500 *per annum*, which, with £1,000 ready money I had remitted my father from the Isle of France, the savings of 20 years' Indian service, and a handsome sum I brought home with me derived from the same source, I naturally imagined would secure the *otium cum dignitate* so beautifully alluded to in one of the odes of my friend Horace. Arriving *via* Cork at Bristol, I found my family elegantly housed in a mansion that cost my father at least £5,000, situated in Portland Square. He boasted largely of his banker's accounts, and handed me the expenditure cash account, which I glanced over and observed a flaming exposition of enormous household expenses to the amount of many thousand pounds; but the rent-roll was carefully withheld, and from motives of delicacy I abstained from all enquiry on this important subject.

Impressed with a full persuasion that all was *couleur de rose,* I resolved to keep my carriage, and asked for £200 to purchase horses. On this demand I observed a tremulous agitation and paleness on my father's countenance that struck me as remarkable, without affecting me with any presentiment that his affairs were not in so flourishing a state as his previous conversation had indicated. He replied that just at that moment he could not supply me, having certain vouchers that required immediate payment. I begged him not to inconvenience himself, as I had a considerable sum with me, which for the present could be appropriated to the exigency. His only answer was, "I deserve to be shot."

The following day he was seized with a paralytic stroke, and in three weeks was a corpse. Now the whole scene of his misfortunes and iniquity were revealed to me; in a word, he had levied a fine and suffered a recovery, by which the entailed estate had been disposed of some years previously, the amount of which had been squandered away in various speculations, and to crown his thoughtless folly, he had become security with the Marquis of Bute for my uncle, who was receiver-general for one of the counties. Having become deficient in his accounts, government seized his property, sold it for half of its real value and compelled the securities to make up the deficit; my father became, therefore, a ruined man. Fortunately he had provided handsomely for my three sisters, who were respectably married. My £1,000 had been drawn out of the navy three *per cents*, and aided in preserving him from the King's Bench, and I was left to commence my career in life *de novo*. Had it not been for the recollection of my children, I should certainly have terminated my existence. My remaining fund of £1,400 was all I possessed in the world.

A major's pay was not to be despised, and I once more rejoined my regiment at Athlone, depressed in mind and hopeless of promotion. Two years before, I had lodged £1,100 in the firm of a London banker, for the purchase of a lieut.-colonelcy, which fell vacant during my voyage from the Mauritius, and had been purchased by the honourable Major Lowther, brother to Lord Lonsdale. I appealed to the Horse Guards for justice. The reply to my humble application was an insulting letter from Sir Henry Torrens (then military secretary to the commander-in-chief), that his Royal Highness was not responsible to me for the officers he chose to promote.

Now, as there was a distinct regulation, framed by His Royal Highness the Duke of York, that no officer of the army should be purchased over by another provided his money was lodged, and that officer regularly returned for purchase in the Regimental Returns, which in both instances I had conformed, I waited personally on the duke to explain the injustice of my case.

He received me very affably, and on hearing my explanation exclaimed, "What! what! what! I never was informed of the affair before; I shall note it down and will see into it." He then made a memorandum and graciously bowed me away. I was afterwards informed that had His Royal Highness been aware that I was inclined to purchase a lieut.-colonelcy liable to half-pay, I should not have been superseded. This was all the satisfaction I was ever allowed for this insufferable injustice. How could a simple individual contend with the powerful interest of a man whose brother sent a dozen members to Parliament! I am of opinion that the poor duke even in this instance was absolutely compelled to break through his own regulations.

I therefore remained 16 years a major, I presume as a punishment for having claimed justice from those who basely infringed their own laws. I then for the first time discovered that both the army and navy were mere tools in the powerful hands of the aristocracy, and that the trade of religion was also equally subjected to their insatiate grasp. When misfortune and injustice assail us mortals, we then begin to analyse the conduct of men in power and draw inferences to their disadvantage.

But all moralising on this subject is absurd, for let the rankest democrat that ever existed be once placed in power and he will probably exceed in injustice and tyranny the actions of the more refined principled aristocrat. Where is the human being who will neglect the welfare of his friends and relations, when by favouring their interests he can form around him a grateful band of staunch adherents? *Humanum est errare* is a motto the spirit of which must ever prevail, and has been predominant ever since the creation of the world, if the actual human passions existed at the time that influence us in the present age.

I pass over three years of my melancholy existence, spent in garrison towns of Ireland, when, in October, 1820, the regiment embarked from Dublin for Liverpool, proceeded on to Manchester, and in the course of three months moved on to Gosport, from whence they embarked for Guernsey and Jersey. In these hospitable romantic little islands I remained upwards of two years, feasting, dancing and drilling—the usual routine, for a military man, in lazy times of peace. I shall ever recollect the friendly attentions of Admiral Sir James Sumarez and his family with sentiments of unaffected gratitude, and also those of the equally gallant and generous Sir Colin Halket, who commanded Jersey as major-general. I served upwards of a year in each.

In the latter end of September we were disagreeably surprised by an order to hold ourselves in readiness to proceed to the West Indies; a few days afterwards our destination was changed for the Rock of Gibraltar. To some of our officers this change was delightful; as to myself, I should have preferred the Isle of Jamaica, Barbadoes or any other of our settlements in the West Indies to the protracted monotonous residence of 10 or 12 years on the barren Rock of Gibraltar. The beginning of October we marched for Fort Cumberland, near Portsmouth, and from this gloomy, desolate station proceeded on the 11th November, 1823, to Portsmouth, and immediately embarked on board the fine vessels the *Ganges* (84) and *Superb* (74), commanded by Captains Brace and Sir Thomas Staines.

This day five years prior we had anchored at the Mother Bank in our three transports from the Mauritius. We sailed the following morning, and anchored in the Bay of Gibraltar on the 24th November, and on the 25th landed 700 stout fellows, the majority of whom were destined never to see their native country again. Fighting is really an agreeable amusement when compared to a lingering, miserable existence of 10 or 12 years in an unhealthy fortress; but more on this subject hereafter. The garrison consisted of five regiments of infantry and a battalion of artillery, with a proportion of engineer officers and sappers and miners, amounting in numerical strength to 4,500 effective men.

A description of the duties and amusements of one day on the Rock will suffice for a twenty years' residence there. In the morning 400 men for the different guards are paraded and marched off with colours and music; drill thrice a day, with an evening parade or field-day. Field officer visits the guards in the course of the morning and after 12 at night, forming a tedious excursion of six miles. At night he is accompanied by a sergeant on foot carrying a lamp, so that in a deluge of rain both are inevitably soaked to the skin. Courts martial, inspecting old buggy barrack furniture, and counting the dollars in the commissariat department frequently occupies him for several hours.

An invitation to dine at the convent or lieut.-governor's house and a ball given once or twice a year by the governor are the only recreations I am aware of for officers, except an evening's ride over the sandhills along the shore towards St. Roque, a town five miles distant from the Rock. We are such creatures of habit that a residence here has charms for many, and I have known officers quit the garrison with sentiments of the most unaffected regret and even exchange into another corps for the purpose of returning to it.

Some old French author asserts that *tous les goûts sont respectables*; it may be so, but I could never discover a single attractive pleasure to render Gibraltar a desirable place of residence, and may its lightning-blasted summits never again impress my mind with those solitary sensations of deep melancholy with which I have so often regarded them! For a field officer there certainly is no station in the British possessions where the duty is so arduous and disagreeable.

The yellow fever is also as radical a disease in the garrison as in any part of the West Indies; not a year passes without numerous subjects in each regiment being affected and dying of this species of plague, which once every five or six years concentrates its venom and carries off thousands of soldiers and inhabitants. I only remained two years on this detestable spot when, depots for regiments having been established in England, as senior major I was ordered home to take charge of this nucleus for the service companies. Selling my horses and furniture at one-third of their original cost, I embarked on a Danish brig, and in three weeks anchored in Falmouth harbour, proceeding thence per mail to Plymouth, where the four companies of the depot were forming.

Scarcely had I collected 200 of this untrained band when, in December, 1825, we were ordered to Ireland, embarked in a gale of wind, and in three days reached Cork harbour, from whence we proceeded in a steam-vessel to Middleton, where we disembarked and marched to Youghal, a dreary, dirty, abominable town on the sea-coast.

As the men were marching through the town, the poor girls with whom the cottages were swarming looked out of their half-formed doors crying, "Plase your honour, give us some of your men for husbands!" Although ragged and abounding in filth and vermin, yet the faces of these wretched beings were in many instances really beautiful; such misery as the peasantry of Ireland offers to view is unequalled in any other part of the universe. These cottage Venuses contrived to marry several of our undisciplined youths in the course of the three months the depot remained at Youghal, a species of heavy baggage that must inevitably encumber every regiment serving in old Erin.

One morning, as three of our subalterns were quietly taking their breakfast in one of the upper barrack rooms, a ball penetrated the window, passed over the table and lodged in the opposite wall. It must have been fired from a considerable distance, as immediate search was made for the detection of the perpetrators of this wanton outrage; but not a soul was discovered in the vicinity of the barrack square.

The generality of the Irish peasantry are good, honest, cheerful creatures; there are, however, amongst them some of a most demoniacal, ferocious nature—indeed this observation may apply to all countries; but I have never heard of, or seen such deliberate assassins, such cool, determined murderers as the Irish, bravely dying for their offences with a malicious, scornful smile on the countenance. I am only surprised that more instances of revenge do not occur, when the degraded state of the nation is considered; their situation is penniless and hopeless, crowds of famishing children barefooted in the midst of winter, the parents ragged and all but naked, living within four mud walls covered with turf, amidst pigs, poultry, cows, and all sleeping together on a mass of straw, moss, or heather, the room or hovel filled with smoke to an absolute degree of suffocation, and their food consisting each day of boiled potatoes mixed with buttermilk.

The lords, the satellites of government, the clergy live in luxury, careless of these outrages to humanity and morality, and nothing but the despair of the populace and the terrible effects of a bloody exterminating revolution will bring them to their senses. "Babblers, we fear you not," exclaim these hereditary legislators; "we have the army, navy, great landholders and holders of funds under our dominion, and with the powerful aid of these engines we defy your armless bands." *Mais, nous verrons*, hunger and necessity will ultimately prove irresistible.

In February, 1826, the depot proceeded to the picturesque town of Fermoy, where the still-hunting duty prevailed to a disgusting degree; requisitions for small parties of men were daily made by the gangers, which generally terminated in the seizure of spirits and stills. One morning a man in a shabby-genteel dress called on me, and in a mysterious, half-communicative manner signified that a still was working in the mountains near Lismore, about ten miles from Fermoy, that he was a gauger and required an officer and six men to accompany him in order to effect the seizure. Having produced his authority from the magistrates, I replied that so small a number of men commanded by an officer was a most unusual circumstance, and positively refused the party unless a sergeant, corporal and twelve men were allowed to accompany him. He objected on account of the expense to government, assuring me that six men were amply sufficient to accomplish the object in view.

At length, after a warm discussion, I succeeded in the proposed augmentation of force, and my own son commanded the party. In the afternoon of the same day they marched off accompanied by the ganger, and the following morning about three o'clock, after a fatiguing journey, reached the miserable hovel that contained the still, which was briskly working at the time. Having upset all the tubs and casks that contained the spirits, a cart was procured and the still placed thereon. Proceeding slowly down the mountain, the party entered a deep ravine between two lofty hills clothed with wood, through which the road led for some distance.

As they proceeded along this dangerous pass large bodies of the peasantry were distinguished on the eminences, on both sides, and soon showered down stones from their advantageous positions on the soldiers below, several of whom were struck down, and finally 11 of them and the officer were seriously injured. Confident in the strength of numerical superiority, amounting to several thousands, the peasantry made a rush at the cart, which they captured and bore off in triumph. The soldiers, still pressed, exclaimed, "For God's sake let us fire or we shall all be killed!"

A stone at this instant striking the officer on the breast with such violence as to fell him to the earth, he reluctantly gave the fatal word "Fire!" and several of the peasantry fell. The party continued retreating and firing by files, closely pursued. Having gained a small bridge over a river, with a gate on each side, they closed and barricaded the gate nearest the populace, keeping up a brisk fire from the bridge; they however collected in large bodies above and below, endeavouring to pass the fords of the river.

As all the ammunition was expended and four of the soldiers so badly injured as to be incapable of marching, a passing car was immediately taken possession of, and the wounded men thus conveyed by a different road from that by which the party had arrived. This manoeuvre preserved them from destruction, as the peasantry had crossed the river and completely blockaded the passage of the road by which it was expected the party would have returned to quarters.

At seven o'clock that evening I inspected this small force after their return to Fermoy. Not a man of them had escaped uninjured; all their clothing was literally torn to atoms, the muskets generally indented with deep bruises, and nine men placed in hospital. The officer was severely wounded in the forehead, with a serious swollen black contusion on his breast, which confined him to his room for many days. The gauger had escaped, but was not heard of until the next morning, when he made his appearance, offering a very lame excuse for quitting the party. I was uncharitable enough to suspect him of some confederacy or collusion with the peasantry, and had the six men proceeded on the expedition, as originally intended, I am persuaded they would have fallen a sacrifice to the fury of these lawless people.

An investigation of this affair was instituted and the military exonerated from all blame. It appeared that between 30 and 40 of these oppressed cottagers had suffered in the skirmish, which from all accounts was a premeditated plan to entrap the raw recruits. It was now considered judicious to remove the depot, as the surrounding country was highly exasperated at this unfortunate massacre; we were accordingly ordered to Bantry, where we arrived about a month afterwards. The Bay, Scattery Island, and the barren, rocky mountains around, presented one of the wildest, most romantic, and beautiful scenes I ever met with in any part of the world. Provisions of all descriptions so remarkably cheap that with an income of £100 *per annum* any single man might live in absolute luxury. I contracted with a butcher for the supply of the troops, at three-halfpence a pound for beef, and the choice pieces might be obtained at twopence.

Now mark the unaccountable inconsistence of us human beings; although this extreme moderate demand for the necessaries to support existence was admitted, yet a large family was emigrating from Bantry to France from motives of economy. I question if the most secluded spot in the latter country can produce anything half so reasonable in any shape as the articles vended at Bantry. On enquiry I found that this economising family, who had never yet quitted the county of Kerry, were induced to adopt this measure from the perusal of some book in which an exaggerated description of Normandy had fascinated them into a persuasion that they might keep their carriage on an income of £300 a year; they tried the experiment, found it fallacious, and, I understand, returned again to their rural abode depressed in spirits and reduced in income.

I could describe the magic residence of Colonel White, brother of Lord Bantry, on the margin of the eastern boundary of the bay, called Glengariff, and all its adjacent wild romantic beauties, was I not fully aware that ninety-nine out of a hundred readers pass over such trash as unworthy of perusal; indeed, one slight well-designed picture gives more real information than the most elaborate wordy description could possibly convey.

I lodged at a marine half-pay officer's cottage, about three miles from Bantry. A whole squad of young children with dependents of all descriptions devoured the substance of this poor fellow, who, shortly after my departure from Inchiclough (the name of his residence) was consigned to the gloomy precincts of a gaol. The beggars who daily passed this dwelling were grateful and satisfied with a few potatoes for alms, but the constant succession of these wandering wretches greatly diminished the resources of the marine officer, who was as thoughtless and indifferent on the subject of economy as the major part of his countrymen.

After three months' residence at this retired spot the depot moved to Kinsale, from thence to Cork, Buttevant, then to Longford, and ultimately to Boyle, where an event transpired of such insufferable injustice, resorted to by a man. high in official authority, that I cannot refrain from dedicating a few lines to the subject. A young man, by name Butler, of prepossessing appearance and eccentric habits almost approaching insanity, had joined the depot at Longford, a few months after our arrival at Boyle. I had detached the senior captains to different outposts when an order arrived from the Horse Guards for a captain and 30 men to proceed forthwith to Cork for embarkation tor Gibraltar, to join the service companies at that station.

Of course Captain Butler was ordered off, being the only captain at headquarters. Now I did not know that he was a *protégé* of the adjutant-general, Sir Henry Torrens; however, three or four days after his departure I was suddenly electrified by an order from this great despot for the commanding officer of the depot to proceed forthwith to London and report himself to the adjutant-general and immediately embark for Gibraltar.

The next day I set off *via* Dublin and Liverpool, reaching London in three days, leaving my goods and chattels to the mercy of chance and some friends for their future destination. Having reported myself at the Horse Guards and solicited an audience at the adjutant-general's office, I was soon introduced to the great man, Sir Henry Torrens, who received me with that stately *hauteur* so peculiar to those in a little brief authority. On explaining the reason of my arrival in London his brow was immediately clouded with a sinister frown, and he remarked that he had no *idea of any commanding officer playing with the service* by ordering young men who had only just joined the depot on foreign service. I replied that Captain Butler was the only officer present at headquarters when the order arrived for the party to proceed forthwith, and that I was not conscious in any one instance of my military career of 30 years of ever playing with the service; that I had honestly performed my duty and only regretted that it should have interfered with his arrangements.

He hastily told me to hold my tongue, adding, "I don't care for your explanations, you shall be off to Gibraltar by the first ship."

"I am ready, sir, to proceed, but cannot admit that I have *played with* the service, and if you consider my conduct in that light I must beg the usual appeal to a court martial to either substantiate or acquit me of this serious accusation."

"I don't care, sir, I don't care, you may get about your business and do as you like."

"Sir Henry, this a species of treatment I cannot tamely submit to," I was proceeding in my observation, when he rang the bell and commanded the attendant to show me the door. I never was so indignant, to be thus used by a man who had been no longer in the service than myself, and merely for performing my duty without partiality, favour, or affection. I waited on Lord Hill, who desired me to commit the whole transaction to paper and forward it direct to him. Having done so, I attended his levee, and on the staircase met Sir Henry Torrens, who cast on me a look that must have petrified me had his countenance been possessed of the attributes of Medusa. Lord Hill expressed himself in a mild, gentlemanly manner on the occasion, regretting the occurrence; however, as the order had been given I must proceed to Gibraltar.

I then applied for three months' leave of absence to arrange my affairs and endeavour to dispose of my commissions advantageously, resolving no longer to submit to wanton insults from any official character. As I did not succeed in this plan, I once more embarked for the regiment. A fine steam-packet of 800 tons received me on board at the Tower, and in five days, touching at Lisbon and Cadiz, I landed at Gibraltar the beginning of September, 1828, and assumed the command of the old 12th. Scarcely had I arrived when strong indications of an unhealthy season were manifested by offensive exhalations from the various drains and a stationary white cloud crowning the summit of the Rock, which even a strong easterly wind failed to remove.

The heat in the garrison was excessive, attended by a close, confined state of the atmosphere, creating an indescribable sensation of suffocation. The rank seaweed on the shore emitted an effluvium disgusting to the olfactory nerves, and everyone complained of a certain supineness or lassitude affecting the whole corporeal system; nor was I exempt from the prevailing feeling, which rendered me incapable of my usual energy of mind and activity of body.

On the 5th September, 1828, a man of the 12th was violently affected by fever and died next day, exhibiting a corpse as yellow as gold, which, though no uncommon occurrence at this period of the year, as many fall victims to this disease annually, yet it was deemed expedient to encamp the 12th Regiment on the neutral ground the following day, when another soldier was affected, sent in to the naval hospital and died in 24 hours. He had been accustomed to frequent that part of the town where the former man had contracted the fever, both of them having associated with girls of the town residing close to Prince Charles Edward's Wall, in No. 24 district.

For ten days subsequent to these events the 12th Regiment performed camp duties on the neutral ground without affording any guards for the town, and were completely free from any fresh case of fever; however, as numerous patients were sent into the naval hospital from the 42nd and 43rd Regiments, from which the town guards were selected, and who still occupied the Casemate Barracks within the walls of the fortress, these corps were directed to encamp close to the 12th Regiment, when the three corps mutually and equally participated in all the requisite duties, both town and camp.

The very first guards the three corps mutually and equally participated in all the convent, provost and main guard; 20 out of the 60 men were the same day seized with the epidemic and conveyed to the hospital. I shall never forget one fine young fellow of the grenadiers, 6ft. 2in. high, about 19 years of age, ruddy complexion, and healthy appearance, who, on being affected with a pain in the loins, came to my tent and with tears in his eyes begged not to be conveyed to the naval hospital, as he should certainly die and leave his aged mother destitute of all support. The orders were positive, which I temperately explained, that all patients were immediately to be taken there. His only remark was "Then I am a dead man."

In 48 hours the poor fellow had ceased to exist. Funeral processions were now seen passing from the town to the burial-place on the neutral ground from morn to night; 70, 80, and sometimes 100 bodies were thrown into the long trenches dug for their reception, and as the camp was within ten yards of this indiscriminate cemetery, the continued melancholy scene, instead of producing a serious effect on the minds of those who had escaped the malady, became in a short time a subject of mirth, and a laughable speculation of insurance of lives for a week was entered into by several gay Lotharios.

As we were one afternoon sitting down to dinner a dead-cart passed by the marquee, and on enquiry who the occupant was, it proved to be our cook, who had just prepared the dinner and instantly fell dead, to the no small annoyance of our gastronomers, as we were next day in great tribulation for a successor and were served with a very indifferent meal. An officer of one of the corps having died of the fever, a fine handsome young fellow, an assistant surgeon of the 73rd, chose to wrap himself up in the cloak in which the deceased had expired and sleep near the corpse the whole night, but this foolhardy display of courage was punished most seriously, for on rising the following morning he was affected with the usual symptoms of fever, which, in a few hours, put an end to his short existence.

Three weeks had now elapsed, and the mortality increased daily, when a transport laden with medical men from England arrived, amongst whom were doctors Pym and Barry, who vaunted much of their abilities in arresting the progress of the disease; it would be superfluous to describe the nostrums and absurd experiments resorted to for this enviable purpose; though they did not succeed, they still attained the principal objects of their hazardous voyage and exposure to the climate, being ultimately knighted for their philanthropic exertions.

Three French doctors also traversed Spain from Paris, the principal, named Chervin, who certainly exposed himself in a most extraordinary manner to ascertain the exact nature of the malady; he not only swallowed the black vomit of several of the patients but also inoculated himself, which last experiment affected him; in this state he courageously directed the remedies necessary on the occasion and recovered. His prescriptions were afterwards adopted by our faculty and eminently tended to alleviate the sufferings and preserve many of the patients. It was generally rumoured that Mons. Chervin contributed more powerfully to eradicate the disease than any doctor on the Rock; in fact, he was thoroughly acquainted with it, having visited the islands of the West Indies and almost every part of the globe where fevers prevailed, thus perfecting his knowledge by dear experience. The lieut.-governor, Sir George Don, highly approved of the fearless exertions of this truly humane Frenchman, expressed in orders on the departure of Mons. Chervin from the garrison. This was all he obtained from the English Government for a journey of nearly 2,000 miles and exposing his life in every possible manner to the dreadful effects of the epidemic fever.

One morning the armourer of the 12th Regiment applied for leave to enter the garrison, as his wife, who was assisting a lady, had contracted the disease. I endeavoured to dissuade him from the attempt, as he could do no good and would inevitably fall a martyr to the disease if he came in contact with his wife. My representations were fruitless; he persisted, proceeded into the town, and in 48 hours fell a victim to his affection, his wife dying a few hours before him. The men selected to attend the patients in the naval hospital died so rapidly, that at length no volunteers offered themselves for this service, as the employment was attended by certain death. Twenty-three soldiers who had acted as orderlies in the hospital ceased to exist in the course of three weeks, and the other regiments were equally unfortunate.

A fine handsome young officer of the 12th, named Werge, had been amusing himself on the neutral ground at a game of cricket, when he suddenly complained of a violent pain in the small of his back, the usual forerunner of the epidemic. I advised him to remain in camp, but he consulted other and younger friends and proceeded to hospital. In extreme excitement he returned to the neutral ground the following day, through a heavy shower of rain, saying he would not die in that pest-house. When I saw him he was pale and cadaverous, but complained of no particular local pain; however, in the afternoon, he was again conveyed to the hospital and next day was buried. I am persuaded if this naturally healthy young man had remained in camp he would have survived, as many others who took this precaution actually did.

On mustering the regiment on the 24th November, 1828, Lieutenant Forsteen, of the 12th, fell out of the ranks with customary symptoms of violent pain in the small of the back, his horse was brought and he chose to ride into the garrison in spite of all advice; he was in hospital only three days, the black vomit came on, and he soon followed his companions to the grave. The fate of this young man had been long anticipated, as he was in the constant habit of frequenting the town and lounging about in the various shops situated in the very centre of the malaria; remonstrances were fruitless, as he only laughed and joked on the subject, and out of sheer bravado would challenge the officers to accompany him to the scene of desolation. *Telle est la nature humaine.*

The field officers on the neutral ground soon became all indisposed except two, thus I was compelled to sleep in the fortress every other night on duty as field officer of the day. I consequently represented this incessant fatigue and exposure as beyond the strength of men past the meridian of life. About nine miles were to be traversed in the course of the day, under a burning sun, and nearly the same distance at 12 o'clock at night to visit the different guards stationed in every part of the garrison, and as there was only one field officer, the whole length of the Rock, the neutral ground, and Catalan Bay were all included in his tour. The lieut.-governor, Sir George Don, immediately appointed several of the senior captains to act as field officers, and candidly acknowledged the justice of my statement.

An order existed that every field officer should visit the hospital at least once a week. I, of course, complied with the regulation; however, when the epidemic was at its height, our surgeon, Mr. Amiel, informed me that they had ceased this tour of duty, as several had been affected by the fever immediately after their visit. As I was conversing with him in the ward amidst the dying and the dead, one of our soldiers was brought in from the neutral ground as a patient; he, however, stoutly declared that he had nothing the matter with him and would not be detained in that pest-house. "Look at me, colonel," said he, "I am as well as any man in the regiment;" and, according to my superficial observation, he certainly appeared in perfect health.

The surgeon looked closely at his eyes, and then whispered to me, "The man is under great excitement and has every symptom of the fever about him, and in my opinion has but a very short period to live." I then quietly told the man to remain a few hours in hospital, when, if he was really not affected by the disease he should return to his duty. He became outrageous, exclaiming he would be damned if he would be sent to hospital for nothing, and in struggling with the orderlies to escape he suddenly tell dead on the floor. Mr. Amiel told me that this man was not a solitary instance of similar incredulity of patients who were actually labouring under the severest symptoms of fever. Having passed the beds of nearly 200 men and spoken kindly to those free from delirium, I came to the hospital sergeant, who, after three weeks of constant attendance on the sick, had been suddenly seized with fever and nausea as he was in the act of holding a basin to receive the black vomit of one of the patients; he spoke cheerfully, expressing strong hopes of recovery, he was, however, a corpse the following day; in him we lost an excellent clerk and a good soldier.

I certainly never experienced more melancholy sensations than in my weekly visits to inspect the state of the hospital; such groans, shrieks, and dying lamentations must have affected the . most obdurate heart., independent of any little personal tremors, that might have agitated the sensitive frame of the visitor. Whenever I quitted this scene of annihilation I was invariably affected with a dizziness in the head and a sense of suffocation of which I was not clear for many hours after.

Sir George Don now issued an order for field officers to discontinue their weekly inspection of the hospital until the virulence of the epidemic had abated. Poor old man, he was upwards of 80 years old, yet he regularly came to the neutral ground twice a week, from his cottage at the south end of the Rock, for the purpose of assembling the senior officers of the regiments and hearing their reports on the actual state of the corps. He now determined to erect temporary sheds on the neutral ground for the reception of the convalescents, and several immense buildings of some hundred feet in length and forty or fifty feet in breadth were soon completed, into which all the patients who had partially recovered were immediately placed.

The advantage of this arrangement was soon obvious, as scarcely any relapses took place, which was continually the case when they were left in the hospital. Having appointed another hospital sergeant to replace poor Butler, he was shortly seized with fever, and in this state escaped from the ward in which he had been placed by direction of the surgeon. Sergeant Edge, the man in question, was sedulously sought for in all quarters for two days without being discovered.

On the third morning after his disappearance, as the corpse of an officer of one of the other regiments was taken to the burial-ground for interment. Sergeant Edge was found lying between the mounds of earth thrown up on lieutenants Werge and Forsteen's graves in a perfect state of nudity; the fever had left him he conversed rationally, but would have died there of sheer exhaustion had he not been thus fortunately discovered. He could give no account of his reasons for hiding himself in this situation, except that the two officers between whose graves he had ensconced himself had always treated him kindly, and that he was desirous of being. interred near them. He was taken to the sheds and speedily recovered, when he resumed his duties as hospital sergeant.

I will now relate one instance of female devotion during this horrid desolating epidemic. A beautiful young Spanish lady became deeply enamoured of one of the English officers, and was heard frequently to declare that she would not survive him if he died. He was at length attacked by the contagion, being attended by her to his expiring moments. His body was conveyed to the usual cemetery for the officers. During this interval she had climbed a high part of the Rock, and, on the first volley of firearms denoting the interment of her lover, she precipitated herself headlong from the dizzy height and was literally dashed to atoms. She was found near Catalan Bay with almost every bone in her body fractured, the leg and thigh bones protruding shockingly from the flesh in pointed splinters. After such devotion who will question woman's love?

The dead-carts were continually parading the streets of the town to receive the corpses, which were interred without any ceremony. To avoid this contamination, a wealthy Jew had secreted ten bodies of his persuasion in a large loft, in consequence of which the precincts of his habitation became absolutely doubly pestiferous from the sickening odours encircling it. The town major was soon informed of this abomination, and instantly despatched a party of police for the purpose of removing the nuisance.

The Jews, however, resisted this authority; the town major was therefore compelled to proceed with a party of the military, when ten bodies in a most putrid state of decomposition were deposited in a cart and conveyed to the usual cemetery; so offensive was the effluvia of these carcases, that it caused the immediate deaths of two soldiers and one policeman. Scarcely a family in Gibraltar escaped the direful effects of this desolating scourge; in about six weeks from its commencement upwards of 4,000 bodies were interred in the long trenches on the neutral ground. Six regiments were then serving in the garrison, one of which (numerically) was swept from the face of the earth, *id est*, 800 men perished, including officers from the different corps.

One morning I met Colonel Payne, of the artillery, who had remained in the town contrary to the advice of his friends; he told me that the fever had neither affected him nor any of his family, although a month had expired since its first breaking out. I remarked that he might not escape before its termination, and advanced several arguments to induce him to encamp, assuring him that I had never slept in the fortress (which my tour of duty compelled me to do about ever third night) without returning to camp with a violent headache and excessive lassitude. He laughed at what he termed my prejudice, persisting that there was no more danger in the town than on the neutral ground. "*Nous verrons, mon ami*," was my reply, and I trotted off on my charger to complete my inspection of the guards.

A few days afterwards he and part of his family were attacked and in the space of 48 hours his body was borne to the officers' burial-ground. It would fill a thousand sheets of paper to recount all the tragical events and scenes of this lamentable scourge. Wherever a common sewer conducted the filth of the town to the sea, there the most inveterate fever appeared to prevail. The governor's chaplain resided in the proximity of one of these, and in a few hours breathed his last. There was one horror amidst this desolating ravage that merits notice.

In passing near the long trenches on the neutral ground formed for the reception of the dead, I one day observed the earth in motion, and on a nearer approach, discovered the hands of a feeble old woman, endeavouring to drag herself from the trench. I immediately procured assistance from our pioneers, and she was immediately withdrawn from this living Golgotha. She had been interred the preceding evening, and the earth having only partially covered her, she had, contrary to all expectation, awoke from her trance just at the time of my passing by. She was taken to hospital, and, strange to relate, recovered and became quite a healthy woman; she was about 50 years of age, and previous to her burial had appeared for several hours in a perfectly inanimate state.

Several instances of this nature occurred during the two months the fever prevailed, and there is no doubt many, in the hurry, confusion and terror that affected the inhabitants, were actually interred in a living state. Sir George Don, lieut.-governor and general in the army came from his cottage, in the southern part of the Rock, to the neutral ground thrice a week in his carriage, passing through some of the most unhealthy parts of the town, yet he escaped the fever although in his 82nd year. He could read the smallest print without spectacles, and a more active, indefatigable old gentleman never existed; in fact, Gibraltar owes all the beauties it possesses to his ingenuity and rage for improvement, which ultimately embellished the most sterile sand and rock with flowers and shrubs of infinite variety and beauty.

He frequently observed that nothing but "Doctor Frost" (alluding to the snow-capped mountains seen in Spain from Gibraltar) would eradicate the fever; and certainly no human efforts affected any change until the latter end of November, when the distant mountains became covered with snow, and from that period the epidemic gradually subsided, until the 10th December, 1828, after which no fresh cases were introduced into hospital and those already suffering soon resumed their wonted health.

Having succeeded to the lieut.-colonelcy of the regiment, after a service of 34 years, I began to reflect that at the age of 50 man is more adapted to the ease and tranquillity of retirement then the harassing and fatiguing duties of military life; I consequently obtained leave of absence, and soon bade *adieu* to that hot-bed of vice, filth and disease, the barren Rock of Gibraltar.

Memoirs of George Elers

Contents

Gazetted to the 90th Regiment	241
Joins His Regiment at Newport	244
Arrival at the Cape	251
Return to India	261
To Seringapatam	274
A Dangerous Journey	285
Gets His Captaincy	296
Lord Wellesley	305
News of Trafalgar and Austerlitz	321

CHAPTER 1

Gazetted to the 90th Regiment

My poor mother had for many winters suffered very severely from asthma, and each winter it grew worse. The misfortunes of my father, added to the separation from her two children, I think, hastened her death. She died one evening after being confined to her bed for about a week. This was about the middle of December, 1795. You may imagine my feelings, left alone by myself, my father and two brothers absent, no one but the three servants with me—the faithful James Pearson, his wife, my mother's maid, and the cook. They (the females) were quite worn out by their attendance, and by a desperate effort I resolved to pass that night in sitting up in the same room with my poor dead mother as the last mark of my respect to her.

My mother was buried in the vault of her family at Bromley, where her brother, John Debonnaire, was placed the September preceding. I wrote to my brother, who was then at Shrewsbury, and he came up to my mother's funeral. My aunt and cousin, the Debonnaires, were very kind to us during this melancholy period, and Miss Debonnaire,[1] with the assistance of a Mr. Hutchinson, a worthy, good man, notwithstanding that he was a lawyer by profession, was my mother's trustee. He arranged the disposal of the lease and furniture of the house, as also of my mother's diamonds, the produce of which was to be divided among us three children.

We were shamefully cheated with respect to the jewels. As a proof, there were three jewellers appointed to value the diamonds and trinkets. It so happened that a bracelet containing my father's picture, set round with sixty brilliants, a most exquisite painting by the famous Smart, was valued at ten guineas only. My brother expressed a wish

---
1. 'My aunt'—*i.e.,* Ann, née Tennant, wife of John Debonnaire; and 'cousin,' their daughter Anne, who married William Tennant, of little Aston Hall, County Stafford.

to have this picture and bought it in. Many years after, on the death of my brother, this picture came into my possession, and I found that the diamonds were worth four times that amount If, therefore, this one article of small value was so far underestimated, how much must we have lost upon earrings, necklace, etc., which were worth much more? I was between eighteen and nineteen when I lost my mother, and the little property I acquired by that sad event I could not receive until I was of age. The same kind friend who procured my brother his commission procured me one also through Mr. Greenwood, the army agent.

When our house was disposed of, I had an introduction to an old lady of the name of Leigh, who had a neat, small house in Store Street, Bedford Square. She resided with her unmarried daughter, an old maid. With these ladies I lodged until the month of April. I used to breakfast with them, and I had an invitation from my kind friend Mr. Hutchinson to dine with his family and pass my time with them whenever I was disengaged. In those days, although seventy years of age, he could drink his wine and enjoy the company of young people, and his wife was just as good-humoured as himself. They had three daughters; one a decided old maid, the second about thirty-two, and the youngest about twenty-eight I used to ride about the town with the ladies in the morning, and played cards with them in the evening, generally getting home to Store Street by midnight.

I was taught to expect that I should see my name in the *Gazette* very shortly, when to my great joy one Saturday in the month of March I saw: 'George Elers, gent., to be Ensign without purchase in the 90th Regiment.' I was highly pleased, and read it over and over again—the first time I ever saw my name in print. I dare say there are many old officers who, if they confessed the truth, once felt as I did on a similar occasion. It was the fashion in those days to be dressed in the evening at the theatres in shoes and stockings and a cocked hat. I was already provided with the hat, and, as you may suppose, I lost no time in mounting the cockade and a rosette for my hair. Colonel Graham was our colonel; he raised the corps, became Lord Lynedoch, and is still alive.

The regiment was stationed in the West Indies. I had not been a fortnight an Ensign when I had the offer of a lieutenancy in the 12th Regiment under Colonel William Picton, one of the Minden heroes. The two lieutenant-colonels were Henry Hervey Aston and Thomas Grey, the former about thirty-five, the latter about twenty-four. They were two of the handsomest men I ever saw, particularly Aston, who was so celebrated as a man of *ton* and fashion. Grey[2] was the son of General Sir Charles Grey, and brother to the statesman, Earl Grey. I purchased this commission, and gave £100 above the regulated price; but it was a great step to get so early, and, besides, I had the advantage of a most particular introduction to Colonel Aston, who, until his lamented death, ever treated me like a father.

My outfit cost me about £300. I had nothing to do but order what I wanted, and the bills were sent in to Mr. Hutchinson, who paid them. No officer, with the exception of Colonel Aston, had such a kit. I had six regimental jackets, besides dress-coats, great-coat, shirts about twelve dozen, and everything in the same proportion.

My lieutenancy was dated April 12, 1796. I waited upon my colonel, who at that time was living at Nerot's Hotel, King Street, St. James's. I was aware, even in those days, of the effect of first impressions, and took great pains to be dressed well on my first appearance before him. His features and fine figure I knew perfectly by sight. I was dressed in black coat and waistcoat, white worsted pantaloons, and neat Hessian half-boots, with a crape hat-band. I was ushered into his dressing-room, where he was putting the last finish to his toilet. I told him who I was. He shook me by the hand, eyed me most critically from head to foot, said I *turned out well*, and finished by asking me the name of my tailor.

I was ashamed to confess it was an obscure one by the name of Weston, then not known, but afterwards the celebrated *artiste* for the Prince of Wales. He recommended me strongly to join my regiment without delay, adding: 'I shall be down myself in a day or two, and I should wish you to learn a little of your duty before we embark for the East Indies, to which place we are under orders.' I saw him step into his curricle with all the grace of an Apollo; he once more shook me by the hand, and told me I should make a very fair light infantryman, and wished me good-morning.

---

2. No 'Thomas Grey' is to be found in the 'Peerage' sub 'Earl Grey;' possibly it is an error for 'William.'

CHAPTER 2

Joins His Regiment at Newport

In a very few days, by the kind assistance of one of my fair friends, Miss N. Hutchinson, everything was packed up in my trunks—canteens and camp equipage, with various letters of introduction and recommendation, among others one from Lady Burnaby to Rear-Admiral Rainier, commanding the Indian Fleet; Sir William Burnaby, an old post-captain, was my brother Edward's godfather, and a very old friend of my father's. Lady Burnaby's sister, a Miss Molyneux, afterwards was married to my first cousin, Dr. William Colston, who is now living, and has the excellent living of West Lydford, Somersetshire, (as at time of first publication).

I started by one of the Gosport coaches, and arrived at the Indian Arms at Gosport in the evening. The inn was all bustle and confusion—plenty of officers, like myself, on the route to join their respective regiments. My regiment was stationed at Newport, Isle of Wight.

The next morning I was much disgusted at the dirty bed and room I had been put into; the chambermaid, I conclude, saw that I was a young Johnny Raw, and that anything would do for such a young one as me. I proceeded to Cowes, hired a chaise, and was put down at the Bugle. I inquired for the regiment, and was told that they were at exercise a short distance out of town. I strolled out to them, when I saw the regiment formed into square and a punishment taking place. I got into conversation with a handsome young officer I had seen in London with some friends of mine a few days before, though I then did not know who he was. He proved to be the Hon. John Meade, a son of the Earl of Clanwilliam.

The punishment over, the commanding officer gave the word: 'Attention! Numbers four, five, six, will stand fast. Remaining companies will wheel back four paces. Right about face! Quick march!' And then, as if by magic, the regiment was formed into open column of companies. The band struck up, the word 'Quick march!' was given, and I, by the side of my honourable friend, marched into Newport, keeping the step like an old soldier instead of a raw recruit. I shall never forget the shrillness of the fifes, the effect of the hollow, martial sounds of the drums which played, and on their ceasing at intervals being taken up by the band. I literally trod on air.

The battalion having been dismissed, my new friend the Honourable introduced me to all the officers, I having previously told him my name and rank. The officers crowded round me, and dear old Jack Picton, the major, came up to me, shook me by the hand, and said: 'You will, of course, join us at our mess at five o'clock?' Next to him came up our paymaster and second. Captain Allen, together with the captain of grenadiers, Captain Craigie. All of these were the oldest veterans in the service, and had served with the regiment at the siege of Gibraltar. I shall never forget their fine martial figures and swarthy complexions.

Major Picton was the very image of his gallant brother. Sir Thomas, who fell at Waterloo, though not so tall—a compact, strong man of about forty years of age, and in height about 5 feet 9 inches. I dined at the mess, and notwithstanding that I drank wine with all the officers who were drinking wine, I did not get tipsy. I was sufficiently on my guard not to make a fool of myself on my first *entrée*. I observed that the officers who drank wine were chiefly the senior ones, and that the subalterns, chiefly very young men and almost all young Irish officers, had lately joined from Irish regiments reduced of very high number—I really think from a regiment numbering as high as 130.

In the course of two or three days Colonel Aston joined the regiment, and redeemed his promise to me, for I was immediately appointed to the light infantry company. I was obliged to send up to London for a sabre and wings instead of epaulettes, and lots of narrow gold lace for my scarlet waistcoat. We wore blue pantaloons edged with scarlet, hats covered over with the finest black ostrich feathers, with a stand-up feather composed of red and black. They looked very handsome, but were expensive, particularly when those who could afford it had about three times the quantity they needed to wear. A good hard shower of rain soon took their smartness off, but they were only adopted by ourselves and the 80th Regiment expressly for the East Indies.

I never shall forget the first time I saw Colonel Aston in his regimentals—his fine military figure, and all his appointments fitting so well. How many hundred officers have I since seen, but not one to be compared with his noble, chivalrous bearing, not even his friend Arthur Wellesley, now the great and illustrious duke!

I was put in orders for the light company, commanded by Captain Woodall; my brother subalterns were two Irishmen, George Nixon and Perceval. Colonel Aston exercised the regiment every morning for about a couple of hours, and the young subalterns were drilled by the second major, Bellairs, a very kind, brave, but indifferent officer. He had been at Gibraltar, but he would have been sadly puzzled to put the regiment through any of the manoeuvres. I think at this time I puzzled the young men of the regiment and made the old ones smile. My looks and slight figure made me appear about sixteen, when in fact I was near nineteen; having, moreover, led a gay life in town, I had acquired quite the manners of one of the initiated in fashionable life, and was very different from the raw Irish lads who composed the greater part of the subalterns.

One of them, of the name of George Eld Derby, a youth of about my own age, thus very gravely addressed the mess one evening after dinner: 'By Jasus, gentlemen, I am conscious you must have the meanest opinion of my courage. Here have I been no less than six weeks with the regiment, and the divil of a duel have I fought yet. Now, Captain Craigie, you are the senior captain of the regiment, and if you plase I will begin with you first; so name your time and place.'

Now, very many of these subaltern officers were of the stamp of my friend Mr. Derby. So a man could not be too guarded in his conduct with such heroes. Nothing, however, occurred unpleasant previous to embarkation; but in the two months spent on board some of the ships' quarrels occurred that were settled by an appeal to the pistols. Several duels took place at the Cape, but none terminated fatally, though some officers got badly wounded. We had no quarrels on board our ship. It is true that within three weeks of our arrival at Madras I received an insult, and immediately sent a challenge to the officer who had given it, and he very wisely made me a most satisfactory apology. My second was a regular Irish duellist, and he was perfectly satisfied with it, as well as myself.

But to return once more to Newport and the charms of the island. I think their market-day was Saturday, when the rural beauties, with their fresh butter, eggs, and chickens, appeared in the market, blooming with youth, freshness, and innocence. What pleasant rides have I taken, and generally by myself, in the most unfrequented and romantic parts of the island, often dining in a fisherman's hut or little, neat, sanded parlour off eggs and bacon and a pint of ale, attended by some of the rural beauties of the island! How well I remember Shanklin Chine, and, looking over the high cliff, contemplating the blue and sparkling sea that I was so soon to be floating over to distant climes, in all probability never again to return!

But these melancholy reflections were not of long duration. I had youth, health, and was naturally of a sanguine disposition, and I had, moreover, money sufficient in my purse to bear all reasonable expenses, with some besides for my less affluent brother officers. I soon found out that some of the juniors found it a hard matter to pay their mess bills, for which I was extremely sorry. I believe it was generally thought that I was a man of fortune, from my *apparent indifference to expense* and my anxiety of having the opportunity of purchasing a company. The first surmise was quite a mistake, for I kept in my pocket-book a regular account of my expenditure and receipts, only I took care that no one should know it.

The day at length arrived for our embarkation. The two flank companies, the colours of the regiment, the band and Colonel Aston, were embarked on board the *Rockingham*, East Indiaman, 800 tons, the Hon. Hugh Lindsay commander. The other part of the regiment was distributed on board the *Hawkesbury, Melville Castle,* and *Airlie Castle*, all Indiamen of about the same size. I think the *Fox* frigate, Captain Malcolm, was to proceed with us to the Cape, and the *Tremendous* (74) into a certain latitude. For it was the very height of the war, and the Dutch fleet was at sea looking out for us. They must have been near us, as they arrived at the Cape only about ten days before us, and the first news we heard on our arriving there was that they had been all captured by Lord Keith.

The bustle and confusion getting on board, which was in the first week in June, the decks covered with knapsacks, officers' baggage, etc., ducks, pigs, poultry, sheep, etc., all quacking, squeaking, crowing and baaing at the same time, was quite ludicrous. The chief officer showed us our cabin. Colonel Aston's cabin was divided from ours, and had a quarter gallery. We had the remaining part of the cabin, with a partition for the other part of the quarter gallery, for our own use and that of the officers of the ship. We were eleven officers stowed away in standing berths and cots in a cabin not more than, I should think, ten feet square, besides the rudder-head, which took up very considerable room. I swung in a cot, as well as Captain Craigie and the surgeon, Dr. Campbell; Meade, Crawford, Robert Nixon, his lieutenants, lay in the standing berths. Woodall, George Nixon, and Perceval were stowed away in the same manner, and Ensign King in a cot. This was our party.

In the morning we were attended by our servants, which just doubled the number of our party in the small cabin of ten feet square, or at most twelve. Eight o'clock was the hour of breakfast, three o'clock dinner, six o'clock tea and coffee, nine o'clock supper; and meals were punctual to a minute. Both subalterns and men kept watch on deck, from eight to twelve, from twelve to four, with two what they call dogwatches—that is, two hours from four to six, and six to eight. After breakfast the men were put through the manual and platoon exercise, and we had parades twice a day, when every man was expected to be perfectly clean. A subaltern of the day was appointed whose duty it was to see the hammocks all stowed away on deck, the decks swept and perfectly clean, and the lights extinguished at nine o'clock.

We had among our passengers four ladies: two very fine girls, the two Miss Smiths, about seventeen and nineteen, just come from the fashionable schools of London, Queen Square and Bloomsbury (they were the daughters of Mr. and Mrs. Petrie, the second in Council at Madras); a Miss Payton and a Miss Chinnery, her friend—the first a very handsome old maid about thirty-six, the other a good-tempered but very plain girl of about my own age.

The superiority of the two Miss Smiths was very obvious. Jemima, the eldest, was a most incorrigible flirt, very clever, very satirical, and aiming at universal conquest. Her sister, Henrietta, was more retiring, and I think more admired; at least, I know Colonel Aston was much struck with her pretty little figure and lovely neck, and she afterwards made a conquest of the future hero, Colonel Arthur Wellesley, who arrived at the Cape with the 33rd Regiment a few months before us. Mamma Payton, too, had her admirers. She was very quiet and matronly, and rolled about her fine black eyes at dinner in every direction.

Without being absolutely vulgar, she had no polish or refinement, and had evidently not been used to fashionable company, while the two Miss Smiths clearly had. As to poor Miss Chinnery, no one ever thought of her. Poor soul! she had neither beauty nor talent; but she was good-natured and inoffensive, and thankful *when* she received attention. There were some fine young men going out as writers, particularly John Byng. His father was afterwards Lord Torrington.[1] He was about my age, and had seen the best and highest society. He was remarkably handsome and a favourite of the Prince of Wales. Writing of that illustrious personage, I cannot resist repeating—pardon my vanity—what I overheard him say to Lady William Russell in the crush-room at the opera—'Look, Lady William, at that handsome boy!!' I was then about seventeen. I am conscious it is a great piece of ridiculous vanity recording this trifling circumstance, which I hope will be the last, as it is the first, instance of such folly on my part.

We had all our respective places at dinner—Captain Lindsay in the centre; at his right hand were placed the two Miss Smiths, and on his left the other two ladies. Opposite the captain sat Colonel Aston, and I on his left. Crawford and Captain Swinton (74th Regiment) sat together on my left. Poor Captain Lindsay a day or two after we were on board said: 'Gentlemen, I propose we should limit the consumption of wine to a pint per man, as I shall not have sufficient otherwise to last out the voyage.' Now, that ought to have been quite sufficient, but in those days it was the fashion to drink, and as our young gentlemen did not like to be limited to any particular allowance there was a dead silence. Captain Lindsay then said: 'It is not the wine I care for, but, as we are now fairly off, I have not the means of getting a fresh supply.'

'Pray don't make yourself uneasy on that head,' said Colonel Aston, 'as I happen to have about a couple of thousand pounds' worth in the fleet, and should you run short I shall be happy to supply you.' We heard nothing further about the wine after that.

Our band played generally every day during dinner and in the course of the evening, when the other ships would sail close alongside of us and exchange a few words, they being attracted by the band and our young ladies. Twice a week we had dancing, and every Saturday night we drank a health to our sweethearts and wives, according to custom. I was always fond of singing, and had a friend who had the most beautiful tenor I ever heard. We used to meet at a friend's chambers in the Temple, and many is the merry night we passed there until morning warned us to depart. Our principal beverage was punch.

My friend was only a clerk in the Stamp Office, but well connected, the *protégé* of Mr. Tickell, patronised by Sheridan, Richardson, etc., and nephew to Mr. Sober, of Baker Street, Portman Square, with whom he lived. His name was Sampson Tickell Wood. He soon sang away the heart of Sarah Sober, his pretty cousin, and ran off with her

---

1. 'John Byng,' third son of the fifth Viscount Torrington; died in 1811.

and married her. Just at this time I mentioned to my kind friend Mrs. Streatfield the indiscretion of the youthful couple, and introduced the lovely Sarah and her spouse to her and Miss S. The Bishop of London was enchanted with his singing, and through my introduction he at length found his way into Carlton House, and from his connection with Sheridan, together with his accomplishments, the junior clerk in the Stamp Office at Somerset House got into many of the gay parties that were given by His Royal Highness.

The consequence of all this was that my friend Sam got into the King's Bench, and his pretty little wife Sarah took the opportunity of again running away; the partner of her flight this second time was Tom Thornhill,[2] a young man of large fortune in Norfolk, who, after Sam's death, married her. I understand Thornhill paid Sam's debts and gave him £2,000 on the condition that he did not prosecute him. All this I learned on my return from India. I saw poor Sam after, but never spoke to him, as I did not approve of that sort of compromise.

When we—that is, the fleet—were lying at the Mother Bank, Colonel Aston kept a sailing vessel, about thirty tons, in case the fleet should get under way, in readiness to convey him on board from Portsmouth, where Mrs. Aston was living. The night before we sailed I was walking the deck in the afternoon, when he said: 'Come, young one, will you come with me and take *your last look* at Portsmouth?' (Poor fellow! it was *his last look*.) I said I should like it much. When we arrived at Portsmouth, he said: 'Call upon me at nine o'clock at Hammond's, in the High Street, as I am now going to take leave of Mrs. Aston. Take care you are not later, and go and amuse yourself till then.' I was punctual, and we went on board the yacht. He was silent all the time we were on board, and, I thought, melancholy.

---

2. 'Tom Thornhill,' Thomas Thornhill, of Fixby, County Yorks, and Riddlesworth, County Norfolk.

CHAPTER 3

Arrival at the Cape

The next morning, June 10, we made sail. In the course of a few days we got into very warm weather—warmer than I ever felt it before. But we amused ourselves, some with walking the deck, others reading, some playing backgammon, others chess, the ladies playing on the piano or drawing. In short, it appeared quite a party of pleasure. We passed Madeira about twenty miles off, and saw the Peak of Teneriffe and the Cape Verd Islands. We only saw one small Portuguese vessel, which we boarded, and got some delicious oranges. We passed the equinoctial line, and went through the wonted ceremony of receiving old Neptune, and paying the usual forfeit by those who passed it for the first time.

Here we were becalmed for ten days or a fortnight. It was intensely hot, and we suffered from a most tormenting skin eruption called the prickly heat. At length the long-wished-for breeze came, and we were once more in motion. Nothing can possibly be more grand and sublime than the rising and setting of the sun in these latitudes, and the moonlight nights are quite delicious. The phosphoric particles in the sea are wonderful, and truly beautiful.

Off the Cape we experienced a gale, and the sea ran very high. It assumed a form I never before saw; what they call the trough of the sea appeared at least a mile long between one wave and the next, which obliged us to fasten down our deadlights. At length one fine morning the man at the masthead sang out 'Land ahead!' This was very early in the morning, and by sunset we had cast anchor in Table Bay, after a voyage of two months. It soon got dark, but the next morning I was up betimes, and the town and huge mountain looked as if hanging over the ship, although we were at least two miles distant. The houses looked very neat and white, though we were too far off to see anything very distinctly.

The regiment did not disembark, but the officers were allowed to go on shore, and a few of the men by turns. We found the Bay full of ships of war: Lord Keith's squadron and the Dutch ships he had captured, together with our little fleet. I only recollect one of the Dutch ships, the *Van Tromp*, where were some officers of the Scotch Brigade. I went to dine with a Major Ewen of that corps, when it suddenly came on a gale of wind, and I was detained there all night. These gales often come on very suddenly, and will in an instant lay a '74' on her beam ends.

I met two old schoolfellows at the Cape; one an acting-lieutenant on board the *Van Tromp* frigate, who had lost a leg in the service. His name was Fisher, and he was son to Dr, Fisher, who lived with Storace, the singer. The other, a young man, was a surgeon of the garrison, who invited me to spend a few days at his quarters, and mounted me upon one of his unshod Cape horses. The horses are never shod. I found it pleasant riding out in the cool of the evening. We used to dine at the house of a Dutch officer by name of Scholts. It was very unpleasant sitting down to such immense quantities of meat swimming in oil, and such a variety of dishes, not one fit to eat, and the Cape wine was execrable. He kept a board and lodging house, where I occasionally met officers of our different regiments quartered at the Cape.

There were the 33rd, newly arrived; the Scotch Brigade; the 78th; 86th—all, like ourselves, destined for India, as also the 80th, a regiment very much resembling ours. I think it was raised by Lord Paget, the present Marquis of Anglesey, (as at time of first publication). The only difference in dress was this: the 80th wore a white ostrich feather, and we black and red. These two regiments were, in point of uniform, exactly alike, and it is not to be wondered at, as Lord Paget and Colonel Aston were great friends, and both had the best possible taste in dress; and I dare say they laid their heads together to dress their regiments as alike as possible.

The regiments of the line in those days were very badly dressed, and on our arrival at Madras we were the pattern for all the East India regiments on the coast. Nothing could be more ludicrous than the dress of the Company's officers at that period, some wearing shoes and buckles on guard; others shoe-strings, their facings not more than two inches broad; epaulettes not fastened to the shoulder, but hanging down upon their breast One of their generals I have seen with a pair of black silk smalls and stockings to match, white waistcoat, and a general's red coat The name of this officer was Sir Eccles Nixon. There were also at the Cape several regiments above the number of ninety-two that I cannot recollect, also the 28th Light Dragoons. We used to make up parties in large waggons to go into the interior. Some of ours went as far as eighty miles.

The farthest I went was on horseback, broiling in the sun, as far as Constantia, the vineyard where they make the celebrated wine. The oranges here were delicious. In the evening we used to dance. Some of the Dutch girls were very pretty, and some wealthy. One of them fell in love with one of our subalterns, and offered herself and I know not how many thousand dollars to the young gentleman. But they were not accepted.

The slave girls are, in general, fine girls, and some very fair, being the offspring of Dutchmen by native women. They (the proprietors) rather encourage than otherwise the intercourse between the officers and their slaves, as a matter of traffic. When Dutch women get married they are pretty, rosy girls of some shape; but no sooner do they get married and have a family than they grow enormously fat and out of all grace and proportion. They are very fond, when young, of dancing.

Captain Ruding, one of ours, a young man of ancient family, and heir to a Leicestershire estate of five thousand a year, just of age, fell in love with Jemima Smith, and after a ten days' courtship was led, nothing loath, to the altar.

Captain Lindsay, on our arrival at the Cape, took a very commodious house in the town for himself and the four ladies. With their attraction the house was filled with all the principal officers, visiting and paying their respects from morning till night, among others the afterwards celebrated hero, Colonel the Hon. Arthur Wellesley, at that time (September, 1796) just turned twenty-seven years of age. At this time he was all life and spirits. In height he was about 5 feet 7 inches, with along, pale face, a remarkably large aquiline nose, a clear blue eye, and the blackest beard I ever saw. He was remarkably clean in his person, and I have known him shave twice in one day, which I believe was his constant practice.

His features always reminded me of John Philip Kemble, and, what is more remarkable, I observed, many years after, the great likeness between him and the performer, Mr. Charles Young, which he told me he had often heard remarked. He spoke at this time remarkably quickly, with, I think, a very, very slight lisp. He had very narrow jaw-bones, and there was a great peculiarity in his ear, which I never observed but in one other person, the late Lord Byron—the lobe of the ear uniting to the cheek. He had a particular way, when pleased, of pursing up his mouth. I have often observed it when he has been thinking abstractedly. He got his brevet rank of colonel on May 1, 1796, as did also his friend Colonel Aston; but Aston was just senior to him. I believe they were both lieutenant-colonels of 1793, and were only three years in that rank.

I believe Colonel Wellesley was very much in debt and embarrassed when he left England, and a small tradesman in Dublin was of great assistance to him by the loan of four or five hundred pounds, which on his arrival in India in due course of time was repaid; and I have heard that on his return from India he walked into the shop of the tradesman, a boot and shoe maker, and asked him if he recollected him. The man said 'No.'

'Well,' said Sir Arthur, who was Secretary to the Duke of Richmond, 'can I be of any service to you?'

The man said: 'I want nothing for *myself*, but I have a son.'

'Give me his name,' said Sir Arthur; 'you did me a kindness once, and I do not forget it.' He got the man's son a place of ;£400 *per annum*. It gives me pleasure to record this anecdote of the Duke of Wellington, who has not a very tender or feeling heart. And in this instance I think he felt himself under an obligation to the man he did not forget, and it was his pride as well as principle, together with the man's answer, 'I want nothing for myself,' that determined Sir Arthur to provide so handsomely for his son. I know of another instance of his liberality of which he told me himself, but without any ostentation, only from my being a friend of the husband of the fair lady to whom his kindness and liberality were directed. Major William Ashley Sturt, of the 80th Regiment, a young man from the Guards, just before he left England, after committing all sorts of follies, concluded by marrying a beautiful woman of the establishment of a notorious woman living in Berkeley Street, a house much resorted to by men of fashion, Mrs. Sturt arrived in the year 1801 at Madras without a sixpence.

I at this time was living, on a visit with Colonel Wellesley, at a palace of Tippoo Sahib's, just outside the fort of Seringapatam. Major Sturt was with his regiment a great distance from Madras, and was far from rich, so in her distress, and being a stranger in a foreign country, she wrote to her old friend Colonel Wellesley, who by return of post sent her an order upon his banker for £400. My dear friend Colonel

Aston was on terms of great friendship with Colonel Wellesley, and introduced me to him, which is the only way I can account for his distinguishing me five years after in the way he did in preference to other officers of my regiment.

After spending two months very pleasantly at the Cape, we proceeded to Madras under convoy of the old *Trident*, a 64-gun ship. We left behind us sick poor Lieutenant-Colonel Grey, who shortly after died there of an abscess. At Eton he received a blow from a cricket-ball, and that eventually caused his death. We carried on with us the 33rd Regiment, commanded by the Honourable Colonel Wellesley, destined for Calcutta. Colonel W. proceeded in the *Princess Charlotte* Indiaman. I had a very narrow escape, some years after, of being captured by the French in this vessel at Vizagapatam. We lost one of our ladies, Jemima Smith, now Mrs. Ruding, having embarked on board her husband's ship, the *Melville Castle*. We continued our voyage, and in about two months anchored in Madras Roads on January 9, 1797. The day was too far advanced to disembark that evening, so it was arranged that the regiment should land the next day after an early dinner.

The appearance of Madras from the roads is not very interesting. The coast is flat both to the north and south as far as the eye can reach, relieved by no object save the cocoa-nut trees and *palmyras*, and the white foam from the tremendous surf constantly rolling in shore, the outer surf commencing at least 200 yards from shore. No ship's boat, I think, could possibly avoid being swamped at Madras. But they have very safe and commodious *masulah* boats, entirely made of the cocoa-nut tree, and manned by four or five *lascars*, who sing in chorus a song that enables them to pull all together; these boats they manage with a dexterity which no English sailor could equal. By way of additional security in case of a capsize, they are attended by two or three catamarans—long pieces of wood lashed together, on the top of which are perched two natives. They are in no danger of being drowned even if they fall off; they float like cork. But the greatest danger is from the sharks that abound near the shore.

We ate our last dinner on board the *Rockingham*, and the regiment landed on the beach of Madras between five and six o'clock in the evening. The men were marched into the barracks in Fort St. George, vacated by the 74th Regiment, while the officers received us on the beach and escorted us to their mess-room in the fort, where a very handsome dinner was provided for us. We had all of us previously dined on board of our respective ships; this second dinner, followed up by large quantities of madeira and claret, had the natural effect of making many of us much the worse for it Then came at a late hour the providing us with beds for the night. Each officer of the 74th seemed to vie with the other as to who should show us most hospitality.

I was taken care of by a Lieutenant Macleod, the Adjutant of the regiment. And now my misery commenced from the mosquitoes. Not having been provided with mosquito-curtains, I was really devoured, hands, feet, and legs, and as for my face, when I looked in the glass I was swelled and disfigured to such a degree that I did not know myself. Colonel Aston was quite sorry to see me such a martyr, and sent me down some curtains which he had by him when he expected to go out to the West Indies. But the mischief was all done in one night. The torment I experienced from these insects drove me almost mad. I tore my flesh to pieces, particularly my legs and feet. These bites, from contact with the stocking, became small ulcers, the marks of which I now bear about me, and prevented me from wearing boots for many weeks, and of course I could not mount guard and take my turn of the garrison duty.

We formed an excellent mess. We had, of course, our own regimental plate. We found two black men, brothers, who agreed to find us an excellent dinner, a dessert, and a pint of madeira each man for ten *pagodas* a head monthly; also twice a week, Thursday and Sunday, a better dinner, consisting of European articles, such as hams, tongues, cheese, etc. But if we exceeded the allowance of wine, beer, etc., we had to pay extra. Thursday and Sunday were the days we received guests. Our members consisted of nearly the whole regiment, amounting to between forty and fifty officers. I have often seen on the days we had company our guests nearly three times out numbering ourselves. It once occurred to me that I sat up all night and went from the mess-table to the morning drill at five o'clock. But that happened to me but once.

The drills, the guards, and the regimental duties of the subalterns were rather severe. For instance, the first five months, during the hottest part of the season, the regiment was formed in the fort, ready on the first dawn of day, when the gun was fired and the gates opened, to march out of the garrison and form on the glacis of the fort. After the reports were collected, we marched round several times both in slow and quick time, saluting, etc. Afterwards many of the eighteen manoeuvres were gone through. Then the senior officers were drilled by Major Picton and the junior by Major Bellairs. After that a few more manoeuvres, and then, the sun getting very powerful, we were marched back to our quarters. I used on getting to my quarters, when I breakfasted at home, to throw off all my clothes and lie down on my cot fairly done up and go to sleep.

I was obliged to get up and dress at twelve to attend the major to practise the sword exercise for an hour; then home, undress, and lie down for a couple of hours; then dress again for a three o'clock dinner, and at five the regiment again formed for exercise, when we continued till it was too dark. And this system continued with little intermission until the month of July, when we were delighted at the prospect of the regiment going on an expedition to capture the island of Manila in conjunction with other troops.

As I have before mentioned, I had a few letters of introduction to the people of Madras. I got some dinners, and that was all. I presented my letter to the old admiral from Lady Burnaby. He said to me: 'Young gentleman, you are in the army, and I can be of no use to you. Had you been in the navy, from the regard I have to Lady Burnaby, I would have taken care of your promotion.' Now. if my poor brother Edward had had the good fortune to have delivered this letter to the admiral instead of me, he would have been pushed on to the rank of a post-captain instead of dying, after hard and gallant services, a lieutenant. Such are the lucky or unlucky events of our lives.

The garden-houses about Madras are for the most part inhabited by the Civil Servants, who live in as much luxury as the climate will allow. Their houses vary in splendour according to the means of their occupiers. For instance, a Member of Council will have a house like a man of large fortune in this country, while the writer will have a much smaller one, consisting of an entrance-hall, wherein he dines and breakfasts, and two bedrooms, one on each side. The largest and best houses are all built on the ground-floor. None of the houses have ceilings, but cloth of pure white is the substitute. But these substitutes for a ceiling are only used in the best houses by the civil servants, who live in every respect better than the subaltern ranks of the army.

Glass windows are seldom used in India, but Venetian blinds and doors are substituted for them to get the benefit of the current of air. I have seen glass doors and windows at Negapatam and Pondicherri, the former a Dutch settlement and the latter a French one; but even there they are not common. The sea-breeze sets in about 2 p.m. and continues until about 4 a.m. Nothing can be more refreshing than that delightful breeze. Every house has a veranda attached to it, where the custom is to take exercise by walking in the extreme heat of the day. The thermometer in the coolest part of the morning is generally in the shade as high as 72°, and increases to 82°. In an officer's tent it generally is from 90° to 100°, and in the tents used by the private soldiers at least 10° higher. When the sea-breeze dies away at night the heat is insupportable, and the stings of the mosquitoes enough to drive one mad.

I was truly miserable the first three years I was in India; my last thought as I lay down to sleep, and the first when I awoke, was England. After that period I got more reconciled to the country. I used to ride in the evening, when we relaxed in our drill, upon the Mount Road and in its environs. The perfume from the hedges was delightful, and the trees are always green and flourishing, notwithstanding the constant heat and never-failing sun. The birds and little gray squirrels are quite tame. I had one of the latter, who used very often to sleep for hours in my coat-sleeve, even when on parade. I had also a small monkey, which was very amusing with its tricks. My dear friend Colonel Aston had only four horses—a pair of large bay horses which he used to drive in the curricle he used in England, wherein I used sometimes to ride, and two saddle horses; one, a dark iron gray, was a heavy, quiet horse, remarkably steady with troops—he was called Blueskin—and the other was a very fine gray Arab, bought of Colonel Winch of the 36th for 500 *pagodas*, and named Diomed. This horse afterwards became the property of Colonel Wellesley, and was left to him by Colonel Aston just before he fought his last and fatal duel.

India in these days is as well known as the Continent of Europe. I shall not, therefore, enter into any particular detail of it, particularly to you, who have passed four or five years there in a similar situation as myself. I have only mentioned my first impressions. How well I recollect the old Nabob of Arcot taking his evening drive on the Mount Road in an old-fashioned English post-chaise with black postillions, his long and venerable white beard, his yellow complexion, turban, and silk dress! He always made every officer he met a profound *salaam*. He lived in some state about two short miles from the fort, at or near a place called St. Thomé.

The Mount was distant from Madras about ten miles. Here was the station of the artillery, and also of the 22nd Light Dragoons, commanded by Lieutenant-Colonel Stapleton Cotton, since for his long and gallant services to his country ennobled as Viscount Combermere.

The Major was the Honourable George de Grey, afterwards Lord Walsingham. This unfortunate nobleman was, together with his lady, burnt to death about six or seven years since at their house in Harley Street. He fell asleep, and the candle ignited the curtains of the bed. De Grey, when I first knew him, was not above twenty years of age.

Colonel Cotton was about five or six years older. The colonel was regarded as a good regimental cavalry officer, and was considered so by the old veteran, General Floyd, commanding the cavalry, who had served as a cornet at the famous Battle of Minden, where my regiment was one of the six who gained a glorious victory over the French, August 1, 1759. We used to have the words 'Minden' and 'Gibraltar' on our regimental colour, and the latter on our breastplates, a great and proud distinction in those days. In these times, under the great modern hero, there is scarce a regiment in the service that has not at least half a dozen such honourable memorials.

When my colonel, General William Picton, received the command of the 12th Regiment, he went to court to return his thanks for the honour conferred upon him by George III. His Majesty said: 'You must thank Captain Picton, who commanded the grenadiers of the 12th Regiment at the Battle of Minden.' I have seen the original return of the killed and wounded on that glorious day. They were very severely handled, very few escaping being either killed or wounded.

When we arrived at Madras we found Lord Hobart the governor of the settlement. He had lately lost his wife, formerly a Mrs. Adderley. With her arrived Miss A. and her brother. Miss A. was one of the most beautiful young creatures I ever saw, and married only a few months later Captain Gardner[1] of the navy. He was son to Lord Gardner, the admiral. I never in my life saw any woman with so beautiful a complexion. When in England I thought Lady Charlotte Campbell very lovely, but she was far surpassed by Mrs. Gardner. They lived very unhappily together; they soon after left India, and on their passage home they had so violent a quarrel that she flung his picture on the deck, stamped her foot upon it, and threw her wedding-ring into the sea. There was also a Mrs. Campbell, the wife of Captain C of the Company's artillery—a very fine woman.

Both these ladies were much admired by Colonel Aston. There was a good deal of what the ladies call flirtation going on among these

---

1. 'Captain Gardner,' Hon. Alan Hyde Gardner, afterwards second Lord Gardner. Married, March 9, 1796, Maria Elizabeth, only daughter of Thomas Adderley, of Innishannon, County Cork. Divorced 1805. She married, secondly, Henry Jadis.

ladies with their admirers, but nothing more—at least, not at that time. They both went home at the same time, if not in the same ship. The lonely Mrs. Gardner afterwards eloped with Mr. Jadis. It is only a few years since a child, born before a formal separation took place, tried to establish his claim to the Gardner peerage. But he lost his claim after a long and severe investigation. It all turned on the possibility of the period of gestation extending to ten months. We used to have very pleasant balls at the Mount. Colonel Aston often drove me over to them, and we used to sleep at Colonel Cotton's house.

CHAPTER 4

Return to India

It was the beginning of the month of August, 1797, when an expedition was prepared to proceed against Manila. I never shall forget the considerate kindness of Colonel Aston respecting my comfort on that occasion. I could not get any native servant willing to embark with me. They have a prejudice against going on board ship. I was embarked on board H.M.S. *Trident*, 64 guns, Captain Milner. Only half the regiment was to proceed at first with the first division. I remember our captain-lieutenant was Captain William O'Brien, the present Marques of Thomond. He was on board the same ship with me, a truly noble and high-spirited young man, a great favourite of mine, universally beloved and respected by the regiment. Colonel Aston sent me a Portuguese servant, but he was so stupid he was not of the smallest use to me. I was obliged to get one of our men to attend upon me. I did not require much—merely cleaning my boots and slinging my cot, fetching water, etc.

I messed with the lieutenants in the gun-room; Captain O'Brien messed with Captain Milner. There were several large Indiamen taken up for the troops, some of 1,500 tons burthen. I had a very comfortable berth in the gun-room—so cool, and no mosquitoes, it appeared quite a paradise. I found the officers excellent good fellows, the senior lieutenant a short, sturdy young man, whom I have often heard say that if ever he got into action he never would strike his colours, whatever disparity of force should exist He blew his ship up after in action, when he could no longer defend her against a superior force. This young hero's name was Rowe. The second lieutenant's name was Gordon, a gentleman, quite young. And the third, Houston, a remarkably handsome young Scotchman, and a great favourite of the Duke of Hamilton's. The Lieutenant of Marines' name was Wilson. The master was an old man, as was the surgeon. All the rest were little more than boys, but good officers.

We had a pleasant voyage of about three weeks to Prince of Wales Island, or Penang, as it is sometimes called; we found here the 33rd Regiment and other troops from Bengal. The settlement of Penang lies at the foot of high land, covered with jungle that looks very beautiful from the sea. It is inhabited by Malays and Chinese. At this time it had not been an English settlement above ten years, and was then in its infancy. I renewed my acquaintance with Colonel Wellesley. The troops were not disembarked, but the officers and a few men were allowed to go on shore. I slept on shore two or three times. Some of the Madras native regiments were encamped there.

In consequence of the hostile demonstrations on the part of Tippoo Sultan, the governor-general was obliged to give up his intention of proceeding against the Manilas, and we had to lie quietly in the roads of Penang until the monsoon was over on the coast of Coromandel. The monsoon commences about the middle of October, and it is not safe for ships to enter the Madras roads ere the first week in January. So we all led a very quiet, stupid life on board our respective ships until the middle of December, when we of the coast troops returned to Madras. My chief recreation was visiting the opposite shore of Kedah, shooting pigeons and sea-gulls, visiting the troopships, fishing out of the stem gallery, sometimes bathing at the foot of a delicious waterfall under the shade of the *palmyra*, the plantain, and other Asiatic trees. This lovely bath was situated about two or three miles from the town. The approach to it was up the mountains, and all under the shade of large forest trees. It is, indeed, a truly delicious retreat No one ever visited Prince of Wales Island without going there.

A change took place before we left Penang with respect to the quartering of the troops on board the ships. I was sent on board the *Princess Mary*, an extra Indiaman of 500 tons, commanded by Captain Nash, and manned solely by *lascars*, with the exception of the officers. The ship appeared so small, so dirty, the duty done so slovenly both by men and officers, so very different from the smartness and discipline of a man-of-war, that it formed a miserable contrast. It was only for about three weeks, but they passed long and wretchedly. On arriving on shore my kind friend Captain Ruding gave me a room in his house.

I forgot to mention during our short stay at Penang that we lost one of our captains, Thomas Hayward Winstone, of an old family in

Gloucestershire, and related to my friend Sir Thomas Hayward of Berkshire. He drank very hard. I had spent the evening with him only a few nights before. He allowed the land wind to blow upon him during his sleep. He awoke ill, and never recovered. I saw him as he lay dead; he had a most stern and severe expression in his countenance. He was opened, and his liver was entirely decayed. His complexion was very similar to Colonel Aston's. His funeral was a military one, the first I ever attended. It made a great impression upon me at the time, he being the first officer we had lost since leaving England. Alas! the loss of how many more shall I have to recount!

I had not been on shore many days when I was taken ill with a decided attack of liver. I was ill about three weeks, and after having taken repeated doses of calomel I recovered. At this time, about February, 1798, some of the old regiments, such as the 36th, 52nd, and 75th Regiments, were ordered home. And some of our officers, being heartily sick of India, effected an exchange. Among those who left were Captains Ruding and O'Brien. In them I lost two kind friends. Alas! in after-life what different fates awaited them—one the heir-apparent to £5,000 *per annum*, the other presumptive heir to an Irish earldom! They each of them succeeded to the fortune and honours they were heirs to, but with far different results. My dear and kind friend Colonel Aston, ever mindful of my comfort, bought a horse of Lieutenant Meade for me, together with a new saddle and bridle, as we received orders to proceed to garrison Tanjore, a distance of about two hundred miles from Madras.

O'Brien was much beloved by the regiment, and he was very much attached to it. But he had too much at stake to stay longer in so precarious a situation as the East Indies. He had a very narrow escape in the West Indies a short time before. The flank companies of the army in 1794 were embarked at Cork for the West Indies. Both of ours went, and Lieutenant O'Brien went also. Our flank companies stormed St. Lucia, and those who were not killed all died of the yellow fever in nine months, with the exception of O'Brien and two of the private soldiers. O'Brien, when he left the regiment, presented some little memorials of his regard to those officers with whom he was most intimate. To me he gave an emerald pin, which I preserved for ten years, and happened to prove to him the care I had taken of it by wearing it at Ascot races, where by chance I met him. It was stolen a few days after this out of my shirt.

We marched out of Fort St. George at gun-fire one morning the latter end of the month of February, and encamped on Choultry Plain, in the vicinity of the fort. Thus I made my debut under canvas in the East. I started with a very modest establishment: a head servant, a second *ditto*, a boy to carry my chair, and *coolies* for my cot, table, etc., a *cooderry currah* and grass-cutter. These two native servants were for the purpose of attending upon one horse, the only one I had. The novelty of a camp life amused me much at first.

We were obliged to be up before daylight; the bugle sounded an hour before dawn. The *lascars* were then busily at work knocking loose the tent-pegs, the servants packing up the trunks, attending their masters and helping them to dress, loading the bullocks with trunks, etc. In the course of another hour the second bugle sounds. The regiment is formed in marching order, the drums and fifes begin to play, and the officers are shortly after allowed to mount their horses and ride by the side of their companies.

The quartermaster and his staff precede the regiment, and fix the encampment about nine, ten, or twelve miles from the last ground, according as he finds favourable ground. One thing is indispensable: the vicinity of water, and it should be near a village. We had a fine large mess tent, and our mess man gave us a good dinner every day, as he used to do in quarters. In the evening the villagers used to come out to our lines to indulge their curiosity, oftentimes accompanied by the dancing-girls, particularly if in the neighbourhood of any celebrated *pagodas*. I think it is about thirty miles from Madras we came to the celebrated *pagodas* of Conjeveram. They are, from their size, architecture and magnificent tanks, really wonderful objects of curiosity. Immense quantities of monkeys inhabit these *pagodas*, where they are considered quite sacred, and jump about these temples in perfect security.

We arrived at Pondicherri, and encamped in the neighbourhood. And here was stationed a native regiment I had met at Penang; with some of the officers I renewed my acquaintance. At this place I acquired the accomplishment of swimming, taught me by one of my company. I was very fond of this refreshing exercise, but never felt comfortable, from my constant dread of water-snakes and alligators. I was bathing once in the vicinity of Tanjore, and heard my servant in earnest conversation with an old Brahmin. I asked him the subject of their conversation. He said: 'Brahmin say, master, that he knows an *old* alligator that has lived in this tank upwards of one hundred years.' I never bathed there afterwards.

We at length arrived at Tanjore. An immense fort it was, and with a still larger *pettah*. There was a regiment of Native Infantry doing duty in that part, commanded by a Colonel Innis. Colonel Aston had a very good quarter in the fort, which had an excellent garden attached to it, with a fine vineyard. The grapes abounded there, and it was a source of great profit, I have heard, to officers whose object it was to make and save money. Not so with the liberal, noble-minded Aston.

The weather on our first arrival was dreadfully hot, and the nights were most oppressive; we were worn out by the heat of day, and unable to get any refreshing sleep from the closeness of the nights, as no cool sea-breeze was to be had here. It was here that Colonel Aston got an attack of liver complaint. I used often to dine with him in his room and take his horse out for exercise in the evening. I think he began to get tired of the climate and the monotony of the life, and I believe, had peace been permanently established in India, he calculated being at home in the summer of 1799, and had made arrangements to that effect. But man proposes and God disposes. His sun was nearly set

About seven miles from Tanjore was a military station called Vellum. There our flank companies were removed under Major Picton. It was a wild and cheerless place, situated on a large, sandy plain, the few rocks in the neighbourhood infested with large snakes of the most dangerous description, among others the *cobra de capello*, the most venomous. After being bit, if no application is made, you die in half an hour. These snakes are of a dirty brown, and are generally from 5 feet to 7 feet in length. When irritated they expand a fleshy substance from each side of the head, which is marked like a pair of spectacles. They throw themselves upright, and can then spring some distance upon you. I had the most miraculous escape of being bitten by one some years after.

During my short stay at this dull and miserable station I had the opportunity of seeing a young widow burn herself by the side of her deceased husband. The funeral pile was about 10 feet high; in the middle of the pile lay her deceased husband, an old and miserable-looking man. The devoted victim was a young creature about seventeen, dressed in white, with all her jewels on and various ornaments of gold. There was a confused noise of singing and shouting, intermixed with the sound of *tomtoms*—that is, a sort of small drum—and at intervals the hollow and sonorous sound of gongs and trumpets. The priests and her friends crowded round her, all speaking to her at once, apparently to distract her attention and to prevent her shrinking at the last moment from sacrificing herself.

There was a small tank of water close to the funeral pile. They led her to this. I was very near her when I saw her quietly take the jewels from her ears, her nose, unclasp her gold bracelets, as well as the bangles from her ankles and every ornament she had on, which were received by her relations.

She then stepped into the water, divested herself of her clothes of pure white, and replaced them with clothes of a yellow colour. She then performed her ablutions, came out of the water, and unassisted walked three times round the pile, followed by the priests and her friends, who at this period appeared to be more urgent and loud in their discourse to her to distract her attention. She then, unassisted, mounted the pile, laid herself down by the side of her husband, and put his head under her arm, turning herself towards them. They then sprinkled large quantities of oil and straw on the pile. The fatal fire was then applied, and amid loud shouts and while the fire reached her I distinctly heard her utter the words '*Narina, Narina.*'

Fortunately, during this horrid ceremony a very high wind was blowing, and I consoled myself in the hope that she was suffocated ere she suffered much pain. I was very near her during the different parts of the ceremony, and could have saved her life by merely touching her, as she would then have been defiled, and would not have been permitted to have the honour of sacrificing herself. But in saving her life I stood the chance of being torn to pieces, and I certainly should have been brought to a court-martial for disobedience of orders, for the English in those days were strictly forbidden to meddle with the customs and prejudices of the natives.

In the neighbourhood of Vellum, on the arid and sandy plains, small stones abound which, in course of ages, get chipped at the angles by accident. These, if given to a lapidary and cut and polished, produce a stone frequently of value, and in polish and lustre far superior to our Bristol stone. I used to amuse myself collecting these sometimes. Major Picton had a leash of English greyhounds, and we used at early dawn to take the dogs out and run foxes and jackals. They run for a mile or two very swift, but I have got several severe falls by my horse getting into false ground and holes and coming suddenly across watercourses and ravines.

An important revolution occurred during our stay at Tanjore. The old *rajah* was deposed, and the young one, by the name of Suffrajeh, brought up and educated by a German missionary of the name of

Schwartz, was placed on the *musnud* in his room. At this time he was one of the handsomest natives I ever saw. This revolution took place without any confusion, noise, or bloodshed, and, I believe, had justice on its side, which is not always the case in political revolutions.

The young *rajah*—about twenty-four—gave us a grand dinner according to the English custom, and as soon as the dessert was placed on the table he was led into the room by Colonel Aston and the Civil Resident, Benjamin Torin, and took his seat at the centre of the table, between the two. I shall never forget the splendour of his dress. It reminded me of the *sultans, caliphs*, and princes I used to read of in the *Arabian Nights' Entertainments*. His turban was richly decorated with jewels, and he had an ornament somewhat like a heron's feather entirely composed of diamonds issuing from his turban. He had a close jacket of the richest *kincob*, a splendid sash, in which was stuck his dagger, ornamented with precious stones, and also a scimitar, the handle and scabbard of which were similarly ornamented. He spoke English very well, and was dignified and graceful in his manners. All the officers got presents; the colonel got a splendid star, and the other officers according to their rank. I got a cloth of gold sufficient for a dress.

All went off extremely well. This ceremony took place soon after we left Vellum. Mr. Benjamin Torin, the Civil Resident, lived a short distance from the Fort of Tanjore. He had come out for the second time in the same fleet that we came in to India. My kind and good guardian, Mr. Hutchinson, who had a house in the vicinity of Englefield Green, where Mr. Torin's family had long resided, was so kind, unknown to me, as to mention my name to him. The consequence was Mr. Torin never gave a dinner-party that I did not get a card of invitation to meet all the senior officers, and among the rest Colonel Aston. These two *dons* used to endeavour to outdo each other in the elegance of their entertainments, and they always, as if by mutual consent, invited me to them.

It was during our stay at Tanjore we lost two officers: Lieutenant Cassidy and Lieutenant William Gahan, the latter one of the finest young men in the regiment. He was much lamented. Our men during our stay at Tanjore were very sickly; every evening we had two or three funerals. I used to amuse myself by looking at the Hindoo women bathing themselves morning and evening, and fetching their water in brass vessels upon their heads, holding and balancing them most gracefully with one hand, the other hanging down or holding up the robe clinging wet and tightly round their symmetrical figures.

Here from early dawn till the shades of night were females of all ages, from the child of ten to the venerable matron. What practice for the chisel of a Canova or a Thorwaldsen! Nothing could be finer than the busts of these women, and as far as the knees they were perfect; but their legs were in general faulty. They had not that lovely roundness that distinguishes the legs of the European women. Yet their hands and feet were certainly small.

The large tank, with some hundred or more steps leading to the water, was just opposite to my quarter, and I used to amuse myself by endeavouring to copy their Grecian attitudes and graceful figures. It was at this place that I acquired great skill in shooting with a pellet bow. I could with some certainty hit anything twenty or thirty yards off. I one day espied one of our officers' servants squatting down smoking a cheroot. I fired, and hit the poor fellow in the mouth. Away vanished the extinguished weed. I was delighted, and laughed very heartily at the man's astonished looks; but I never after repeated the foolish experiment.

We received orders to march from Tanjore to a station called Arnee about the month of October, as the army was to be formed in that neighbourhood to be in readiness to act against Tippoo Sultan if he did not comply with certain requisitions made to him by government in February ensuing. We arrived at Arnee during the rains, and here, unfortunately, my dear Colonel Aston left the regiment, and proceeded on leave to Madras, leaving the regiment under the command of Major Picton. Among the officers we received in exchange from other regiments was a Lieutenant Hartley of the 36th. He was a middle-aged man, and from having been some years in the country had acquired a good deal of local information and experience. He was a fine looking fellow, with honest and blunt manners and good temper. He was frequently consulted by the colonel on matters connected with different customs pursued by the 36th Regiment, and by degrees acquired some influence and favour with the colonel, Most unfortunately for the latter, they corresponded during this temporary absence of the colonel from the regiment

It appears that Lieutenant Hartley had some difference with Major Allen, who was our paymaster, on the subject of his accounts, and represented the business in his letters to Colonel Aston in his own way. Colonel Aston in his reply to Hartley said: 'If Major Allen has used you as you say, I think he has not treated you *liberally*,' or words to that effect There is no doubt that Colonel Aston, when he made use of this term, never dreamed that Hartley would have so far abused his confidence as to read his letter to different officers of the regiment, which he did; and this coming to the ears of Major Allen, a man of a high sense of honour, he immediately consulted his friend and countryman, Major Picton. Major Picton at once issued an order for all the officers to assemble at his quarters to investigate the difference between Major Allen and Lieutenant Hartley.

And that result proved from the investigation that Major Allen's accounts were perfectly clear with Lieutenant Hartley, and that he (the major) did not merit the observation Colonel Aston made upon Hartley's representation. The minutes of this court of inquiry were immediately forwarded to Colonel Aston, who in a state of great excitement made up his mind to join his regiment at once, for the purpose of issuing a very severe order against Major Picton for presuming to take advantage of his (Colonel A.'s) temporary absence to call a meeting of the officers without his sanction. But previously to doing this he consulted his friend Colonel Wellesley, and showed him the order he intended to issue.

Colonel Wellesley said to him: 'You have asked my advice. By no means issue the order.'

Aston replied: 'I have made up my mind, and will do it.'

'Then why, if you had made up your mind to do so, consult me on the subject?'

And they left each other mutually dissatisfied. Colonel Wellesley related this conversation to me two years afterwards. Colonel Aston, on joining the regiment, issued the order. Major Picton immediately applied for leave of absence, to consult his friends as to what course he ought to take.

It was during his absence that I lived a good deal with the colonel at a bungalow he had a short distance from the fort of Arnee, and Colonel Cotton, who commanded the 22nd Light Dragoons at Arcot, came over and passed a few days with Colonel Aston. Colonel Cotton asked permission for me to return with him to spend a few days in hunting and shooting, and I then saw my dear colonel alive for the last time. After dinner on that day the conversation turned on a fatal duel that had just taken place in the island of Ceylon. The circumstances were rather remarkable, but I forget the parties' names. The person who gave the offence received the fire of his adversary, and then, apologizing to him, acknowledged he had been to blame.

But he had no sooner done this than he addressed the second of his adversary, and said: 'But you, sir, I have an account to settle with. You insulted me in the *manner* in which you delivered your friend's message. Be so good as to take his place and give me satisfaction for the insult.' He did so, and was shot dead the first fire. Colonel Aston remarked that if such results oftener took place, fewer duels would be fought on frivolous occasions. In the course of the evening, soon after coffee, some pistol-bullets lying on a table, someone of the party took one up, observing what an unpleasant thing it would be to have one in one's body. Poor Aston, with a foreboding tone, as I thought, replied; 'That has been the fate of many better than you or I.'

After spending a very pleasant ten days at Arcot with Colonel Cotton, one evening as we were drinking our wine an express arrived from Arnee stating that Colonel Aston had that morning (Sunday) fought a duel with Major Allen, and had been shot, but that he still lived. The colonel and I were much distressed at this unfortunate news, and ere the day dawned we were on our horses on our route to Arnee. I had not the nerve to enter his bedroom, but I heard his dreadful groans all over the house. He sometimes said: 'I can bear pain, but sickness unmans me.' I used to attend the doctor's report every hour in the day. From the first they gave little hope of his recovery, until about the fifth day, when the extreme pain began to subside, and there appeared some faint hopes of him.

But this cessation of pain was occasioned by mortification having taken place, and at about six o'clock in the evening of the seventh day he ceased to exist. Colonel Wellesley arrived two or three days after the duel, and I heard Aston say: 'Ah, my dear Arthur, is it you? I shall now die happy.' Immediately after his death, I went to the couch he was lying on, attended by Dr. Campbell, the surgeon. He turned down the sheet that covered him and pointed to where the bullet had entered his side. It was a dark and livid mark, not a hole, but the skin split in a triangular form, on a level with and 6 inches from the navel. The bullet went through the liver and passed entirely through the vertebra of the backbone, then took an oblique direction downwards, and lodged in the muscles of the hip.

Major Picton sent him a challenge on the Saturday preceding, and he met him, attended by Captain Craigie as his second. Major Picton's second was Lieutenant Crawford. Major Picton's pistol missed fire, and he threw it down on the ground in a rage. The colonel told him to 'try again,' The seconds very properly would not allow this, and, on Colonel Aston's firing in the air, they would not allow the business to proceed further. They shook hands, but the colonel said: 'Remember, the order must stand; no rescinding.' He afterwards said: 'Well, Picton, you and your friend must come and dine with me today, and all must henceforward be forgot.'

The next day was Sunday, and on that day it was customary for the captains of their companies to wait on the commanding officer with the state of their companies. Major Allen, who was only a major by brevet, presented his at the breakfast-table, and remained until every officer had retired. When alone with Colonel Aston, he said: 'I wish to consult you, colonel, about exchanging out of the regiment. From certain unpleasant circumstances that have lately occurred I find my situation, after the reflections you have applied to me, not what it was.' Colonel Aston said: 'If you ask my opinion, I think, as senior captain, you would be wrong to quit the regiment; and with respect to your feelings, I am ready to atone in any way you wish.'

'Will you, then, give me a meeting?' demanded Allen.

'Certainly, instantly. But allow me to say you have been very tardy in demanding it. I have been some days with the regiment without assuming the command of it, to give you and others who feel grieved an opportunity of satisfying themselves.'

Previously to going out, which was very shortly arranged, he sent for the adjutant, and desired him to go to all the officers and to say that if any one of them felt themselves aggrieved he was ready to satisfy them instantly, one after the other, and finish the business altogether.

The colonel and Captain Craigie happened to arrive on the ground a few minutes before Captain Allen and his second, an assistant-surgeon of the name of Erskine. Captain Allen apologized for keeping him waiting, adding: 'I am sorry, upon my soul. Colonel Aston, it should ever come to this.'

Colonel Aston merely said: 'Take your ground, sir.'

The distance was measured. Allen fired, and from the circumstance of the colonel standing perfectly upright with his pistol levelled, the seconds concluded that the ball had passed him. The colonel dropped his pistol arm, and said: 'I am wounded, but it shall never be said that the last act of my life was that of revenge.'

Poor Allen ran up, threw himself on the ground, and was quite overcome by sorrow and remorse. The colonel was assisted into his *palanquin*, and met one of his officers, a Lieutenant Falla, soon after himself killed before Seringapatam. 'Well, Falla,' said the colonel, 'I have got a confounded lick in the guts, but I hope I shall get over it.'

I have seen many dead men, but never saw one that looked like poor Aston. He appeared just as though he were asleep—his long, dark eyelashes closed, and the sweetest smile upon his lips. It seemed to give the assurance that his immortal soul had taken its flight to the realms of bliss. The passage from death to the grave is very rapid in that warm climate, and ere twenty-four hours had expired he was in his last earthly resting-place.

He, of course, had a military funeral; his own regiment and a native regiment and a company of the artillery attended. Minute guns were fired, and every demonstration of respect paid. His beautiful Arab charger was hung with crape, and his boots pendant from the holsters. When the body was brought out of the house the horse was standing near the door. At the sight of the coffin he started back, reared up, and fell over. It appeared that even the horse felt sensible that he had lost his master.

There is no doubt that when Colonel Aston left England he had settled all his affairs by disposing of his property, but not that part which he had in India, consisting of horses, wine, plate, furniture, etc These he left to his friend Captain Craigie, with the exception of the Arab horse Diomed, which he left to Colonel Wellesley. He also desired that my note of hand to him for a considerable sum might be destroyed, as well as a miniature of a lady and several papers. These were thrown down a deep well in the garden. His stock of clothes, etc, that he bought in England was immense; I have heard from fifty to one hundred pairs of boots. I remember on the passage out I had a painful boil on my arm; the scar I have to this day. He lent me a loose jacket to wear. I said I was afraid I should deprive him of it, as there were no laundresses on board ship. He said: 'Never mind; I have two hundred more.' His tailors made for me when I returned home—the Croziers, of Panton Square—and they assured me they used to take him home thirty coats at a time. And if they did not fit exactly he used to kick them out of the room.

Such a sensation his untimely death made that it was long the topic of conversation. In him I lost the best and kindest friend I ever had. I should now have been, barring the casualties of war, a general, with orders and decorations, like many of those now wearing them, who were only subalterns when I had the rank of captain. He always assured me I should be his A.D.C.

The two majors were placed in arrest, sent down to Madras, and tried by a court-martial. They were admonished, and Allen was tried in the Civil Court and acquitted. They both returned to their duty with the regiment. But poor Allen never held up his head afterwards. He died in less than three months of a raging fever.

CHAPTER 5

To Seringapatam

Soon after the death of my dear friend Aston I lost both health and spirits. I joined the army, but kept my tent, from a violent attack of the liver, attended with burning fever. I had no *palanquin*; none but officers of the highest rank could afford to keep one, and I was too ill to sit on my horse. Colonel Cotton and the Hon. Major de Grey were kind enough to send one of theirs to me every morning to convey me to the new encampment.

I got as far as Vellore, when I was obliged to go into quarters while the army were halting for a few days, and when they marched I made an effort to join them. I never shall forget the Pass of Amboor, surrounded by immense mountains: the hottest part of the season, an army of 25,000 men, and ten times that number at least accompanying it with bullocks, horses, elephants, etc., for the transport of the baggage, heavy artillery, etc No clean water to be had but the colour of the dirtiest puddle, and this for a poor sick devil.

I clung to the army as long as I could hold up my head, and when we came to the foot of the *Ghaut* that divides Mysore from the Carnatic I was ordered with other sick officers and men to proceed to the fort of Kishnagherry. I was put down more dead than alive at the house of Scott Jackson, the paymaster of the district He came out for the second time in the same fleet with myself. He received me in the most kind and hospitable manner. He was a gentlemanlike, elegant young man, and he paid me ever)' attention. I had also two clever medical men to attend me—a Dr. McMorris, still living, (as at time of first publication), and a Dr, Orde, long since dead.

I had been living about a month with Jackson, when we heard news from the army. Among the casualties in my regiment was the death of poor Falla from a cannon-ball, a twelve-pounder, from the fort of Seringapatam, three miles distant from our trenches. It rolled in and buried itself in poor Falla's groin. It was the most remarkable wound ever seen, and the general conversation of the army, for the shot was not to be seen, the flesh swelling completely over it George Nixon, Lieutenant of Grenadiers, lost his arm and part of his side by a rocket, and the same rocket struck the legs of his brother Robert, making a dreadful deep wound. George died, but Robert recovered.

There were two detachments of the army in our vicinity, or, more correctly speaking, only one—Colonel Read's. The other, under Colonel Brown, was several marches off, hastening to join Colonel Read, bringing up rice and other stores for the use of the army. I joined Colonel Read with other sick officers and men who were convalescent, but had to wait with Colonel Read for the junction of Colonel Brown several days. Had we proceeded alone *without waiting*, we should have been present at the capture of that fortress. We arrived three days too late, and had the mortification of hearing the cannonade going on without being present at it The long and fatiguing marches of this army caused me to have a relapse, as I had not perfectly recovered.

I was seized with a confirmed dysentery, and on arriving with my regiment I was ordered into the palace of the Lai Bagh, which was one of the country palaces of Tippoo Sultan, converted into a hospital, in the gardens of which was a mosque shaded by cypress-trees, where lay the remains of his father, Hyder Ali, his wives and children, and lastly, deposited only a few days before, the body of Tippoo Sultan. These beautiful gardens, shaded with luxuriant trees and broad gravel walks, were dug with deep trenches, and yet from the hardness of the ground not sufficiently deep for graves for the poor soldiers who were carried when dead out of the gorgeous palace to be interred in these *ready-made* graves, and from their being so very shallow the jackals came at night and pulled them out again. I have often seen an arm with the red sleeve hanging out of a grave, the soldiers always being buried in their uniforms.

On my arrival sick at the palace I found all the private soldiers lying on the bare ground, some in the agonies of death. It was a shocking sight to behold. The heat and smell were dreadful. The upper rooms were assigned to the officers. Captain Buckeridge of ours and Lieutenant Perceval went into this hospital sick. They both died there; indeed, few who breathed this pestiferous air ever came out alive. Fortunately for me I was obliged to return to camp, there not being any vacant corner to place me in. I thought it mattered very little where I died, for I did not expect to live more than a few hours. My inside appeared to be all gone, and part of the intestines absolutely given way.

The whole camp teemed with death and contagion. The flies and insects settled upon everything that was eatable, and the bullocks and other animals dying continually, these flies were continually feasting upon their carcases, and then settled upon our faces and provisions. I lay in this deplorable state for two or three days, when a Lieutenant Ashton brought me a couple of bottles of port wine which he had purchased at some deceased officer's sale. From the moment I took two glasses of this precious wine I gradually recovered, all owing to its astringent and nourishing properties. This certainly saved my life. These two bottles of wine fetched a large price, such was the scarcity of wine in general, but more particularly port, which is never tasted in India but as medicine.

On my arrival before Seringapatam I found a new lieutenant-colonel appointed from the 74th Regiment, known in that regiment by the sobriquet of 'Old *Sour Crout*.' Never did man merit the name better. He was a zealous, brave old man, and looked like a gentleman, but nothing pleased him. He was an old officer, and his name was Robert Shawe. He often used to boast that the Honourable Colonel Wellesley was his subaltern when he commanded the light infantry of the 76th Regiment. He was certainly, without any exception, the most peevish, waspish, disagreeable old gentleman I ever fell in with, and the most difficult to please. How happy I was to leave his tent whenever my duty obliged me to come in contact with him! He had a rich Milesian brogue. A favourite phrase of his was: 'Sir, don't *spake* when I am *spaking!* What a contrast to poor dear Aston!

At this time I was very near getting a company by purchase. A company became vacant in England, and old Shawe gave out an order that those subalterns wishing and able to purchase should send their names into the orderly-room. I knew I had the money in England, but the whole sum (£1,500), must be placed down immediately. It so happened that my name appeared to be the first for purchase, and I believe the only one. Old Shawe sent for me, and said: 'I *persave*, sir, you are the first officer for purchase. Where is your money?'

'In England, sir.'

'That will not do; it must be lodged at a house of agency in Madras.'

'Very well, sir.' So I returned to my tent and thought of all my friends in India. None struck me so likely as my kind friend Benjamin Torin at Madras. I wrote to him explaining my situation, and told him I had that sum in the English Funds, and if he would take my bills on his friend Mr. Hutchinson, and advance me the money, I should be eternally obliged to him. By return of post he sent me the kindest answer, saying he had lodged the sum of £1,500 for me in the house of Harrington and Co. of Madras.

There was in the regiment a very deserving young Irishman of the name of Eustace, and a favourite of Colonel Aston's, chiefly from the circumstance of his having, when quite a boy, been very near taken prisoner by the French on the Continent, and defending a gun very gallantly and narrowly escaping from the French. Major Craigie requested Eustace to go to me and beg me to resign my right to the purchase, as Major Craigie would arrange the purchase for him. I did not like to take the advantage which I had over him under the peculiar circumstances, and I resigned my right in his favour. I did not get my company for four years after this, and then by purchase, and Captain Eustace got his majority and lieutenant-colonelcy in a few years after for nothing, which I should have had if I had insisted upon my right to purchase the company. Such is the lottery of our service.

Writing of lotteries puts me in mind of my first cousin, Miss Debonnaire, who was intimate with a Jew, a stockbroker of the name of Ricardo, and father of the celebrated rich financier, a man unrivalled in his way in the House of Commons, who acquired an immense fortune by his financial skill and good management. She desired old Ricardo to purchase her a ticket in the lottery, and told him he should have half of it. The old man took one of his little sons with him, and told the boy to purchase a ticket while he sat in the carriage. The boy had several tickets to choose from. He selected one, and this ticket came up a £20,000 prize.

Miss Debonnaire gave Ricardo the £10,000, besides making many handsome presents. The little boy got a watch-chain and seals, value fifty guineas. Lady Curtis a handsome new carriage, and she sent me £100. She soon after married her cousin, William Tennant, Esq., a widower with one only son, with a good estate in Staffordshire called Little Aston Hall, worth £6,000 or £7,000 *per annum*. This gentleman, notwithstanding his fine estate, was in want of £10,000, and on her marriage she made him a present of that sum; the rest of her fortune was settled upon herself. She had also a jointure of £700 *per annum*, which, considering he had but one son and his large fortune, was a very inadequate provision for her, particularly after her liberal conduct to him upon their marriage. They spent the honeymoon at Bath, and their turn-out was in the best style—never less than four horses and two post-riders.

Very few men were better judges of a horse than Mrs. Tennant, and her taste in building carriages was perfect. She never had a carnage more than three years at the utmost. Houlditch, of Long Acre, used to build for my uncle and aunt, and also for my cousin Nancy, as we used to call her. She afterwards patronized Windus, a City man. During her stay in Bath she went into a bookseller's shop, where she purchased another ticket, and this proved a prize of £5,000. Her husband did not survive his marriage more than two years, and his son shortly after married the Hon. Charlotte Pelham, daughter of Lord Yarborough, with whom he got a fortune of not more than £15,000 or £20,000, which is all, I believe, he ever received, though his lordship's fortune was £120,000 *per annum*.[1] Young Tennant in his early years was a delicate and sickly child. Had he died, all his estates would have reverted to my cousin, Mrs. Tennant And she said if they had we should have been her heirs.

About a month after the siege a poor child about ten years old, found in the fort in rags and poverty, was proved to be a lineal descendant of the prince who formerly ruled over the Mysore country, who, many years before, had been deposed by Hyder and had had his country taken from him. The English Government took this favourable opportunity of restoring this poor child to the *musnud* of his ancestors. The city of Mysore is distant from Seringapatam about ten miles, and our regiment was selected to preside over his inauguration. It is the custom to give presents on such ceremonies, and on this occasion I got a shawl; so that in the space of one year I was present at the restoration of two *rajahs*.

The army broke up, and we were marked down for Bangalore, whither we marched, and encamped on the glacis of the fort. I drew a bill on England for £300, and my kind friend Mr. Torin honoured it. I believe the reason I did this was that the officers having their prize-money to spend and I having none, having missed the storm by three days only, I could not do as they did. For had we not awaited the arrival of Colonel Brown's detachment. Colonel Read, whom I belonged to, would have been in time for the storming. It was considered a very hard case by all the army, and after keeping us from receiving it for years, it was at length granted to us; but I did not receive it until the

---

1. The writer slightly exaggerates Lord Yarborough's income.

year 1807, and without one shilling interest, which was our due.

There are a certain class of people with an army called prize agents. There is no doubt this interest found its way into their pockets. The sum I received was about £430; a captain received £800, a major £2,000, a lieutenant-colonel £4,000, a major-general £12,000, and the commander-in-chief one-eighth of the whole prize-money captured. The idea at first was that every officer in the army had made at least from £10,000 to £20,000. And even General Baird, whom I dined with, expressed his disappointment at receiving so small a sum as £12,000. He expected at the very least £100,000. The wealth captured was enormous, and consisted of all sorts of property from every court in Europe. There was splendid china from the King of France, clocks, watches, shawls of immense value, trinkets, jewellery from all nations, pearls, rubies, diamonds and emeralds, and every other precious stone made up into ornaments—even solid wedges and bars of pure gold.

A soldier offered me *one* for a bottle of brandy. Many of the officers received part of their prize-money in jewels at a fixed valuation. I saw an emerald in its rough and uncut state valued at £200. Many of our soldiers acquired by plunder what would have made them independent for life if properly managed, I heard that one of them soon after the storm staggered under as many pagodas as he could carry—to the amount, it was said, of ;£10,000. A soldier of the 74th Regiment got the best prize, consisting of two pairs of the *sultan's* armlets, composed of large diamonds of an oval shape, each diamond as large as a full-grown Windsor bean. This man had been confined sick in the hospital, and had come out of the sick list in time to be at the storm.

Soon after May 4 Dr. Pulteney Mein, the surgeon, was called out of his tent to speak to this man, who said to him: 'Your honour, I have got some large white stones, and a black fellow has offered me 1,500 *rupees* for them. If you will give me that sum for them they are yours.'

Mein was a liberal, honest, but wary Scotchman. He knew the value of 1,500 *rupees*; he was not so sure of these white stones. After some hesitation he said: 'Well, it's like purchasing in the lottery; I will give you your price.'

Rumours soon spread in the army of the prize which he had got, and an order was published by the commander-in-chief for all officers to give up their plunder for the general benefit of the captors. Mein tied these valuables up in a muslin handkerchief, and wore them next his skin for upwards of two years. Meer Allum, a Mahratta prince, offered him an enormous sum for them. However, he realized upwards of £2,000 *per annum*, nothing near what he had been offered by the prince; and he was generous enough to give the soldier an annuity of £200, which the poor man did not live long to enjoy.

I often have mused upon what trifles will turn the scale and have an influence upon our future fortunes. Had Colonel Wellesley been an obscure soldier of fortune, he would have been brought to a court-martial, and perhaps received such a reprimand for bad management as might have induced him in disgust to have resigned His Majesty's service, whereby one of the greatest soldiers England ever had would have been lost to the country. But Colonel Wellesley, fortunately for himself and his country, was brother to the Governor-General of India, and that was enough to wipe away any neglect or bad management, if any existed; but which, in Colonel Wellesley's case, I believe did *not* exist, and might have happened to any man, however experienced and vigilant.

Within a short distance of Seringapatam a large wood or tope lay between the fort and our army. The enemy were strongly posted there, and it was necessary to dislodge them. Colonel Wellesley was ordered on this service with the 33rd Regiment and a regiment of native infantry. The colonel that evening had dined with General Harris, and at night he proceeded to execute the orders he had received to drive the enemy out and take possession of it. The night was dark as pitch *forward*, and in the *rear* towards our camp the fires and lights burnt brilliantly, which increased the darkness in front. The force under the colonel moved towards the wood cautiously and silently, when suddenly a fire from all directions was poured in upon them. 'Where's Colonel Wellesley?' resounded on all sides, and the colonel was nowhere to be found. The officers were trying to find the colonel, and the colonel vainly endeavouring to find them. All was confusion, and they were surrounded both by friends and enemies firing on each other.

Colonel Wellesley, finding it impossible from the utter darkness of the night to discern any object, and despairing from this ever to form his force together, returned to camp, and repaired to the dining tent of General Harris overcome with despair at his failure. He eagerly inquired for the general. One of the servants said; 'Master, General Sahib, gone to sleep.' In a state of distraction Colonel Wellesley threw himself, with all his clothes on, *on the table* (at which a few hours before he had dined), awaiting the dawn of day.

General Harris, having received the report of this *untoward* business, immediately called his staff, and General Baird was sent for to take the command of a new force to dislodge the enemy. Baird said: 'No; Colonel Wellesley has failed, not through the want of skill or bravery, but from circumstances. He is a young man, and if I supersede him it may cast a slur on his future career as a military man. Let him have the command by daylight, and I will answer for it he will carry the wood and drive the enemy out as well as I can.'

The command was given to Wellesley, and he achieved it, as Baird foretold. The night attack which was so unfortunate was on April 5; and on May 4 the fort was stormed, and General Baird commanded the storming party and took possession of the fort, where he remained as commanding officer for about ten days.

I received all the *former* part of this narrative from the Colonel's A.D.C., Captain Hughes, of the 74th Regiment. With respect to the unjust affair of the superseding poor Baird in the command of Seringapatam, I heard it from Colonel Wellesley's *own statement*, in the apartment of the palace, the Dowlet Bagh, where the scene occurred. Colonel Wellesley said, in his rapid manner of speaking: 'I went down to Baird one morning early, and found him at breakfast with his staff. "General Baird, I am appointed to the command of Seringapatam, and here is the order of General Harris." Baird immediately rose, and addressing his staff, said: "Come, gentlemen, we have no longer any business here." Wellesley said: 'Oh, pray finish your breakfast.'

This is all that Colonel Wellesley told me about this curious scene. Some two years afterwards, upon General Harris's return home, and on attending the Duke of York at one of his levees at the Horse Guards, Harris, who was not very quick in a difficulty, was asked quickly and suddenly by the duke: 'Pray, General Harris, what reason had you for superseding General Baird in the command of Seringapatam and giving it to a junior officer?' Poor Harris stammered, and was at a loss for a reply, and the duke turned his back upon him, and began a conversation with some officers.

Having received my £300 for my bill from Mr. Torin, the first thing I did was to buy a charter—cavalry saddle, Gibson's bit, holsters all complete—for which I paid £120. My horse, which I bought of my[2] Captain Woodall, cost £100, and my pony I exchanged with

---

2. By 'my' captain the author evidently refers to Captain Woodall's being in command of the Light Infantry Company to which he himself belonged, see chapter 2.—(Original) Ed.

Dr. Campbell for Colonel Aston's duelling pistols, as *they* involve no charge for maintenance, and I saved the keep of the pony, and they completed my cavalry equipment. My charger was full 15 hands high, colour a very dark chestnut, a beautiful shoulder, high crest, a hollow back, very blood-like racing hind-quarters, with a showy blood tail. His having a hollow back was a bad point, but when one was on his back with a cavalry saddle and being well thrown on his haunches, nothing could be more delightful and easy to ride. He had great spirit, but was of good temper.

I left Bangalore for Madras in company with an old officer who went by the name of Cornet Kippen, I suppose from his holding that rank so many years, for at the time I knew him he was a captain of native cavalry. He was uncouth in his manners, but sociable, and he used to entertain me during our journey with various Indian anecdotes. I afterwards heard one of him and General Baird laughable enough. The cornet was a man of very great curiosity; he happened one day to be in General Baird's tent when he was answering some letters he had just received from England. Turning suddenly round, he saw the cornet peeping over his shoulder reading them. All the reproof he gave him was: 'Mr. Kippen, here are others of a later date !'

On our march one morning we observed at a distance a group of natives digging at a mound of earth, and one of them kneeling down; and as we came up to the man he very suddenly withdrew his hand, having been bitten in the finger by a snake. In the course of two or three minutes the man began to feel great pain and sickness. The natives tied a bandage very tight round his arm, and applied a small gray stone to the punctures in his finger. In a few minutes he was relieved from the pain, and in the course of half an hour the stone was taken off the wound, and the man declared he felt quite well. I purchased this stone of the natives, and they told me if we had any milk and put the stone into the milk, it would cause the milk to bubble up as though it were boiling. They pulled the snake out of the hole, and it proved to be a large *cobra de capello*. I drew my sword to kill it, but they would not allow me. They said that the man bitten would die if I killed the snake. The natives of India never kill them, and they are generally worshipped and preserved.

A melancholy accident happened in the gardens of the palace. A doctor named Scheltky belonged to the Scotch Brigade. Dr. Campbell, of my regiment, and Dr. Scheltky had their tents pitched close together near the hospital. Dr. S. one night came into Dr. Campbell's tent nearly undressed to smoke a cigar and chat for half an hour before going to bed. On his return Campbell heard the doctor cry out: 'I have either been hit by a stone on the leg or I have been bitten by a snake.' Campbell brought a light, and in one corner of the tent lay coiled up a large snake. Campbell got his gun and killed it. It was not a cobra, but was most beautifully marked with rings as far as the centre of the body, and it had a long tail gradually ending in a point. Poor Scheltky died in great pain three days afterwards. There are about forty-seven or fifty different species of snakes in the East Indies, of which not more than seven are venomous. The *cobra de monil* is reckoned by the natives as the most deadly. It is not more than a foot and a half long. The snake-snatchers are in great dread of this snake.

My friend the cornet parted from me about forty or fifty miles short of Madras, and I was left to pursue my journey with only my servants for company. I missed the cornet very much. I passed one or two days in a *choultry*, confined to it by incessant rain, it being the very middle of the monsoon, and my entry into the fort of Madras was very inauspicious. Turning short round, through the Wallagah Gateway, my horse, from the slippery state of the roads, slipped down on all fours. Neither of us, very fortunately, received any hurt. I know not what took me into the fort, for there was only one tavern, and that, like all others, very bad and ruinously expensive.

I went finally to one of the taverns in the Black Town; I found out that they were dirty and expensive, and not very respectable, only frequented by unfortunate midshipmen, who had no friends to receive them ashore, and who spent in two or three days' residence more than what their pay amounted to in twice as many months. So I went out to live at St. Thomé, about two miles from Madras, close to the sea. And here I found Captains Crawford and Nixon of ours, and Captain Dalrymple of the 74th, all living together most comfortably in a fine house. So I was in no want of society.

After living here till the beginning of January, my regiment had moved from Bangalore into the Carnatic, and had arrived at a station called Wallajahbad, forty miles from Madras. I joined my regiment at this station, got into a good quarter, and found a good billiard-table, a good regimental library, and excellent shooting and hunting. The snipes are capital eating. A good shot will bring home thirty brace a day. I never killed more than seven brace; but I was not a good shot The exercise in the heat of the sun is very hard work indeed, and trying to the constitution. We had moderate drills and evening parades, and in the middle of the day we amused ourselves visiting each other's quarters and gossiping under the long verandas. We had also a very good mess. We spent our time very pleasantly. I bought a beautiful little pony, so that I now had a good charger, and the pony was so quiet that I could shoot off his back.

Our regiment received orders about June to march to Poonamallee, about fifteen miles from Madras, there to remain till further orders. It was reported that it was destined to go on an expedition to Batavia. I was first for detachment, and I was ordered to remain at Wallajahbad with the sick men, about fifty in number, and a guard of about twenty or thirty men, together with the assistant-surgeon, Dr. Erskine, and a sick officer, Lieutenant Langford. This poor man had only dined with us twice, when he took to his bed and died. I saw him when dead. He looked sad and sorrowful, different from Winstone, who had the most stern expression of feature, or from poor Colonel Aston, who looked as if he were asleep with a sweet smile.

I buried this poor man by reading the Burial Service over him and firing three volleys over the grave. I had this melancholy office to perform over several of the soldiers. I found myself very dull here, separated from my regiment, though it was a source of great profit to me, as I made a considerable sum from the bazaar, from my situation as commanding officer over seventy or eighty men.

CHAPTER 6

A Dangerous Journey

At length I received my orders to join, with all the sick, the headquarters of the regiment at Poonamallee, and there I heard to my great joy that old Sour Crout's appointment to our regiment was not approved of at home, and that he was to go back to his own corps, the 74th, and also that we might expect a fine young man to join us, a Lieutenant-Colonel George William Richard Harcourt,[1] whose kind and amiable manners were to restore harmony and good-humour to the corps after poor Aston's melancholy business. In a very short time Colonel Harcourt arrived from England, bringing with him both officers and men for the regiment He was a tall, thin young man of about twenty-eight years of age, with a pale face, slight and elegantly turned figure, small aquiline nose, large whiskers and light brown hair, without powder.

His manners were perfectly polished, and he seemed to say: 'I am come to make you all happy and heal all your differences.' He had commanded the 40th Regiment in the West Indies, and had been wounded severely some short time before. He brought out with him a young man as a servant, to whom he was much attached. He also brought out a fashionable curricle, which I sold for him two years later to Colonel Wellesley. He arrived with plate, books, and everything in the best possible style. I was one of the first officers of the regiment he saw, and he seemed pleased with my stud and paid me some compliments upon my riding. We were all highly delighted with our new and young colonel, and so he appeared with us. We were soon after, to our great annoyance, divided.

Two companies were sent to sea, supposed destined, in company

---
1. George William Richard Harcourt, younger son of John Harcourt, of Ankerwyke, County Bucks. A major-general in the army; died unmarried.

with other troops, for Batavia, and three other companies were sent to the southward, under Major Picton, against some turbulent Polygar *rajahs*. The remaining five companies with Colonel Harcourt, the flank company's band and colours, marched to the Mysore country. We had a very pleasant march through the Carnatic, and we kept up our mess until we arrived at the Ghauts, when it was too much trouble and difficulty for our mess men to carry it on further, and then we divided ourselves into small mess parties, and provided for ourselves as well as we could. My brother sub., Robert Sale, now a colonel in the 13th Regiment, messed with me, and Colonel Harcourt and Captain Nixon and Crawford messed together, and they often gave us capital dinners find breakfasts.

During our march, after we had entered the Mysore country, an unfortunate dispute took place between a Lieutenant Price and Captain Nixon. I do not know the origin of the quarrel, but Price was a hot-headed young Irishman, and committed himself in a way that obliged Colonel Harcourt to put him under arrest. And he was in this situation when Colonel Wellesley happened to come across us on his march down to the Carnatic, he being appointed to proceed with troops destined to join Sir Ralph Abercromby in Egypt. Colonel Wellesley, who then commanded the troops in Mysore, gave orders that a general court-martial should assemble for the trial of Lieutenant Price, and, poor fellow, he was broke. It was a most distressing sight seeing him every day riding without his sword, and, after the sentence, deprived of his two epaulettes, being a lieutenant of grenadiers.

All this scene was distressing to Colonel Harcourt, but he was obliged to report what had taken place, with so unpleasant a result. This made Captain Nixon very unpopular with a few of the junior pan of the regiment, and there was a hot young Irish assistant surgeon, a Mr. Washington Price (no relation to the officer of that name who had been broke), who was particularly violent against Nixon. A fierce quarrel broke out many months after at Seringapatam, which ended in a duel at Warriore, near Trichinopoli, in the Carnatic.

After marching for some time about the Mysore country, we were ordered to proceed to Seringapatam previously to an army of about 5,000 men being formed under the command of Colonel Stephenson, of the Madras Cavalry, to proceed to the Cotiote country against the Rajah of that name. The army was divided into three brigades. Colonel Harcourt commanded one of them. Our five companies and the 77th Regiment were the First Brigade, and I was appointed Colonel

Harcourt's brigade-major. The Cotiote country lies distant, I should suppose, from Seringapatam about sixty to eighty miles due west, and between it and Mysore lies a small territory called Coorg, the *rajah* of which has always been at peace with the Company, while the Rajah of Cotiote has invariably been hostile, and it was in the early part of 1797 when he surprised a battalion of native infantry and they were all massacred.

No favourable opportunity having occurred to avenge this barbarity, our force was destined for that purpose. The country is by nature very strong, filled with thick jungle, with no roads and deep rivers, and not ground enough clear from wood to encamp too men. We were led to expect a very unpleasant service, as it proved to be. In a few marches we crossed the frontier of the enemy's country. The roads were very bad, and in getting into the country of Cotiote the pioneers were constantly employed, and our progress was very slow, not more than a mile, or at most two miles an hour. A broad and rapid river ran on our left, and we could not see, from the thickness of the jungle, more than a few yards from our flanks.

It was on January 9, 1801, that we commenced hostilities. The road took a sharp turn to the left, and brought us nearly in front and in view of this rapid and deep river, the name of which I forget, when from the opposite banks the enemy opened his fire from the tops of the trees upon our advanced guard, which was supported by the grenadiers of the 12th Regiment. We could not see a man, but could perceive the fire from the top of the trees. Some of the grenadiers plunged into the stream, but were obliged to return for fear of being drowned. We poured in platoon after platoon upon them, but could make no impression until we brought up a gun, and the *juice of the grape* by degrees silenced them.

We did not lose many men, considering. I saw two of our grenadiers lying lifeless, being shot through the head, and several others lying dead. Colonel Harcourt took it very coolly, as he was accustomed to engagements, laughing and taking his snuff as usual. As for myself, I was very well content when it was all over and the rascals fairly off. Our loss was very inconsiderable, not above thirty men altogether.

On this march we established a strong post on halting, and built a strong stockade there. The post and village were called Manantaudi. Here we remained three weeks, sending out strong parties to scour the country, and we used to have a good deal of bush fighting, and the natives used to fire at us from behind trees. One man of my company was shot through the lungs in this way; the ball entered his chest and out at his back. The poor fellow died in the course of the night. He was close to me when he was shot.

I had been with the army about three or four months upon this service when, in crossing a river one day, I suddenly got into deep water and fell in over head and ears. I was very hot at the time, and the next day I had a regular attack of what they call jungle fever. We had nearly effected our object. The enemy fled in all directions, and there was scarcely a man to be seen. Our men got sickly from this unwholesome country, where the sun never penetrated, and the miasma arising from the rotting vegetation proved very prejudicial to their health. We were, therefore, expecting every hour to receive orders to march and do the garrison duty of Seringapatam. We were not above forty miles from a place on the coast of Malabar called Talatcheri, and to this place I went for change of air.

I found here a Mr. Waddell, of the Bombay Civil Service, who very kindly showed both myself, Colonel Harcourt, and Captain Crawford much hospitable attention. These two only remained here a day or two, when they returned to the regiment, leaving me to stay a few days more for the benefit of the sea-breeze. We had a Captain Macleod lately appointed to us, an old officer in bad health, living at Talatcheri. I called upon him, and saw a most beautiful Arab horse tied up in his yard. I fell in love with him, and Captain Macleod agreed to accept in exchange for this Arab a very handsome mare of mine, which I had bought of an officer of the 19th Light Dragoons, and for which I had paid 100 *pagodas*; I also paid Captain Macleod about 70 *pagodas* extra.

This Arab had a most beautiful head, a large dark eye like an antelope; he was a silver-gray, with a dark mane, and long square tail of the same colour. He had broken knees, and was very apt to trip, but he was the quietest creature in the world. Often have I laid down by his side at night when he has been sleeping. He was just 14.2. This horse afterwards proved a little fortune to me.

Colonel Wellesley having been superseded in command of the Indian force for Egypt by General Baird at Bombay, by order, I believe, of his brother at Calcutta, landed either at Talatcheri or Cannanore, attended by his *A.D.C.*, Captain West, of the 33rd Regiment, and his Persian interpreter, Major Ogg, of the Company's service. I saw him, and he said to me: 'Elers, I think it will be better for you to accompany me to Seringapatam, where I shall go directly, and where your regiment will follow to be stationed there, and you can live with me until they arrive.' I thanked him, and I joined him at Cannanore. I had with me my horses, servants, baggage, and camp equipage.

Colonel Wellesley's health at this time was not very good. He had had a touch of the jungle fever in the Bullum country, and I believe at Bombay a violent eruption came out all over his body; but when I saw him he was getting convalescent, but was rather subject to slight touches of fever and ague. No one but those who have experienced these attacks are sensible how they undermine the constitution. They will turn a young man's hair gray very soon. I was but twenty-four years old when my favourite servant Francis, a Portuguese Christian, said: 'Master getting quite old gentleman. I see two, three, four gray hairs.'

I said: 'Pull them out, you rascal.'

'Oh no, master; me pull out, *tousand* come.'

Colonel Wellesley was just thirty-two, and I saw some about his temples mixed with his fine crop of light-brown hair. Colonel Wellesley had a magnificent tent to dine in, the largest I ever saw. It took thirty *lascars* to raise it

When we left Cannanore we had only a guard of six troopers; between us and our friend the Coorga *rajah's* country lay part of our enemy's, the Cotiote country. Colonel Wellesley and I dashed on together first, unaccompanied by his staff or the troopers, when he observed to me: 'Now, Elers, if we are taken prisoners, I shall be hanged as being brother to the governor-general, and you will be hanged for being found in bad company.' We had not to go above thirty miles, when we safely reached the territory of the Coorga Rajah. I felt my mind much relieved, for, notwithstanding the joking way in which the colonel treated it, we should most assuredly have been put to death; and in that case he would never have fought the Battle of Waterloo, or I recounted my adventures.

Before I entirely take leave of this part of the Malabar coast, I must relate an accident that happened to a man of the 77th Regiment. From the confined nature of the ground, overrun with jungle, it was difficult to find a vacant spot to pitch a tent, and there was no regularity in the pitching of the tents, officers' and privates' being close together.

One day I was in Colonel Harcourt's tent, when a shot whizzed close by us. I ran out, thinking we were surprised; but on inquiry I found that the armourers' forge of the 77th Regiment was pitched together with a tent where some tailors of the same regiment were at work close together. One of the armourers had a pistol to repair for an officer, and he, not aware that it was loaded, put it into the fire. It exploded, and the ball entered the temple of an unlucky tailor sitting at work in the next tent. It went in at one temple and out at the opposite; but the poor tailor recovered from this extraordinary wound, and I saw him alive and well six months after, but with the loss of both his eyes.

On the night we arrived in the country of the Coorga Rajah we were sitting drinking our wine after dinner, congratulating ourselves that we had arrived there, when, looking through the tent doors, we saw the forest suddenly illuminated with torches, and many men carrying all sorts of game on bamboos. This was a present from the Rajah of Coorg to Colonel Wellesley, giving him a very small specimen of his day's sport, and hoping that he would spend a few days with him, as he was hunting in his country. Among the specimens of the game sent were eleven elephants' tails, cut off that day; a large snake; a boa-constrictor, 16 feet in length, lashed to a long bamboo, and carried by six or seven *coolies*; cheetahs, tigers, foxes, jackals, etc., and three immense carp. The *rajah* had an annual hunt, and we happened to arrive on his hunting day. He sent his *salaam*, and said he should next day come and pay his respects to the colonel. The next morning he sent two of his tents, and they were pitched close to ours. They were red and green striped. He also sent chess and backgammon boards of the handsomest sort, inlaid with ebony and ivory, and the chessmen of the finest kind, carved in ivory, with rose-water, betel, etc.

The *rajah* arrived soon after breakfast, preceded by a guard of about one hundred men, clothed in green, and armed with bows and arrows, the *rajah* himself mounted on a charger, with English boots and pantaloons, the rest of his dress Eastern. He was a man of middle age, and spoke a little English. The two chiefs got off their horses, and immediately embraced three distinct times. They then retired to their tents and conversed in Persian, Major Ogg acting as interpreter. In one part of the conversation I admired Colonel Wellesley's quickness in detecting Major Ogg giving an erroneous interpretation to a speech of his to the *rajah*. The colonel was clever in quickly acquiring languages, but spoke none very correctly, and I believe this applies to his Spanish and Portuguese at the present time.

The poor *rajah* urged that he had ever been faithful to the English, his country and revenue small, that the Company took from him by way of *kist* 5,000 *pagodas* annually, and he wished the colonel to intercede for him with the governor-general to remit it altogether, which the colonel, to the great joy of the *rajah,* promised to do. He pressed the colonel to spend a few days hunting with him, but the colonel told him he was most anxious to arrive at Seringapatam, but he promised him he would visit him at a more favourable opportunity. They parted with mutual expressions of goodwill and friendship, and Colonel Wellesley, wishing to make him a present according to Eastern custom, was much puzzled what to give him, not being prepared. He gave him a handsome English rifle, which the *rajah* was much pleased with, and said would be of great use to him on his hunting excursions.

Colonel Wellesley was so anxious to arrive at the fort that the two or three last marches were so long and rapid that my servants and baggage were left behind, and I arrived at Seringapatam at the palace of the Dowlet Bagh without a single suit of clean clothes. He desired his head servant, an old fellow of the name of Vingetty, to give me whatever of his clothes I wanted, such as shirts, trousers and waistcoats, which fitted me very well, and, above all, he ordered him to give me a good room and cot to sleep on. It was a back-room, and looked into the gardens of the palace. I was much pleased to lie down and recover from the fatigue I had gone through, for I was nearly knocked up from following the great man in his rapid movements. When the dinner-hour arrived he placed me on his left hand, and said: 'That is your place;' and there I sat every day for the next three months. We sat in the centre of the table, his *A.D.C.,* Captain West, at the top of the table, and Captain Barclay, the deputy adjutant-general, at the bottom. This comprised the family, but there were always other officers, guests, altogether from eight to a dozen, every day.

Colonel Wellesley kept a plain but good table. He had a very good appetite, and his favourite dish was a roast saddle of mutton and salad. This dish was placed opposite to him, and he generally made his dinner off it. He was very abstemious with wine; drank four or five glasses with people at dinner, and about a pint of claret after. He was very even in his temper, laughing and joking with those he liked, speaking in his quick way, and dwelling particularly upon the few (*at that time*) situations he had been placed in before the enemy, the arrangements he had made, and their fortunate results, all of which were applauded by his staff, who had shared in the glory and peril.

This generally formed the topic of conversation after dinner. He was particularly severe upon any neglect of the commissariat department, and openly declared that, if he commanded an army, he should not hesitate to hang a *commissary* for any dereliction of duty. He was very apprehensive of being superseded in his command of Mysore; and when a General Frazer of the King's service had at that time just landed in India, he was apprehensive he might take his command from him. He said: 'We want no major-generals in Mysore.'

I remember one day, on our march from Cannanore, he received an overland despatch from England.. The chief item of intelligence was that the Earl of Mornington, then Marques of Wellesley, had received a pension of £5,000 a year for his services and judicious arrangements with respect to the war with Tippoo Sahib. The next was a brevet giving the old colonels the step of major-generals. He was all hope and animation. 'Do you happen to have an Army List, Elers?'

I said 'Yes,' and I ran to my tent and fetched it for him, saying: 'I am sorry to tell you, colonel, it does not include you as a major-general. You are within about five or six of it.'

He said sorrowfully: '*My highest ambition* is to be a *major-general* in His Majesty's service.' This was uttered to me in May, 1801. Fourteen years afterwards he had fought the Battle of Waterloo, conquered Bonaparte, was a Prince, a Duke, a Knight of the Garter, Grand Cross of the Bath, a Grandee of Spain, and a Grand Cross of, I believe, every order of knighthood in Europe. His humble friend, I, George Elers, at that time took his hand and said to comfort him: 'Never mind, colonel; the next brevet must bring you in, and in a few days you will have the command of Seringapatam, where honour and wealth attend on you!'

A few days after our coming to Seringapatam arrived rather a pretty and lively woman, a Mrs. Stephenson, the wife of Colonel Stephenson, awaiting her husband's arrival from the Cotiote country. With his usual gallantry and politeness to the fair, apartments were assigned to the lady by the colonel, and she made for some time a very pleasant addition to our circle.

I used to go out sometimes with the colonel on his elephant. He had a very handsome *howdah* to it, and the elephant was entirely covered over with superfine scarlet cloth, hanging within two feet of the ground. I think the *howdah* was a present from Colonel Close, of the Company's service. When Colonel Wellesley was first appointed to the command of Seringapatam, Tippoo Sahib's hunting establishment was found in the fort, and the colonel wrote to government about it. The government did not wish to be at the expense of keeping it up, and Colonel Wellesley kept them at his own charge. They consisted of several leopards and cheetahs, with their keepers, regularly trained for the purpose of hunting the antelope on the plains of Seringapatam. It is very well to see it once, but it is poor sport.

The Company go out on elephants and on horseback. The cheetahs are placed with their keepers on what are called *hackerries*, or small open carts drawn by bullocks; they are hoodwinked and ready to be let slip when a herd of deer appear. The antelope is a very shy animal, and will not allow you to approach nearer than some two hundred yards. This having been accomplished, the *hackerries* stop, and the man takes the bandage off the cheetah's eyes. He leaps like a cat upon the ground, and sinks down upon his belly, wagging his tail. He fixes his eyes upon one particular deer, steals along for thirty or forty paces, and then crouches down.

After doing this two or three times the herd take themselves off full gallop, all but one unfortunate, whose eyes have been fascinated by the cheetah. He endeavours to escape; he makes a feeble effort, when the cheetah in a few bounds overtakes him and fastens upon him. The keeper runs up, throws the winkers over the cheetah's eyes, and preserves the antelope from being eaten up; but life is extinct. He takes out a knife, and, extracting the entrails, they are given to the cheetah as a reward for his pains. All the motions of a cheetah are exactly like those of a cat upon a lawn springing after birds.

We had a billiard-table at the palace, and I used to play sometimes with Captain West. I once remember playing two games with Colonel Wellesley, in both of which I beat him. We used to get up early in the morning and attend the garrison parade, and Colonel Wellesley used, of course, to be saluted by the Guards as they marched off. His dress at this time consisted of a *long coat*, the uniform of the 33rd Regiment, a *cocked hat*, white pantaloons, Hessian boots and spurs, and a large sabre, the handle solid silver, and the mounting of the scabbard of the same metal, but all gilt He never wore powder, though it was at that time the regulation to do so. His hair was cropped close. I have heard him say he was convinced the wearing of hair powder was very prejudicial to health as impeding the perspiration, and he was doubtless right.

Major Woodall joined our regiment about this time, bringing up with him a lady he had lately married;[2] she was a Miss Cochrane, a natural daughter of the Earl of Dundonald, and now married to Sir George Tuite, Baronet.

---

2. Janet, widow of Major Thomas Woodall, of the 12th Regiment, married, June 8, 1807, Sir George Tuite, Bart..

About this time an unpleasant business took place at Seringapatam, which obliged Colonel Wellesley to act as prosecutor at a general court-martial ordered to take place at Seringapatam upon three officers of the artillery of the Company's Service—*viz.*, Lieutenant-Colonel Saxon, Lieutenant-Colonel Mandeville, and Captain Macintire. I believe the whole court-martial was composed of field officers drawn from all parts of the coast I remember one, Colonel the Hon. G. St. John, and there were some field officers of the 84th and 86th. It made an addition to our dinner-table, but all the day the colonel was occupied from ten o'clock until four at the court, and I saw little of him.

The trials lasted a month, and the colonel executed this unpleasant duty with all that tact and judgment which has so much distinguished him in after-times of much greater difficulty and importance. The charges laid to these officers were peculation and defrauding the Company at the arsenal of bell metal, etc, to a large amount. They were all sentenced to be dismissed the service and sent home immediately. I was very sorry for the fate of poor old Saxon; he had, I believe, risen from the ranks. Poor devil! he had dined at the colonel's table but a few days before he was put under arrest, little thinking what was so soon to happen to him. An officer by the name of F——, of artillery, was appointed to Captain Macintire's post, bringing with him a very young and rather pretty woman for his wife.

Colonel Wellesley had at that time a very susceptible heart, particularly towards, I am sorry to say, married ladies, and his pointed attention to this lady gave offence to, *not her husband*, but to the *aide-de-camp*, who considered it highly immoral and indecorous, and a coolness took place between West and the colonel, and they did not speak all the remaining time I lived with the colonel. Lady Tuite, then Mrs. Woodall, interfered in the same officious way, which the colonel did not forget; for in after-times, upon meeting him at a large party, when she held out her hand to shake hands with him, he put both his hands behind his back and made her a low bow.

For my own part, I abhor the seduction of innocent girls, and think it wrong to intrigue with married women; but if I witness anything going on between two people, and the *husband* does not see or choose to take notice of it, I think none but a father or a brother has a right to interfere. You are sure to get into a scrape and make enemies of all parties. And as for Colonel Wellesley, he never in these matters interfered with others, but, on the contrary, once kindly assisted me in a little affair of gallantry I had, but not with a married woman. But this was in a spirit of gratitude, I having assisted him on a like occasion. The colonel, in after-life, proved most grateful to the lady, and provided by his interest for some of her children.

CHAPTER 7

Gets His Captaincy

Having lived with the colonel for about three months, and my regiment having established a good mess in the fort, I told him that if he would provide me with a good house I would not trespass on his hospitality farther. He gave me a good quarter, consisting of three rooms and offices for my servants and stables for my horses. I used to wait upon him occasionally with the report of the main guard, and at other times used to go uninvited to breakfast with him, when he invariably said, in his quick way: 'Elers, will you dine here today?' I am sure he could not say I ever refused him.

About this time, September, 1801, my friends Colonel Harcourt and Captain Crawford procured permission to visit Calcutta, the former to see his old friend the Marques of Wellesley, and Captain Crawford on a trip of pleasure and curiosity. The colonel had left the regiment but a short time when, about the beginning of October, we received orders to proceed to the Carnatic, to a station Trichinopoli, about two hundred miles south of Madras. Just previously to this I sold Colonel Wellesley the curricle Colonel Harcourt brought from England, and he was quite pleased with his purchase. He soon got a pair of horses to run in it. He said it was a much safer conveyance than a buggy, for where two horses could go, the wheels could follow.

One night at the mess, just before we left Seringapatam, the conversation turned upon the powers of English horses on long journeys. I said I could ride my Arab horse fifty miles for three days in succession, even in that climate. My friend Sale offered to bet me 500 *pagodas* I could not do it. I laid the wager, and was to do it *exactly one week after* our arrival at Trichinopoli. Having made the wager *this way*, I made it very much against myself; but I finally overcame all difficulties, and won my wager with great ease. In the first place, it was the very height of the monsoon, raining sheets of water. I took my horse under the cover of my own tent during the night, and in the day he was, like his master, obliged to rough it.

The pass—that is, the descent from the Ghauts down into the Carnatic—was full of sharp rocks, and there was great danger of laming my horse, besides either of us falling sick. However, we arrived all safe, and I got a piece of ground marked out all round a most extensive cantonment, measuring exactly six miles, and had my grooms' ready to rub down, with water, etc., all ready, and I started one morning at one a.m., and finished my first fifty miles with ease by five o'clock in the afternoon. In short, I completed my task with great ease and won my wager.

On arriving at Trichinopoli, which is situated at the foot of an immense rock, we were placed in cantonments about a mile from the fort, at a place called Warriore. I found Major Picton here with the three companies that had been on service to the southward among the refractory Polygars, and also the two companies that had been to sea, to the eastward, where they had gone as far as Batavia. We were all very happy to see each other again.

About this time I heard from Colonel Harcourt, who said that he and Crawford were well and very happy, and were living with the governor-general; they were then to take a trip up the country, many hundred miles from Calcutta, visiting the upper provinces of Bengal. Major-General Brydges, a Company's officer commanding the Southern Division of the army, lived in the vicinity of Trichinopoli; also an old gentleman of the name of Darke, formerly very rich, and to whom the Nabob of Arcot was indebted for many *lakhs* of *rupees*. He had one only daughter,[1] married to General Floyd, who had been long stationed here in command of the 19th Light Dragoons.

By this lady he had Julia, married to the great statesman, the present Sir Robert Peel, Bart. Captain Prescot, of the artillery; William Hawkins, Esq., of the Civil Service; Colonel Browne, the officer commanding the detachment proceeding to Seringapatam; Major Lennon and wife; Wallace and wife, a French lady, the former a civilian; and Mr. Irwin and lady, his assistant, besides several other officers and their ladies, so that we had a very good society, and used to get up subscription bails that were very well attended. But our grand effort was establishing some subscription races, and Captain Laing, of the Company's

---

1. Rebecca Juliana, daughter of Charles Darke of Madras. Married, January 29, 1771, Sir John Floyd, Bart.

service, and Lieutenant King, of ours, were the chief promoters of some races here that would have done credit to any town in England. The general commanding set a good example by his liberal subscription, as also Mr. Hawkins, and all the officers composing the garrison. We collected a sum sufficient to give amusement for three days, with public breakfasts, ball, etc.

The first day a plate of £100 was run for between Captain Laing's bay Arab, Little Jem; Mr. Irwin's Dragon, a bay Arab; and Lieutenant Elers' gray Arab, Aboukir—two-mile heats. This was allowed to be one of the finest races ever run. I rode my favourite gray, and had never ridden a regular race before. The other two horses were ridden by men of the regiment who had been professed jockeys. The first heat I lost by not more than a head, and the second heat I won by the same distance. These heats were contested with Little Jem. The third horse, Mr. Irwin's, had no chance. Everyone thought I was certain of winning. But I was very much exhausted, for my horse evinced, particularly in the second heat, a disposition to bolt, and I could scarcely keep him on the course, particularly within a few hundred yards of the winning-post, which was the more provoking.

We went off for the third heat, and I evidently had it all my own way until I came to a certain spot; I was at least six or seven lengths before Little Jem when my hands got cramped, my reins relaxed, and my horse swerved from the course, and Little Jem, I had the mortification to see, passed me in a canter and won the race. The owner of the third horse, Dragon, who, I believe, was distanced the second heat, came up to me and gave me a challenge to run the next day for a thousand pagodas, and said he merely lost the race by the badness of his jockey. I said 'Done!' and it was settled to be run the next day. I well knew the great superiority of my horse, and that I only lost the race from the cramp I got in my hand. But to make this race certain I went immediately to the man who rode Little Jem, and secured him to ride for me.

The next day, just as the horses were saddling, Mr. Irwin began to quake, and he begged me to let the stake be only for one-half of the original bet I did not like to take any advantage, and consented. I won the race with the greatest ease; and on the third day I won with the same horse a handsome cup of £50, which I brought to the mess. It held eight quart bottles. It was emptied several times on that night in honour of Aboukir.

After the races we had an elegant breakfast, and afterwards dancing; and we had amusements for the men, such as jumping in sacks and running after a pig with his tail soaped. And on the retirement of the ladies we concluded the sports of the day with chicken hazard. I won more *rupees* that day than I could well carry home, but which, as I recollect, I contrived to do, walking in the heat of the sun, as I had no conveyance. This was the happiest week I ever passed in India; everything seemed to prosper with me. I lived in the same quarter with Colonel Picton, and used always to breakfast with him.

In the middle of the day we used to drive to the fort of Trichinopoli, where Mr. Hawkins had a capital house, a good billiard-table, good *tiffins*, and the house always full of pleasant people. Among others was a worthy old man by name Peter Key; he was a gray-headed, retired old captain of Native Infantry. He came out for the second time with us in the same fleet, and used to call us 'his boys.' He lived a great deal with Mr. Hawkins. Mr. H. was a good man, a great oddity, but much respected. He was an Irishman, and a brother to Admiral Whitshed, and son to the late Bishop of Raphoe.

About this time an unpleasant affair took place between Assistant-Surgeon Washington Price and Captain Nixon, arising from a quarrel which took place some months before at Seringapatam. Nixon came to me and borrowed my pistols, the brace that were Colonel Aston's. Mr. Price and he met, and Captain Nixon's shot took effect in the fleshy part of Price's hand, hit the stock of his pistol, and the ball lodged near the top of the arm and was cut out directly. And there the business ended. Captain Nixon soon after obtained leave and went home.

We had not been at Warriore above six months when the regiment was moved to the barracks and cantonments formerly occupied by the 19th Light Dragoons on Trichinopoli plain, a short distance only from Warriore. There were no barracks for the officers, but they lived in detached bungalows wherever they could get them. Mr. Hawkins lent me a capital house and gardens of his called Belfont, something more than a quarter of a mile from the barracks and the same distance from the mess-room. But I had plenty of horses and a chaise. I think I had we horses at this time. One of them was a Pegu pony, black as jet, the most beautiful creature I ever saw. He was one of three that Major Woodall brought from Pegu with him. He cost me a large price. I used always to ride him to parade, and at night he was always sent for me to the mess-room to bring me home.

About this time poor Major Woodall left us sick for Madras. I bought a very pretty portable library from him, consisting of *Bell's Plays* and others, about sixty or seventy volumes, enclosed in wooden cases, with locks and keys, that shut up for travelling, besides a good deal of furniture, etc. Poor fellow! he died shortly after at Madras.

About this time (June, 1802) I received a letter from Colonel Harcourt, telling me he was on his way overland to England with despatches of great importance from the governor-general, and that I should see him back very shortly. He went, and did not remain in England more than three weeks. It was about three months after this that I received a kind letter from Colonel Wellesley to say he had written to Mr. North, the Governor of Ceylon, to procure me a company in some Malay corps raised for His Majesty's service in the island of Ceylon, but that he had not received any answer. Colonel Wellesley strongly recommended me to apply to my friend Colonel Harcourt to use his influence with the governor-general for that purpose. I think there was a coolness between Colonel Wellesley and his brother the marquis at that time, or I think he would have applied to him himself in my favour.

Soon after this Major Picton, as commanding officer, received the intelligence that Captain Hastings Frazer had got promoted out of our regiment at home, and that his company was for sale. At this time I had three or four lieutenants senior to me, among others one of the name of Cavendish, a distant relation of the Duke of Devonshire, and a connection of Lord William Bentinck, the Governor of Madras. Poor Cavendish went down to Madras and endeavoured to interest his lordship in his favour, but without success. I cannot account for it, for Lord William I ever found very kind and obliging to me as far as hospitality went. However, this company was kept vacant for *some months* to give Cavendish the chance of procuring the money, which was not acting fairly towards me, as I ought to have been a captain of the early part of 1802 instead of May, 1803.

I should have got the rank of a brevet-major before I quitted the service if I had been a captain of 1802. Major Picton at length was obliged to forward my name to General Lake on May 6, 1803, for my promotion to the vacant company. At this time the Bengal Army, under General Lake, was most actively employed in the great Mahratta war against Holkar, while General Wellesley was as much engaged against the other chieftain Scindiah, in the north-west part of India. General Lake was so much engaged that from the time my recommendation went off, the first week in May, we had no promotions published until the last week in November, when at length, to my great joy, I found myself in orders as a captain in the 12th Regiment

I had reduced my little fortune very considerably, when I gave Mr. Hutchinson the most positive orders to sell out of the funds all the stock I had in the three *per cents*. I think it was just *previous* to the peace, or perhaps just after war was again declared, and when the people were threatened with invasion. However, the stocks, the three *per cents*. were down to 48, and I believe they never were lower, and this reduced my little fortune nearly one-half. So I was determined, directly my recommendation went off for my promotion, that I would live with the greatest economy, I sold off my stud, in the first place, buggy, horse and harness, and discharged my Hookah Bedar, and lived very quietly at the mess. I still kept up a good *tiffin* and plenty of negus, called *sangaree*, for any officers that would call upon me. In the course of seven months I had saved considerably more than two hundred pounds, and continued to do so for some time.

I asked leave to visit the coast about this time, and I went to Negapatam, and on my return called for a few days on a Captain Blackburne, the military resident at Tanjore. He had a good billiard-table, and played well. I found a Brahmin here who professed to paint miniatures, and I sat to him, and sent home the picture and a gold Trichinopoli chain as a present to my cousin, Mrs. Tennant. But she valued neither—the picture she gave to one of the Miss Hutchinsons, and the gold chain she gave to the Hon. Mrs. Tennant. Colonel Brown was so kind as to take charge of these things, and had the miniature very handsomely mounted on his arrival in England. Colonel Archibald Brown was a singular man. He was a Scotchman; a fine, military figure, six feet high, very rich, very generous, very friendly, even to excess with his purse. He never stirred out of his fine large quarter, and saw very little company; but kept a good table, and he took a great fancy to me—perhaps it was partly on account of our going up together to the siege of Seringapatam.

However, he was always delighted when I called upon him, but most particularly so when I would leave my own mess and call to dine with him, *uninvited*. We always dined *tête-à-tête*, when we had our cool bottle of claret, and he used to entertain me with his early adventures in India, the wars of Sir Eyre Coote, the defeat of Baillie's detachment, and the wars of Lord Cornwallis.

Among his other military stories was one that took place about the year 1795. He commanded a force that took a small Dutch settlement to the eastward. The governor, a Dutchman, invited him to come and live with him and his family. He contracted a friendship with this man; and lent him a *considerable* sum of money to pursue some mercantile speculation, which did not prove fortunate. The merchant when he borrowed the money gave the colonel his bond for it The poor merchant suffered much unhappiness at the debt he had incurred with Colonel Brown, and the little prospect he had of redeeming his bond. Colonel Brown, in the most generous way, said: 'My dear friend, do not make yourself uneasy. Here is the bond. I will now destroy it. If you are ever able to discharge it, do so. If not, I shall never ask you.'

There was another instance of his generous nature. Mr. Hawkins was once regretting his improvidence in his earlier career, which prevented him from returning home as others did with an independence. 'My dear Hawkins, share with me what I have got I have enough for both of us.' So said this generous, excellent man Colonel Brown. I always felt happy in his society. His sentiments were so noble and chivalrous, they quite inspired one to emulate them. Colonel Brown returned home about the latter end of the year 1802, and when I returned in 1806 I found him living in a good house in Sackville Street. When Colonel Brown left me in India I lost a sincere and kind friend, whose memory I shall ever honour. He died at his house in Curzon Street at an advanced age, leaving a sister and a nephew of the name of Knox, in a house of agency at Madras, the heir (*sic*) to his fortune.

In May, 1803, I obtained leave of absence to visit Madras. I went in a *palanquin*, and visited Pondicherri on my way down, and put up at the commanding officer's house, Colonel Keith, a widower with one daughter, a lovely girl of about eighteen. I remained there one night and went to a ball. Colonel Keith gave me news of my elder brother, then a captain in the 43rd Regiment. I believe he knew my brother in the West Indies. The journey down to Madras, a distance of two hundred miles, appeared very tedious; and as I had but one set of bearers to my *palanquin*, I was many days on the way.

At last I arrived at Madras, and after reporting myself at the adjutant-general's office I waited on the governor, Lord William Bentinck, lately arrived from England. My reception was very kind, and he asked me to come and dine with him the next day. I was introduced to Lady William and her brother, the Honourable Edward Acheson and Colonel Monckton, the two *aides-de-camp* of Lord William. I remember we had some of the finest Hermitage I ever drank. I went out to St Thomé, and lived at the garden house of Captain Kerby Dalrymple, where his brother, Captain D. of the 19th Regiment, was also living. Kerby Dalrymple was one of the Seringapatam prize agents, had sold out of the army, and had turned merchant. He kept his carriage, a post-chaise, and lived very handsomely.

When I was not engaged playing piquet with his brother, I used to go with Kerby to the fort in his carriage, and return in the evening. Captain Hugh Dalrymple was at that time a very fine player at this game, and I was a pupil of Major Picton's, with whom I used often to play from morning until night Major Picton used to play whist and piquet for very large sums and with great success.

This Hugh Dalrymple some years after arrived in England, and at Graham's Club he used to play with the celebrated Major Aubrey. The present Marques of Hertford matched Dalrymple against Aubrey, and won of Aubrey £40,000 and Dalrymple won of Aubrey £10,000. It is not to be wondered that Dalrymple beat me, but I lost only a very trifling sum to him. With the regiment I used to play pools with Colonel Picton and Captain Crawford for small stakes. So I was in very good practice, and was a tolerable match for most players—that is to say for those who were not regular blacklegs. I returned to my regiment, and brought up with me a very handsome buggy and beautiful dun pony to run in it.

Soon after my arrival, one night on returning from the mess, on getting into bed I had occasion to go into the garden. My servant Francis said: 'Pray stop, massa. Let me get lanthorn. Sometime bad snake bite massa.' I paid no attention to this prudent advice, and as I opened the door Francis put the lanthorn into my hand, by the light of which I saw, curled round the seat, an enormous *cobra de capello*. I instantly shut the door, loaded my gun, and on opening the door gently, he was laid coiled up in one corner. I shot at him and nearly cut him in two, and he gave a loud hiss and sprang out between me and Francis, and with large bamboos we despatched him.

The next morning I cut off his head, and by way of experiment placed the leg of a live chicken between his jaws, and compressing them, inserted the fangs in the fleshy part of the chicken's thigh. The poor chicken did not live three minutes after. There never was a spot more likely for snakes than this garden, it was so luxuriant in vegetation, being well watered from a neighbouring spring. I had a most narrow escape of my life.

On the departure of General Brydges for England, the command of the Southern Division of the army devolved upon a Colonel Pater, a very good-natured but enormously fat man, of the cavalry. He and Colonel Picton were great friends. I recollect his orders were couched in the most ridiculous inflated language that made us all laugh.

Chapter 8

Lord Wellesley

About July, 1804, I received a letter from Colonel Harcourt, giving me an invitation to come and pay him a visit at Cuttack. He had been some time before appointed secretary to the governor-general, when he was appointed to the command of about five thousand men sent against this country, lying about three hundred miles to the southward of Calcutta towards the Carnatic. He had built a good house at Cuttack, and was established there with a staff and everything comfortable about him, and desired me to get six months' leave of absence and join him, when he would give me an Arabian horse to ride and furnish me with a *hookah* to smoke, which we were both very fond of. After procuring my leave of absence, I began to make preparations by selling off my horses, buggy, furniture, *hookah*, books, only reserving a small quantity of plate, which I unfortunately took to Madras with me. I say unfortunately, because I lost it (the plate) through doing a kind action.

I lent it to a captain of our regiment who, with *his wife,* had just arrived from England. He died a few months after, and his widow would not return it to me or pay me for it, and I had no acknowledgment to say it was lent and was to be returned. But she was not a lady, and was only living with him as his mistress. I also lost a new tent. I left it with the regiment, and Colonel Forsteen, at that time only a captain, bought it, and placed the money in the paymaster's hands, a Lieutenant Jagger. He died, and I lost this also. I forgot to mention that when I sold off my stud the first time upon resolving to save all I could, a young, dashing civilian, a sad, wild young Irish boy, and a natural son of the Earl of Buckinghamshire, came into my stable and wanted to purchase the *whole lot.* I sold him two horses, and my favourite Arab horse, Aboukir, was one. I got his note of hand for 500 *pagodas* for them, which I never should have got but through a rich black man, who, to get 'master's favour,' as they say, cashed the bills. This hopeful youth's name was Ellis, and he died some years after a great deal in debt.

I felt very sorry to leave the regiment I felt a certain presentiment that I never should see it or the officers again. I loved the old regiment and many of the men. I used to practise manly games with them in the heat of the sun, particularly the game of cricket, quoits, and a game called long bullets. At the latter game Sale could beat me, but at quoits there were only two men in the regiment could beat me, and they belonged to my own company—Sharpe, a Yorkshire man, and Ostler, an Essex man, who taught me, and also the art of swimming. I was in those days very active, and few could beat me at leaping, either over a garter or in distance. I could leap both backwards and forwards eighteen feet, when to my utter astonishment a man, by name Burchinhoff, of my company, beat me by five feet.

Among other little pets I kept was a small tiger, which I had as soon as it could see. I remember it had a most unpleasant smell, rolling among the carrion its dam brought into its lair. I had also a small alligator, not more than a foot long. But of all my pets, my favourite was the most beautiful terrier I ever saw. He was small, jet black-and-tan, with a little white on his breast. I gave him the name of Jack, after the name of a very great pet and favourite of Colonel Wellesley's, a terrier who once followed Colonel Wellesley to Chitteldroog from Seringapatam, a distance of more than a hundred miles. When the colonel arrived at the foot of Chitteldroog, they fired a salute in compliment to him. The dog was frightened, and ran away, and the colonel gave him up for lost. A few days after he received a letter from Seringapatam to say that the dog had found his way back. In India there are no beaten tracks or roads, which renders it the more extraordinary. This little dog of mine accompanied me by sea and land to Calcutta and back to Madras.

Trichinopoli has ever been famous for robberies committed by a set of thieves living in the hills, called *bhils*. These robberies were of the most impudent and daring description. They strip themselves entirely naked and oil themselves all over; so if they are caught they slip through your fingers like an eel, and so make their escape. A report was current that they entered the barracks where the 19th Light Dragoons lay one night and stole all their pistols, sabres, etc., when the men were asleep. We had not been in these quarters long when scarcely a night passed upon which they did not pay us a visit. They came to my stable and took a new saddle. It was bound round with a metal resembling silver upon the cantle of the saddle. They tore this off, and considerably damaged the saddle in doing so. I recovered the saddle. They had thrown it away among some rocks. They seldom came into the quarters in the night, but about two hours before daybreak, as they conclude people are generally sounder asleep at that time. Dr. Campbell one night was determined not to go to sleep all night, and having loaded his pistols, laid them on the chair by the bedside.

At their usual hour they paid the doctor a visit. Two of them came into the bedroom, and the doctor began to snore, pretending to be fast asleep. They, thinking this was so, began to examine the combs, razors, brushes, etc., very coolly, and after they had gratified their curiosity one of them took up a light trunk, put it on his head, and leisurely walked out of the room with it. His companion got another trunk, put it on his head, and followed. Dr. Campbell then jumped out of bed, and as the poor wretch was running away fired at him at the distance of a few paces. The ball entered his back and came out at his breast. After this he ran off so strong that Campbell thought he had not hit him. At last he fell. I saw him groaning and lamenting, lying under the shade of a milk hedge, crying out to us most piteously to cure him, and he would show us where all the thieves were and deliver up all the plunder. He did not die till sunset. After that we had no more robberies.

While I was in the Mysore country I had a large sum of money belonging to the men of my company. I had it in a trunk, and gave it and the key to my head servant. One day the servant was not to be found; he had been tired of long marches and a camp life, and had fairly run off. I, of course, gave up all thoughts of finding my money; he had taken the keys with him, and I was obliged to have the trunk broken open, and to my great joy the money was all safe. It was considerably more than a hundred pounds. The man thought that if he *left* the keys, a common and universal practice when a servant runs away, they might fall into bad hands, and I should have been plundered, and he would have had the credit of having robbed me.

The native servants are generally great thieves, although some are as remarkable for their strict honesty and fidelity. It was my good fortune to possess one of the latter. He came to me to be hired while I was living with Colonel Wellesley. He was a Portuguese Christian by the name of Francis. He was an ugly man, and I told him so. He said:

'Massa must not mind ugly face; I got good heart, and will serve massa faithfully.' I took him, and he lived with me until I went on board the ship that carried me to England. On the deck of that ship, the *Hawkesbury*, he said with the tears in his eyes: 'Massa, if I had not wife and children, I never would leave massa, but go England with massa.' He was the best of servants, so clever, so faithful, and so honest. He understood the dressing of a *hookah*, and dressed mine for some years. I made him a present of my *hookah* among other things when I left India. He understood the care of horses, and was also a good cook. In short, he was as a servant quite invaluable.

I shall now, after this long digression, resume my narrative.

I took leave of my regiment at Trichinopoli on August 6, 1S04, and proceeded in a *palanquin* to Madras. I took a passage in the *Princess Charlotte*, East Indiaman (the same ship that brought Colonel Wellesley from the Cape) to Vizagapatam, laden with I know not what cargo; but she was proceeding to that place for the purpose of bringing down bales of longcloth to Madras, and we were to be convoyed by the *Wilhelmina*, of 18 guns, under the gallant Captain Lambert. The *Wilhelmina* could only have protected us against privateers, which swarmed between Madras and Bengal.

It was very lucky for us that we did not meet with Admiral Linois, who, in the *Marengo*, of 84 guns, and two heavy French frigates, was cruising about for plunder, and arrived at Vizagapatam two or three days after I had safely landed at that station, and Captain Lambert, having safely conducted the *Princess Charlotte* to Vizagapatam, had started upon another cruise. Colonel Alexander Campbell, of the 74th Regiment, was the commanding officer of this station, and I lived at his house. I had been there about two days, when the *Centurion*, of 50 guns, arrived for the purpose of protecting the *Princess Charlotte* with a valuable cargo of cloth for Madras.

The *Centurion* was at Madras, commanded by Captain Spratt Rainier, the admiral's nephew; he was, unluckily for him, left sick at Madras, and Commander Lind took the ship in charge on this occasion. I remember Captain Lind, who was an ugly little old-fashioned fellow of about fifty, dining with us on the day he arrived with his purser and one of his lieutenants.

According to my usual custom, I was up by daylight, and, looking seaward, I saw three large ships, hull down, standing in to the bay. Captain Lind with his purser had slept at the house of the Honourable Alexander Murray, of the Civil Service, and after reporting what

I saw to Colonel Campbell, I went to Mr. Murray, who with his wife and Captain Lind were at breakfast. Mr. Murray's house was situated very high above sea-level, and commanded the view of the whole bay. I told Captain Lind of the ships, and he got up from the table and looked at them through a glass. He said he could not make out what they were, but thought they looked very suspicious. He begged Mr. Murray to lend him his carriage to convey him to the beach.

After he was gone about half an hour, the ships were getting very close to the *Centurion*. They approached one after the other, the two frigates first, when the first French frigate, running close alongside, discharged her guns at the *Centurion*, and I distinctly, saw her boats that were lashed upon her quarter fly up like chips. The *Centurion* soon got up her anchor, and we distinctly heard the cheers of the British sailors as they continued to pour their broadsides into the two French frigates. The *Centurion* stood out to sea, engaging the two frigates at the same time. At this crisis we saw the *Centurion* tack and stand inshore. The purser and myself naturally concluded the *Centurion* would run ashore to prevent her falling into the hands of the enemy. He began to cut his capers about the room, and said he was a ruined man, all his hard earnings lost.

When the *Centurion* was standing inshore, we saw Captain Lind under a heavy fire in a small boat get on board, and instead of running the ship ashore, which we every minute expected, he let his anchor go with springs on his cable close inshore. The French frigates also came to an anchor, but at a long and cautious distance, one on the quarter, the *Marengo* amidships, and the other frigate ahead. Many of the shot went over the *Centurion*, and were found up the country. I saw many heavy shot of 68 pounds that were afterwards brought in. Soon after they took up this position they sent their boats and took possession of the *Princess Charlotte*. A country ship called the *Burnaby* ran ashore, and soon went to pieces in the surf.

Soon after the action commenced, I ran down to the beach and offered my humble services to Colonel Campbell. He gave me the command of two 12-pounders, with some invalid artillerymen to serve them. When the French took possession of the Indiaman some of the carpenters were on board the Indiaman belonging to the *Centurion*, who had gone to do some work early in the morning; and instead of going on board again they pulled ashore, giving as an excuse that they were afraid of being taken prisoners. Colonel Campbell ordered me to take these carpenters back to the *Centurion*, and to take charge of his son, who was to go with me on this service. We got on board the *Centurion*, and the first person I saw was Captain Lind, his face black with powder and his shirt-sleeves tucked up, in a most prodigious heat. He said he was very glad to get his carpenters back, for the ship was making large quantities of water, and their pumps were all at work.

I saw the deck torn up with grape, and two ports on the larboard quarter knocked into one, and all their boats destroyed. I saw the mouth of one of the guns half taken off, which, on the ship rolling, sent it through the deck, and it came out between the legs of one of the men who was steering at the commencement of the action. One of the little middies showed me an escape. He had by a round shot carrying away part of his jacket. I saw several large trunks of clothes destroyed by the shot.

At length, having executed my orders and gratified my curiosity, I asked the captain if he had any further orders for me, when I took my leave. I went on shore, and the French squadron with their prize stood out to sea soon after I left the *Centurion*. Considering the long time the *Centurion* was under fire her loss was very trifling. I have often thought that when Colonel Campbell wrote his despatch to the Madras Government he might have mentioned my name as having volunteered my humble services to him. For I was merely a visitor on leave of absence, and had no occasion to do what I did. Captain Lind got his post rank and was made a C.B., and afterwards knighted, and his first lieutenant a commander.

The *Centurion* was obliged to go to Bombay to be repaired, but not into dry dock. She soon afterwards proceeded to England, where she went under thorough repair; a 68-pound shot was found buried under her counter. If this shot had rolled out at sea, she would have gone down stem foremost.

I proceeded the rest of my journey, about two hundred miles, in a *palanquin*, stopping at the house of a Mr. Carr, a civilian at Balasore, where I stayed one night. There I saw a beautiful woman, the daughter of Mr. Rock, who was married to my old school-fellow Henry Parry, living with Mr. Carr. She was very lovely and accomplished, but her mother was a native woman. I regretted this for the sake of Parry at the time, and I still more regret it now, having since renewed my acquaintance with him, and knowing his kind and affectionate disposition. He has since united himself with an amiable woman, with whom he lives very happily.

I at length joined Colonel Harcourt, who received me with the greatest kindness. He had built a large house and kept many servants, some of whom were in scarlet and gold with scarlet turbans, who, bearing large silver sticks, formed a lane upon all occasions of ceremony, particularly when we proceeded every day to dinner. I was quite astonished, not having seen anything of the kind all the time I was in India; but when I arrived at the Government House at Calcutta, I saw exactly the same thing.

So that this was adopting Lord Wellesley's princely style of living. I was introduced to all his staff, consisting of Lieutenant Ashe, his *A.D,C.*; Major Andrews, Brigade Major; Mr. Fortescue, a civilian, a cousin of Lord Wellesley's: Mr. McInnis, Persian interpreter; and Major Brown of Calcutta, commanding a small detachment of cavalry raised and formed by himself, something on the plan of our volunteers; and, lastly, a Mr. Blunt of the Bengal Infantry, and Baron Kutzleben[1] (a relation or connection of the present Lord Wrottesley), who was the junior *A.D.C.*

This was our family, and we always had besides many officers of the fort and civilians to dine with us, together with their ladies, and we used sometimes to have a ball. We used to get up every morning by gunfire and ride until the hour of breakfast. Colonel Harcourt gave me an Arab horse, but I did not much like him, and also a *hookah* and a Hookah Breda. Both the colonel and myself were very fond of smoking; the perfume is delicious, and very different from the horrid, vulgar smell of a pipe of common tobacco, which I abominate. I am not very fond of cigars, even when they are good, which at present is by no means common. More than one-half are spurious.

I here formed an intimacy with an old Bengal civilian, a Mr. Melville, and I renewed this intimacy afterwards in England; also with Mr. Grame, another civilian. I used to be very fond of riding a black horse of Mr. Fortescue's, one that he used to hunt the wild hog with. He was exactly like an English horse, and formerly belonged to Lord Lake as a charger, and was ridden by him at the Battle of Lasswarry. Fortescue was a good horseman and very fond of spearing the wild hog, and was quite an adept at the sport. I used sometimes to ride with Colonel Harcourt upon his elephant, which is not a very pleasant conveyance; the motion is very fatiguing. The country about the fort of Barabetty, which was taken by assault by Colonel Harcourt a short

---

1. Son of Christian, Baron of Kutzleben, Minister to the Landgrave of Hesse Cassel, married, 1780, Dorothy, daughter of Rev. Sir Richard Wrottesley, Bart., grandfather of the first Lord Wrottesley.

time before I came, is very luxuriant, abounding in rich pasture-land and very pleasant to ride upon on account of its turf.

One day after *tiffin* Major Andrews and the baron proposed to me to play chicken hazard. I consented; I won of both of them a considerable sum of money, for which I was very sorry, particularly for poor Kutzleben, who was four or five years younger than myself and a *protégé* of Colonel Harcourt's. But I was not to blame, as they both teased me to play; and beginning to play only for a mere trifle, which they lost, and they both wishing to get back that little, and I not wishing to win their money, we played double or quits, till they lost, Kutzleben £300 and Major Andrews £250. I told them to pay me whenever they pleased, and they gave me their bills in England for the sums, which were duly honoured on my arrival there.

On my route up to Cuttack I saw the celebrated Pagoda of Juggernaut, whither the Hindoos are in the habit of taking long pilgrimages from the remotest parts of India to pay their devotions to the idol and to procure holy water. They are sometimes two years and upwards on these journeys. There are poor, devoted religious enthusiasts at this place who undergo various self-inflicted punishments to propitiate their gods, such as smearing themselves all over with honey and partly burying themselves in the earth to be eaten up by the flies.

Others will make a vow to raise their hand clenched above the head and never to hold it down again. I have seen one of these men, his arm entirely withered away, nothing but the muscle and bone appearing, and the nails having in the course of years forced themselves through his hands and appearing out at the back of his hands, several inches through; and they looked like the large claws of a hawk, only larger. Others will throw themselves down under the wheels of carriages, particularly of an enormous high one containing their idols; this immense carriage, twenty to thirty feet in height, is drawn by hundreds of the natives in religious procession, and some of these fanatics will throw themselves under the wheels of this high carriage for the purpose of being crushed to death, while others will bury themselves alive to secure their salvation.

Having spent upwards of two months with my friend Colonel Harcourt, I proposed to visit Calcutta, and return from that city by sea to Madras. Major Brown, who lived in the Writers' Buildings, was about to proceed there, and gave me an invitation to come and live with him. Colonel Harcourt gave me letters to most of Lord Wellesley's Staff—to Captain Doveton, commanding his bodyguard; to

Sydenham; Colonel Shawe; Colonel Calcraft, the Town Major; Captain Bradshawe, *A.D.C.*, and Captain Armstrong, *A.D.C.* I arrived at Calcutta December 13. The approach to Fort William from the river is truly beautiful, the grass sloping down from the garden houses to the edge of the river, and large vessels anchoring close to the shore.

The magnificent palaces, and, towering above them all, the Government House, that from the whiteness of the *chunam* had the appearance of marble, and the freshness of the grass on the esplanade of an evening, where all the fashionables meet in the cool of the evening in their carriages, *palanquins*, or on horseback, struck me, unused to such gay sights, as perfectly delightful. Here the company linger, enjoying the cool of the evening, until dusk, when they go home, where a good dinner and plenty of cool claret and Madeira are waiting for them.

Major Brown was living as a bachelor, very quietly and very pleasantly. He was an agent for the salt-works, and he had also the command of a troop of volunteer cavalry in the service of the governor. I presented my letter to the town major, who was celebrated all over India for the excellent—nay, luxurious—table he kept. He perfectly understood good living and the art of cookery, which he superintended himself— at least, all those things which required to be attended to very particularly, such as roasting English hams and basting them with champagne.

The first day I called upon him he asked me to dine with him. I was engaged to dine with Lord Wellesley. So he said; 'You had better not go there; you will not get anything worth eating there. His cooks don't understand the thing.' Colonel Calcraft's dinners were truly *recherché*. I never ate anything in India so good as the various delicacies of his table. I often used to dine with him. The first dinner I ate at Lord Wellesley's he placed me on his right hand, and the celebrated Indian diplomatist, Colonel Collins, was on his left. He gave me a very gracious and flattering reception, keeping me in continual conversation. The immense hall was brilliantly lighted. After drinking a moderate quantity of wine, coffee was introduced, after which he took my arm and walked about.

At length we sat on a sofa, and he said: 'Captain Elers, I shall never give you any more formal invitations; from this day a knife and fork will constantly be placed for you during your stay in Calcutta at my table.' How often have I since repented that I did not avail myself of his kind and flattering invitation! But my motive for not going was that I was living with Major Brown, and did not like to dine out unless upon some express invitation, and so leave the major to dine by himself I remember during my stay at Calcutta an old officer of the Artillery died at Calcutta, a connection of Major Brown's, who requested me to go to the station of the artillery at Dum Dum and attend the funeral, as he was too ill to go himself, since it was at a distance of ten or twelve miles.

I also paid a visit to Barrackpore, a country residence of the governor. It consists of a good house and a beautiful park, laid out quite in the English style. I used to go to the dinners and parties of Sir George and Lady Barlow, Sir John and Lady Anstruther, etc.; besides these pleasant dinners we had several balls and other parties in constant succession.

One evening, just before dinner, I sauntered into a public billiard-table close to the Writers' Buildings, where Major Brown lived, and I saw a gentleman dressed in the uniform of a captain of an Indiaman. He pressed me very much to play a game with him. I told him I had not time to play more than a game, as I had not dined, and as I was living with a friend whom I did not like to keep waiting. He then begged me if I was disengaged to meet him there after dinner to play, which I agreed to. He was there punctual to his time. When we began to play he proposed to play for gold *mohurs*, which I told him was a great deal too high a stake for me, and that I would not play for more than one *rupee* a game.

I played for two or three hours, and continually lost, and, like all foolish young players, increased my bets as I lost, until at length, after having lost more than two hundred *rupees*, I observed that I thought he ought to give me odds. To which he made a sarcastic reply that he did not see anything *in my face* to induce him to give me odds. I felt much annoyed at losing my money and getting quizzed into the bargain, and yet something persuaded me that I was the better player of the two. So I was resolved to persevere. I called for some Madeira and iced water, and, having refreshed myself, set to with renewed vigour. I soon regained all I had lost, and had won of him three or four hundred *rupees* besides. He then asked me to give him odds, and I retorted upon him the galling reply he had made to me. He played on, and as he lost increased his bets, till at length, towards morning, he was so beaten and jaded he proposed to leave off, and asked me to give him his revenge the next day, which I agreed to do.

He then gave me his card and address, and told me he commanded the *John Palmer*, East Indiaman, taken up by the government to take the Persian Ambassador up the Gulf, and that the government was paying the owners daily an immense sum for demurrage. He at this time owed me upwards of a thousand *rupees*.

We met at about ten o'clock the next day and played until dinner, and again after dinner until very late, I having continued to win, and he increasing his debt to me very considerably. We went on in this way for two or three days, when he said he would try once more, and should he not be able to reduce his debt to me, he would leave off and come to some arrangement with me for the settlement of what he had lost. We met, and we played three or four hours, and getting still beaten, he said he had had enough of it. At this time he had lost upwards of twenty thousand *rupees*, and to liquidate this sum he offered to pay not more than one-third down and the rest on his return from the Gulf—by bills.

I expressed my dissatisfaction at this proceeding. I told him, and with truth, that he had brought it all upon himself, as he had proposed and pressed me to play for large stakes, contrary to my habits; and that I, having at first lost to him and requesting to receive very trifling odds to put us more on an equality, he had refused to do so; that I had played on to give him a chance for several days to recover what he had lost; and that having done so, instead of paying me, he offered me a comparatively trifling sum and bills for the remainder payable in Calcutta. I told him, moreover, that I was about to proceed to England, and that I might never see him again. I also added that my commission was a sufficient guarantee to him if he had won of me, and that I should have paid him any sum I had lost to him. In short, I told him I would not accept the terms. I went to my friend Colonel Calcraft, and told him the whole story. He said he would make every inquiry about him, and if he had the means of paying he should.

In the meantime Captain Read sent to me a friend of his, who said, after paying me some compliments as to my giving my opponent every chance of winning his money back: 'My friend is very much in debt and much embarrassed, and has a wife and child; and he has commissioned me to say he will give you an order endorsed by Messrs. Alexanders of Calcutta to Messrs. Harington of Madras for 1,200 *pagodas*, provided you will give him an acquittance for the remainder.' My kind friend Calcraft made every inquiry, and having done so, he strongly advised me to accede to these terms, which I did. I heard after that if I had accepted his bills they would have all been paid, for he returned to Calcutta, got a large prize in the lottery, and was with his ship remarkably lucky, made a great deal of money, took a fine house in London, set up his carriage and servants, went again to India in the *John Palmer*, and on returning home was wrecked off the Isle of France and perished!

One night at a ball I met Captain Pelly, commanding the Honourable Company's ship the *United Kingdom*. I got introduced to him, and he told me that if I was about to proceed to Madras he would give me a passage. He was a handsome, fresh-coloured young man about my own age, rather inclined to be fat, and a brother of Major Pelly of the 16th Light Dragoons. I took leave of all my hospitable friends at Calcutta, and hired a boat to convey me to Diamond Harbour, where the Indiaman lay, a distance of 100 miles. The first night we came to anchor off Saugor Island, an island full of jungle and infested with royal tigers. I heard them roaring all night long, and it is not unusual for them, when very hungry, to swim off to the boats and endeavour to get on board, which is not a very difficult thing to do if the boats are small, as was the case with mine. However, they made no attempt that night, and I got safe on board the *United Kingdom*.

I here found a Mrs. Maxtone, the wife of an old Madras civilian, and two young ladies, her daughters. And when we stood out to sea we fell in with a ship proceeding to Calcutta with Dr. Wybrow and his wife, the former belonging to the Regiment De Meuron of the Madras establishment. A boat put them on board of our ship, thereby saving them a great deal of trouble and loss of time. This poor lady, Mrs. Wybrow, encountered much prejudice at Madras in consequence of her husband, Mr. Wybrow, having kept a celebrated Columbine at the theatres, who had assumed his name, when he was quite a young man. I did everything in my power to show them attention and introduce them on my arrival at Madras.

Captain Pelly lived very well on board, and kept an excellent table, and I thought would have married Caroline Maxtone, from the flirtation going on during our short voyage of three weeks. But it was not to be; the young lady afterwards got married to a young civilian, well known by the name of Paddy Moore.

I obtained leave to proceed on my private affairs to England; part of my regiment was doing duty at Seringapatam, and a detachment was sent into the Rajah of Travancore's country, where there was some disturbance. Some part of the regiment proceeded by sea, coasting along the Malabar coast. A melancholy occurrence took place on this occasion. A boat full of men, under the command of Sergeant Tildsley (a capital drill, by-the-by, for the manual and platoon), was induced by the representatives of some of the Travancore people to land at a village, saying that the regiment were landed and waiting for them two miles up the country. They landed, and were surrounded before they could make the smallest resistance; their arms and knapsacks were taken from them, they were tied back to back and thrown into a deep tank, and, of course, all drowned, to the number of thirty. The regiment afterwards went to this village, where they took a dreadful revenge, sparing neither young nor old.

I found that it was very uncertain when my leave would be received by the commander-in-chief of Madras from Lord Lake in Bengal, as his lordship was much engaged at the siege of Bhurtpore, where the natives had most obstinately beaten him off in three different attacks, and after all he did not succeed in reducing that fortress. It was reserved for my gallant friend Lord Combermere to effect that many years after. Under this uncertainty, and not wishing to be idle, I requested leave to do duty as a captain in the 73rd Regiment, Lieutenant-Colonel Moneypenny commanding.

I forgot to mention that during my stay in Bengal Sir John and Lady Theodosia Craddock arrived from England, the former as Commander-in-Chief of the Madras Army, bringing with him Captain Rennel as his *A.D.C.* The 17th Regiment also arrived at the same time, commanded by Colonel Stovin. They relieved H.M.'s 22nd in the duty of Fort William. The 22nd were commanded by a Colonel Mercer, a very tall man. Many of the men were from Essex, and were for the most part very young lads.

During my stay with Colonel Harcourt at Cuttack, the famous retreat of the detachment under the Hon. Colonel Monson took place, after his endeavour to form a junction with the army under Lord Lake. This famous retreat, before an overwhelming force of the enemy, was the subject of conversation of the whole army. At that time it did not occur to me that Colonel Monson had married a relation of mine in Calcutta some years before, and now a son by that marriage, William John Monson, is the heir-presumptive to that barony.

It was a most unfortunate circumstance that Lord Lake, when he appeared before the fort of Bhurtpore, which, by-the-by, was only a mud one, did not listen to the proposal of the *rajah*. He offered to pay the expenses of the war with Holkar if Lord Lake would not persevere in his attack on this fort, as he was determined to defend it to the last extremity, and at the last moment to blow the fort, himself, his wives, and children up before he would allow it to be taken from him. He made a resistance against the victorious army of Lord Lake that was without example in Indian warfare.

The siege was going on in its full vigour when I was at Calcutta, and it was not taken when I landed at Madras more than a month after. Lord Lake made three distinct attacks upon it, and each storming party was beaten off with dreadful loss of life. Upwards of 5,000 men were killed and wounded, and the loss in officers was very great The people at Madras made very long faces. It showed what natives were capable of in the way of resistance. Lord Lake, after all, was obliged to give up the conquest of this, as it at first appeared to him, insignificant fortress. H.M.'s 76th Regiment suffered very considerable loss in these attacks, particularly the flank companies. At this time the Congreve rockets and shrapnel shells were not known, which, fortunately for Lord Combermere, were used by him in the reduction of this fort years afterwards.

When Sir John Craddock arrived in India he informed me he had brought out the decorations of a Knight Grand Cross of the Bath for my friend Major-General Wellesley, and also the thanks of the House of Commons for his famous victory of the Battle of Assaye on September 23, 1803. A story is told that Sir John got General Wellesley's servant to bring his master's coat to him, and placed the Star of the Order upon it before he got up in the morning, and then enjoyed Sir Arthur's surprise. I know I was one of the first to give him joy of his blushing honours. In fact, I knew he had the Order before he did.

I must here relate a story told me by Colonel Calcraft about our late excellent King, William IV, When Calcraft was in England, on leave of absence, he attended most of the fashionable parties where the Prince of Wales was in the habit of going. At that time the Duchess of Cumberland gave large supper-parties, previous to which faro and other games of chance were played by the young men of fashion, and Calcraft used to act as croupier for the Duchess. One night after supper, the Duke of Clarence, who at that time had very boisterous spirits, suddenly attacked Calcraft, asking him to drink a glass of wine and making use towards him of a most offensive expression.

The ladies all stared, and the duke again applied the offensive appellation. A dead silence took place when Calcraft rose, and, addressing H.R.H., said that whatever the difference there might be with respect to their rank, he would not allow such offensive expressions to be applied to him, and that if H.R.H. again made use of them, consequences would ensue very unpleasant to both of them.

The Prince of Wales, who happened to be present at supper, got up, and in his dignified manner said: 'Mr. Calcraft, I insist that you instantly leave the room. Any disrespectful language applied to my brother in my presence I consider as an insult to myself.' Poor Calcraft was obliged to leave the room. The next day the prince gave a grand dinner at Brighton, and all his particular friends were, of course, invited, and among them, but for this unfortunate scene, would have been Calcraft; however, he thought he would go and take his chance of an invitation. He went down, but received no card, and was for some time excluded from all *fêtes* given by the prince. At length the prince forgave him, and it was all forgotten.

My kind and good friend Colonel Aston was, in the early period of his life, on terms of very great intimacy with the prince after the business with Chifney the jockey at Newmarket, who rode one of H.R.H.'s horses. As for the Duke of Clarence, he quite disliked him; he said he never by any chance or accident spoke the truth. One day the duke met him in St. James's Street, and said: 'Well, Aston, which way are you going?'

'First tell me,' said Aston, 'which way are you going?'

'Oh, I am going down St. James's Street.'

'Are you?' said Aston; '*in that c*ase I am going up. Good-morning to you.'

I have heard that when the Prince of Wales was informed of the death of poor Aston, the intimate friend of his youth, he was much affected, even to the shedding of tears.

Aston was unlucky in being engaged in so many duels, and people, of course, concluded, although mistakenly, that he was quarrelsome. He was by no means so, but he was very fond of quizzing odd-looking people, and having the advantage of birth, fortune, youth, and figure, he thought, perhaps, that people not having these advantages were fair game. Hence the scrape he got into with an Irishman one night at Ranelagh. Aston was walking in the Rotunda with some men of fashion, when they met FitzGerald, who, by his accent and queer, unfashionable appearance, caught the eye of Aston, and every time he met FitzGerald he took off his hat and bowed low to him, inquiring how he left all his friends in Ireland.

The Irishman stared, and declared upon his conscience he had never set eyes upon the gentleman in his life. His companions cleared away the mist by informing him that it was the famous Hervey Aston, who was quizzing him. This enraged the Irishman, and he began to be saucy and showed fight; and Aston gave him a most dreadful beating, and he then held him up towards the lights, and said 'he would do.' The Irishman, of course, called him out, and shot Aston through both cheeks, carrying away one of his double teeth, the Irishman very facetiously observing that 'now *he would do*' What a narrow escape this was for Aston!

Another duel he fought was with Mr. Home Sumner. It was during the Ascot races. Riding past the Bush Inn at Staines, he saw two ladies, giggling and laughing, leaning out of the window; he, happening to have an orange in his hand, threw it at them, but missing them, hit Mr. Sumner, who was in another part of the room. Sumner came to the window in a great rage, and said he would give five guineas to any man who would inform him who threw the orange. 'Well, then, it was I who threw it,' said Aston. Down came Sumner in a fury, puffing and blowing, and in the meantime Aston got off his horse, and Sumner giving some language that gave offence, Aston pitched into him and beat him as usual.

Of course a duel followed, and poor Sumner got hit on the hip. Aston had fought three other duels in England, with the circumstances of which I am unacquainted. He once told me he had a battle with some impudent footmen at the little theatre in the Haymarket, who were insulting modest women by using indecent language as they were leaving the theatre. He cut one of his knuckles against the teeth of one of these miscreants. It must, no doubt, have been very severe for him to have recollected so trivial an affair.

On our passage down the Bay of Bengal to Madras, Lieutenant Bentinck Doyle, of the *St. Fiorenzo*, a fine frigate, under the command of my friend Captain Henry Lambert, late in the command of the little *Wilhelmina*, came on board our ship, stating that they were cruising in these latitudes in the hope of falling in with the *Psyche*, a French frigate, commanded by a brave Frenchman, who had done our trade much harm by his enterprise. His name, I think, was Surcouff. Captain Lambert fell in with him two days after, and took him by boarding; Lieutenant Doyle headed the boarders.

Chapter 9

News of Trafalgar and Austerlitz

During my stay at Madras I was ordered to attend, as a member, a general court-martial upon two officers of the 34th Regiment, Major Yeaman and Lieutenant Sands. The former was a major by brevet only. I had seen these two officers tried in a civil court for murder before I went to Calcutta. They were tried before Sir Henry Gwillam at Madras for the murder of Captain Bull, of the 34th Regiment, who fell in a duel with Lieutenant Sands, to whom Brevet-Major Yeaman acted as second. After the judge summed up the jury retired, and were absent one hour. They were both saved by the perseverance of a person of the name of Hope, a very rich merchant, who kept a European shop.

This man had once been a private soldier in India, but had made a fortune of £100,000. The whole jury wanted to bring in the prisoners guilty, but Hope saved them and brought the jury over to his side, and when they came into court, Hope, who was the foreman, pronounced 'Not guilty.' A dead silence prevailed. It was really awful. I never shall forget Sir Henry Gwillam saying: 'Not guilty! A most merciful jury! Prisoners,' he said, 'had you been found guilty, you never would have seen the sun rise again. You have had a most narrow escape of your lives. Let it be a warning to you.'

Captain Bull was a remarkably fine young man, and of very quiet and gentlemanlike manners; but it was his misfortune to be sent on a detachment with the above officers, together with others, who made themselves so disagreeable to him that he withdrew his name from this detachment mess. They took offence at this, and desired him to state his reasons for so doing. He gave as a reason that he was every day expecting a young lady from England to whom he was to be married, and he wished to live more economically in order to meet the expense that he should necessarily incur.

They would not receive this as an excuse; they said it was an affront to the whole mess, and they took up dice to throw who should call this poor young man out and who should be the second. The lot fell upon Lieutenant Sands, and Major Yeaman as the second. A Lieutenant Johnson of the 34th was second to poor Captain Bull, who was killed at the first fire. It excited universal indignation throughout the whole Presidency. They were afterwards tried by a court-martial of which I was a member, and they were broke. I also recollect a Lieutenant Moore of the 34th Regiment, who was tried by the same court and broke for some offence. He was in a dreadful state of health, and only survived his sentence a short time. Of this court-martial, I remember Colonels Fancourt and Dodwell of the 34th were members amongst others, the former father to Major F., late a popular M.P. Colonel F.'s end was very melancholy. He was assassinated commanding the fort of Vellore shortly after I left the country in a mutiny of the *sepoys*.

The field officers and Captains of His Majesty's regiments gave an invitation to Sir Arthur Wellesley to dinner on his return to England, and Lord William Bentinck was asked to meet him. There was a Captain Skerrett of the 65th Regiment, an Irishman, a handsome and remarkably gentlemanlike young man, but very tenacious of his dignity, and he took it into his head that Lord William had neglected him by not inviting him to some of his parties. It happened that Skerrett had a very fine voice, but invariably made it a great favour to sing. Lord William and Sir Arthur Wellesley were sitting together, and someone suggested asking Captain Skerrett to sing, as to which, as usual, he made a great fuss and refused—'Got a cold,' etc.

At last someone said that if Lord William were to ask him he could not refuse, so an unfortunate *A.D.C.* went to Skerrett and told him that Lord William wished to see him. Up jumps the gallant captain. 'You sent for me, my lord? What are your commands?'

'Pray sit down. Captain Skerrett. Sir Arthur Wellesley and myself have heard you sing an excellent song, and hope you will do us the favour to sit down and give us one tonight.'

This foolish young man, instead of doing as he was requested, considered himself highly affronted and his dignity compromised. So he jumped up and attacked the *A.D.C.* who brought the message to him. Lord William sent to the town major, a Major Thompson, and whispered to him to put Captain Skerrett under arrest, but not immediately, so that it might not interfere with the harmony of the company, but before Captain Skerrett left the room for the night, to prevent the possibility of his fighting a duel with the *A.D.C.*

Now, I do not believe it was ever the intention of Skerrett to do this; it was only to show his consequence and independence, and to mark that not even for the governor would he condescend to sing. The evening, with this exception, passed off with great harmony, and a great deal of wine was drunk, and many got very tipsy; and unfortunately for me the town major got so *blind drunk* that on my stepping into my *palanquin* he came up to me and put me under arrest, and insisted upon receiving my sword.

In vain I assured him that my name was not Skerrett, that I had nothing to do with the disagreement that had taken place between Captain S. and the *aide-de-camp*, and that he was acting under an erroneous impression. Nothing would convince him, and I went to my quarter in Portuguese Square highly indignant and, from having drunk a large quantity of wine, in a state of great excitement. Unfortunately for me, I heard the sound of dice in one of the officers' quarters, where two subalterns were playing, one of them an officer of the 73rd, the other of the 34th. I am sure both together by their united efforts could not have paid me twenty *pagodas* had I won it I sat down to play with them, and foolishly lost a good deal. This was entirely owing to my excited feelings from wine, but more particularly from the rage I was in by being put under arrest by mistake; and all this from the folly and conceit of Captain Skerrett in refusing to sing when asked by Lord William Bentinck.

It created much merriment at my expense with Lord William, Sir Arthur Wellesley, and others, who were amused at the stupid drunken mistake of the Town Major, Thompson. *I* was the *only sufferer*, my usual good fortune in this business having deserted me. I did duty with the 73rd Regiment, and was an honorary member of their mess. With the exception of some of the senior officers, they were by no means a pleasant set of people to be associated with. They were on very bad terms with each other. Colonel Moneypenny was a gentlemanlike man, and his adjutant, Chamberlain, I liked; I also liked Captains Morris and Gordon, and a few others, but there appeared to be no harmony among themselves.

Taken individually, there was nothing exceptionable against any of them, but I never was happy amongst them, and I was almost glad that I got ill and was prevented from messing with them, or doing any more duty with them, during the last two or three months I was in India; for I was detained waiting for the opportunity of getting off for many months, and did not go until September 10.

I got a good quarter in the fort fronting the sea, and opposite Colonel Trapand's, of the Company's Engineers. This Colonel Trapand was quite a character. He was a remarkably small man, with a large face and a long nose, inclining to the Roman. He was to a certain degree clever and accomplished, quite a gentleman, by origin of an old French family, and he was very fond of drawing in water-colours, but in such a coarse way that his trees and water looked very like scene-painting. He was a great boaster—there was no ill-nature about him—to a certain degree very pompous, but he was very harmless and inoffensive. To me he was ever a source of great entertainment, and I was the last month or two very often with him, both at breakfast, *tiffin*, and dinner.

In the cool of the evening I used to ride out with him in his post-chaise. There lived with him a good-natured lieutenant of Engineers named Garrard; he very unexpectedly went to England, and in the same ship that I did.

There was living at Madras at this time a civilian named James Balfour. He had been suspended the Service for taking a horse as a present from some of the natives. He got restored, and as I had parted with all my horses, he was so kind as to tend me one to ride, and I fed him. He was a great, tall, rough brute to ride, but he was better than none.

The Honourable Basil Cochrane had for many years held the contract for supplying the navy with meat, provisions, etc, and made a very handsome fortune; but he kept open house for every officer in the navy, from the poor mid to the post-captain. This must have reduced his means of saving a very large fortune, which he might otherwise have done.

My friend 'James Balfour, soon after I left India, got Cochrane's situation. He only held it a very few years, and he had made £300,000, and left a Scotchman by the name of MacConnachy to act for him at an allowance of £6,000 *per annum*. Balfour made this enormous fortune in about four years, as he told me. He bought a house in Grosvenor Square, became an M.P., and married a daughter of the Earl of Lauderdale.[1] He did not, like Cochrane, keep open house, or, if he did, it was only the doors and windows.

About a month before I left India the old veteran the Marques

---

1. James Balfour of Whittingehame, N.B., married Lady Eleanor Maitland, daughter of James, eighth Earl of Lauderdale; died 1845.

Cornwallis[2] arrived on board the *Medusa* frigate, under Sir John Gore. They had a remarkably quick passage out. The field officers and captains got up a congratulatory address upon his return to India, the scene of his former active services as governor and commander, to which he returned a very suitable reply, adding that nothing could have induced him, at his advanced period of life, to have returned to India but the commands of his sovereign and the wishes of the Court of Directors. He looked very healthy, with a fine florid complexion and a disagreeable cast in one of his eyes. He did not stay long at Madras, but proceeded to Bengal, where he died somewhere up the country soon after. I do not think he lived more than six weeks altogether after his arrival.

During the last month I was at Madras some of the regiments of H.M.'s Service were ordered to hold themselves in readiness to proceed to Europe. All these regiments had served in India upwards of twenty years—*viz.*, the 73rd, 74th, and 76th; the two former came home at the same time that I did. I saw several regiments land at Madras about this time from England—*viz.*, the 53rd, 59th, 66th, 67th, and 69th. Some of these went on to Bengal, but the 69th relieved the 73rd at Madras. My friend Captain Crawford at this time arrived at Madras, and he also had obtained leave to return to Europe.

The last fortnight I spent in India was with a worthy old surgeon whom I knew at Trichinopoli, who was at this time a member of the Medical Board, and as I had sold off everything I had, such as furniture, etc., he asked me to come and live with him at his garden-house, a mile or two from the fort. And there I remained with him, only going into the fort by way of passing the time until the hour of dinner. Captain Crawford and myself made a bargain with Captain Timbrell, of the *Hawkesbury*, for a passage, and we got a large cabin between us, where we slung our cots. It was the last aft on the starboard side. This cabin cost us something more than £200 each, and part of the 74th Regiment's poor, worn-out old men came on board with us; also the colours of the regiment, and Lieutenant-Colonel Swinton, commanding officer.

The officers were Captains Mein, Boswell Campbell; Lieutenant White, and several others whose names I cannot recollect; Captain Monteith, cavalry; Garrard, Engineers; Ritso, late Captain H.M.'s Service; Ensigns Garrard and Roebuck, Engineers; Garrow, Civil Service; Dr. Ainsley. We had also General and Mrs. Cunningham, Company's

---

2. Charles, first Marques Cornwallis, died 1805.

Service (the old general was absolutely dying when he came on board, but he lived for years after); two squalling brats of boys, a constant torment to their poor mother, who was quite worn-out nursing them and the poor old man, her husband, who was about forty years older than herself; a Mrs. Ure, the wife of a Dr. Ure, of Hyderabad, who had two fine children of three and four years old under her chaise, the children of Colonel Kirkpatrick, of Hyderabad, by a princess, to whom report said he was married.

Her Highness would not part with her children until £10,000 had been settled upon each of them. They were a boy and a girl, and they had a faithful old black man, who was very fond of them, to attend upon them. Mrs. Ure had an infant of only a few months old, nursed by a young native woman, immensely fat, and she had also a young European woman as her maid. The children of Kirkpatrick were consigned to their uncle. Colonel Kirkpatrick, of Nottingham Place.

It was my fortune to have this black and white party consigned to my care on landing in England. Having taken leave of my good old friend Dr. Richardson, at whose house I had been living, and having given away my favourite little dog Jack to the youngest Miss Maxtone, I bade *adieu* to all my Madras friends, and went on board the *Hawkesbury*, East Indiaman, accompanied by my faithful black servant Francis, who there, poor fellow! look leave of me. We did not sail till the next morning.

It will be, perhaps, scarcely believed that I, who had been so miserable and pining to get home the first three years of my being in the country (and no poor Swiss ever felt more the absence from his native country than I did during those three years), was at the time I found the shores of Madras fast receding from my view affected even to tears. I felt as if I was leaving my only home and the only friends I had. I could scarce believe it possible that I could have such feelings until the actual moment arrived of our sailing.

Captain Timbrell was an excellent captain—none could be better. The chief mate, Mr. Johnstone, was rather consequential, and the second mate, Mr. Cowles, was a good-natured, honest fellow. We were under the convoy of Captain Draper, of the *Weymouth* frigate, a very troublesome gentleman, fond of bullying the poor skippers under his command. We had the *Baring*, Indiaman, and the *Montrose*, under Captain Patterson, a young man. Nothing of consequence occurred till we got off the Cape, when we buried poor Lieutenant White of the 74th; and as we experienced cold weather of) the Cape, the poor invalids of the 74th died daily. We spoke an American off the Cape, who told us he had spoken Admiral Linois and his squadron only a few days before, and that they were looking out for us.

We bore down to the southward, and one night soon after the *Montrose* and ourselves agreed to cut and run, and not venture to go to St. Helena, for fear of meeting with Linois. We bore down to the Island of Fernand de Noronha, on the Brazil Coast, within three degrees of the equator.

It is the Botany Bay of Portugal, and inhabited by 1,500 convicts, with a small military force. Not one woman on the island, and the most dreadful crimes committed. I did not land there, but visited a very small island about three miles off, the only man upon which is a poor wretch banished there for some horrible crime—perhaps murder—who receives from the larger island a week or ten days' provisions at a time. I went on this island and stretched my legs for about ten minutes one evening.

On returning on board, there was a great swell, and our Indiaman, as the boat went under her stern, looked an enormous height out of the water. I had some difficulty in getting on board again. It requires great activity to catch the exact moment when the wave lifts you up near the gunwale, and in a moment you sink a dozen feet at least; and if it is difficult for a man with *two* hands, what a difficulty it is for him who has but *one*, which was the case with poor Captain Boswell Campbell, who lost his arm in action, and was still suffering exquisite pain from some of the nerves that had been amputated! He would cry out in agony in walking the deck if anyone came near him on the side on which he had lost his arm, and particularly when we arrived off the Cape during the cold weather.

This brave officer, who lost his arm at Assaye, had the misfortune to fall out of his berth two or three days before we arrived in England. He never came out of his cabin afterwards, and died at the moment when the man on the look-out hailed 'Land!' It was a most melancholy sight to see the poor soldiers, three and four in the course of the week, and also three or four officers of the 74th, thrown overboard in their cots with a 24-pound shot placed at their feet, and the splash which followed as they sank into the deep. The men were sewn up in their hammocks, and made a similar exit.

During the latter part of our voyage we experienced very bad weather, and were obliged to have the dead lights up, and were scarcely able to sit at dinner. We fell in with vast quantities of seaweed from the Gulf of Florida, and had such adverse winds that it was thought at one time we should have been obliged to go to the West Indies. We fell in with a ship from England that sent us some papers containing the interesting intelligence, and at the same time melancholy news, of the Battle of Trafalgar, and simultaneously that of the great victory of Bonaparte at Austerlitz. My dear brother Edward, your brave father, at Trafalgar, was third Lieutenant of the *Orion*, 74, under Captain (now Admiral) Sir Edward Codrington. I think he commanded on the main-deck, and towards the latter part of the action a 74 lay helpless with her bowsprit across the broadside of the *Orion*. The men were about to pour a broadside into her from the guns of this deck, thinking she was a Frenchman, when my brother sang out that it was one of our own ships.

My dear brother had fought a very gallant action about a year before in the *Arrow*, of 18 guns, against two frigates somewhere between Lisbon and Gibraltar. The *Arrow* was protecting a very large convoy. She was sunk alongside the frigates, and her officers and crew were sent prisoners to Alexandria. My brother was a prisoner six months, when he came home in a cartel and was appointed to the *Orion* a short time before Lord Nelson's last and celebrated action. He was unfortunately only second-lieutenant of the *Arrow*, or he would have been promoted, but Lloyd's voted him a sword. When the *Arrow* went down, he swam with his writing-desk, the only thing he saved, on board the Frenchman; and I heard him say that just before the action, seeing he must be taken, he went to his cabin and rigged himself out in his best clothes. There was a clergyman's wife on board going to join her husband, a Mrs. Miller, whom he was very kind and attentive to in her distress. My brother was also in Lord St Vincent's action, February 14, 1797, as a mid on board the *Prince George*. He had also seen much boat service.

Oh, what a delightful sight it was, the view of the white cliffs of dear England! It was nearly ten long years since I last saw them. I was then nineteen years of age; I was now, in February, within a few months of twenty-nine, the most interesting period of my life spent broiling in an unhealthy climate. Already at this early age my hair had begun to turn gray, my skin had grown the colour between an orange and a lemon, and my forehead had assumed wrinkles. But my health was tolerably good, and my spirits as buoyant as when I was nineteen. And when I recollected the officers and men of my own regiment whom I had followed to their graves, I could not help thinking of the mercy of Providence that had protected me through so many dangers both by sea and land, and allowed me once more to put my foot on my beloved country.

Sketch Map
SHOWING PLACES IN INDIA
MENTIONED IN THE NARRATIVE

Historical Record of the Twelfth or East Suffolk Regiment of Foot from 1793

Contents

Historical Record from March, 1793, Drogheda   337

Historical Record from March, 1793, Drogheda

A revolution had taken place in France; men of violent republican principles had seized on the reins of government, beheaded their sovereign, and involved Europe in another war. The pernicious doctrines of liberty and equality had been disseminated in the French West India Islands, and the European planters had solicited the protection of the British arms against the fury of the *mulattoes* and negroes. War was commenced to arrest the tyrannical proceedings of aggression pursued by the French republic; a British army was sent to Flanders under His Royal Highness the Duke of York; additional forces were sent to the West Indies, and in November the flank companies of the Twelfth Foot, commanded by Captains Tweedie and Perryn, Lieutenants Mathews, Leister, Leister junior, and O'Brien, embarked for the West Indies.

The deliverance of the French West India Islands from republican domination, was undertaken in January, 1794; the flank companies of the Twelfth joined the expedition under General Sir Charles Grey, K. B. (afterwards Earl Grey), at Barbadoes, and were engaged in the attack of Martinico. A landing was effected at three different points in the early part of February, and after some sharp fighting, in which the 1794 companies of the Twelfth signalised themselves, particularly the grenadier company, forming part of the brigade commanded by Prince Edward (afterwards Duke of Kent), which captured Fort Royal by escalade on the 17th of March, and carried Morne Tartisson by storm, the island was captured. In his despatch, Sir Charles Grey stated,—'All the officers and soldiers of this little army merit the greatest praise.' The loss of the Twelfth Foot was limited to a few private soldiers killed and wounded.

From Martinico the flank companies of the Twelfth sailed with the expedition against St. Lucia, where the troops arrived on the 1st of April, and the companies of the Twelfth took part in the reduction of that island, which was accomplished in three days without loss.

The flank companies were afterwards engaged in the capture of Guadeloupe and its dependencies, in which service they lost several men. The rapid success with which the British empire was thus extended, by the addition of three valuable islands and their dependencies, excited great admiration; and Sir Charles Grey stated in his despatch, that he 'could not find words to convey an adequate idea, or to express the high sense he entertained, of the extraordinary merit evinced by the officers and soldiers in this service.'

While the flank companies were engaged in the capture of the French West India Islands, the regiment was withdrawn from Ireland to reinforce the troops under the Duke of York in Flanders; it embarked from Drogheda on the 7th of March, landed at Parkgate on the 14th, re-embarked at Greenwich on the 1st of May, and landed at Ostend on the 6th of that month.

On arriving at the seat of war, the regiment was ordered to join the corps under the Austrian General Count Clerfait, who commanded the troops in West Flanders, and it was attached to the division under Major-General Hammerstein, together with the thirty-eighth and fifty-fifth regiments, and the Eighth Light Dragoons.

The Twelfth regiment, commanded by Major Frederick Bowes, consisting of eight hundred and fifteen rank and file, took part in numerous operations, and was engaged in the general attack on the French positions on the 17th and 18th of May. On the latter day, the Twelfth were engaged in driving the enemy from Werwick, and in forcing the passage of the River Lys, on which occasion they highly distinguished themselves; but the operations on the above two days were not successful, from the want of a more perfect combination in the movements of the several divisions, and from the superior numbers of the enemy.

In division orders, dated Camp near Tournay, 20th May, 1794, Major-General Whyte stated 'he had great pleasure in informing the British troops, that General Count Clerfait has highly approved of their spirited conduct in the field, and great exertions in going through such excessive fatigues, as they necessarily have had since their first movement from Ostend. Major-General Whyte laments the loss sustained by the Eighth Light Dragoons, whose spirited and distinguished gallantry, led on by Lieut.-Colonel Hart, has gained them the highest honour; and he desires his thanks may be accepted by the commanding officers, and all the officers and men of the Thirty-Eighth and Fifty-Fifth regiments; and also by Major Bowes and the officers and men of the Twelfth regiment, whose conduct has been highly approved of by Major-General Hammerstein, under whose immediate command they served. To Lieut.-Colonel Hart, who led on the squadron of the Eighth Light Dragoons to the attack, at Rousbeck, his best and distinguished thanks are due; and also to Lieut. -Colonel M'Donald, who led on the Fifty-Fifth regiment to support the attack on the front. He is perfectly convinced the same praise would have been due to Lieut. Colonel Pitcairn of the Thirty-Eighth, had they been called into action.'

The Twelfth Foot continued to serve under General Count Clerfait, and when the French besieged Ypres, with thirty thousand men, with a covering army of twenty-five thousand, the regiment was engaged in the attempt to relieve that fortress. The Austrian advance-guard was repulsed at Olglede on the 7th of June; but the French were defeated in their attempt on Rouselaer. Still entertaining hopes of being able to raise the siege, Count Clerfait attacked the French again on the 13th of June, at Hoogledge, and Major-General Hammerstein engaged a body of the enemy, of very superior numbers, at Kootmarke, and was repulsed. He afterwards retreated to Bruges, detaching the Eighth Light Dragoons, and Thirty-Eighth and Fifty-Fifth Foot to Ostend.

The very superior numbers of the enemy gave them so great an advantage, that the allied army was forced to commence retrograde movements. The Twelfth Foot remained with Major-General Hammerstein's division until the 9th of July, when the following paragraph appeared in the division orders issued at the camp at Contiche,—

> As the Twelfth British regiment is going to leave Major-General Hammerstein's brigade, he takes this opportunity to assure the regiment of his best acknowledgments for the good and gallant behaviour it has shown during the time the general has had the honour to command it; he likewise thanks it for the readiness and good will with which it has borne so many and great fatigues.

On its removal from Major-General Hammerstein's command, the regiment was formed in brigade with the thirty-third, forty-second, and forty-fourth foot, under Major-General Balfour. In August it was in position near Breda, and in the beginning of September retired to the vicinity of Bois-le-duc.

In the middle of September the enemy advanced in great force, and attacked all the British posts on the right; the outpost at Boxtel, being most advanced, was forced, and the troops of Hesse D'Armstadt, who occupied it, sustained a severe loss. The post, occupied by a detachment of the Twelfth regiment, was environed and assailed by very superior numbers; it was defended with great gallantry for a short time, but the soldiers were unable to withstand so overwhelming a force as that by which they were assailed. The regiment had a few soldiers killed and wounded, and Lieutenant Eustace, three sergeants, one drummer, and forty-four rank and file taken prisoners. The British troops afterwards retired beyond the River Maese.

In the meantime, the flank companies had been engaged in the defence of the island of Guadeloupe, where about two thousand French troops had arrived from Europe, and being joined by a multitude of mulattoes and blacks, among whom the doctrines of liberty and equality were disseminated, they gained possession of part of the island, and frightful outrages were perpetrated. The companies of the Twelfth were engaged in an attempt to regain possession of Grand-Terre; but the troops employed in this service were not sufficiently numerous. The Twelfth had Lieutenant John Leister and several soldiers killed, and others wounded.

The companies of the Twelfth were employed in the defence of Guadeloupe under great disadvantages, and they were nearly annihilated. The island was given up in October, and the few remaining officers and soldiers proceeded to St. Domingo.

Meanwhile the Twelfth regiment, serving under the Duke of York, in Holland, was exposed to much suffering and privation. The Dutch, having imbibed the revolutionary doctrines of equality, beheld the advance of the French without alarm, and surrendered their fortresses without much resistance. The British troops had no chance of ultimate success, yet they held their positions with firmness, and they did not fail to impress the enemy with a just idea of British valour. The Twelfth were in position near Nimeguen in September, and afterwards attempted to defend the passage of the Waal.

During the winter the River Waal became frozen, so as to admit the immense masses of the enemy to pass on the ice, and the British were obliged to retreat through Holland to Germany. The sufferings of the soldiers during this retrograde movement were very great; long marches, exposed to snow-storms and tempests, along roads choked with ice and snow, and a deficiency of provisions, put to a severe test the strength of the officers and soldiers.

In March, 1795, they arrived at Bremen, where the hardships they had endured were ended. The Twelfth regiment lost so many men during the campaign and retreat through Holland, that its numbers were reduced from eight hundred and fifteen to four hundred and twenty-five rank and file.

The regiment embarked from Bremenlee on the 11th of April, landed at Gosport on the 12th of May, and marched from thence to Portchester, where it was joined by Lieutenant O'Brien, one sergeant, and one private soldier from the West Indies; being the only surviving individuals of the two fine flank companies which proceeded to the West Indies in 1793.

Every effort was made to recruit the regiment as speedily as possible, and on the 2nd of July, it was reviewed by His Royal Highness the Duke of York, who expressed his approbation of its appearance.

On the 19th of October, the regiment embarked from Southampton, and sailed to Spithead, where it remained a few days, and afterwards put to sea. On the 5th of October, it landed on the Isle de Dieu, in conjunction with a small force under Major-General Needham, and a body of French emigrants, accompanied by the Count D'Artois, brother of the King of France. No circumstances occurred to favour any further attempts connected with this enterprise, and in December the regiment left the island; it was exposed to several violent storms at sea, but arrived safely at Southampton in ten days, and marched from thence to Iron-hill barracks.

The regiment was stationed in the neighbourhood of Southampton, and in the Isle of Wight, until the 8th of June, 1796, when it embarked in the *Rockingham*, *Hawksbury*, *Airly Castle*, and *Melville Castle* Indiamen, under the command of Lieut. Colonel Henry Harvey Aston, in order to transfer its services to the East Indies. The regiment sailed from St. Helens on the 27th of June, and on the 19th of September anchored in Table Bay, Cape of Good Hope; that colony having been captured from the Dutch a short time previously. The regiment remained on board, but small parties landed daily for the benefit of their health. While the Indiamen were in Table Bay, a dreadful hurricane threatened the destruction of every ship, and they all sustained some injury, several losing their anchors. Serious apprehensions were entertained for the safety of the regiment; but providentially it did not sustain any loss, and it sailed from the Cape of Good Hope on the 10th of November.

On the 10th of January, 1797, the Indiamen anchored in Madras roads; the regiment landed on the following day at Fort St George, and mustered eight hundred and seventy rank and file, whose appearance excited admiration.

The regiment was employed on garrison duty at Fort St. George until the middle of August, when it embarked for Manilla, the capital of the Spanish settlements in the Philippine Islands, situate on the banks of a bay, at the mouth of the River Pasig, in the island of Luconan. On the 23rd of August six companies proceeded on the voyage; the other four companies were embarked on board of men-of war, and were about to follow, when orders were received for their disembarking, in consequence of intelligence from the Mysore country, indicating a projected irruption into the British territory by the celebrated Tippoo Saib.

The six companies continued the voyage, and arrived in September at the Prince of Wales's Island, called also Penang, or Betel Nut Island, situated off the west coast of the Malay peninsula, from which it is separated by a narrow strait. At this place a large fleet was assembled, with a numerous body of troops, from the Presidencies of Bengal, Madras, and Bombay, for the expedition against Luconan and the other Philippine islands; the Prince of Wales's Island having been selected for the rendezvous of the forces to be employed in this enterprise. The prospect of the services of the troops being speedily required in more important military operations on the continent of India, occasioned orders to be issued for their immediate return.

Towards the end of September, the *Express* sloop arrived with despatches from Madras, and in a few days afterwards the six companies of the Twelfth sailed from the Prince of Wales's Island. They encountered contrary winds, and it being found impossible for the transports to contend against the north-west monsoon, the Twelfth returned to the island in October. They again sailed for Madras on the 15th of November, and landed at Fort George on the 12th of December; during their absence the other four companies of the regiment had exchanged a few shots with a French squadron, which had appeared in Madras-roads, and succeeded in driving an Indiaman on shore under the works of the fort.

Among the various schemes of aggrandizement entertained by the republican government of France, was the wild and extravagant idea of being able to gain possession of the British territory in the East Indies. To strike an effectual blow at the naval, commercial, and colonial greatness of the British nation, was an object of primary consideration with the French directory, and to excite the jealousy of the native princes of India, and induce them to take up arms against the English, was one of the means used to accomplish this 1793 object. In the ruler of the fruitful province of Mysore, the celebrated Tippoo Sultan, the French found a chieftain eager to seize on the first opportunity for being revenged on the British, who had punished his former aggressions by depriving him of a considerable portion of territory, and inflicting a fine equal to three and a half millions sterling.

This chief entered zealously into the design to drive the English out of India., and endeavoured to induce other princes to join in the enterprise. After the discovery of the designs of the enemy, hostilities were delayed some time, and the Twelfth regiment marched for Tanjore, the capital of a well-cultivated province in the Carnatic, where it arrived on the 1st of March, 1798.

The regiment was reviewed at Tanjore, by Major-General Floyd, who expressed in orders to Colonel Aston, the officers, and soldiers, 'the satisfaction he received on inspecting the eight companies of the Twelfth regiment of infantry at the station;' and added 'In the masterly hands of their commanding officer, there is every reason to expect that His Majesty's Twelfth regiment of infantry will, whenever called upon, be ready and disposed to renew in the east the glories of Minden and Gibraltar.'

Preparatory to the grand enterprise of driving the English out of India, General Bonaparte was sent with a French army to Egypt; many French officers and men were introduced into the army of Tippoo Sultan, and other measures were adopted calculated to forward the design. Under these circumstances the Governor-General of India, Lord Mornington, deemed it necessary to assemble a body of troops on the coast of Coromandel, and to engage the Nizam of the Deccan to furnish an auxiliary force. The Twelfth regiment marched from the fortress of Tanjore, on the 22nd of July, to join the army assembling under the orders of Lieut.-General Harris.

On the 1st of January, 1799, the regiment joined the camp of the army advancing towards Mysore, and negotiations having failed, the troops penetrated the territory of Tippoo Sultan in the beginning of March. The Twelfth, Seventy-Fourth, and Scots brigade, formed the first brigade of infantry under Major-General Haird.

During the night of the 7th of March, the regiment was employed, under Major-General Baird, in an attempt to surprise the camp of a body of the enemy's cavalry, but the Mysoreans obtained information of the design and made a precipitate retreat.

On the following day, the light company of the Twelfth, commanded by Captain Woodhall, took possession of Neldroog without opposition.

The British advanced direct upon the capital of the Mysore country, Seringapatam[1] and Tippoo endeavoured to harass the march by skirmishes, and impede the progress of the troops by burning villages and laying waste the country. The regiment having entered upon active warfare, the commanding officer issued the following order:—

> As the Twelfth regiment, from having the honour to be the eldest King's regiment with the army, is more liable to be called on for immediate service than other corps, the commanding officer expects the officers, non-commissioned officers, and private men, will be ready, night or day, to turnout at the shortest notice, and to parade under arms without noise or confusion. On all sudden alarms the light infantry is instantly to accoutre without waiting for orders, and to be in readiness to march whenever their services may be required.

On the 27th of March, as the *lascars* were pitching the tents of the army on a fine plain beyond the fort of Malleville, they were suddenly assailed by a heavy cannonade from an eminence in front; at the same time the advance piquet, under Captain McPherson of the Twelfth regiment, was attacked by a force of very superior numbers, but repulsed its assailants with distinguished bravery. The army arriving on the plain, advanced in close column of regiments towards the eminence, upon which large bodies of Mysorean cavalry and infantry were formed, who withdrew their heavy guns, but annoyed the advancing columns with rockets.

As the British columns approached the height, they formed line, and ascended to the summit, which was abandoned by the enemy, but a short distance beyond the eminence appeared the army of Mysore in order of battle. As the Twelfth moved forward, a large body of Mysorean cavalry formed in the shape of a wedge, having an elephant with a *howdah* on his back in front, appeared advancing to charge the

---

1. The proper name of that city is Siri Runga Patan.

regiment, and the British line halted to receive the attack. Immediately afterwards two other very large bodies of the enemy were discovered in two topes, or woods, preparing to support the first charge. Lieut.-General Harris, seeing the danger which menaced the regiment, placed himself in its rear, frequently repeating the words, 'Steady, Twelfth!' 'Steady, old Twelfth!' and when the wedge approached within a hundred yards of the line, the Mysoreans discharged their carbines and pistols, but without doing execution.

The Twelfth remained steady, with their muskets at the recover, until the enemy arrived within about thirty yards, when a well-directed volley, followed by a rapid file firing, carried destruction into the enemy's ranks; a rampart of killed and wounded men and horses lying along the front of the regiment. The rear of the wedge was embarrassed by the killed and wounded in front, and could not continue their charge. The elephant was severely wounded, his conductor killed, the chiefs on his back had fallen, and he turned round and directed all his fury upon the Mysoreans, overturning everything in his retrograde movement, and producing great havoc with a prodigious chain, which he swayed.

A few Mysorean horsemen broke through the regiment, but they were instantly shot in its rear, and the British artillery arriving, and opening its fire, the enemy's cavalry fell back; at the same time the British line advanced, and decided the fate of the day at that part of the field; a distant cannonade, however, indicated that the battle was raging elsewhere.

The left of the right wing was opposed to Tippoo's infantry, and gained a complete victory; between seven and eight thousand Mysoreans being put *hors de combat*: the loss of the British did not amount to so many hundreds.

In general orders issued on the same evening, it was stated:—

> The commander-in-chief congratulates the army on the happy result of this day's action, during which he had various opportunities of witnessing its gallantry, coolness, and attention to orders.

And in brigade orders:—

> Major-General Baird, with the most heartfelt satisfaction, congratulates the brigade on the victory obtained this day over the enemy; it is sufficient for him to say, that the valour of the corps fully answered his expectation.'

On the following morning, the army continued its advance upon the capital of Mysore, and the enemy used various stratagems to retard the movement until the approach of the rainy season should render the siege of Seringapatam impracticable. The water was found impregnated with poison; many men were taken seriously ill, and several horses fell down dead while in the act of drinking; the smoking ruins of villages, and other scenes of devastation presented themselves; at the same time large bodies of hostile cavalry hovered round the army, and the camp was often annoyed by rockets; but the British forces moved steadily forward, and on the 3rd of April they arrived within four miles of Seringapatam,—a city and fortress, which had attained considerable strength and splendour under Hyder Ali and his son Tippoo Sultan: it is situate at the upper end of an island, four miles long, and a mile and a half broad, in the River Cavery.

About six o'clock on the evening of the 3rd of April, the Twelfth regiment, with the flank companies of the Seventy-Fourth and Scots brigade, assembled under Major-General Baird, to beat up the enemy's cavalry encampments: they were out all night without effecting the surprise of any of the enemy's detachments; but about three o'clock on the following morning they came suddenly upon a numerous body of Mysorean cavalry, when they rushed forward and bayoneted nearly every man before the Mysoreans could mount their horses, which were led into the British camp at six o'clock, at the moment the army was about to commence its march.

On the 4th of April, the army arrived in sight of Seringapatam; the soldiers had skirmished with the enemy's cavalry and rocket men, during the march, and in the evening a general order was issued, in which it was stated:—

> The commander-in-chief takes this opportunity of noticing the high sense he has of the general exertion of the troops throughout the long and tedious march, with the largest encampment ever known to move with any army in India; and in congratulating them on a sight of Seringapatam, he has every confidence that a continuance of the same exertions will very shortly put an end to their labours, and place the British colours on its walls!

The army took up a new position on the 5th of April, and in the evening the Twelfth regiment was ordered to advance, supported by two battalions of *sepoys*, and take possession of a *nullah*, or bed of a river or aqueduct, about a mile and a half in front of the camp. The night was very dark, but the regiment had scarcely cleared the outposts, when the air was illuminated by hundreds of fire-balls thrown up by the enemy, who thus detected the advance of the British troops, and immediately commenced a heavy fire of musketry and rockets, under which the Twelfth continued to advance in open column of companies.

Suddenly, regular platoon firing was heard in front, and showers of bullets assailed the regiment on both flanks and in front, when it formed line. The trampling sound of approaching troops occasioned the regiment to prepare to charge with the bayonet, which was about to be executed, when it was discovered that the approaching troops were one of the battalions of *sepoys* which had been ordered to support the Twelfth. This battalion had lost its road, moved to the front, and become exposed to the attack of very superior numbers of the enemy, whom it had engaged upwards of an hour, which accounted for the platoon firing heard in front; it was retreating, bringing off its killed and wounded, under Major Colin Campbell, and being pursued, formed in the rear of the Twelfth regiment.

When the pursuing Mysoreans discovered, by their fire-balls, the line of Europeans before them, they fell back to a greater distance, but without any relaxation in their fire, and so many spent balls struck the officers and soldiers of the Twelfth, that they were ordered to sit down to await the approach of day for the completion of the enterprise; the *nullah* was at some distance, and it could only be approached by a road of difficult access. The regiment did not fire a shot, but large quantities of ammunition were sent from the camp; the incessant firing having given rise to the expectation that the soldiers must have expended their cartridges.

About two o'clock on the following morning the enemy's firing ceased, and at four the Twelfth advanced. When the morning light appeared, the regiment found itself in the rear of a long mud wall and fragments of a ruined village, three hundred yards from the *nullah*, which was occupied by thousands of Mysoreans and French, with large masses of infantry on both flanks. Under these circumstances, the regiment halted, and the pioneers threw up an embankment on both flanks, to preserve it from enfilade.

This work was scarcely completed, when daylight enabled the Mysoreans to discover the position and insignificant numbers of the regiment, compared with their host, and they endeavoured to destroy it by a storm of bullets, but the soldiers were sheltered by the mud walls, and very few cannon-balls from the fort took effect, on account of the distance. Lieut.-General Harris, observing the unequal contest, ordered the artillery to fire on the enemy's ranks, the balls passing over the heads of the Twelfth, and the British line advanced. The commanding officer of the detachment, Lieut.-Colonel Shaw, saw the line moving steadily forward to his support, and having entire confidence in the valour of the Twelfth, he resolved to attack the opposing legions with the bayonet; he cautioned the soldiers to prepare, and giving the word 'Charge, Twelfth,' they sprang from behind the mud wall, raised a loud shout, and rushed forward towards the *nullah*.

The Mysoreans were confounded by the suddenness of the attack; they saw the sparkling steel bayonets of the Twelfth approach, and abandoned their post in a panic. As the Twelfth rushed forward, several lines of Mysoreans fired volleys at them, but the balls struck the sand many yards from the regiment, and in five minutes the *nullah* was captured. The enemy rallied behind a high bank, and made a show of a design to retake the post, but the Twelfth and *sepoys* ascended the bank, and kept up a well-directed file firing, which occasioned the Mysoreans to retreat: a party of French were also driven from a post on the left of the regiment. The *nullah* being thus carried, the artillery of Seringapatam opened a heavy fire, which obliged the soldiers to take shelter in the bed of the river. The post thus captured, was designated 'Shaw's Post,' in honour of the commanding officer of the detachment, Lieut.-Colonel Shaw of the Seventy-Fourth foot.

When the Twelfth rushed forward to storm the post, the army suspended its advance, awaiting the result, and a brigade afterwards drove a body of the enemy from a wood on the right of Shaw's Post. A breastwork was subsequently made to cover the troops from the guns of Seringapatam, and the Twelfth had the honour to break ground before that important fortress. About seven o'clock in the evening, the regiment was relieved by the Seventy-Fourth Foot: Its loss was Lieutenants George Nixon and T. Falla, and ten rank and file killed; Captain Whitler, Lieutenants R. Nixon, Percival, King, and Neville, and a considerable number of non-commissioned officers and soldiers, wounded.

The siege of Seringapatam was prosecuted with vigour; and in the early part of May, a practicable breach was ready, when the Twelfth were selected to take part in storming this important fortress. For this service, the flank companies of the European corps left in the camp, the Twelfth, Thirty-Third, Seventy-Third, and Seventy-Fourth regiments, three corps of grenadier *sepoys*, two hundred of the Nizam's troops, a hundred of the artillery, and the corps of pioneers, the whole under the orders of Major-General Baird, took post in the trenches, to make the attack during the heat of the day on the 4th of May, when the Mysoreans were likely to be surprised.

At one o'clock the signal was given, when the forlorn hope sprang forward; six flank companies, and the Twelfth regiment, also issued from the trenches at a running pace, and were followed by the remainder of the storming party; they passed the rocky bed of the Cavery River under a heavy fire, crossed the glacis and ditch, ascended the breaches in the *fausse braye* and rampart in gallant style, and overcame all resistance, with a resolution and valour which proved the innate bravery of the officers and soldiers. The Mysoreans were unable to withstand the prowess of the British troops, and they were overpowered at all points.

During the heat of the conflict, Captain Woodhall was detached with the light company of the Twelfth, and a few men of the battalion companies, to reinforce the troops fighting upon the inner rampart; this party proceeded by a narrow path, passed a deep ditch to the inward wall, and flanked and took in reverse the enemy's traverses, which were defended by the *sultan* in person, who was forced to retire. As Tippoo and his suite were passing the small gate on the northern face, into the body of the town, the light infantry of the Twelfth arrived at the inner side of the gate, and fired upon him and his followers with such effect, that the gateway was choked with killed and wounded, and the body of the *sultan* was afterwards found among the slain. After the firing had ceased at all other points, resistance continued to be made at the palace; but upon assurance of safety to the sons of Tippoo, the enemy surrendered, and the capture of this important city and fortress was achieved.

The regiment had seventeen men killed, and forty-nine wounded during the siege, and Lieutenant Shawe was shot through the leg in the assault; the following officers died during the siege from extraordinary fatigue and the effects of the climate; Major Allen, Captain Buckeridge, Lieutenants Percival and Gahan, and Assistant Surgeon Bacot.

On the following day it was stated in orders:—

The commander-in-chief congratulates the gallant army he has the honour to command on the conquest of yesterday; the effects arising from the attainment of such an acquisition as far exceed the present limits of detail, as the unremitting zeal, labour, and unparalleled valour of the troops surpass the power of praise for services so incalculable in their consequences: he must consider the troops well entitled to the gratitude of their country.

The governor-general stated in a letter to Lieut.-General Harris:—

With the warmest sensation of admiration, affection, and attachment, I offer my cordial thanks, and zealous congratulations to you and all the officers and privates composing the gallant army, which has achieved this glorious and decisive victory, with a degree of energy, rapidity, and of skill, unparalleled in this quarter of the globe, and seldom equalled in any part of the world.

In general orders by government, it was stated:—

The Right Honourable the Governor-General in Council, having this day received from the commander-in-chief of the allied army in the field, the official detail of the glorious and decisive victory obtained at Seringapatam, on the 4th May, offers his cordial thanks and sincere congratulations to the commander-in-chief and all the officers and men composing the gallant army which achieved the capture of the capital of Mysore on that memorable day.

His Lordship views with admiration, the consummate judgment with which the assault was planned, the unequalled rapidity, animation, and skill, with which it was executed, and the humanity which distinguished its success.

Under the favour of Providence and the justice of our cause, the established character of the army had inspired an early confidence that the war, in which we were engaged, would be brought to a speedy, prosperous, and honourable issue; but the events of the 4th of May, while they even surpassed the sanguine expectation of the Governor-General in Council, have raised the reputation of the British arms in India to a degree of splendour and glory, unrivalled in the military history of this quarter of the globe, and seldom approached in any part of the world.

The lustre of the victory can be equalled only by the substantial advantages which it promises to establish, by restoring the peace and safety of the British possessions in India, and a durable foundation of genuine security.

The Governor-General in Council reflects with pride, satisfaction, and gratitude, that in this arduous crisis, the spirit and exertions of our Indian army have kept pace with those of our countrymen at home; and that in India, as in Europe, Great Britain has found in the malevolent designs of her enemies, an increasing source of her own prosperity, fame, and power.

The territory subject to the late Tippoo Sultan was divided: to Great Britain was allotted the capital and several extensive districts; another portion was given to the Nizam; and a third to the Mahratta power; the remainder continued to form an independent state under a descendant of the ancient rulers of Mysore. Thus was the hostile combination against England confounded, British territory extended, and its power and revenue increased. The Twelfth regiment was afterwards rewarded with the royal authority to bear the word *Seringapatam* on its colours, to commemorate its gallant conduct during this war, and the officers received medals from the East India Company.[2] The regiment captured eight stand of colours from the troops of Tippoo Sultan at the storming of the capital.

After encamping a short time near Seringapatam, and afterwards near Yarriagoranelly, the regiment marched into garrison at the captured fortress; but while it was stationed there, a partisan, named Dhoondia, excited the Mysoreans to take arms in opposition to the allied powers, which occasioned orders to be issued for the Twelfth Foot again to take the field. This partisan assembled an irregular force, and gained possession of several fortified places. When a small body of troops was sent against him, he fled, and was pursued to the frontiers of the Mysore country.

The regiment was afterwards encamped near Seringapatam, where it was joined in December, 1800, by the Seventy-Seventh Foot, some battalions of *sepoys*, and a proportion of native cavalry, forming a small

---

2. The following regiments received the Royal permission to bear on their standards, colours, and appointments, the word "Seringapatam," in commemoration of their gallantry in the storming and capture of that city and fortress on the 4th May, 1799; *viz.*—the 19th and 22nd (late 25th), Light Dragoons; the 12th, 33rd, 73rd, 74th, 75th, 77th regiments, and the Scots Brigade, afterwards the 94th regiment.

army under Colonel Pater, for the purpose of reducing the warlike tribes of the Wynaad country,—a mountainous district overrun with woods, and comprising about twelve hundred square miles, situate in the province of Malabar.

Leaving the vicinity of Seringapatam on the 26th of December, five companies of the regiment arrived at Manantoddy on the 9th of January, 1801, and were employed until the 23rd of that month, in stockading the small hill fort, and in making arrangements for entering the woody districts of the Wynaad country.

From Manantoddy the Twelfth proceeded to Peria Colgum, where they constructed a redoubt: they afterwards marched to Lackerry Cottah, at which village another redoubt was constructed.

The little army under Colonel Pater traversed the country in almost every practicable direction, ascending hills, cutting roads through almost impenetrable jungle of bamboos, skirmishing with the warlike inhabitants, and forcing them to submit, in which service the Twelfth had several men killed and wounded: the climate, and extraordinary fatigue undergone by the troops, also occasioned the loss of many lives from disease. The Wynaad country having been forced to submit, and the hostile *rajah* taken prisoner, the companies of the Twelfth regiment employed in this service returned to Seringapatam.

The regiment quitted Seringapatam in the middle of October, 1801, and proceeded to Trichinopoly, a celebrated city and fortress, situate on a hill, or rock, three hundred and fifty feet high, on the south bank of the river Cavery, opposite the island of Seringam, famous for its magnificent Hindoo temples.

At Trichinopoly the regiment was joined in January, 1802, by the remains of two companies, which had embarked on board of His Majesty's ships, at Madras, for Batavia. These companies had suffered severely from the climate of the island of Java; and of the five officers and one hundred and twenty-five men who embarked at Madras, only three officers and sixty-three soldiers returned; Lieutenants Gordon and Neville and sixty-two men died of fevers, and other diseases.

Three companies had been stationed under Major John Picton, at Vellore, in the Carnatic, the residence of the family of the late Tippoo Sultan, consisting of his brother, twelve sons, eight daughters, and an immense number of women; and these companies were afterwards employed against the insurgent sect called the Polygans, in which several non-commissioned officers and soldiers were killed and wounded; Lieutenant William Firth was also wounded, and Lieutenant

Parker died of the jungle fever. After the performance of this service, the three companies joined the regiment at Trichinopoly, where the Twelfth were 1803 stationed during the years 1803 and 1804. 1804

In August, 1805, the regiment marched to Seringapatam, where a very fatal fever broke out in 1806, when the Twelfth removed to an encampment at some distance from the fortress; but they lost many officers and soldiers in that and the following year.

In April, 1807, more than half the surviving officers and men were suffering from disease, when an order arrived for the remainder to march to the coast of Malabar, and occupy quarters at the port of Cannanore, where the regiment was stationed upwards of eighteen months.

At Cannanore the health of the men was restored, and when inspected in 1808, by Colonel Cuppage, a district order was published, in which the colonel expressed his thanks to Captain Eustace and the officers and men of His Majesty's Twelfth regiment, for their handsome appearance at the review. The dress, steadiness, and general appearance of the men, marked the great attention paid to their discipline, and their uniform good conduct and friendly disposition towards 'the natives reflect every credit on the corps.'

While the Twelfth Foot were at Cannanore, some disputes, of a tedious and complicated character, occurred between the British and the Rajah of Travancore, a province situate at the south-west extremity of Hindoostan. In 1795, a treaty of alliance was concluded between the British and the *rajah*, who agreed to subsidize three battalions of *sepoys* for the defence of his dominions; when the disputes with the *rajah* came to a crisis, these battalions were at the port of Coulan (or Quilon), and they were threatened with destruction by the natives, together with every person in the British interest. While the execution of these menaces was delayed, the Twelfth regiment embarked, towards the end of December, 1808, in *potamars* (small undecked vessels), to proceed along the coast a distance of three hundred miles to Coulan, in the Travancore country.

Four of these boats, having three companies and a half on board, arrived at their destination in a few days, and were immediately landed, to the great joy of the *sepoys*. A severe gale of wind dispersed the boats containing the other companies of the regiment, and several of them were wrecked on the coast of Cochin, a small province on the north of Travancore, but by great exertions the soldiers were saved; others gained the port of Cochin, where they remained until the storm was over. One *potamar*, containing Sergeant-Major Tilsey and thirty-three rank and file, was driven on the coast of Travancore, near Alleppi, when the natives sent off several small canoes.

The soldiers, believing they had arrived at the friendly port of Coulan, went on board the canoes two or three at a time, but on landing they were overpowered by the natives, their wrists broken with an iron bar, their hands tied behind them, and they were cast into a dungeon, where they remained several days without food. They were afterwards conducted, when scarcely able to walk, to a high ground near the sea, and precipitated into a watery grave. The sergeant-major was reserved to the last, and as he witnessed his companions in arms successively hurled headlong into the deep, he struggled to release himself, and tore pieces of flesh from his shoulders with his teeth, exclaiming 'Let me die like a soldier!' but the barbarians derided him, and eventually put an end to his torments in the same manner as the others. A negro youth, who accompanied this portion of the regiment as cook, witnessed this tragic scene, and was menaced with the same fate, but was spared, and he afterwards made known the fate of the party.

Another *potamar*, having nearly a company on board, under Lieutenant George Blanchard Gray and Adjutant Hayes, approached the coast a few miles from Coulan, and were, in consequence of the shattered state of the vessel, deciding on the propriety of landing, when a volley of musketry from the shore announced the hostile intentions of the natives. The vessel was bound together with some large tents, to prevent its splitting, and it arrived safely at Cochin, but went to pieces in the harbour. All the *potamars* being damaged, other vessels were procured to continue the voyage.

The officers and men of the regiment, who arrived at Coulan on the 29th of December, joined the *sepoys* encamped near the town. On the evening of the same day, the Travancoreans attacked the piquet under Captain Clapham of the *sepoys*; the fire of musketry and artillery indicating a sharp conflict, Lieut.-Colonel Chalmers, commanding the troops at that station, detached Ensign James Keappock, and forty men of the Twelfth, to support the *sepoys*, and the enemy was forced to retire, leaving about eighty men dead on the scene of conflict.

The Travancoreans were excited to rage and fury against the British, who had thus gained a footing in the heart of their country; they assembled in immense multitudes before the camp, kept up an incessant fire on the piquets, and heavy columns menaced the encampment; the soldiers were thus kept constantly ready for action, and they lay on their arms night and day.

On the 8th of January, 1809, the remainder of the regiment arrived at Coulan, excepting one company, commanded by Lieutenant Thomas Thompson, left with six hundred *sepoys* and several guns for the defence of Cochin. The men of the Twelfth, with the *sepoys* and guns which had arrived, were landed as expeditiously as possible; but the force was obliged to remain encamped on a sandy plain near the sea, enclosed by an almost impenetrable forest of cocoa-nut trees, from the want of means for carrying on active operations. The resident prohibited the felling of the trees to conciliate the natives; but this produced no advantage, and the wood afforded shelter to the Travancore an marksmen, who annoyed the camp with their fire, keeping the troops in a constant state of alarm; the outposts were also frequently attacked by parties of the enemy.

Before daylight, on the 15th of January, a tumultuous noise in the wood proclaimed the approach of an immense number of men, and at break of day the Travancoreans commenced an attack along the whole front of the British line, at the same time heavy columns were seen among the trees threatening both flanks. Thinking the attack was a surprise, the enemy fired his artillery at the tents; but when sufficient light enabled the Travancoreans to see the British ranks, they immediately directed their guns on the Twelfth regiment, as if desirous of annihilating the Europeans first. Thus perilously exposed to the enemy's numerous artillery, the British instantly advanced the right wing of the Twelfth and two battalions of *sepoys* against the enemy's left, and the left wing of the Twelfth, with one battalion of *sepoys*, against the right of the enemy's line.

The whole force was instantly brought into close action; but the British had only five small field-pieces to answer the fire of the forty guns brought into action by the enemy: the British musketry was, however, well directed, and the incessant peals which echoed in the woods announced a vigorous contest, which was continued for several hours, during which clouds of barbed arrows, from the enemy's local troops, inflicted painful wounds on the British soldiers.

About midday, the Twelfth were ordered to charge with bayonets, and capture the enemy's artillery; they rushed forward with distinguished bravery, the soldiers shouting "Remember our murdered comrades at Alleppi" as they precipitated themselves upon their opponents. The Travancoreans made a resolute defence, many of them being bayoneted at their guns; and a discharge of grape-shot, from one field-piece, killed eleven grenadiers of the Twelfth regiment. During this contest many distinguished acts of gallantry were displayed by the officers and men, and Ensign Keappock, being attacked by two opponents, slew them.

Finally both wings of the regiment were triumphant; heaps of Travancoreans fell beneath the bayonets of the Twelfth, who captured eighteen brass field-pieces. The loss of these guns intimidated the enemy, who retired about three o'clock in the afternoon, leaving five thousand killed and wounded on the field of battle. The British were unable to follow up the advantage, from the want of stores, which prevented their quitting the coast.

The enemy appears to have been very confident of success on this occasion, and to have been intent on the annihilation of the Europeans; several Travancoreans of their Carnatic brigade were taken prisoners, and ropes being found in their possession, they were questioned on the subject, when they confessed that the cords were brought for the purpose of hanging the British soldiers, and that the British officers were to have been trampled to death by elephants.

The regiment had fifty men killed and wounded; no officers were killed, but the following were wounded Captain Richard Bayley, Lieutenant M. J. Molloy, and Surgeon Robert Erskine.

On the succeeding day, the following statement was published in orders:—

> It is with the greatest satisfaction that Lieut.-Colonel Chalmers congratulates the troops he has the honour to command, on the glorious success obtained yesterday, against the attack of an enemy whose force did not amount to less than thirty thousand men. He begs leave to offer his most particular thanks to Lieut. -Colonel Picton, who commanded the right wing of this little force, with a wing of the Twelfth regiment, and to the officers, non-commissioned officers, and privates, whose gallantry and high discipline have, on all occasions, appeared conspicuous. Lieut.-Colonel Chalmers has to offer his thanks to Major Hamilton, who commanded on the left, with a wing of His Majesty's Twelfth regiment, and to the officers, non-commissioned officers, and privates, whose gallant conduct needs no further comment, than that they belonged to His Majesty's Twelfth.

The political resident, Colonel C. Macauly, stated in a letter to Lieut.-Colonel Chalmers:

> I have received the details of the victory over the united force of the Divan an achievement that reflects signal honour on the discipline and animated valour of the troops under your command, and sheds fresh lustre on the British arms.

A numerous army of opponents continued to hover near the British force at Coulan, and it was deemed advisable to cut down many of the trees, to throw up a breastwork in front of the encampment, and to construct a redoubt, which was armed with the guns taken from the enemy.

In the meantime, the company of the Twelfth under Lieutenant Thompson, with the battalion of *sepoys*, commanded by Major Hewett, left for the defence of the port of Cochin, had been attacked by the troops of the *rajah* of the province of Cochin. During the action, the *sepoys* gave way, and the company of the Twelfth had to maintain a desperate struggle with very superior numbers. The enemy was repulsed, and the inhabitants of Cochin were preserved from a general massacre, with which they had been menaced for being favourable to the British interests; they openly attributed their preservation to the distinguished heroism of the company of the Twelfth, which had half its non-commissioned officers and private soldiers killed and wounded; Lieutenant Thompson was severely wounded, and died a short time afterwards.

The Twelfth regiment and *sepoys* continued to resist the armed population of Travancore and the numerous forces of the *rajah*; but being constantly harassed by the approach of bodies of the enemy, the physical powers of the soldiers became diminished, and their numbers decreased by disease; but the innate valour of the troops remained unabated. Before daylight on the 31st of January, the Travancoreans made another effort to surprise the camp; but a rocket announced their approach, and the British were under arms, as they usually were, at three o'clock in the morning: many of the cocoa-nut trees had been cut down to enlarge the plain, and as the enemy's heavy columns emerged from the wood, a sharp cannonade was opened upon them; but they formed line under fire and advanced, when the guns of the redoubt rent chasms in their ranks.

Undismayed by the storm of grape and bullets which smote their ranks, the Travancoreans pressed forward, and endeavoured to establish several guns on a rising ground; but the artillery of the redoubt dismounted their ordnance. After keeping up an irregular fire of musketry for some time, they withdrew from the front, and concentrating on the right, renewed the attack with greater vigour, when the left wing of the Twelfth regiment was detached under Captain William Henry Forssteen, to aid the *sepoys* on that flank. On the arrival of the Twelfth on the right, a charge with bayonets was executed with great vigour and the Travancoreans fled from the field, leaving one brass six-pounder behind them; several other guns were preserved by the swiftness of the elephants.

On the following day, the troops were thanked in orders 'for the steady and cool manner in which they met and repulsed the attack of the enemy.' After this defeat, in which they lost an immense number of men, the Travancoreans did not hazard another general attack; but they frequently endeavoured to surprise the piquets in the night, in which they were always defeated.

On the 13th of February, the Nineteenth regiment arrived from Columbo; and the troops were only prevented advancing up the country from the want of stores and the means of conveyance. A small supply having arrived, they advanced in two columns, the first composed of the Twelfth and a battalion of *sepoys*, commanded by Lieut.-Colonel Picton; and the second, of the nineteenth and a battalion of *sepoys*, under Lieut.-Colonel Stewart, and by a combined attack they captured the enemy's stockade and extensive breast-works, in gallant style, on the 21st of February.

In the meantime another British force had penetrated the Travancore country under Colonel St. Leger, and this army arrived at Travandapatam, the capital, without meeting with serious opposition. The refractory *rajah* made overtures for peace, and the Twelfth regiment returned to Coulan, detaching the flank companies to the capital.

The regiment commenced its march for Seringapatam, on the 23rd of May; but was forced to halt several days in consequence of the heavy rains of the Malabar monsoon, which rendered the rivers impassable, swept away part of the regimental baggage, and drowned several men in the rapid currents which rushed along the low grounds. On the 24th of July the regiment arrived at Trichinopoly.

In Europe, the war with France was being prosecuted with vigour, and in the month of March, 1810, the flank companies of the regiment were completed to one hundred rank and file each, and marched under Captain Forssteen, for Madras, to take part in an expedition against the French island of Bourbon, situate in the Indian ocean, about four hundred miles east of Madagascar. In June the expedition arrived at Rodriguez, and in July came in sight of the island of Bourbon, when the surf was so high as to render a landing dangerous; an attempt was., however, made; the light infantry of the Twelfth in a small schooner, and about three hundred men of the Thirty-Third and Sixty-Ninth regiments in boats, approached the shore and effected a landing with the loss of a few men drowned; but the schooner and boats were dashed to pieces, the soldiers' ammunition damaged, and many of their arms lost.

As no more men could be landed, Lieutenant Foulkstone of the Sixty-Ninth regiment volunteered to swim through the surf and convey orders to Lieut.-Colonel Macleod, to take possession of St. Marie. This order was instantly obeyed, and the light infantry of the Twelfth distinguished themselves in storming the batteries, in which service they had two private soldiers killed; Lieutenants John Spinks, and John B. Whannell, with five rank and file wounded. The grenadier company of the Twelfth, and other corps afterwards landed at Grand Chaloupe, and by their spirited conduct, particularly the gallant behaviour of the Eighty-Sixth regiment, the reduction of the island was speedily accomplished.

While the flank companies were engaged in this service, the regiment was stationed at Wallajahbad, from whence it marched, in August, to St. Thomas's Mount, and in September to Madras, where it embarked on board the *Russell*, of seventy-four guns, and the *Cornwallis*, *Hesper*, *Cornelia*, *Bucephalus*, and *Clorinde* frigates, to take part in the expedition against the Mauritius, or Isle of France, another island in the Indian sea, belonging to France; the grenadiers and light infantry of the regiment also embarked from St. Paul's in the island of Bourbon, to share in the enterprise.

On the 28th of November the armament approached the Isle of France, and the troops effected a landing in the bay of Mapon, when one brigade was ordered into a large wood, through which it was necessary to pass. The light company of the Twelfth under Captain Forssteen, preceded by a section under Lieutenant Ashe, penetrated among the trees, and skirmished with a French piquet, in which service two men were killed, and Lieutenant Ashe and three private soldiers wounded. After a march of nine miles, the light infantry of the Twelfth halted on some low ground surrounded by jungle.

The weather was very hot, water could not be procured, and the sufferings of the soldiers, in consequence, were very severe; but on the following day some alleviation of suffering was obtained by sucking the dew from the herbage, and advancing to the powder mills, within five miles of Port Louis, the capital, clear streams of water were discovered. While halting at this place, the piquets were attacked by the enemy, when the rifle company of the Twelfth, and the light infantry of the Fifty-Ninth, dashed forward, and drove back the French skirmishers, wounding General de Caen.

On the following morning the army advanced, the grenadiers of the Twelfth being in front., and the light infantry on the flanks, under Captains Firth and Forssteen, Lieutenant Keappock commanding the leading section of grenadiers. While advancing along a narrow road, through a country covered with underwood, the army was suddenly assailed with grape shot, from an eminence; but a charge with bayonets forced the French to withdraw. Arriving at some open grounds, the British formed line, when the French abandoned their guns and retreated towards the town, leaving a body of troops on a mountain on the British left. The Twelfth were ordered to storm the height, and they raised a loud shout, and soon gained the summit, when the French fled, leaving a gun behind them.

The officers and soldiers of the regiment evinced great heroism in these services; Lieutenant Keappock was wounded in the side, but continued at his post until a shot in the head forced him to retire; his honourable, though dangerous post, was taken by Lieutenant Jenkins, who received a severe contusion on the breast by a ball, but continued at the head of the leading section.

In this short but brilliant and decisive service, the regiment had Major Jeremiah O'Keefe, one drummer, and sixteen rank and file killed; Lieutenants Keappock and Ashe, three sergeants, and twenty-eight rank and file wounded; five men missing.

The French governor, General de Caen, seeing no prospect of being able to make effectual resistance, surrendered the island. This enterprise was thus successfully accomplished, and the conduct of the Twelfth regiment was commended in orders, also in the public despatch of Major-General Abercromby.

After the surrender of the Isle of France, the flank companies proceeded to Port Louis, and the battalion companies descended the Long Mountain, and embarked from Tortue bay, in the *Psyche* frigate, for Grand Port, where they were joined by the flank companies, after being separated eleven months.

General Picton died on the 14th of October, 1811, in his eighty-fourth year, and was succeeded in the Colonelcy of the Twelfth foot, by Lieut.-General Sir Charles Hastings, Baronet, from the Seventy-Seventh regiment of foot.

The regiment was stationed in the Isle of France during the years 1811 and 1812.

In the meantime the war with France was approaching to a crisis; Napoleon Bonaparte had attained the summit of power, and the efforts of Great Britain were commensurate with the importance of the contest; the army was augmented, and in the autumn of 1811 a *second battalion* was added to the Twelfth regiment of four hundred and fifty-one officers and soldiers, into which the recruiting companies of the regiment were incorporated.

In the autumn of 1812, the second battalion proceeded to Ireland.

In April, 1813, the first battalion embarked from 1813 Port Louis, for the island of Bourbon, where it was stationed nearly two years.

During this period the tyrannical power of Bonaparte had been overthrown, and the Bourbon dynasty restored to the throne of France. On the re-establishment of peace in Europe, the island of Bourbon was restored to the French monarchy, and in consequence of this arrangement the regiment embarked from St. Denis on the 3rd of April, 1815; the French soldiers, who arrived from Europe to take possession of the island, landing as the British went on board the ships prepared to receive them.

The Mauritius, or Isle of France, was retained by the British government, and the Twelfth Foot having been selected to form part of the garrison of that valuable island, immediately proceeded thither.

Soon afterwards, Bonaparte quitted the island of Elba, in violation of his engagements, and regained the throne of France, when the powers of Europe took arms against the usurper, and his veteran legions were overpowered in the field of Waterloo by the allied army under Field Marshal His Grace the Duke of Wellington, on the 18th of June, 1815. To replace the losses of the British Army at Waterloo, additional forces were sent to the continent, and the second battalion of the Twelfth regiment, which had returned to England a few months previously from Ireland, embarked for Flanders on the 27th of June, under the command of Colonel Julius Stirke; it landed at Ostend and advanced to Paris, where the campaign was terminated by the restoration of the Bourbon dynasty to the throne of France. Peace being again established in Europe, the battalion returned to England in December.

In June, 1815, the rifle company of the first battalion proceeded to Bengal, and formed part of a field brigade assembled for service; it, however, returned to the Mauritius in November.

In January, 1816, the second battalion again proceeded to Ireland.

The first battalion continued to form part of the garrison of the Mauritius during the year 1816, and the first six months of 1817; on the 1st of July of the latter year, a serious fire broke out at Port Louis, when the exertions of the garrison to extinguish the flames, called forth the admiration and thanks of the inhabitants, which were communicated to the troops by the governor.

Transports having arrived to convey the regiment to Europe, a general order was published, in which it was stated:—

> Major-General Sir Edward Butler, in taking leave of the Twelfth regiment, feels himself highly gratified in stating, that its conduct, during its services in this island, has, in every particular, been such as to meet with his highest approbation, and he begs to assure Lieut.-Colonel Forssteen, the officers, non-commissioned officers, and men of the Twelfth regiment, that they carry with them his warmest wishes for their prosperity and welfare.

The regiment sailed from Port Louis on the 25th of July, arrived at Portsmouth on the 10th of November, and afterwards proceeded to Cork, where it landed on the 26th of December, after an absence from Europe of nearly twenty-two years.

A representation of the distinguished services of the regiment in the Travancore country, and other parts of India, with its gallantry at the capture of the islands of Bourbon and Mauritius, procured for it the royal authority to bear the word "India" on its colours.

www.ingramcontent.com/pod-product-compliance
Lightning Source LLC
Chambersburg PA
CBHW030217170426
43201CB00006B/120